BY THE SAME AUTHOR

Ramesses the Great
Tutankhamun's Trumpet
A World Beneath the Sands
Aristocrats and Archaeologists
Writings from Ancient Egypt
The Nile
The Rise and Fall of Ancient Egypt
The Egyptian World
Lives of the Ancient Egyptians
Dictionary of Ancient Egypt
Genesis of the Pharaohs
Royal Annals of Ancient Egypt
Early Dynastic Egypt

THE
LAST DYNASTY

Ancient Egypt from
Alexander the Great to Cleopatra

TOBY WILKINSON

W. W. NORTON & COMPANY
Independent Publishers Since 1923

First published in Great Britian in 2024 by Bloomsbury Publishing.
Copyright © 2024 by Toby Wilkinson
Maps and family trees © 2024 by Michael Athanson

All rights reserved
Printed in the United States of America
First American Edition 2024

For information about permission to reproduce selections from this book, write to Permissions, W. W. Norton & Company, Inc., 500 Fifth Avenue, New York, NY 10110

For information about special discounts for bulk purchases, please contact W. W. Norton Special Sales at specialsales@wwnorton.com or 800-233-4830

Manufacturing by Lakeside Book Company

ISBN 978-1-324-05203-6

W. W. Norton & Company, Inc.
500 Fifth Avenue, New York, NY 10110
www.wwnorton.com

W. W. Norton & Company Ltd.
15 Carlisle Street, London W1D 3BS

10 9 8 7 6 5 4 3 2 1

To John and Peter

Contents

Note on Proper Names	ix
Note on Dates	xi
Macedonian and Ptolemaic Rulers of Egypt	xii
Timeline	xiii
Ptolemaic Family Tree	xxii
The Ptolemaic and Seleucid Royal Houses in the Second and First Centuries	xxiv
Maps	xxvi
Introduction: Questions of Identity	1
Prologue: Hail the Conquering Hero	7

PART I APOTHEOSIS (323–221 BC)

1 Rise of a Dynasty	21
2 Brave New World	39
3 Grain, Gold and Glory	59
4 The Life of the Mind	81

PART II CRISIS (221–145 BC)

5 Fragile State	103
6 Rebellion and Retrenchment	121
7 The Hinge of Fate	137
8 One Country, Two Cultures	157

PART III NEUROSIS (145–80 BC)
 9 Out of Joint 173
 10 Mother's Ruin 189
 11 Keeping the Faith 209

PART IV NEMESIS (80–30 BC)
 12 Fight for Survival 229
 13 Dangerous Liaisons 249
 14 Serpent of Old Nile 267

Epilogue: To the Victor the Spoils 285

Notes 291
Sources 301
Bibliography 315
Acknowledgements 331
Index 333
Image Credits 347

Note on Proper Names

Choosing how best to render the names of places and people from the ancient world is a complex task, and largely a matter of personal preference.

For Ptolemaic Egypt, there may be three different versions of a place name to choose from: ancient Egyptian, Greek and modern Arabic. Hence the town called by the Egyptians Khemnu ('eight-city', after a local group of eight deities) was known to the Greeks as Hermopolis (after Hermes, the Greek equivalent of the Egyptian god Thoth) and corresponds to the present-day city of Ashmunein (which, interestingly, harks back to the original Egyptian name). Depending on the vagaries of archaeology and history, places may be better known by the Greek form (examples include Heliopolis, Sais and Sebennytos) or the (anglicised) Arabic form (Karnak, Luxor, Dendera and Edfu).

In this book, which deals with a period in which Greek was the language of government in Egypt and throughout the eastern Mediterranean, the Greek forms of place names have generally been used, both for well-known sites (Memphis, Thebes) and for more obscure locations (for example, Karia, Kilikia, Kyrene and Tarsos, rather than Caria, Cilicia, Cyrene and Tarsus). Where the Latinised or anglicised version is so familiar that using any other variant would merely obfuscate, the commonplace forms have been retained: hence Egypt, Karnak, Cyprus, Rhodes, Athens, Carthage and Babylon – and, indeed, Rome.

A similar approach has been taken with personal names. Less familiar characters (such as Antipatros, Kassandros, Seleukos and

Antiochos) are rendered in their Greek forms (instead of the Latinised or anglicised Antipater, Cassander, Seleucus and Antiochus), but common spellings have been retained for the most familiar names (principally Alexander and Philip, Ptolemy and Cleopatra, but also Herodotus, Julius Caesar, Mark Antony and Octavian).

The ordinal numbers ascribed to each of the Ptolemies (I–XV) and Cleopatras (I–VII) are a modern convention. In their own time, each Ptolemaic ruler would have been known by his/her name and cult title, hence Ptolemy Soter (Ptolemy I), Ptolemy Epiphanes (Ptolemy V), and so forth. Scholars are generally of the opinion that Ptolemy VII Neos Philopator did not enjoy an independent reign, but was only incorporated into the Ptolemaic ruler cult after his death. None the less, the traditional numbering – with Ptolemy VI being succeeded by his brother Ptolemy VIII – has been followed here.

Note on Dates

All dates are BC unless otherwise stated.

Dates in ancient Egypt were expressed in terms of a king's years on the throne, with each regnal year beginning on the date of accession. A date in the format 306/5 indicates that a single (ancient) regnal year spanned two (modern) calendar years.

Macedonian and Ptolemaic Rulers of Egypt

Alexander III ('the Great')	332–323
Philip III Arrhidaios	323–317
Alexander IV	323–310 (nominally 304)
Ptolemy son of Lagus: as satrap	323–304
as king Ptolemy I Soter	304–284
Ptolemy II Philadelphos	284–246
Ptolemy III Euergetes	246–221
Ptolemy IV Philopator	221–204
Ptolemy V Epiphanes	204–180
Ptolemy VI Philometor	180–145
Ptolemy VIII Euergetes II	145–116
Ptolemy IX Soter II	116–107
Ptolemy X Alexander	107–88
Ptolemy IX Soter II (restored)	88–81
Ptolemy XI Alexander II and Berenike III	80
Ptolemy XII Neos Dionysos	80–58
Berenike IV	58–55
Ptolemy XII Neos Dionysos (restored)	55–51
Cleopatra VII and Ptolemy XIII	51–47
and Ptolemy XIV	47–44
and Ptolemy XV	44–30

Timeline

Date	Events in Ptolemaic lands	Events elsewhere
367	Birth of Ptolemy son of Lagus	
332	Alexander III of Macedon conquers Egypt (November)	
331	Alexander visits Siwa oracle Foundation of Alexandria (April)	
324		Mass wedding in Susa
323	Alexander dies, succeeded by Philip III Arrhidaios (June) Ptolemy becomes satrap of Egypt	
321	Alexander's body brought to Egypt Wars of the Successors between Alexander's generals (until 301) Ptolemy gains Kyrenaika	
317	Philip III killed, succeeded by Alexander IV	
315	Ptolemy invades Cyprus	
312	Battle of Gaza	
311	Alexandria becomes capital of Egypt; Satrap Stela	

Date	Events in Ptolemaic lands	Events elsewhere
310	Alexander IV killed	
Ptolemy I		
304	Ptolemy adopts royal titles (Ptolemy I)	
301	Ptolemy gains Koile-Syria	
300	Euclid's *Elements*	
299	Ptolemy provides for burial of Apis bull	
297	Demetrios of Phaleron arrives in Alexandria, helps found Mouseion	
285	Ptolemy names his son as co-ruler	
Ptolemy II		
284	Ptolemy II becomes king	
280	Pharos lighthouse completed	Colossus of Rhodes completed
279	Grand Procession (Ptolemaieia)	
275	Ptolemy II annexes Lower Nubia (Dodekaschoinos)	
274	First Syrian War (until 271)	
273	Egypt and Rome exchange embassies	
270	Canal from Nile to Red Sea dredged and repaired	
267		Chremonidean War (until 261)
264		First Punic War (until 241)
261	Zenon becomes agent for Apollonios	
260	Second Syrian War (until 253)	
259	Revenue laws and nationwide census	

Date	Events in Ptolemaic lands	Events elsewhere
Ptolemy III		
246	Ptolemy II dies, succeeded by his son Ptolemy III	
	Third Syrian War (until 241)	
238	Synod and decree of Canopus	
237	Foundation of temple of Horus at Apollonopolis (August)	
Ptolemy IV		
222	Ptolemy III dies, succeeded by his son Ptolemy IV	
219	Fourth Syrian War (until 217)	
218		Second Punic War (until 201)
217	Battle of Raphia (June); synod and decree (November)	
214		First Macedonian War (until 205)
210	Rome sends embassy to Alexandria	
205	Revolt in Lower Egypt	
	Revolt in Upper Egypt, Horwennefer proclaimed pharaoh	
Ptolemy V		
204	Ptolemy IV dies, succeeded by his son Ptolemy V	
202	Fifth Syrian War (until 195)	
200		Second Macedonian War (until 196)
197	Ptolemy V crowned at Memphis; synod and decree (March)	
194	Ptolemy V marries Cleopatra I	
186	Revolt in Upper Egypt defeated, Ankhwennefer captured (August)	

Date	Events in Ptolemaic lands	Events elsewhere
184	Revolt in Lower Egypt defeated (March)	

Ptolemy VI and Ptolemy VIII

Date	Events in Ptolemaic lands	Events elsewhere
180	Ptolemy V dies, succeeded by his son Ptolemy VI	
175	Cleopatra II appointed co-ruler	
172	Ptolemaios enters the Sarapieion as a recluse	
171		Third Macedonian War (until 168)
170	Sixth Syrian War (until 168)	
	Ptolemy VIII (younger brother of Ptolemy VI) declared co-regent	
168	Day of Eleusis (July)	
167		Maccabean Revolt (until 160)
165	Failed coup attempt by Dionysios Petosarapis	
164	Revolt in Upper Egypt; Ptolemy VI flees to Cyprus	
163	Ptolemy VI restored; Ptolemy VIII flees to Rome	
155	Ptolemy VIII draws up his will leaving Egypt to Rome	
150		Fourth Macedonian War (until 148)
149		Third Punic War (until 146)
146		Rome destroys Carthage, conquers Greece
145	Ptolemy VI dies in battle, succeeded by Ptolemy VIII	

Date	Events in Ptolemaic lands	Events elsewhere
142	Dedication of temple of Horus at Apollonopolis	
	Cleopatra III appointed co-ruler	
141	Failed insurrection (May)	
132	Civil war between Ptolemy VIII/ Cleopatra III and Cleopatra II	
126	Dryton draws up his third will (June)	
124	Civil war ends, triple monarchy restored	
121		Roman armies enter Gaul
120	Menkhes village scribe at Kerkeosiris (until 111)	
118	Amnesty decree (April)	

Ptolemy IX and Ptolemy X

Date	Events in Ptolemaic lands	Events elsewhere
116	Ptolemy VIII dies, succeeded by his elder son Ptolemy IX	
	Cleopatra II dies	
	Roman tourists visit Philae	
112	Roman senator Lucius Memmius pays official visit to Egypt	
107	Ptolemy IX deposed by his brother Ptolemy X	
101	Cleopatra III killed	
96	Kyrenaika passes to Rome	
88	Revolt and destruction of Thebes	
	Ptolemy X deposed and Ptolemy IX restored (September)	
86	Second coronation and jubilee of Ptolemy IX	First Mithridatic War (until 85)
83		Second Mithridatic War (until 81)

Date	Events in Ptolemaic lands	Events elsewhere
81	Ptolemy IX appoints his daughter Berenike III co-ruler	

Ptolemy XI

Date	Events in Ptolemaic lands	Events elsewhere
81	Ptolemy IX dies (December), succeeded by Berenike III	
80	Ptolemy XI (son of Ptolemy X) appointed co-ruler	
	Berenike III and Ptolemy XI killed	

Ptolemy XII

Date	Events in Ptolemaic lands	Events elsewhere
80	Ptolemy XII (son of Ptolemy IX) succeeds as king of Egypt	
75		Third Mithridatic War (until 63)
63		Rome conquers Judaea
60		First Triumvirate
59	Roman embassy to Alexandria	
58	Rome annexes Cyprus	
	Ptolemy XII deposed by his daughter Berenike IV with Cleopatra Tryphaina co-ruler for one year	
55	Berenike IV deposed and Ptolemy XII restored (April)	Julius Caesar lands in Britain
54	Work begins on temple of Hathor at Tentyris (July)	
52	Ptolemy XII appoints his daughter Cleopatra VII co-ruler	

Cleopatra VII

Date	Events in Ptolemaic lands	Events elsewhere
51	Ptolemy XII dies, succeeded by Cleopatra VII and her brother Ptolemy XIII	
50	Decoration of roof chapels at Tentyris	

TIMELINE

Date	Events in Ptolemaic lands	Events elsewhere
49		Caesar crosses the Rubicon
48	Pompey killed in Egypt (September)	
	Caesar arrives in Alexandria and meets Cleopatra (October)	
	Cleopatra deposed in favour of her sister Arsinoe	
47	Ptolemy XIII dies, succeeded as co-ruler by his brother Ptolemy XIV	
	Birth of Ptolemy Caesarion	
46	Cleopatra travels to Rome to stay with Caesar	
	Birth of Imhotep (July)	
44		Assassination of Caesar (March)
	Ptolemy XIV dies; Ptolemy XV Caesarion appointed co-ruler	
43	Low Nile flood leads to famine (until 41)	Second Triumvirate
42	Death of Taimhotep (January)	Battle of Philippi ends Roman civil war
41		Cleopatra visits Antony at Tarsos
40	Birth of Alexander Helios and Cleopatra Selene	
39	Imhotep proclaimed high priest of Ptah	
37	Cleopatra proclaims a renaissance	
36	Birth of Ptolemy Philadelphos	
34	Donations of Alexandria	
31		Battle of Actium (September)

Date	Events in Ptolemaic lands	Events elsewhere
30	Octavian conquers Egypt (1 August) Mark Antony dies, Cleopatra VII takes her own life (10 August) Ptolemy XV Caesarion killed	
29	Temple services begin at Tentyris (February)	Octavian's triumph in Rome

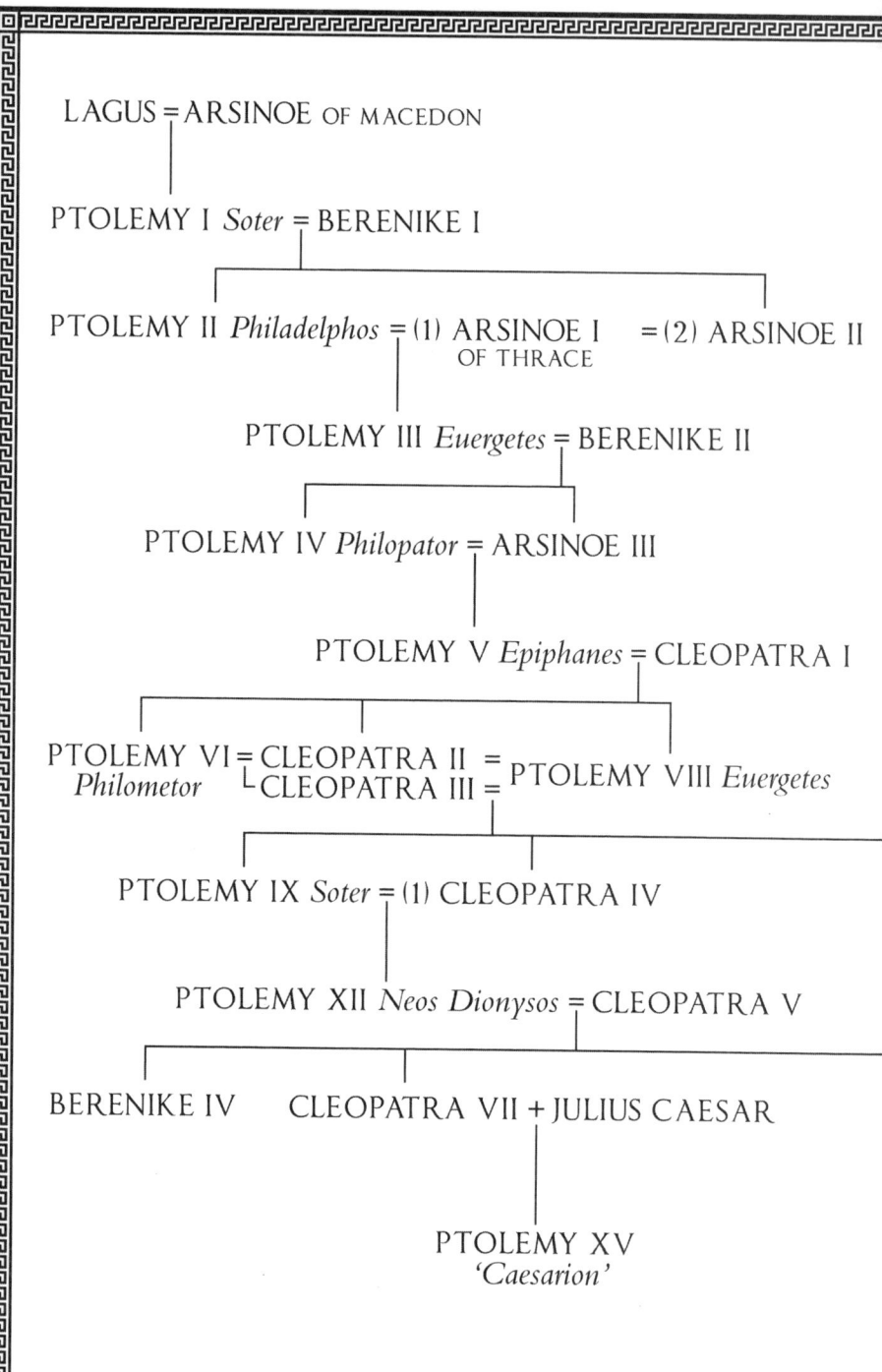

THE PTOLEMAIC ROYAL HOUSE

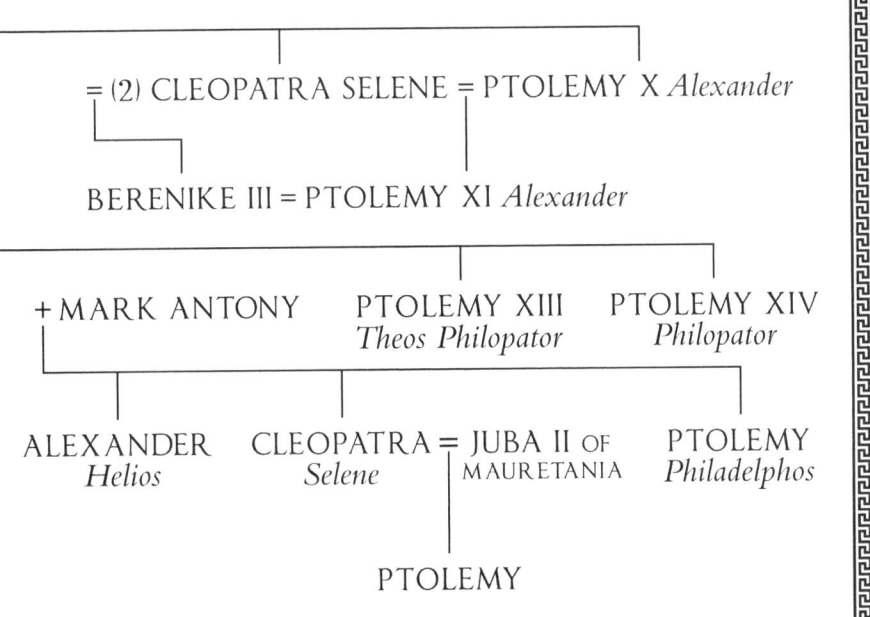

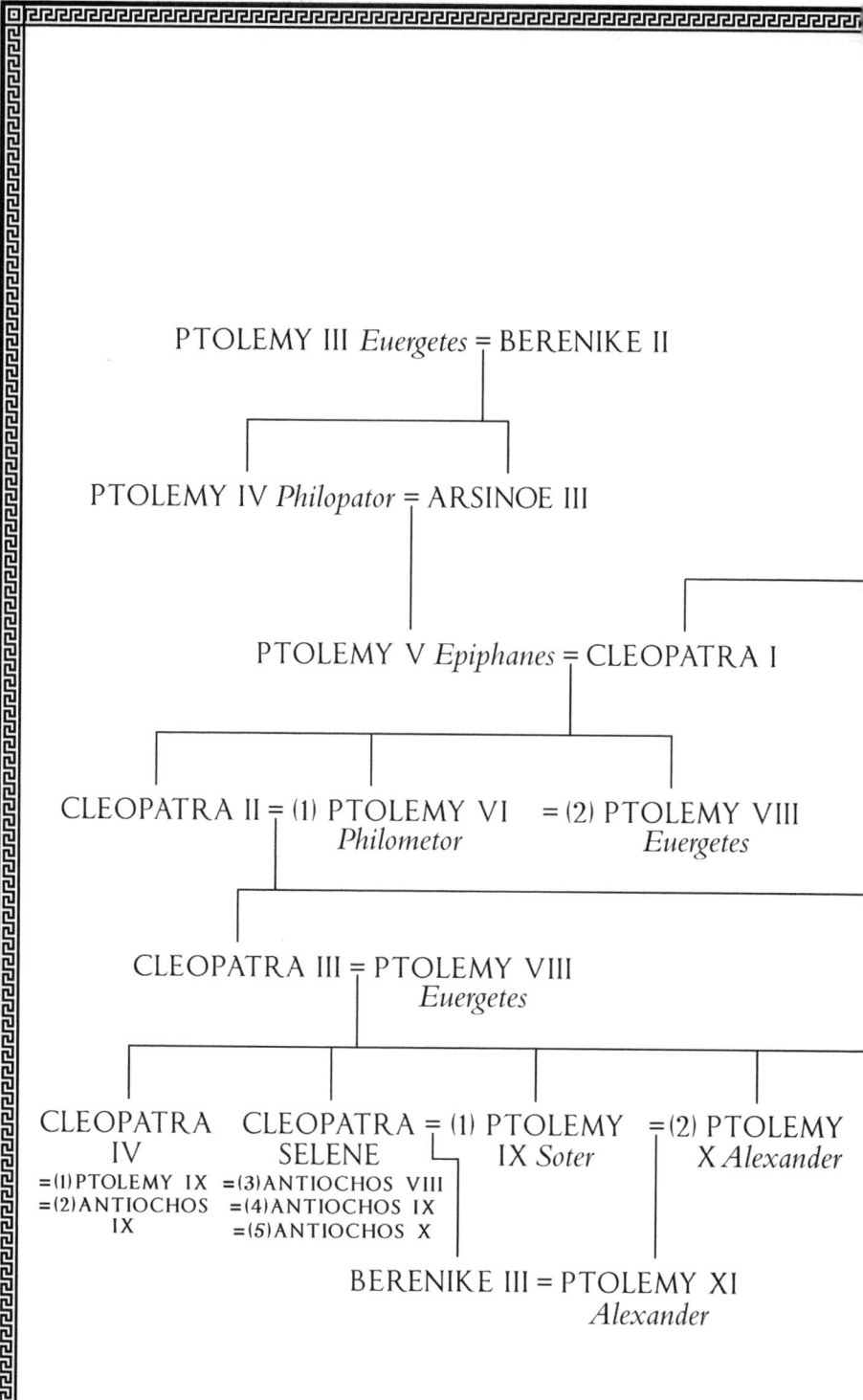

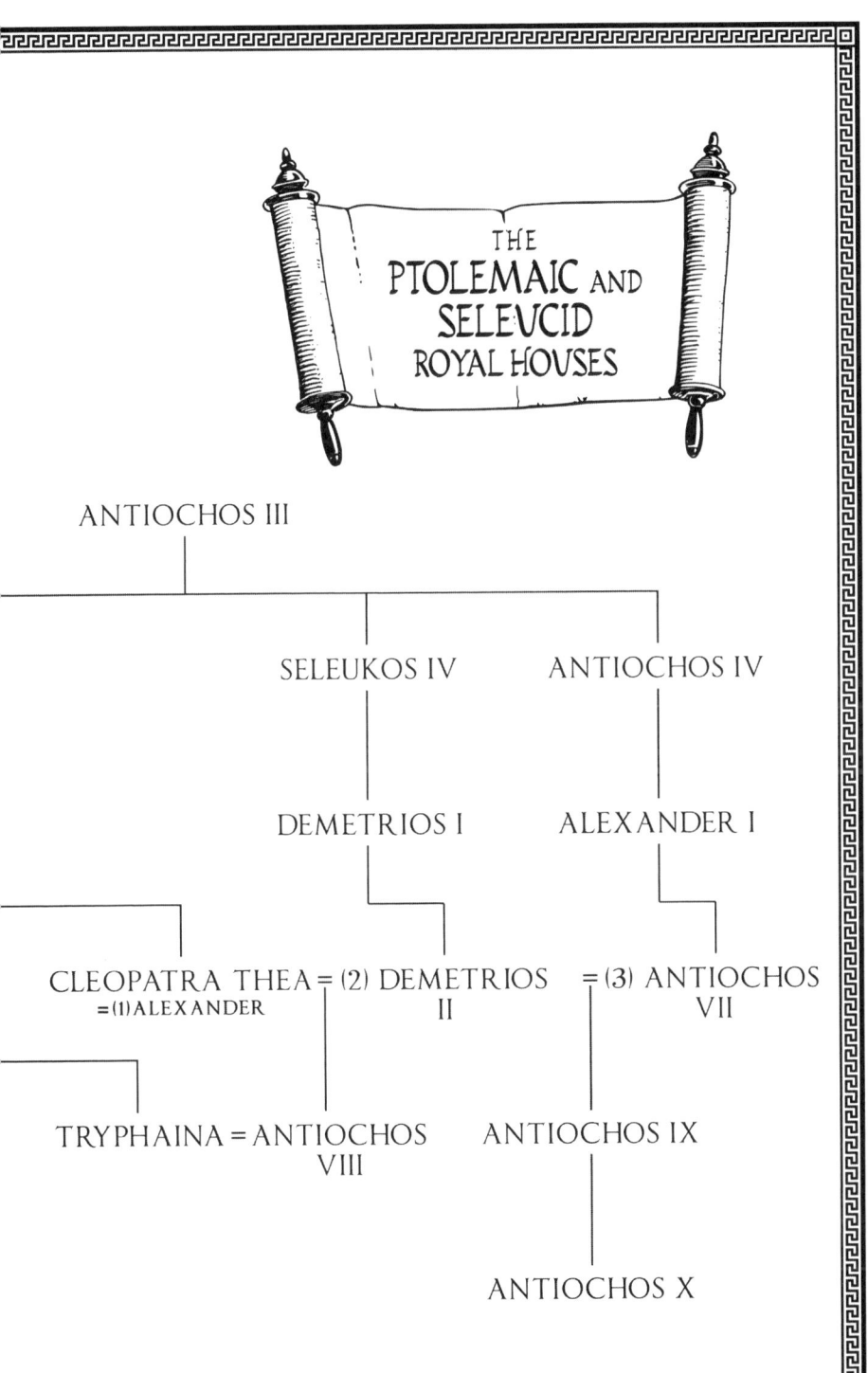

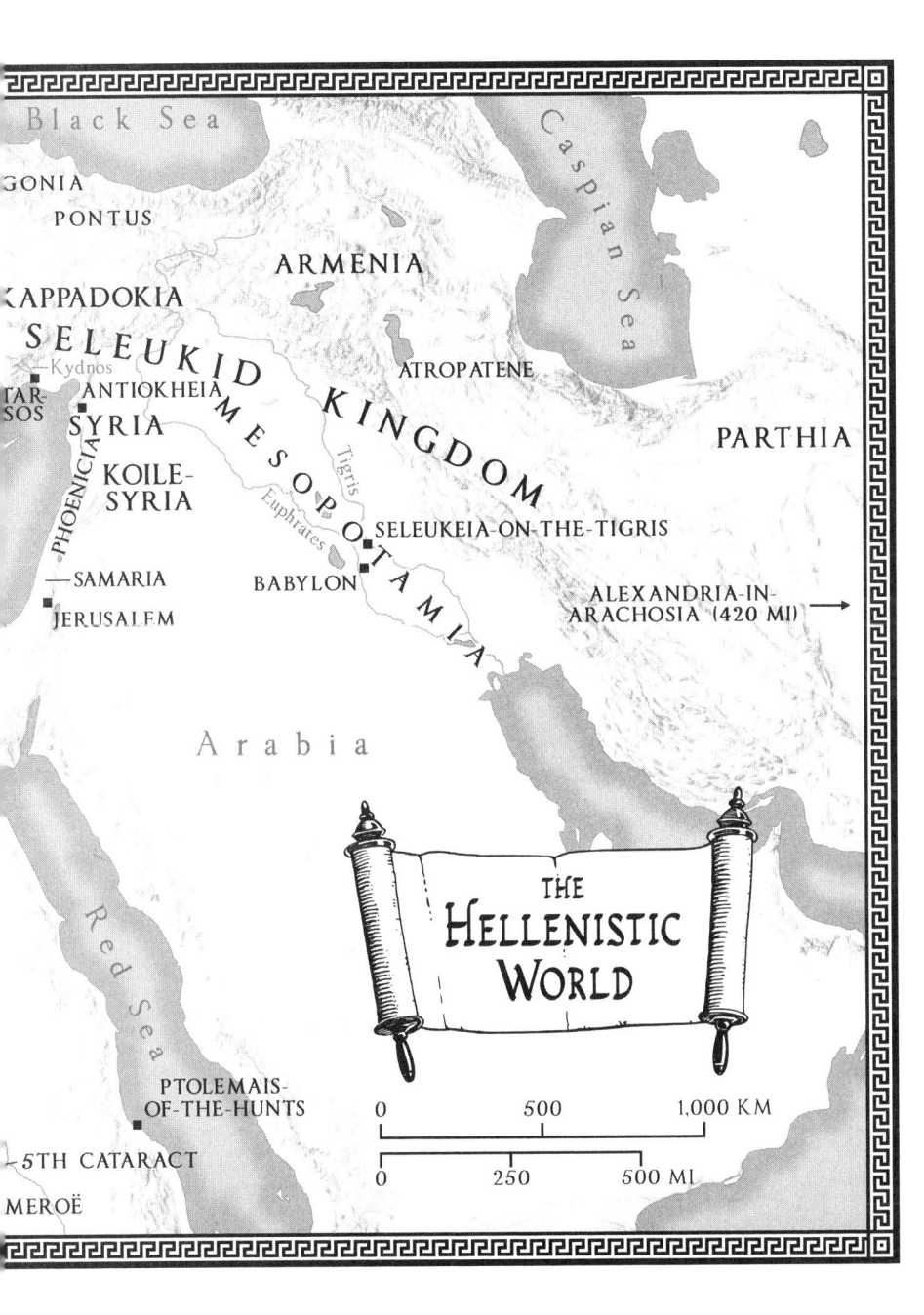

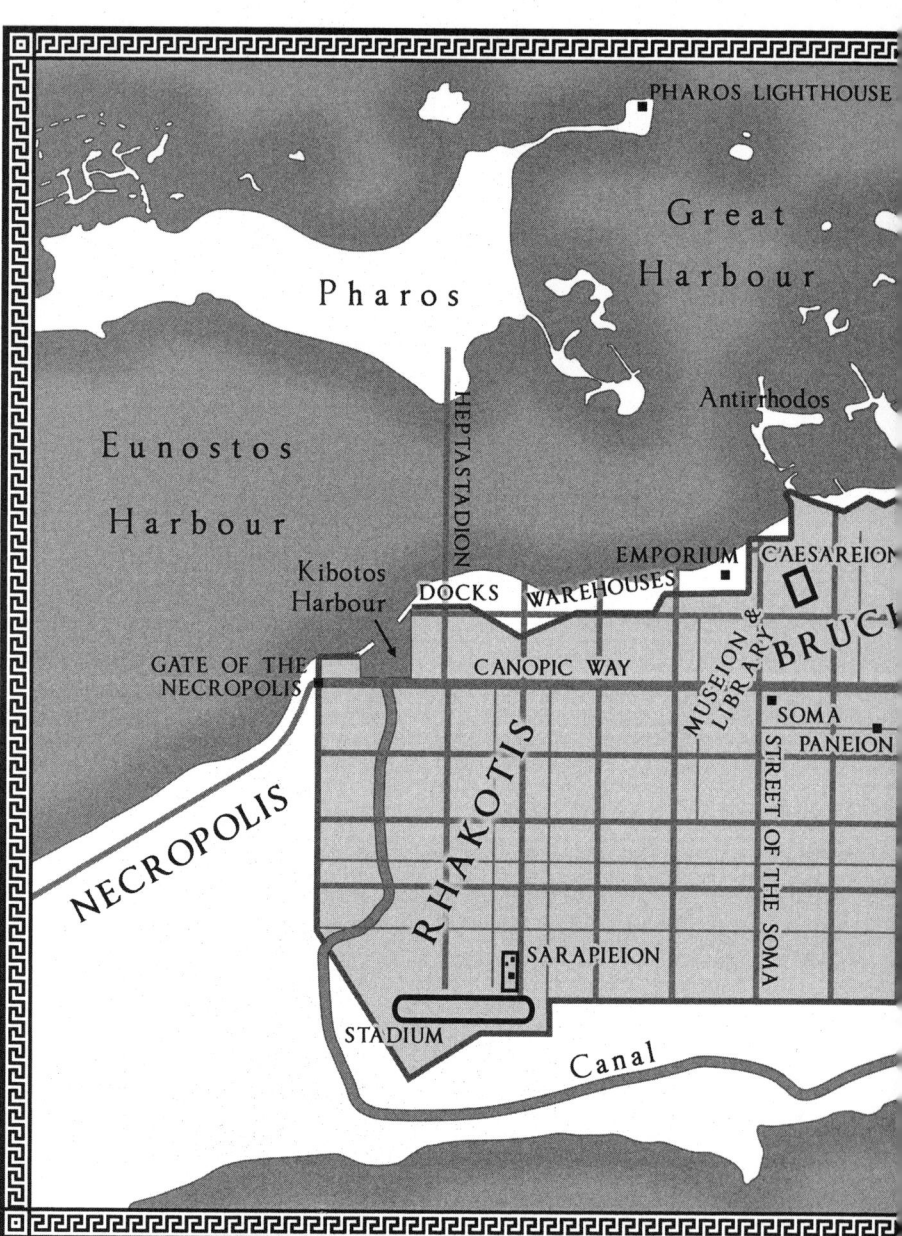

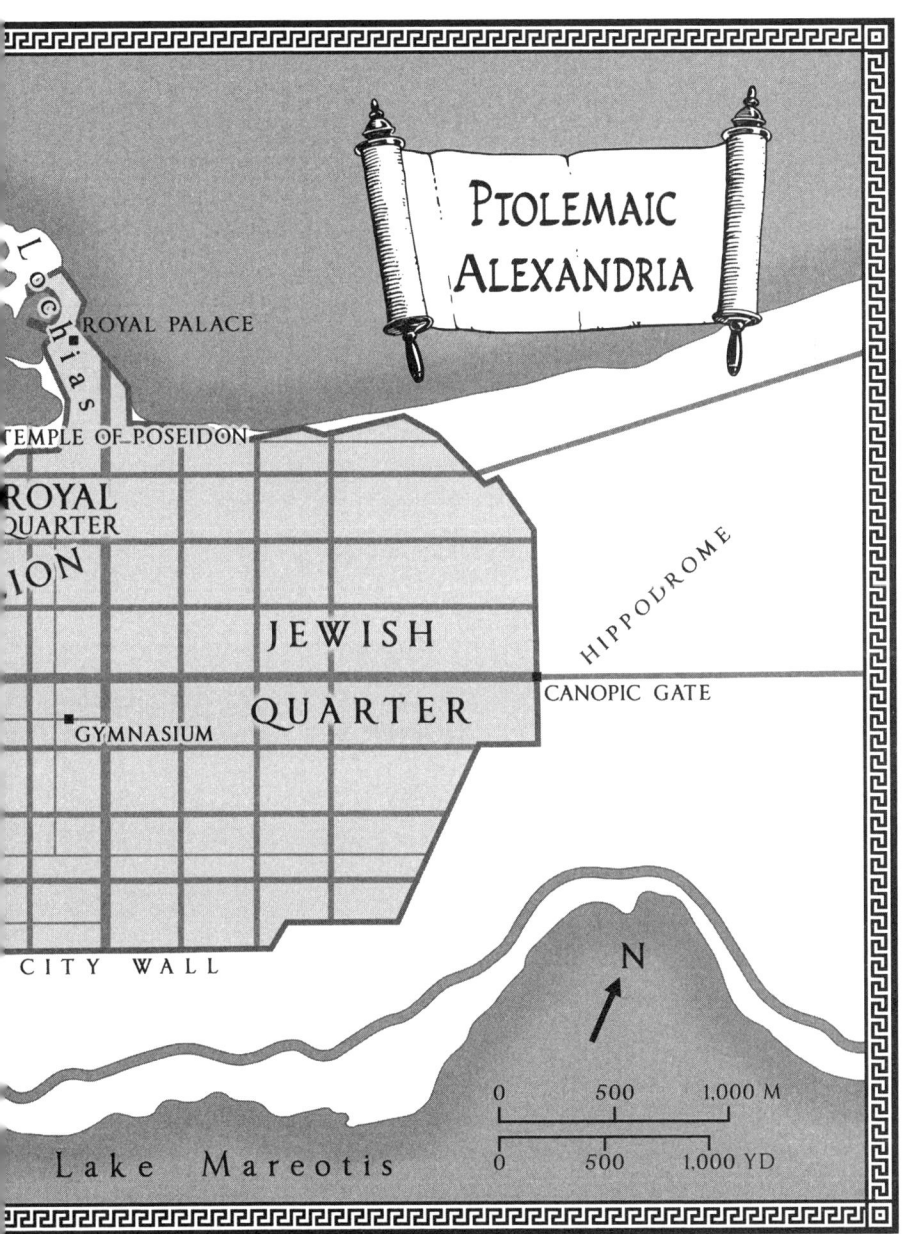

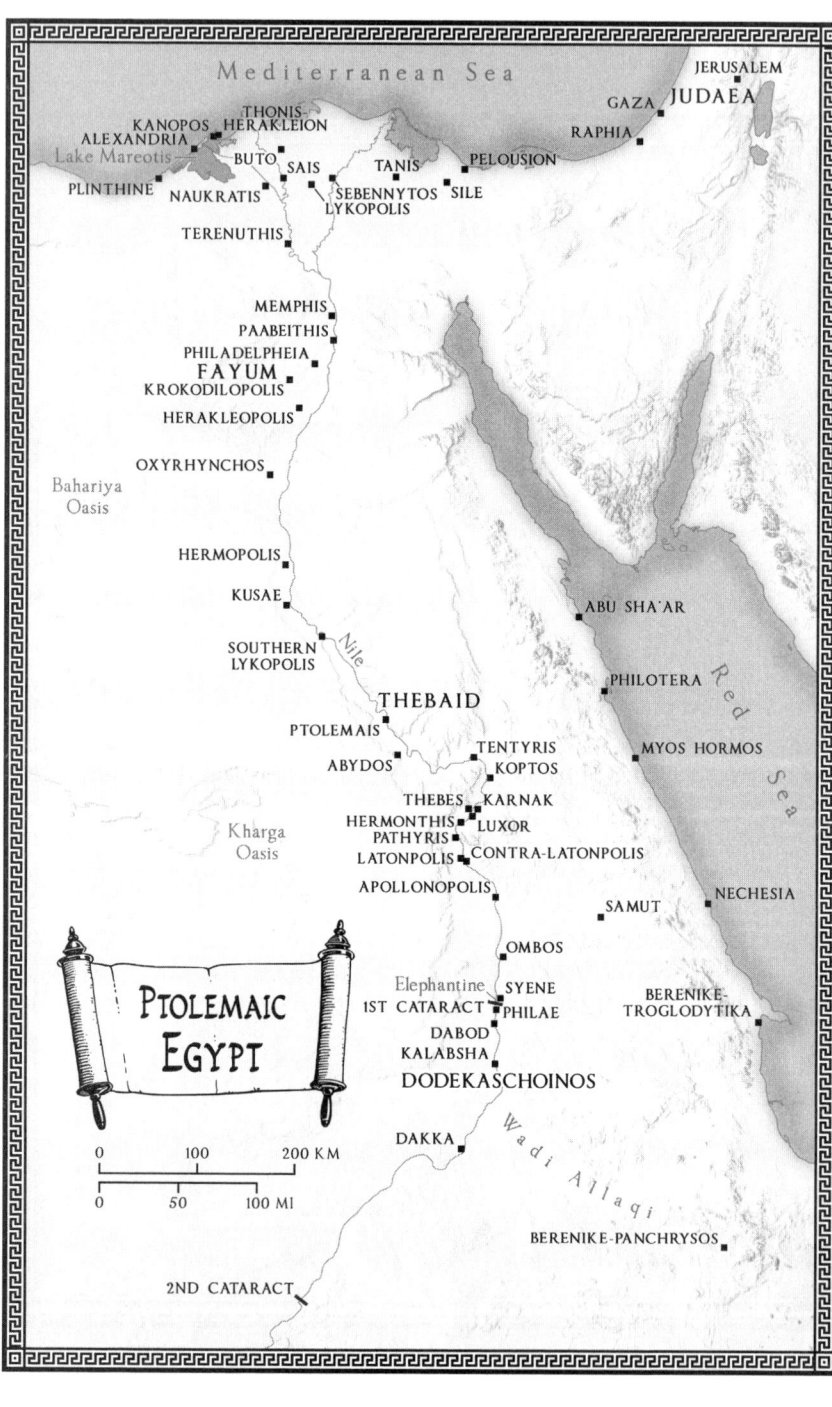

Introduction: Questions of Identity

On 10 August 30 BC, Queen Cleopatra and her two ladies-in-waiting found themselves alone at last in a chamber of the royal palace in Alexandria. A sprawling complex of opulent rooms and airy courtyards, the regal residence occupied a promontory on the Mediterranean shore of Egypt. From its windows, there were stunning views out across the harbour, filled with boats from every nation; to the soaring Pharos lighthouse on its rocky outcrop, its summit topped with a gleaming statue of Zeus; and to the open sea beyond. Outside the palace walls, the buzzing, cosmopolitan city, founded by Alexander the Great some three centuries earlier, was now the liveliest metropolis in the world, where people and ideas from Europe, Asia and Africa met in a heady mix. Its library and temple of the Muses had nurtured the finest minds, advancing knowledge in every sphere of human enquiry. And, at the heart of everything, the royal quarter, powerbase of the monarchs who had created Alexandria and the empire of which it was the crown jewel.

But on this day, the dynasty that had ruled the Nile Valley for longer than any other in its 3,000-year history was about to come to an end. Enmeshed in increasingly complex geopolitics, Egypt had found itself backing the wrong side in a power struggle between foreigners that would reshape the entire ancient world. Faced with invasion on two fronts, the country had fallen. Roman troops were occupying Alexandria, and all escape routes were blocked. Egypt's deposed sovereign, Cleopatra, had been taken prisoner and incarcerated in her own palace, watched over day and night by their captors.

The queen's powers of persuasion had been the defining characteristic of her twenty-year reign, and she now put them to use one last time, convincing the bored guards that she posed no threat. Then, as soon as their backs were turned, 'She put on her most beautiful apparel, arranged her body in most seemly fashion, took in her hands all the emblems of royalty, and so died.'[1] By the time the sentries returned, it was too late: 'they found Cleopatra lying dead upon a golden couch, arrayed in royal state. And of her two women, the one called Iras was dying at her feet, while Charmion, already tottering and heavy-handed, was trying to arrange the diadem which encircled the queen's brow.'[2]

The precise manner of Cleopatra's death was a mystery,

> for the only marks on her body were slight pricks on the arm. Some say that she applied to herself an asp which had been brought in to her in a water-jar, or perhaps hidden in some flowers. Others declare that she had smeared a pin, with which she was wont to fasten her hair, with some poison… In this or in some very similar way she perished, and her two handmaidens with her.[3]

The turbulent life, tumultuous reign and tragic death of Cleopatra – the seventh queen of her royal house to bear that name – fascinated her contemporaries and captivated imaginations across the world in the 2,000 years since. To the Romans, who inherited her kingdom, she was the author of her own demise:

> By love she gained the title of Queen of the Egyptians, and when she hoped by the same means to win also that of Queen of the Romans, she failed of this and lost the other besides. She captivated the two greatest Romans of her day, and because of the third she destroyed herself.[4]

Rome's staunch republicans took an ever-dimmer view. To them, Cleopatra was the embodiment of luxury and licence, an oriental despot brought down by her own moral turpitude.

Cleopatra's own people saw things rather differently. To her Greek-speaking subjects, immigrants and their descendants from across the eastern Mediterranean, she had been a noble scion of her dynasty. Her distant forebear, the Macedonian general, Ptolemy son of Lagus, had served as one of Alexander the Great's closest lieutenants before forging an empire from the conqueror's legacy. Subsequent Ptolemies had turned Egypt into the greatest of the Hellenistic kingdoms, and Alexandria into a beacon of prosperity, culture and sophistication. There had, of course, been ups and downs over the centuries; but Cleopatra VII had seemed to be on the right side of history. She had regained for the crown many of its former territories, and put on displays of pomp and pageantry to outshine any sovereign. In short, she had epitomised the magnificence of monarchy.

To the native inhabitants of Egypt, whose ancestors had tilled the fertile soils of the Nile Valley for countless generations, Cleopatra had been a true pharaoh. Though of Greek Macedonian heritage, she had understood the importance of honouring the traditional deities of Egypt. She had built and beautified temples, observed the ancient rites and festivals and paid her respects in person to the sacred animals that were such a distinctive and defining characteristic of Egyptian religion. Like every pharaoh, she had herself been hedged with divinity. Reigning as the living Isis, the earthly incarnation of the universal goddess and mother of the world, Cleopatra had been the very model of Egyptian kingship.

In short, what you thought about Cleopatra, in her own lifetime and immediately after her death, depended on your own background.

Likewise, in our own age of contested views, questions of identity swirl around the queen on every side. Was she beautiful? (Not, it would appear, by the standards of modern aesthetics.) Was she African? (Partly: though born on the continent of Africa, where her forebears had lived for over two centuries, she was of Macedonian Greek heritage. She was queen of Egypt, but not an Egyptian queen.) Was she a fearless defender of women's rights or a lascivious whore? (Neither: such modern labels cannot be readily applied to the distant past, and to do so risks turning complex historical figures into one-dimensional actors in our contemporary drama.)

If we are to understand Cleopatra, as a product of her own time and place, we have to ask a different set of questions. What were the cultural and political cross-currents that shaped Mediterranean history in the centuries leading up to her life and reign? How did the markedly different population groups in Egypt live alongside each other? What was the nature of the Ptolemaic monarchy? What sort of a city was ancient Alexandria? Were the rise of Rome and the fall of Egypt inevitable? By examining Cleopatra's complex inheritance – across the full sweep of Ptolemaic history, from Alexander the Great to the queen's own reign – this book seeks to answer such questions.

Alexander the Great and Cleopatra: two of the most recognisable names from history. Yet the period of three centuries between these two great lives is surprisingly little known outside specialist academic circles. Even for scholars, the Ptolemaic period falls between two stools: too late for Egyptologists, too early for Roman historians; 'the gap between where classical Greece ended and imperial Rome began'.[5] Those who do approach Ptolemaic Egypt generally do so by way of the classical evidence: Greek papyri and the (heavily biased) accounts of Greek and Roman commentators. They tell of a vibrant, cosmopolitan country, buzzing with commerce and new ideas, a land of innovation and opportunity. But this material reveals only one side of the story. Ptolemaic Egypt was a country of (at least) two cultures. The art, architecture, artefacts and inscriptions produced by and for the indigenous population give a different account: of a land that cherished its ancient customs, but also sought to reinterpret and reinvent them to suit the changing times. A land of tradition and quiet evolution.

The source material for Ptolemaic history is rich and diverse. Alongside the well-known (but often heavily biased) accounts of ancient historians, geographers and commentators – writers like Polybius, Diodorus Siculus, Strabo, even Julius Caesar himself – there are inscriptions on statues, stelae and temple walls, and literally thousands of papyrus documents. Ancient Egypt was always an obsessively bureaucratic country, and it has been estimated that a single government office under the Ptolemies might have used up to twenty rolls of papyrus a day. Fortunately, the dry climate of Egypt is particularly conducive to the preservation of organic materials, and the papyri that have been recovered – dumped on ancient rubbish heaps or upcycled into cartonnage for mummy cases – illustrate life in Ptolemaic Egypt in extraordinary detail. Some fifty archives of papyri have been unearthed dating from the period between Alexander and Cleopatra. The single largest find was made just before the First World War in the ruins of an ancient town, by peasants digging for mudbrick to use as fertiliser; it comprised over 2,000 separate documents, and sheds light on everything from agriculture and irrigation works to internal trade and local government. Another archive was discovered among the wrappings of mummified crocodiles in an ancient cemetery.

In addition to texts, there are objects. Royal and private sculpture, far from presenting a degenerate version of Greek or pharaonic antecedents, includes some of the most innovative and compelling works of art to have survived from the ancient world. Yet this aspect of Ptolemaic Egypt is surprisingly little known. From small votive objects to entire temples, the material evidence reveals the rich cultural inheritance of the Nile Valley under the Ptolemies. Elements that existed long before Alexander's conquest sit alongside new fashions brought from other eastern lands. Artefacts speak of ancient social structures co-existing with new economic and political institutions.

Inscriptions and material remains alike confound any notions of Hellenistic Egypt as a pale imitation of its pharaonic forerunner, speaking instead of an undoubted 'Ptolemaic brilliance'.[6] This book aims to bring that brilliance to life, revealing afresh extraordinary events, remarkable achievements and larger-than-life personalities. The narrative follows the birth, flourishing, decline and fall of Ptolemaic power from Alexander the Great to Cleopatra. It is arranged in four parts, corresponding to the four main phases of Ptolemaic history: the golden age of Ptolemies I–III, when a great kingdom was forged; an era of transition under Ptolemies IV–VI, when the empire began to fray at the edges, buffeted by foreign wars and internal revolts; the crisis years of Ptolemies VIII–XI, when the country, riven by dynastic disputes, became fatally weakened; and the endgame, played out under Ptolemies XII–XV and the great Cleopatra, when Ptolemaic rule witnessed one final flourish before succumbing to the power of Rome.

Getting under the skin of Ptolemaic Egypt is challenging, but immensely rewarding. For what emerges, whether in the hallowed halls of Alexandria's Great Library among the finest intellectuals of the Greek-speaking world or in the temples of the Nile Valley among the native Egyptian clergy, is a period of unusual dynamism and creativity. A period that shaped, not only Cleopatra's life and reign, but the world of ideas we still inhabit. A period like no other in history.

Prologue: Hail the Conquering Hero

In the autumn, the season of new growth, as green shoots began to appear in the well-watered fields along the banks of the Nile, a foreign ruler from across the sea made his way to Egypt's ancient capital. He did not come alone, but was accompanied by a sizeable detachment of his own soldiers; for this warrior had just conquered Egypt by force of arms, and was heading to Memphis to claim his prize and receive the homage of his new subjects.

In the city's main temple, dedicated to the local creator god Ptah, there was a special area set aside for his living embodiment, a sacred bull. The beast had its own stall, its own priests and lived a life of pampered bovine luxury. It was revered not just as Ptah's avatar but also as the guarantor of royal authority and national prosperity. Its cult stretched back to the dawn of history, an unbroken thread that had endured – through war and famine, invasion and turmoil – unchanged and unchanging. The sacred bull asserted by its very presence in the heart of Memphis that the Egypt of the pharaohs lived on.

As the animal paced back and forth in its stall, the attendant priests must have felt a degree of apprehension. Would their country's new ruler respect age-old tradition by venerating the bull in their care? This latest conqueror was no native Egyptian, so could hardly be expected to hold any particular allegiance to the Egyptian gods. The priests remembered only too well the recent rule of the hated Persians, who had shown scant regard for Egypt's animal cults, cementing the people's fear and loathing for foreign overlords. Another new king might be no better. As the sound of horses' hooves and marching men came into earshot, the moment of truth had arrived.

Gaza, gateway to Egypt: between September and November 332, Alexander III of Macedon, known to posterity as Alexander the Great, besieged and captured the fortress city in southern Palestine. Militarily, it was not a vital objective, and his troops could easily have circumvented it on their way to the Nile Valley. But Alexander believed that capturing Gaza, long regarded as impregnable, would burnish the credentials of his army as an unstoppable force. However, there may have been another reason why the city's capture was deemed important, even necessary: some eleven centuries earlier, Egypt's greatest warrior pharaoh, Thutmose III, had captured Gaza from its Palestinian inhabitants and established it as a forward military base for subsequent campaigns of conquest in the Near East. In doing so, he had renamed the city, with typical pharaonic bombast, 'Captured by the Ruler'. Alexander was well read, well advised and well aware of Egyptian history. Capturing Gaza not only sent a message to his arch-enemies, the Persians, it also announced to the Egyptians – nominally Persian subjects for the past decade, but fiercely proud of their own history and identity – that here was a new conquering hero, a worthy successor to the mighty pharaohs of the past.

The city, its defending troops bolstered by Arab mercenaries and with stores of food laid up, held out stubbornly against Alexander's army for two months; its stout walls, surrounded on all sides by soft, sandy ground, had successfully resisted other armies before; but eventually, Macedonian resolve, tactics and weaponry prevailed. Alexander ordered a high mound to be constructed all around the city, giving his siege engines the opportunity to attack Gaza's walls in their upper courses, where they were thinnest and weakest; while tunnels dug secretly under the fortifications hastened their collapse. The Gazan troops fought and died to a man. Eventually, the city fell.

What happened next betrayed Alexander's ruthlessness, and more than a streak of cruelty. Since boyhood, he had been captivated, if not a little obsessed, with Homer's epic tale of the Trojan War. He is said to have carried a copy of the *Iliad* with him at all times, annotated by his boyhood tutor, Aristotle. One of many episodes that lodged in his mind was Achilles' treatment of the defeated Hector, whose body had been tied to a chariot and driven round the walls of Troy – three times for good measure. Alexander now seized the opportunity to live out his Homeric fantasy. The unfortunate victim was the defeated Arab governor of Gaza, the eunuch Batis. He was attached to a chariot while still alive, and dragged round the walls of the city until he died an excruciating and humiliating death. No doubt the Macedonian soldiers jeered while the Gazan women and children looked on in horror. They themselves were promptly sold into slavery before the city was repopulated from surrounding villages, and retained by Alexander as a fortified military base.

News of Gaza's fall and Batis' fate must have travelled fast. By the time Alexander and his army reached Pelousion, on Egypt's northeastern border, after a march of seven days and 130 miles, the waiting Persian governor, Mazaces, knew he had no option but to surrender. (He was no doubt thinking of his own skin, as much as the fate of the Nile Valley.) Egypt had sent a large number of troops to support its Persian overlord, Darius III, at the fateful Battle of Issos in November the previous year; as a result, the country was now denuded of fighting men, unable to offer even token resistance to the Macedonian force. Tipping the scales even further in Alexander's favour was his fleet of warships, which had set sail from Phoenicia when he left Gaza, and was already moored off Pelousion. The Egyptians were outnumbered at sea and on land. As Alexander's biographer later wrote:

> When Mazaces the Persian ... ascertained how the battle at Issos had resulted, that Darius had fled in disgraceful flight, and that Phoenicia, Syria, and most of Arabia were already in Alexander's possession, as he had no Persian force with which he could offer resistance, he admitted Alexander into the cities and the country in a friendly way.[1]

Moreover, Mazaces is said to have surrendered the entire contents of the Egyptian state treasury, a sum of 800 talents.

Alexander, having received the submission of Egypt, might have been expected to move on to the next military goal (as he had after each of his previous victories), and pursue the Persians eastwards. Instead, for reasons that remain hazy, he turned southwards and headed for Egypt's capital. Whatever his motivations, it seems clear that Egypt, the most ancient and sophisticated of the civilisations of the ancient Near East, held a special allure for the Macedonian conqueror. In particular, traditional pharaonic ideology – of an omnipotent, transcendent monarchy established by divine right – appealed to Alexander's developing self-image.

And so, in November 332, after installing a garrison at Pelousion and ordering his ships to sail upriver, Alexander himself set off overland. His first stop was at the cult centre of the sun god Ra, long regarded by the Egyptians as the ultimate creator god and the patron deity of divine kingship. The Egyptians called the place Iunu, but Alexander and his Greek-speaking successors would know it as Heliopolis, 'sun city'. From there, with the Nile on his right, he continued marching towards the capital: 'He reached that city through the desert, after getting possession of all the places on the march through the voluntary surrender of the inhabitants. Thence he crossed the stream and came to Memphis.'[2]

In the temple of Ptah, the priests attending the sacred bull need not have worried. Alexander was not only intrigued and entranced by Egyptian religion, he also had an instinctive understanding of the power of propaganda. If he were to hold Egypt, he needed to be accepted and welcomed by the Egyptians as a legitimate pharaoh. This in turn required him to behave like one. By delivering Egypt from Persian rule, he had made a good start. Where the Persians had acquired a reputation – perhaps unfair, but widely held – for dishonouring the Egyptian gods, Alexander would go out of his way to honour them. He therefore paid appropriate reverence to the sacred bull of Memphis – called Hep in Egyptian, rendered as Apis in Greek – and ordered his troops to respect Egyptian sensibilities by not encroaching on the necropolis overlooking the city. A scrap of papyrus, pinned up at the entrance to the cemetery by Alexander's general, bore the brief but clear instruction: '[Order] of Peukestas: no entry, priestly property'.

Before departing Memphis, Alexander also observed the traditional rites of pharaonic accession, which had been carried out in the city since the foundation of the Egyptian state. At every accession, the new pharaoh would adopt and proclaim his official names and epithets: different elements in a five-fold titulary that summed up the multi-faceted roles of an Egyptian ruler. True to form, Alexander's choice of titles showed his awareness of Egypt's history and his desire to be seen as a legitimate king. His throne name, 'Ra's chosen one, beloved of [the god] Amun' (Egyptian *setepenra-meryamun*), deliberately harked back to the fabled, glorious reign of Ramesses II, combining two epithets first borne by that illustrious pharaoh some nine centuries earlier. Alexander's other royal titles followed more recent precedent, recalling the reign of Nakhthorheb, Egypt's last native pharaoh who had lost his kingdom to the Persians twenty years before Alexander came to the rescue. Most telling of these was the epithet 'he who drives out the foreigners' (Eg. *teken-khasut*). The message could not have been clearer: though foreign himself, Alexander intended to rule the Nile Valley as an Egyptian king, giving the people back their independence after two decades of submission under a foreign yoke. As a later commentator put it, 'since the Persians had committed impieties against the temples and had governed harshly, the Egyptians welcomed the Macedonians'.³

Alexander's concern to uphold and associate himself with the traditional rites of Egyptian monarchy was likewise reflected in his carefully chosen patronage of the country's cults and temples. As part of his programme for Egypt, he ordered new work at the great religious complex at Karnak (Eg. Ipet-sut, 'the most select of places'), the country's foremost sacred site in Upper Egypt, heartland of pharaonic kingship. Among the myriad courts, pylons and shrines within the Karnak complex, he chose as the centrepiece of his patronage the royal cult chapel built by the warrior pharaoh Thutmose III. By restoring the work of a great conqueror of the past, Alexander was aligning himself with the venerable Egyptian tradition of muscular, militaristic kingship. Another of his projects at Karnak was to commission a set of reliefs for the small temple of Khonsu. Again, the choice was deliberate: in ancient Egyptian religion, Khonsu was regarded as the son of Amun, the greatest god of the entire pantheon. Moreover, on the walls of Khonsu's temple, Alexander had himself depicted wearing the leopard skin of a high priest. Conqueror, son of god and high priest: here was a new king who understood what it meant to rule as a pharaoh.

The remaining elements of Alexander's work at Karnak focused on restoring parts of the ceremonial route used by the cult statue of Amun when the god travelled from his main temple to his subsidiary residence at nearby Luxor (Eg. Ipet-resyt, 'southern sanctuary'). And it was Luxor that Alexander chose for his principal project in Egypt's religious capital: a new shrine to house Amun's divine image. This new holy of holies, dubbed the 'great chamber', was erected in the thousand-year-old sanctuary first constructed by the pharaoh Amenhotep III as a monument to his deified self. As the accompanying inscriptions explained: 'He [Alexander] has created the great chamber anew in beautiful white sandstone after it had existed since the time of ... Amenhotep'.[4]

It was an acknowledgement of the history of the building and the essential continuity of Egyptian kingship. Moreover, Alexander must have known – his advisers would surely have informed him – that the holy of holies at Luxor was the spot where the pharaohs of old would 'recharge' their divinity each year by communing in private with the image of Amun. Alexander would also have known that the chamber next to the sanctuary bore a relief, commissioned by Amenhotep III, depicting the divine birth of the pharaoh. This was a concept that held a particular appeal for the ruler of Macedon, who, through exposure to Near Eastern cultures, increasingly saw himself as an oriental king, appointed by god and imbued with divinity. In the same vein, Alexander commissioned an entirely new temple in the Bahariya Oasis, dedicated jointly to Amun-Ra and Horus, falcon god and protector of kings.

But he also knew that his new Egyptian subjects were not the only audience he had to placate. His own army, and the wider Greek-speaking world that was following his progress with a mixture of wonder and apprehension, regarded oriental customs as debased and debauched, the concept of divine kingship as self-aggrandising and anathema to Greek sensibilities. Alexander had, somehow, to appeal to both cultures. As part of his extended accession rites at Memphis, he therefore staged gymnastic and musical contests in the Greek tradition with, it is said, 'the most distinguished artists in these matters coming to him from Greece'.[5] Sporting and artistic gatherings, such as the four-yearly Olympic Games, had been a central, and wildly popular, feature of Greek culture for centuries. Alexander was giving his followers what they expected, and appreciated, from a mighty conqueror. From the outset, he strove to maintain the delicate balancing act required of any foreign ruler of Egypt.

In addition to great agricultural wealth, the lustre of an ancient religion and the allure of divine kingship, Egypt offered Alexander a prize that nowhere else in the Near East could: definitive answers to the existential questions that obsessed him concerning his descent and his destiny. In Egypt's far reaches, deep in the Libyan Desert, lay the oasis of Siwa. At the centre of the oasis was a temple, dedicated to the god Amun (Ammon in Greek), whom the Greek-speaking world equated with their own god Zeus. Alexander felt a particular connection with Zeus-Ammon, whose cult had been celebrated in his Macedonian homeland for the best part of a hundred years. Moreover, the temple of Zeus-Ammon had a further appeal, being the site of a famous oracle, which promised answers to worshippers' most vexing questions. The oracle was renowned throughout the Greek-speaking world and enjoyed an illustrious pedigree: in the fifth century it had been celebrated by the poet Pindar and consulted by the great Spartan general Lysander. Little wonder, perhaps, that 'Alexander was seized by an ardent desire to visit Ammon in Libya, partly in order to consult the god, because the oracle of Ammon was said to be exact in its information... Accordingly he made the expedition to Ammon with the desire of learning his own origin more certainly.'[6]

Alexander left Memphis for Siwa in early 331, accompanied by his army. According to later reports, they first travelled down the Nile to the Mediterranean shore, then advanced westwards along the coast before striking inland, across the desert, towards the oasis. Rains are said to have kept Alexander's army well watered, and this deliverance from drought was taken as a sign of divine providence. However, the shifting sand dunes of the northern Sahara made wayfinding difficult; 'Alexander's army lost the way, and even the guides were in doubt about the course to take.'[7] One fanciful account of the journey claimed that two serpents appeared and led the army onwards, all the way to the oracle and back again; another gave the credit to a pair of ravens, flying in front of the army as guides. Whether by act of god, skilful navigation or simple good fortune, Alexander and his escort did arrive safely in Siwa, and the king was ushered, alone, into the inner sanctum of the temple to consult the oracle. Having put his questions, Alexander moved to an adjacent room where he was greeted by the high priest of the temple and acclaimed as the son of Zeus-Ammon.

Modern investigations at Siwa have revealed the workings of the oracle. Above the sanctuary there was a hidden chamber where a priest could secrete himself and listen to the questions put by worshippers. He could then relay these to the high priest, who had the job of pronouncing the god's answers, before a public proclamation was made to those waiting patiently outside the temple. In Alexander's case, the later sources are contradictory, and not a little cagey, about precisely what he asked the oracle, and what responses he received. One account simply states that he 'heard what was agreeable to his wishes'.[8] Another provides a much more detailed, though surely heavily embroidered, version of events:

> When Alexander was conducted by the priests into the temple and had regarded the god for a while, the one who held the position of prophet, an elderly man, came to him and said, 'Rejoice, son; take this form of address as from the god also.' He replied, 'I accept, father; for the future I shall be called thy son. But tell me if thou givest me the rule of the whole earth.' The priest now entered the sacred enclosure and as the bearers now lifted the god and were moved according to certain prescribed sounds of the voice, the prophet cried that of a certainty the god had granted him his request... Alexander was delighted with these responses.[9]

The one certain fact that emerges from Alexander's visit to Siwa is his recognition by the oracle as the son of Zeus-Ammon. In a coordinated programme of legitimation, this declaration was subsequently confirmed by two further oracles in Greek-speaking Anatolia (present-day Turkey), that of Apollo near Miletos and of Athena in Ionia. That the region had recently been conquered by Alexander must have offered a measure of confidence in its oracles' likely pronouncements. Having himself declared the descendant of Zeus would have burnished Alexander's credentials with his Greek followers, while being recognised as the son of Ammon/Amun would have legitimised his accession as pharaoh. Indeed, it is likely that the verdict from Miletos was reported on Alexander's second visit to Memphis, in March 331, when he may have taken part in a full-scale coronation ceremony according to traditional Egyptian rites. At about this time, he started to issue coins which showed the ram's horns of Amun sprouting from his curly Greek locks. An encounter in a remote oasis had transformed him from man to god.

His divinity and descent confirmed, his destiny assured, Alexander's thoughts turned once again to conquest, and the imperative to pursue the Persian king Darius and his forces to the furthest reaches of their crumbling empire. Alexander, by his own admission, was driven by an inner yearning (Greek *pothos*) to achieve each new, seemingly impossible goal. And, before leaving Egypt, he had one more act to accomplish, one further piece of his legacy to set in place.

Though raised in the mountains of Macedonia, Alexander's outlook was a Mediterranean one. All the territories he had conquered to date, including Egypt, encircled the Sea of the Greeks (as the Egyptians called it). If his new empire were to flourish, its prosperity would be built on maritime trade. Egypt's traditional capital, Memphis, was well situated for riverine traffic plying the Nile, but it was too far from the sea to be a major player in Mediterranean commerce. To secure Egypt's future wealth and cement its place at the heart of a great maritime empire, a new, seaward-facing metropolis would be required. Alexander knew of just the spot.

In Book 4 of the *Odyssey*, Alexander's favourite author mentioned an island named Pharos, a little way off the Egyptian coast, just beyond the north-western extremity of the Nile Delta. There seems to have been a coastal port in the area in former times, and it was to this region that Alexander now led his troops. According to one account, his initial idea was to build a new city on Pharos itself, but it was soon discovered that the island was too small for his grand designs. He is likely to have reconnoitred the surrounding area, from the established port of Kanopos, at the mouth of a major branch of the Nile, to the great inland body of water known as Lake Mareotis. Having weighed up the advantages and disadvantages of different locations, on 7 April 331 (according to later tradition) Alexander finally decided upon his chosen site: a narrow isthmus, its landward approaches guarded by the lake, its seaward by a series of rocky islets, including Pharos:

> The position seemed to him a very fine one in which to found a city, and he foresaw that it would become a prosperous one. Therefore he was seized by an ardent desire to undertake the enterprise, and himself marked out the boundaries of the city, pointing out the place where the agora was to be constructed, where the temples were to be built, stating how many there were to be, and to what Grecian gods they were to be dedicated, and specially marking a spot for a temple to the Egyptian Isis. He also pointed out where the wall was to be carried round it.[10]

Alexander's specific decision to honour the goddess Isis in his new city, alongside the Greek gods of his forebears, is telling. The cult of Isis, one of Egypt's most ancient, had enjoyed an upsurge in popularity with ordinary Egyptians in the first millennium BC, but was also beginning to spread across the eastern Mediterranean. It had reached the Athenian port of Piraeus as early as 333, and Alexander was quick to appreciate the goddess's universal appeal. A temple to Isis, combining Egyptian and Greek architectural features, would therefore appeal both to native Egyptians and to Greek-speaking settlers: a cult to knit together the peoples of his new province.

There seems little doubt that Alexander chose the location of his new foundation and personally laid out its main features: the principal avenues and temples, the market place and the city wall. A story started to circulate that, there being no sand available to mark out the boundaries, 'One of the builders hit upon the plan of collecting in vessels the barley which the soldiers were carrying, and throwing it upon the ground where the king led the way; and thus the circle of the fortification which he was making for the city was completely marked out.' When birds flew down to eat the barley, soothsayers prophesied that the city would prosper, 'especially from the fruits of the earth'.[11]

Unlike most of Alexander's other colonial foundations, which were situated and planned as military outposts, the city by the sea that later bore his name – Alexandria – was established for commercial reasons. Deep water immediately offshore provided anchorage for the biggest maritime vessels, while canals debouching into Lake

Mareotis gave access to the interior of Egypt, via the Nile. A further benefit of the site's coastal location was its advantageous climate: 'by selecting the right angle of the streets, Alexander made the city breathe with the etesian winds so that as these blow across a great expanse of sea, they cool the air of the town, and so he provided its inhabitants with a moderate climate and good health.'[12] Having dictated the city's overall layout, Alexander was content to delegate the rest of the urban planning to his architect, Deinokrates of Rhodes.

Alexander's parting gift to Egypt was to reorganise its administration. He appointed a Persian and an Egyptian, named in later sources as Doloaspis and Petisis, as civilian governors of the northern and southern regions (Lower and Upper Egypt); when Petisis declined to serve, Doloaspis received the whole country. The major garrisons were placed under separate command, and entrusted to members of Alexander's elite band of Macedonian Companions: Pantaleon from Pydna was given Memphis, and Polemon, son of Megakles, originally from the Macedonian capital Pella, was given Pelousion. The outer fringes of Egyptian territory, the coasts bordering Libya and Sinai, were given their own Greek-speaking governors, Apollonios and Kleomenes respectively. In the Nile Valley and Delta, the native provincial governors (Gr. *nomarch*) were left in place, but were ordered to pay taxes to Kleomenes, who was also to supervise the building of Alexandria. Finally, those sections of the army that were to stay behind in Egypt were placed under the command of two generals, Peukestas and Balakros.

This series of appointments had the effect of maintaining native traditions of local government, while placing the main levers of power in trusted hands, and also dividing up civilian, military and economic authority. As a later commentator noted, 'Alexander was said to have divided the government of Egypt among so many men, because he was surprised at the natural strength of the country, and he thought it unsafe to entrust the rule of the whole to a single person.'[13] It was an important lesson, but one that many later rulers of Egypt would learn the hard way.

In the spring of 331, having spent barely six months in Egypt, Alexander departed the country to resume his campaigning. Over the next eight years, the internal urgings that drove him ever onward would carry him to Persia, the Hindu Kush and the borders of

India: the limits of the known world. He never returned to Egypt, but Egypt never left him. When he died in Babylon on 10 June 323, he left instructions for his body to be buried in the temple of Zeus-Ammon at Siwa, the place which could be said to have given his life its meaning and purpose.

Of all Alexander's conquests, Egypt seemed to offer the brightest prospects for an ambitious successor. All the pieces had been put in place by Alexander himself: legitimacy in the eyes of the native population, acclamation by Greeks and Egyptians alike, a well-structured administration, and the foundations of a great commercial city to exploit Egypt's riches and link it with the rest of the Mediterranean world. Yet Alexander himself left no dynasty to take forward his plans or inherit his empire. His dim-witted half-brother and a posthumous son by Alexander's Persian wife Roxane would reign after him, but in name only. Alexander's real heirs were the trusted generals who had campaigned alongside him, all the way from Macedon to Babylon. One of them, in particular, had accompanied him to Egypt – to the shrine of Apis at Memphis, to the oracle at Siwa, to the site of the future Alexandria – and had been struck by the fertility and promise of the Nile Valley. Perhaps *he* might now pursue, and build upon, his late commander's extraordinary vision.

The general's name was Ptolemy.

PART I

APOTHEOSIS (323–221 BC)

1
Rise of a Dynasty

Ptolemy was born in 367 BC into a respected family from Eordaia, a mountainous region in the west of the Kingdom of Macedon. His father Lagos (a name meaning 'leader of people') was a member of the royal court, while Ptolemy's mother Arsinoe ('of uplifted mind', in other words 'intelligent') was herself of noble blood and an intimate of the ruling Macedonian royal family, the Argead dynasty. Indeed, a later myth suggested that Ptolemy was the result of an extramarital liaison between Arsinoe and the future king of Macedon, Philip II.

Lagos and Arsinoe named their son Ptolemaios, from the Macedonian form of the Greek word *polemos* ('war'). It was an apt and prescient choice. The Macedonian nobility prided itself on its resilience and resolve, and in the years before Ptolemy's birth his country had already started to flex its muscles, attacking the neighbouring region of Thessaly. Ptolemy grew up at the royal court and, after Philip II became king in 359, imbibed the overtly martial culture and expansionary philosophy that would eventually see Macedon extend its borders to the ends of the earth. But it was Philip's son, Alexander, born a decade after Ptolemy, who would have the greatest influence on the course of his life. The two took lessons together, learning the arts of war but also being introduced to the full richness of Greek scholarship by Alexander's tutor, Aristotle. Philip II had summoned the philosopher to his court for the express purpose of teaching his son; Ptolemy, therefore, was something of an accidental beneficiary, but took Aristotle's lessons and example to heart.

The fellow students, Ptolemy and Alexander, became inseparable: almost like an older and a younger brother. When Alexander succeeded his father as king of Macedon at the age of twenty, in 336, he gathered around him a close-knit group of Companions – Macedonian men who shared his upbringing, outlook and vision, and on whom he knew he could rely. Ptolemy ticked every box. He was soon appointed a member of the royal bodyguard, and would be at his friend's side throughout the next decade as Alexander first reasserted Macedonian control over its neighbours, then assumed leadership of all the Greeks, and finally invaded the Persian empire. Ptolemy accompanied Alexander to Egypt in 332, and continued in his retinue until the very end. In the campaigns of 327 against the mountain peoples of the Hindu Kush, Ptolemy commanded a third of Alexander's army; later, he was one of the commanders of the Indus fleet. Ptolemy loyally followed his master's lead by marrying a Persian bride, Artakama, at the mass wedding arranged by Alexander in Susa in 324 (he divorced her soon afterwards); and Ptolemy was there by Alexander's side when the king died in Babylon in June 323.

By the time he was in his early forties, therefore, Ptolemy had studied philosophy with the greatest thinker of the age, learned firsthand the arts of war and empire-building from the greatest conqueror the world had ever known, and proved his own worth as a battlefield general. His loyalty to Alexander was never in doubt, but Ptolemy was also politically astute and ambitious for himself. Within a matter of months, he would deploy all his education and all his experience to emerge as the greatest beneficiary of Alexander's extraordinary legacy.

Alexander's untimely demise threw his embryonic empire into chaos and confusion. On his deathbed, he handed his signet ring, the instrument of his rule, to the highest-ranking general in his bodyguard, Perdikkas. But the Companions knew that, without Alexander's driving ambition and personal charisma, his vast conquests – stretching from the shores of the Aegean to the banks of the Indus – could never be held together by a single ruler. The late king's leading generals therefore started to debate how best to divide the spoils between them. Ptolemy, demonstrating his capacity for strategic thinking and imagination, suggested a loose confederation, with each of the territories ruled by a satrap (following the Persian model), and a Council of the Satraps that would meet occasionally to pass empire-wide resolutions. The proposal was rejected: within days of Alexander's death, his successors' selfish motives were already coming to the fore. Instead of a confederation of friendly states, the generals agreed, inevitably, to divide the empire between them.

The Settlement of Babylon, as it has come to be called, resolved to recognise Alexander's half-brother Arrhidaios as king (under the regnal name Philip III), to rule jointly with Alexander's child by Roxane, yet unborn, if it turned out to be a boy. It did, and was duly named Alexander (IV). But this whole exercise was a political fig leaf, designed to perpetuate the fiction of an hereditary Macedonian monarchy vested in the Argead dynasty while the generals secured their own interests. Arrhidaios was mentally impaired, Alexander a baby. Neither could rule in reality. The machinery of government was instead entrusted to a triumvirate comprising Antipatros (appointed regent of Macedon, which by now included much of mainland Greece), Perdikkas (still clinging to Alexander's signet ring) and Krateros, a respected field commander. Nominally under their supervision, but in truth independent rulers, the senior military officers were allocated the various regions of the empire as satrapies – some twenty-four in total. Lysimachos, a member of the royal bodyguard, received Thrace; the splendidly named (and no doubt disarmingly disfigured) Antigonos the One-Eyed, who had served under Philip II and had been appointed satrap of Phrygia by Alexander, added Pamphylia and Lykia in southern Anatolia to his territory; Eumenes of Kardia received Paphlagonia and Kappadokia in central Anatolia. These were all nice rewards, plum regions of the familiar Greek-speaking world. But the real prize lay elsewhere, on the outer edge of the empire: Ptolemy saw to it that he was awarded Egypt.

Before the end of 323, Ptolemy had made his way to the Nile Valley. There he found Kleomenes – whom Alexander had left in charge of the eastern border defences, the building of Alexandria and, most importantly, the country's finances – exercising control as satrap. Ptolemy knew that, if he were to gain full control of Egypt, Kleomenes would have to be removed; he also knew that he wouldn't go voluntarily. The solution was to accuse Kleomenes of corruption – not an outlandish accusation, given the wealth that flowed through the satrap's hands – and have him summarily removed from office. This had the added advantage of furnishing Ptolemy with the contents of Egypt's treasury, reputed to be some 8,000 talents, or ten times the amount handed over to Alexander when he had conquered Egypt just nine years earlier.

True to his military instincts, Ptolemy immediately began enlisting mercenaries to reinforce Egypt's garrisons and build up his own army. Egypt had the advantage of formidable natural borders, surrounded on all sides by desert and sea, but they were not impenetrable. History and recent experience alike had shown that. From the moment Ptolemy arrived in the country, he embarked upon a carefully calculated programme to strengthen Egypt's defences.

He began with its western approaches. For much of the first millennium, Egypt had been subject to attacks by Libyan tribes. With their renowned martial skills, they had even seized the kingship, ruling as pharaohs for some 250 years in the tenth to eighth centuries. Securing Egypt against further Libyan attack was a necessary prerequisite before Ptolemy could turn his attention to the more lucrative lands of the eastern Mediterranean. The leading city of eastern Libya was Kyrene, a Greek colony founded in 631. Over the following three centuries it had become the capital of a prosperous state, Kyrenaika, ruled first by a line of kings and then, from the mid-fifth century onwards, as a republic. An early opportunity to win control of Kyrene and its hinterland presented itself to Ptolemy in 322, when a force of Spartan mercenaries deposed the city's ruling oligarchs and sent them into exile. Ptolemy seized the chance to intervene. His army, under the general Ophellas, marched to Kyrene, executed the leader of the mercenaries, restored the oligarchs and occupied all of Kyrenaika as a 'friendly force'. In regaining its autonomy, Kyrene lost its status as a free city. From now on, it would form an integral part of the Ptolemaic domains.

Despite this early military success, Ptolemy realised that, to secure his position in the long term, force of arms would be necessary but not sufficient. He also needed to build up his political capital. In official inscriptions, therefore, Ptolemy maintained the official line that Alexander's half-brother and son were now the reigning kings. (Egyptian scribes dated monuments to Philip III until the announcement of his death in 316, and thereafter to Alexander IV.)

Showing due respect for Alexander's heirs was politically astute. The Greek-speaking world had recognised Alexander as their leader because of his brilliance as a military leader; he was their best and only hope of defeating the hated Persians. But Alexander's successors had not won their satrapies by their own bravery on the field of battle; they had simply carved up Alexander's empire in a grubby free-for-all. In Greek eyes, Ptolemy remained a satrap, subject to the rule of a king. He dared not claim more – not yet, at least. For the time being, Alexander's personal legacy remained the most powerful guarantor of legitimacy. With this in mind, Ptolemy hatched an audacious plan; if successful, it would secure not only his control of Egypt but also his pre-eminence in the post-Alexander world.

Alexander had left clear instructions that his body should be buried in the temple of Zeus-Ammon at Siwa. But very soon after his death, the idea seems to have gained traction that he should be interred in his homeland, alongside his father, in the ancestral royal cemetery at Aigai (present-day Vergina). Before any burial could take place, however, there was the small matter of moving Alexander's body from Babylon; moreover, he had indicated that, when the time came, nothing less than a spectacular funeral train, with a glittering hearse at its centre, would suffice. While the embalmers set about preserving Alexander's body for the long journey ahead, construction started on the hearse. Babylon, it seems, was not the most convenient place for such a complicated project, and work dragged on for nearly two years.

Eventually, some time in 321, the cortège set off, bound for the hills of Macedon. But, halfway along the route, in Syria, it was hijacked by Ptolemy's agents and diverted southwards to Egypt. The hearse and its precious cargo were taken at once to Memphis. There, Alexander was buried alongside his pharaonic forebears. Presiding over the whole occasion was the satrap Ptolemy. He now had Alexander's mortal body – an immensely potent, nay holy, relic – casting its aura and power over his realm. It was a talisman that none of the other satraps could hope to replicate. Nor would Ptolemy, with his love of learning and history, have been ignorant of Egyptian tradition, which dictated that the person who carried out the burial of a pharaoh became the rightful heir and successor.

The interception and seizure of Alexander's body provoked an immediate hostile response from Perdikkas who, as official regent of the empire, feared Ptolemy's ambition. But Ptolemy had anticipated such a response, building his defences and armed forces to fend off any attack. Moreover, Perdikkas had already alienated most of the other successors. His attempted conquest of Kappadokia antagonised Antigonos the One-Eyed, satrap of the neighbouring provinces. Then Perdikkas agreed to marry the daughter of Antipatros, but soon broke off the engagement in favour of an even more prestigious match, Alexander's sister. Antipatros' very public humiliation won Perdikkas no friends in Macedon. Finally, Krateros was feeling increasingly ignored and shut out of decision-making by the regent. So, when Perdikkas decided to invade Egypt in 321, to clip Ptolemy's wings, he found himself without allies.

The attack came, as expected, from the north-east, Perdikkas' army entering Egypt near Pelousion. The aggressors had the advantage of war elephants from India, the battle tanks of the ancient world; but Egypt's defenders knew their territory and were well prepared. In an initial clash, Ptolemy himself, leading his troops, managed to gouge out the eye of Perdikkas' elephant. The regent headed southwards, towards Memphis, but it was a fateful decision. As his army tried to cross the Nile, the quicksand of the riverbed gave way under their feet; 2,000 men lost their lives, either drowned or eaten by crocodiles. Demoralised and facing annihilation, the remaining troops mutinied and went over to Ptolemy's side. The hapless Perdikkas was swiftly dispatched by his remaining officers. Ptolemy was magnanimous in victory, welcoming Perdikkas' battle-hardened veterans with open arms.

With Perdikkas dead, the regency was now up for grabs, and may have been offered to Ptolemy. Wisely, however, he is said to have refused it: with the fracturing of Alexander's empire an inevitability, trying to hold it together was a fool's errand. Antipatros was confirmed as regent of the whole empire, and moved swiftly to reallocate the satrapies. Ptolemy was confirmed as satrap of Egypt and Kyrenaika, and was also granted dominion over any lands further to the west of Kyrene that he might conquer in the future. Babylon, meanwhile, was allotted to Seleukos, Perdikkas' former deputy and one of his assassins.

As the pieces of a lasting settlement started to fall into place, the rivals continued to plot and manoeuvre, sensing that a permanent division of the empire was inevitable and seeking to maximise their own advantage. The resulting Wars of the Successors dragged on for over four decades, characterised by shifting allegiances, internecine battles and broken treaties. The jockeying for position intensified after Antipatros' death in 319, when he passed over his own son Kassandros and left the regency to Polyperchon, whom the successors promptly refused to recognise. In the ensuing free-for-all, Antigonos the One-Eyed defeated and killed Eumenes, thus winning control of most of Anatolia, and extended his control eastwards. In response, Seleukos fled Babylon and entered into an alliance with Ptolemy, Lysimachos of Thrace and the vengeful Kassandros of Macedon. Sensing an advantage, Ptolemy annexed Syria and Phoenicia, withdrawing his troops soon afterwards but leaving behind garrisons to guard a buffer zone with Egypt. As with his pre-emptive move against Kyrenaika, Ptolemy was following established pharaonic precedent: the greatest pharaohs of the past had pursued a similar policy of establishing protectorates in Syria and Palestine, to prevent any full-scale incursion into Egypt from that quarter.

And still the contenders continued to fight among themselves. In 317, Alexander's redoubtable mother, Olympias, had her stepson Philip III Arrhidaios murdered. This cleared the way for Olympias' grandson, Alexander IV, to reign as sole monarch. Unfortunately for Olympias, she had misjudged the mood, and was herself condemned to death for regicide. By early 316, Alexander IV was under house arrest in Macedon. Its new ruler, Kassandros, wanted no competition, especially from the sole surviving member of the Argead dynasty.

Ptolemy took advantage of the chaos and confusion to extend his writ still further, invading Cyprus in 315 with assistance from his brother Menelaos and his new-found ally Seleukos. The island, situated between Egypt, Phoenicia and Anatolia, was of the utmost strategic importance, commercially and militarily. Ptolemy knew that defending his interests and building a great trading nation would require a strong navy; an effective navy, in turn, would need bases across the eastern Mediterranean. Cyprus not only offered an excellent location, it was also rich in natural resources, notably copper, timber and grain. Within two years of invading, Ptolemy had formally annexed Cyprus.

In the meantime, the satraps of Asia had started to agitate against Antigonos the One-Eyed who, since his victory over Eumenes, was in the ascendant. In 314, they demanded that he cede Lykia and Kappadokia to Kassandros, Phrygia to Lysimachos, all of Syria to Ptolemy, and return Babylon to Seleukos. Pushing their luck even further, they required Antigonos to share all the booty he had captured in his campaigns of expansion. He refused on every count. The result was war – again. After another five years of intermittent fighting, Antigonos had consolidated his power in Anatolia, while Seleukos had regained Babylon and the eastern provinces. The concluding peace treaty, before its ink was even dry, had been violated by both Kassandros and Ptolemy: Alexander's successors now sensed that they were entering the endgame.

What precipitated the final scramble for territory and influence was the news coming out of Macedon. In the late summer of 309, rumours started to circulate that Alexander IV had been murdered, along with his mother Roxane, on Kassandros' orders. The boy was in his fourteenth year, approaching maturity, and was judged too great a threat to be left alive. With all of Alexander the Great's relatives gone, the fiction of a unified empire crumbled to dust. His surviving lieutenants entered a desperate contest for final advantage.

In Libya, Ptolemy extended his control westwards as far as the Gulf of Sirte, to gain access to the lucrative trade between Greek coastal cities and inland Africa. When the governor of Kyrenaika, Ophellas, was killed in a revolt, Ptolemy installed his own brother, Magas, to secure the province. A similar decision was taken with respect to Cyprus, where Menelaos was appointed governor and made titular King of Salamis (a city-state on the east coast of Cyprus) – a nice bauble to buy his continued loyalty. It proved a bad choice. In 306, Menelaos was unable to resist an invasion led by Antigonos' son Demetrios. Cyprus fell to the invaders, and would not be restored to Ptolemaic control for another twenty years.

Antigonos was cock-a-hoop at having wrested control of such a strategic possession from the mighty Ptolemy and took the decisive step of assuming the title of king; he bestowed the same title on his son Demetrios. To date, none of Alexander's successors had dared to claim the mantle of royalty, even as they were busy carving out their kingdoms. Perhaps fearing the opprobrium of the wider

Greek-speaking world, they had maintained the fiction that Philip III and Alexander IV were the only legitimate kings after Alexander the Great's death. That pretence was now dead in the water. In response to Antigonos' move, Ptolemy was acclaimed king by his own army, and formally recognised as such by January 304. Kassandros of Macedon, Lysimachos of Thrace and Seleukos of Asia soon followed suit.

The Age of the Successors had ended. The Hellenistic Age had begun.

Being a king in the Greek-speaking world was relatively clear-cut, if not exactly straightforward. Gaining recognition as a ruler through 'spear-won' territory, in other words military conquests, was customary. However, Ptolemy's core territory – Egypt – had been conquered by Alexander; hence Ptolemy's keenness to associate himself with his former master, not least by bringing Alexander's body to Egypt to demonstrate continuity from his own reign. By 311 at the latest, Ptolemy had relocated his capital – and with it, Alexander's remains – to Alexandria, further strengthening the association. All the while, even after Alexander IV had been eliminated, Ptolemy continued to call himself satrap, a clear indication of his loyalty to the Argead dynasty and Alexander the Great's memory. The Greek title *basileus*, which Ptolemy and his fellow dynasts finally adopted in 306/5, signified royal status, but carried no particular geographic connotation. From shortly after this date, coins issued by the Ptolemaic mint dropped the inscription *Alexandrou* ('of Alexander') in favour of *Ptolemaiou basileôs* ('of King Ptolemy'), and Ptolemy's head, wearing the Macedonian royal diadem, replaced that of Alexander. In Greek eyes, Ptolemy was now a king *in* Egypt, but he was not exactly king *of* Egypt. Greek kingship was a matter of individual prestige, won by force of arms. To Egypt's native inhabitants, by contrast, kingship and territory were inextricably linked. Being pharaoh meant being 'Lord of the Two Lands', the master and defender of the Nile Valley and Delta. This fundamental contradiction between Greek and Egyptian concepts of kingship, between the personal and the national, would shape the monarchy under Ptolemy I and every one of his successors – shape and, at times, strain.

Nowhere is the tension better displayed than on a remarkable monument dating from 311, during Ptolemy's time as satrap of Egypt.

Known as the Satrap Stela, it remains the single most important historical source for the period. Superficially, the stone slab follows the long-established pharaonic tradition of royal inscriptions. At the top is a representation of the king offering to the gods, under the protection of a pair of outspread wings. Below, some twenty lines of carefully cut hieroglyphs record the king's names and titles, a paean of praise for the ruler and, finally, the main purpose of the stela, the reaffirmation of a royal grant of land to the temples of Buto, an important town and cult centre in the north-western Nile Delta. All quintessentially Egyptian. However, a closer look reveals the confusion engendered by a situation entirely unprecedented in Egyptian history: an absentee king (Alexander IV) and a non-royal ruler (Ptolemy). Attempts to reconcile this state of affairs with Egyptian royal and religious protocol required some linguistic somersaults.

The inscription starts, entirely properly, with the names and epithets of the reigning king and the official date, Year 7 of Alexander IV. But it then concedes the messy reality: 'He is king in the Two Lands and the foreign lands. His Majesty is among the Asiatics while a great chief is in Egypt, whose name is Ptolemy.' Next follows a whole series of laudatory epithets, usually applied to a pharaoh, but here descriptive of the 'great chief' Ptolemy:

> He is a youthful man, strong in his two arms, effective of counsel, mighty of armies, stout hearted, firm footed, who attacks without turning his back, who faces up to his opponents when they fight, precise of hand when he has grasped the bow without shooting astray, who fights with his sword in the midst of battle, there being none who can stand in his presence, an active champion whose arms are not repulsed, with no reversal of what issues from his mouth, who has no equal in the Two Lands or the foreign lands.[1]

The text goes on to recount victorious campaigns against Syria and Nubia but, again, they are ascribed to Ptolemy, not King Alexander. Up to this point, the scribes had been scrupulous in referring to Ptolemy as 'great chief' or 'great ruler of Egypt'. However, when the text came to the key decision to confirm the donation of land to the temples of Buto, the scribes' linguistic ingenuity and cultural flexibility gave way. Ptolemy now becomes 'His Majesty'. The reason is simple: in Egyptian theology, only one person could make grants of land to the gods, and that was the king. Ptolemy had reaffirmed the grant, so Ptolemy must be acting as king. A de jure king 'among the Asiatics' and a de facto king acting like a pharaoh; it was all too confusing. No wonder the stonemasons left empty the royal cartouches (name rings) at the top of the stela.

Only after Ptolemy had formally claimed royal titles was the contradiction finally resolved. Egyptian documents took 305/4 as the first year of Ptolemy I's reign – even if other sources referred back to the time of Alexander's death, some eighteen years earlier, when the 'spear-won' territory of Egypt had passed by right from Alexander to his general.

To cement his legitimacy in the eyes of his Egyptian subjects, Ptolemy chose the next anniversary of Alexander's death, 12 January 304, as the date for his formal accession. He made sure to hold this in Memphis, traditional capital of Egypt, not in Alexandria, which the Egyptian scribes insisted on referring to – somewhat tortuously and not a little contemptuously – as 'the fortress of … Alexander, whose former name was Rhakotis, on the shore of the Sea of the Greeks'. Rhakotis, incidentally, meant simply 'building site': ever since Alexander had founded the city in 331, that is what it had been. Native Egyptians would continue to refer to the city by its pejorative nickname even after construction work had finished.

The royal grant recorded on the Satrap Stela demonstrates a significant degree of continuity between the old pharaonic ways and the new Ptolemaic dispensation. The scribes who composed the text, and the priests who benefited from its measures, were well versed in traditional Egyptian cultural practices, the duties expected of a king and the appropriate language in which to describe them. The classic texts used in scribal training had survived recent political vicissitudes unscathed. Neither a decade of Persian domination nor a further decade of Macedonian rule had succeeded in weakening, let alone supplanting, the proper decorum of Egyptian kingship. It is no coincidence that Ptolemy's decision to re-dedicate lands around Buto to the city's main temples reaffirmed a decision taken by the last native pharaoh, the short-lived and shadowy Khababash. He seems to have been a rebel leader who led a revolt against Persian rule some time in the 340s and succeeded in winning recognition as king, at least in parts of the Delta. By referencing Khababash's donation, and indeed repeating it, Ptolemy – when he was still, officially, only satrap – was deliberately connecting himself with the line of legitimate pharaohs stretching all the way back to the dawn of Egyptian history; and publicly distinguishing himself from the Persian kings of recent times. Ptolemy was a foreigner, for sure, but a foreigner who understood and respected Egyptian traditions, and intended to maintain them.

Another monument created during Ptolemy's tenure as satrap was a great gateway on the island of Elephantine, situated in the Nile at Egypt's southern frontier. The local temple, begun before the Persian conquest, had been left unfinished at the outbreak of hostilities; Egypt's Persian rulers had shown no interest in completing it, so there it remained, partly built, an affront to the god. Ptolemy ordered its full realisation, and the great portal still stands today. When Ptolemy became king, he continued in the same vein, paying particular attention to the cult buildings begun, or completed, by the kings of the thirtieth dynasty, the last native royal house to rule Egypt before the Persian takeover.

Alexander had taken pains to contrast himself with the hated Persians by honouring Egyptian cults. On assuming royal titles, Ptolemy I followed suit: one of his first acts as king was to issue a decree forbidding the alienation of temple property. But he also went a stage further, making temple building and beautification a major part of his government's programme. Although time has not been kind to Ptolemy's pharaonic building projects, his name has been found at sites the length and breadth of Egypt, suggesting an extensive, ambitious and concerted programme. He is known to have built or added to temples at a host of sites in the Delta: Tanis, Paabeithis, Naukratis and Terenuthis. In his choice of locations and dedications, Ptolemy was keen to associate himself with royal tradition and popular cults, a winning combination. Further south, he patronised a temple at Tebtunis in the Fayum dedicated to the crocodile god, another cult that had gained huge popularity. In the central stretch of the Nile Valley (Middle Egypt), he likewise chose sites that had been inaugurated or enlarged under the thirtieth dynasty: places like Kusae and Oxyrhynchos. At the major cult centre of Hermopolis, Ptolemy had already added to the temple of the local god Thoth in the early days of his satrapship, when Philip III Arrhidaios was still nominally king.

Ptolemy did not simply add to earlier buildings or slavishly copy them for his own projects. He also contributed to the ongoing development of Egyptian sacred architecture, taking forms first introduced in the thirtieth dynasty and elaborating them. The most striking example is the type of shrine known today as a birth house. This was originally conceived as a minor addition to a principal temple. Resembling a small shrine with its own forecourt and access path, the birth house stood apart from its parent temple and was the setting for periodic celebrations of the pharaoh's divine birth. Under Ptolemy I, the birth house became a fully fledged temple, albeit in miniature, and started to play a part in the daily cult ritual of the main temple. Under Ptolemy, for the first time in four decades, pharaonic religion and culture were given a new lease of life.

The renaissance of Egyptian civilisation points to a crucial feature of Ptolemy's reign: the influence of members of the old Egyptian elite in both religious and civic spheres. Alexander had recognised the advantages of leaving indigenous officials in place, albeit with strong supervisory oversight by his trusted Macedonian lieutenants. Egypt was simply too large a country, with too ingrained a set of customs and practices, to be ruled by a foreign, Greek-speaking elite without the active cooperation of the old guard. Where Alexander had accepted much of the status quo ante as a practical necessity, Ptolemy actively cultivated the native upper class, not only to strengthen his grip on power but also to restore the vibrancy of pharaonic culture. An historian himself, Ptolemy was interested in learning about the ancient civilisation of the country he had inherited, drawing inspiration from historic precedent.

In Egypt there had always been a few bold souls who, in the face of foreign domination, had attempted to act as interlocutors. Whether through self-interest or a genuine concern for cultural preservation, men like Udjahorresnet had successfully negotiated the continuation of pharaonic rites and traditions in his home city of Sais at the time of the first Persian invasion in 525. He had diligently cosied up to the Persian conqueror Cambyses in order to persuade him of the political expediency of respecting Egyptian culture. Under Ptolemy I, Udjahorresnet's successors found themselves pushing at an open door. Unlike the Persians, Ptolemy intended to make Egypt his permanent home and dynastic seat. He would be a resident pharaoh, not an absentee one. The easiest way to win over the native elite was to maintain key features of the thirtieth dynasty regime. This was most powerfully signalled by bringing the body of Nakhthorheb, the dynasty's last ruler, to Alexandria. His sarcophagus was interred within the sacred precinct where Alexander had been reburied. There could have been no clearer indication of Ptolemy's determination to present himself as the legitimate heir of both his illustrious forebears, Egyptian and Macedonian.

The evidence for high-ranking Egyptians remaining in the government under Ptolemy and his immediate successors is extensive. The great-nephew of the first king of the thirtieth dynasty retained power in his ancestral seat of Sebennytos. He oversaw it and the neighbouring border town of Sile as governor, while also holding high military office as 'great first-ranking officer of His Majesty's army'. His uncle, Nakhthorheb's eldest son and heir, served as commander-in-chief, which was an extraordinary state of affairs given that Nakhthorheb himself had supported the Persians in their fight against Alexander. Even more striking is the case of Somtutefnakht from the Middle Egyptian town of Henen-nesut (Gr. Herakleopolis); he continued to hold high office under Ptolemy as head of a local priesthood even though he had himself fought on the Persian side at the battle of Issos. Clearly Ptolemy was not a man to hold a grudge: the army he massed at Gaza in 312 to attack Antigonos' forces is said to have included 'a large number of Egyptians',[2] including, no doubt, veterans who had honed their skills fighting *against* the Macedonian army.

The accommodation went both ways. The receptiveness of the Egyptian elite to Macedonian rule is most clearly illustrated by the family of Padiusir (Gr. Petosiris) from Hermopolis. In Egyptian religious practice, it was common for members of prominent families to participate in the life of their local temples by holding part-time roles, clerical as well as lay (although the distinction is not always clear-cut). This helped build a family's social capital within the community and also brought financial benefits (for example, a share of the offerings presented to the resident deity). In pharaonic Egypt, as in medieval Europe, a single family might effectively monopolise roles in its local cult over several generations, reinforcing its place in the social hierarchy. Padiusir's family was a good example, holding high office in the local cult, that of the ibis god Thoth, for at least five generations, spanning the latter part of the thirtieth dynasty, the Second Persian Domination (343–332), the conquest of Alexander and the start of Ptolemaic rule. The story starts with Padiusir's grandfather, Djed-djehuty-iufankh ('Thoth said he will live'), and his son, Nes-Shu, who served under Egypt's last native dynasty. The baton then passed to Nes-Shu's two sons, Djed-djehuty-iufankh the younger and Padiusir himself. In the 340s and early 330s, the latter carried out his duties in the temple of Thoth with exemplary diligence, even as Egypt itself seethed against Persian control. In his own words: 'I spent seven years as controller for this god, administering his endowment without fault being found, while the ruler of foreign lands was protector in Egypt, and nothing was in its former place, since fighting had started inside Egypt, the south being in turmoil, the North in revolt.'[3] Padiusir further boasts of having restored the temple of Thoth to its former condition, reinstated the proper rites, restaffed the priesthood, and generally maintained the traditional forms of worship against all the odds and despite the neglect and depredations of the Persians.

At the end of his biographical inscription, composed at the time of his death, Padiusir's tone changes markedly, and he speaks of having been 'favoured by the ruler of Egypt' and 'loved by his courtiers'. Although the ruler in question is not named, this can only refer to the new dispensation under Ptolemy, when the Egyptian elite found themselves once again in favour at court. The extent to which old families like Padiusir's embraced Macedonian rule is demonstrated in his tomb chapel (at present-day Tuna el-Gebel). Decorated by his son and grandson, it displays an amalgam of Egyptian and Greek styles and motifs. Alongside chapters from the Pyramid Texts and *Book of the Dead*, hymns to the sun and newly composed religious texts lauding the old gods of Egypt, there is a depiction of the family members gathered around the tomb, dressed in Greek-style clothing with fashionable Macedonian hairstyles; some of them are shown full face, in keeping with Hellenistic art. Because Ptolemy had signalled his respect for Egypt's hallowed traditions, the Egyptians seem to have respected him and his ways in turn. Such friendly cohabitation seemed to bode well for Ptolemy I's new realm.

People like Padiusir and his descendants continued to worship their old gods, patronise their old temples and run the affairs in their old provinces. And the Ptolemaic court at Alexandria had Egyptians in high places, too. One whose influence was felt at the very heart of Ptolemy's government was a priest from Sebennytos, named in Greek sources as Manethon but better known by the Latinised form, Manetho. His Egyptian name probably meant 'beloved of the great god' – an apt name for a priest of the old religion. The fact that Manetho came from the home town of the thirtieth dynasty, and may even have been related to the erstwhile royal family, must have helped his cause. According to later accounts, he served as high priest of the Ra at Heliopolis, one of the most important temples in Egypt, but it was as an historian, not a cleric, that he achieved lasting fame. Some time in the early period of Ptolemaic rule, Manetho was commissioned to write a history of Egypt.[4] Histories of nations, people and great men were a genre beloved of the Greek-speaking world, but alien to ancient Egyptian literature. As high priest, Manetho had access to temple records, notably the lists of long-dead kings and the annals recording the main events of their reigns. With this material, he painstakingly compiled a great work named (in Greek) the *Aigyptiaka* ('history of Egypt'). Charting the history of the Nile Valley from mythical times to the coming of Alexander, it was arranged in chronological order and presented in three volumes. Only fragments of it have survived, excerpted in the works of later authors, but its revolutionary treatment of Egyptian history has proved remarkably enduring. Manetho was the first to divide Egypt's countless kings into thirty 'dynasties' (from the Greek *dynasteia*, 'governmental power'), and his basic structure is still used by Egyptologists today.

Although composed by an Egyptian steeped in pharaonic culture, the *Aigyptiaka* was a work aimed at a court composed largely of Macedonians and Greeks. It was intended not only to appeal to their (and Ptolemy's) love of learning, but, more importantly, to frame their new home, the land of Egypt, in accessible and understandable terms. Simply put, Manetho's challenge was to explain Egypt to the Greeks, by writing a Greek-style history of Egypt. If there is one defining theme of Ptolemy I's reign, it is his delicate balancing act to placate both populations, indigenes and immigrants alike. Every one of his major policies at home seems to have been devised with an eye to maintaining this balance. Perhaps the policy that lasted the longest and achieved the most impact was in the realm of religion. It was even more ambitious than the compilation of a complete history of Egypt: it was nothing less than the invention of a new god.

Ever since hijacking Alexander's body, Ptolemy had basked in the conqueror's reflected glory. His annexation of, first Kyrene, then Cyprus, and his decisive interventions in the Wars of the Successors had burnished his credentials across Greek-speaking lands. The zenith of his reputation in the wider Mediterranean world came in 305/4, more or less at the same time as his formal accession at Memphis. Demetrios, fresh from his capture of Cyprus, decided to attack another Greek island state, Rhodes. Deploying a monstrous battering ram operated by a thousand men, and a wheeled siege tower nicknamed 'taker of cities', Demetrios besieged the Rhodian capital for weeks, but it bravely held out, its defences bolstered by troops sent by Ptolemy. (He was, after all, no friend of Demetrios.) A compromise was eventually reached, and the grateful Rhodians bestowed on their friend Ptolemy the title Soter ('saviour'). He appreciated the gesture and henceforth used the title invariably.[5] Back in Egypt, when translated into hieroglyphics, 'saviour' gave Ptolemy a god-like air. But his Greek-speaking subjects, understanding its political origins, were less awestruck. What Ptolemy wanted was an aura of divine majesty that all his people would respect.

From the very moment he accompanied Alexander to Memphis, in the autumn of 332, Ptolemy had been struck by the Egyptians' unshakeable devotion to the city's sacred bull, Apis. The respect Alexander had shown for the beast had cemented his legitimacy in Egyptian eyes, and Ptolemy followed suit when he became Egypt's ruler. An Apis bull – perhaps the very one that Alexander had worshipped – died of old age in 299, early in Ptolemy's sole reign. His response was to provide a loan, from the government treasury, of fifty talents of silver to help defray the costs of the seventy-day period of mourning and mummification, and the burial of the bull in its special underground catacomb in the hills above the capital. The gesture must have been deeply appreciated by the priests of Apis and the bull's many indigenous worshippers.

The enormous popularity of the living Apis, and of its deceased predecessors, known to the Egyptians as Usir-Hep (Gr. Osiris-Apis or

Osorapis), gave Ptolemy an idea. Perhaps an incarnation of Osorapis, portrayed in the human form customarily adopted by Greek gods, might appeal to Egypt's Greek-speaking population. Then, perhaps, one and the same god might bind together both parts of society, in one community of worshippers. The result – one of only a few historically attested examples of an invented deity – was named Sarapis. In character, he cleverly merged aspects and roles of three major Greek gods: Zeus (king of the gods and royal patron), Hades (god of the underworld) and Dionysos (god of vegetation, pleasure and fertility). If later commentators are to be believed, the theology of the Sarapis cult was devised with the assistance of Manetho, while the god's Greek attributes – including his representation as a bearded Zeus-like figure wearing a Dionysiac corn-measure for a crown – were formulated by Timotheos of Athens, a noted interpreter of sacred mysteries who had been brought by Ptolemy to Alexandria to advise on religious policy.

The promotion of Sarapis was carried out by Ptolemy himself. The new god was named patron of the king's capital and protector of his dynasty. In Alexandria, on an eminence overlooking the city, a new temple was built, named the Sarapieion; above ground it resembled a classical Greek temple, complete with statues of Ptolemy and his family in Greek style, but below ground it had a series of galleries and catacombs, inspired by Egyptian funerary architecture.[6] In the capital and throughout the subject territories, Ptolemy I and his successors fostered their personal identification with Sarapis, whose cult combined elements to suit every audience. To their Egyptian subjects, the Ptolemaic king and queen were Sarapis/Osiris and his consort Isis – the ancient divine couple reincarnated on earth. To people of Greek and Macedonian descent, Ptolemy was the heir of Zeus and the incarnation of Dionysos, blending the kingship of the former with the triumphal luxury of the latter.

Backed by dedicated royal propaganda, the cult of Sarapis soon spread far and wide, reaching coastal Anatolia and the shores of the Caspian Sea. Despite the plethora of ancient Egyptian and Greek deities recognised by Alexander and his successors, it was an invented god who came to stand for Ptolemaic Egypt throughout the Hellenistic world.

And what a world it was.

2

Brave New World

When Alexander the Great came to the throne at the age of nineteen, his Macedonian realm was relatively small and insignificant. It had only recently expanded beyond its core, a mountain kingdom on the northern edge of the Greek world. When he died, just thirteen years later, his empire, won at the point of a sword, stretched from the Adriatic to India, from the Black Sea to the Nile cataracts. From coastal Libya to Central Asia and the Hindu Kush, all the known world was under his sway.

But such an extensive and disparate series of conquests, with nothing in common other than the person who had conquered them, was always going to be hard to rule. With Alexander's death, the task became impossible. The interminable Wars of the Successors were fought, not to win the whole of Alexander's empire, but to secure the best portions of it. When the main beneficiaries declared themselves kings, it was an acknowledgement that Alexander's dream of a unified, multinational superstate had evaporated.

What remained, when the dust settled, was a patchwork of rival kingdoms ruled by fiercely competitive dynasts. Across the eastern Mediterranean, northern Africa and western Asia, the countries that emerged in Alexander's wake were different from anything the world had seen before. Their rulers spoke Greek, but most of their populations conversed in a dizzying range of tongues, from Berber and Phoenician to Aramaic and Persian. Countless native gods and goddesses competed for worshippers with the traditional deities of the

Greek pantheon. And the Hellenistic kingdoms, as they are known, had at their disposal an extraordinary range of natural resources: tin and iron, glass and cedar, ebony and ivory, lapis lazuli and gold – a veritable cornucopia of which the citizens of ancient Athens or Sparta could only have dreamed.

Egypt, too, was part of this brave new world. The Nile Valley, though ancient in its roots and proud of its native customs, found itself an integral part of a much larger whole. Since the dawn of civilisation, the Egyptians had been open to international trade and cultural connections with foreigners – but on their own terms. Now they were mere pawns in a bigger game of Mediterranean power politics. While Egypt defined and shaped the Ptolemaic dynasty, the wider geopolitical landscape would play a decisive role in determining the currents of Ptolemaic history.

From the moment Ptolemy secured for himself the satrapy of Egypt, in the days following Alexander's death, his foreign policy had but one aim: to guarantee the defence and territorial integrity of his new realm. He knew only too well – if not from history, then from recent personal experience – that Egypt was not as inviolable as it liked to think. It was always vulnerable to attack: from the east via the Sinai land bridge, from the north by any well-equipped naval force, from the west along the Libyan coastal route, and from the south by land or river. Egypt's seclusion was imaginary. So, by diplomatic and military means, Ptolemy devoted his energies to securing his kingdom for his successors.

His world was envisaged as a series of concentric circles, radiating out from Egypt. Furthest away, to be managed and contained, were the other kingdoms ruled by Ptolemy's erstwhile colleagues. Foremost among these, in prestige if not in promise, was Alexander's own heartland and homeland, the Kingdom of Macedon. Though remote and isolated, Macedon had three distinct natural advantages over other parts of the Greek-speaking world: a more favourable climate for agriculture, an abundance of timber and rich mineral deposits, especially of silver and gold. These resources had fuelled Macedon's rise under Philip II and would continue to make it an attractive proposition for ambitious rulers throughout ancient history. Thanks largely to the enduring afterglow of Philip II and Alexander the Great, Macedon emerged from the Wars of the Successors relatively intact, and it continued to bask in the reflected glory of the now defunct Argead royal house. But Macedon's strength was also its weakness. Anyone who wished to lay claim to Alexander's mantle had first to secure his ancestral throne, while the Greek-speaking cities of the Aegean that had rallied to Alexander's side against the Persians were suspicious of Macedonian hegemony after his death. The result was decades of turmoil within and beyond Macedon's borders. This suited Ptolemy rather well.

Kassandros inherited the title 'King of the Macedonians' from his father Antipatros, who had been placed in charge by Alexander himself; but another ambitious father and son, Antigonos the One-Eyed and Demetrios, had designs on the Macedonian throne. The latter eventually succeeded in taking control in 294 after an invasion of Celtic tribes from the north had destabilised the country. Although Demetrios' descendants (named the Antigonids, after the dynastic founder) would continue to rule Macedon for the next 126 years, it was never an easy ride. The kingdom faced unrelenting pressures on multiple fronts. Incursions from the north remained a constant threat, while the Greek-speaking world to the south resented Macedon's presumption of overlordship. Athens was particularly hostile, although unable to mount effective resistance. Political alliances formed, dissolved and reformed as diverse groups sought to undermine and challenge Macedonian power. Confederations such as the Aetolian League in north-western Greece and the Achaean League in the northern Peloponnese proved a perpetual headache for Macedon's rulers. The Ptolemies, for their part, were only too happy to send money and grain to support anyone who might prevent Macedon from regaining its former glory, but without risking Ptolemaic troops in a direct intervention. The result was a century and a half of proxy wars, and a century and a half of Greek disunity.

Across the wider Aegean, countless islands and city states, once proudly independent before the coming of Alexander, resumed something of their former autonomy; but in the new world of great-power politics, they had to balance a desire for freedom with a need for protection. The various Leagues offered some of the latter but rather little of the former. Indeed, the League of Islanders ended up being taken over by Ptolemy I, ushering in a thirty-year period of Ptolemaic hegemony in the Cyclades. Ptolemy could afford to play these islands and states off against each other; apart from one or two that offered safe anchorage for the Ptolemaic navy, they had little strategic importance. They were useful pawns in a bigger game; potential allies to rein in Macedonian ambitions. When Aegean islands sought to curry favour with Ptolemy, for example by erecting a shrine in his honour, it was mere recognition of the political reality. The price of protection was flattery.

The outstanding exception was the island state of Rhodes, which held a dominant and influential position in the eastern Mediterranean throughout the Hellenistic era. The island had been conquered by Alexander early in his reign, but was also one of the first territories to reassert its independence after his death, expelling the Macedonian garrison. Ptolemy's defence of Rhodes in 305/4, during the year-long siege by Demetrios, had been no demonstration of altruism. Rather, his rare, direct intervention in another state's affairs – which won him the laudatory epithet 'saviour' – showed the importance of Rhodes to Egypt's commercial interests. These links went back hundreds of years, at least to the reign of the twenty-sixth dynasty pharaoh Ahmose II (570–526). They reflected Rhodes's strategic location, its role as an entrepot between Greece, Anatolia, Syria and Phoenicia, and its favourable position for direct trade with Egypt. The four-day route between Rhodes and the Egyptian coast remained open to vessels all year round, unlike other Mediterranean shipping lanes that were characterised by shifting currents and unreliable winds. The fact that Rhodes also lay more or less directly north of Alexandria gave commercial ties a further boost. (The island that lay nearest the harbour of Alexandria was named Antirrhodos, 'opposite Rhodes'.) Rhodes also maintained its own strong naval force and played a key role in countering piracy on the high seas, which was a persistent threat to maritime trade. The island's navy had a special class of extra-fast vessels called 'protection ships' which patrolled the major shipping routes in squadrons.

In the same spirit of innovation, the Rhodians pioneered a new form of commercial activity, involving consortia of traders rather than lone merchants. This allowed for whole cargoes to be traded rather than broken up and sold off piecemeal. It was a fundamental change, and challenge, to the organisation of international trade, and it made Rhodes a magnet for ambitious and entrepreneurial businessmen. The island replaced Athens as the most important commercial city-state of the Greek world, and it became a centre of international finance as well. All these advantages made Rhodes a key ally. Egypt, for its part, was a major supplier of grain and a wealthy, powerful country. In other words, each had something the other needed. The friendly relationship between Rhodes and Egypt was a defining characteristic of Ptolemaic rule, a rare constant in the otherwise unpredictable ebb and flow of Hellenistic power politics.

The next major piece in the outermost circle of the Ptolemaic world was the disparate set of territories that, just a few decades earlier, had been ruled by mighty Persia. Known today by historians as the Seleukid kingdom after its founder Seleukos I, a contemporary of Ptolemy I,[1] its ruling dynasty was just about its only unifying feature. The kingdom – empire would be a more accurate term – stretched over an area of some 1.5 million square miles, from the shores of the Aegean to present-day Afghanistan, and from the Caspian Sea to Phoenicia. Even after Seleukos ceded his easternmost lands to the Indian emperor Chandragupta Maurya in 303 in exchange for war elephants, the former Macedonian general remained overlord of a population four times that of Egypt. This made the Seleukid kingdom a powerful and dangerous adversary. In particular, Seleukid power threatened Egyptian access to the Phoenician ports that were so crucial for commerce. Hence, while the Ptolemaic relationship with Macedon was merely disputatious, its rivalry with Asia verged on the mutually destructive.

Ptolemy and his successors in Egypt were lucky that the Seleukid kings had to devote virtually all their time and energy to holding their realm together. With a standing army of no more than 70,000 men, this was no easy task. The empire was so extensive and disparate, it required not one but two capital cities: the new foundations of Antiokheia (named after Seleukos' father Antiochos) on the River Orontes in Syria and Seleukeia (named after himself) on the River Tigris in Babylonia (present-day Iraq). But central government could only be exercised effectively in the immediate hinterlands of the two cities. Further afield, large swathes of territory remained largely independent of Seleukid control. Tribal chiefs continued to hold sway in the countryside, dynasts and priests in the ancient city and temple states of Mesopotamia. Such long-established patterns of feudal government barely acknowledged the empire's new Greek-speaking overlords, and deep-rooted cultural patterns undermined any attempt at centralised government.

Seleukos and his immediate successor tried hard to change the political landscape of their realm by establishing scores of Greek colonies at strategic locations for defence and trade. Many were named after members of the royal family: Seleukeia, Antiokheia, Laodikeia (after Seleukos' mother), Apameia (after his Iranian wife) and Stratonikeia (after his Macedonian wife). One settlement, on the banks of the River Oxus in distant Bactria (present-day northern Afghanistan), must have presented an odd picture with its Greek-style gymnasium and statues by renowned Greek sculptors; it could have been lifted, stone by stone, from Macedonia or the Peloponnese. Another brave outpost of Hellenism was established at Alexandria-in-Arakhosia (present-day Kandahar). The idea behind such places was that they would attract adventurous and ambitious settlers from the Greek homelands in search of a new and better life. But most of these new foundations failed to take root: the cultural and political headwinds were simply too strong. The few new cities that did prosper retained a deep loyalty to the Seleukid royal house, and served as a bulwark against restive native populations. While Greek colonists, who were largely male, frequently took local wives, racial co-existence was not matched by cultural accommodation. The cities remained resolutely Greek in character.

Seleukid control was always shakiest at the empire's peripheries and strongest at its core. In the west, Anatolia was never fully conquered; the peninsula's northern provinces of Bithynia and Pontos and its central province of Kappadokia had their own proud leaders who vigorously defended their autonomy and resisted rule by a foreign power. Even the great city state of Pergamon on the Aegean coast continued to be ruled by its own local dynasty, paying only nominal allegiance to the Seleukid kings. Syria, on the other hand, with its close trading links across the eastern Mediterranean, was swiftly Hellenised. It produced a remarkable series of Greek philosophers, notably the Stoics; and its capital Antiokheia became one of the greatest cities of the ancient world.

Babylonia, too, displayed a strong loyalty to the Seleukid regime, helped by its people's hatred of the Persians whom Alexander had conquered. In a rare demonstration of cultural accommodation, Seleukos rewarded the Babylonians' loyalty by allowing them to retain their own governmental, legal and social structures, and by honouring the temples of the local gods: Marduk, Anu and Nabu. In turn, Babylonian astronomy and mathematics had a profound influence on Greek learning, while a local priest, Berossus, compiled a three-volume history of his native land, the *Babyloniaka*, to explain its history and customs to the Greek-speaking ruling class.[2]

Mesopotamia was also of great importance economically. All the land routes of the Fertile Crescent met at Seleukeia-on-the-Tigris, which emerged as a major centre of commerce and banking; while the surrounding country was a rich agricultural zone, producing food and textiles for export. Seleukid rulers profited enormously from their control of trade routes connecting the Mediterranean, Arabia and India, facilitated by a unified coinage across the empire.

While Mesopotamia was only too glad to throw off the Persian yoke, Iran felt very differently. The Persian heartland did everything it could to retain its distinctive culture intact, actively resisting Hellenisation. Whenever the central government was distracted by internal affairs, the Iranian lands broke away, one by one. The vast province of Bactria was lost for ever within fifty years of the establishment of the Seleukid kingdom, followed soon after by the Iranian plateau and eastern Mesopotamia.

It was such fissile politics that kept the Seleukid kings preoccupied most of the time. Nonetheless, in those brief moments when internal stability was restored, the Seleukids invariably took the opportunity to attack the Ptolemies, or Ptolemaic interests along the eastern Mediterranean coast. Phoenicia with its ports was particularly hotly disputed, as was the territory south of the River Eleutheros (present-day Nahr al-Kabir). The result was a seemingly endless succession of 'Syrian Wars' – historians recognise six, although to those living through them they must have seemed like one long, protracted conflict – that raged for over a hundred years, distracting and dominating the foreign policy of many of Ptolemy I's successors.

The Macedonian and Seleukid kingdoms were familiar adversaries – their rulers, after all, were Ptolemy's erstwhile colleagues – but the land to the south of Egypt presented an altogether different picture. The Kingdom of Kush, an ancient state which could trace its origins back to the beginning of the second millennium, controlled most of the Nubian Nile Valley upstream of the First Cataract (the northernmost of six sets of rapids interrupting the river's flow). Although never part of the Hellenistic world (its roots and outlook being African rather than Mediterranean), it was an important neighbour, trading partner and potential rival to the Ptolemies, and one they could not afford to ignore.

Originally centred at the site of present-day Kerma, just above the Second Cataract, the Kingdom of Kush had subsequently moved its capital to Napata, located below the Fourth Cataract and dominated by the holy mountain of Gebel Barkal. Within the city of Napata, Egyptian influences abounded: the principal temple was dedicated to the Egyptian god Amun, and the Kushite kings of the first millennium came to regard themselves as torchbearers of pharaonic culture. While Egypt itself was buffeted by a succession of foreign infiltrations and invasions, the Kushites believed that they were maintaining the true religion, unsullied by alien influence. By the time Ptolemy I claimed the Egyptian throne, the bonds between Kush and Egypt had grown weaker, and the centre of Kushite rule had retreated yet further south, to a site between the Fifth and Sixth Cataracts. Here, at the city of Meroë, close to the confluence of the Atbara and the Nile, the desert track across the great bend of the Nile reached its southern terminus, while other routes east to the Red Sea and west to Kordofan and Darfur converged. As a result, Meroë controlled trade routes by land and river in all directions, and was ideally situated to profit from the trade between sub-Saharan Africa and Egypt. From the beginning of the third century, Meroë expanded as the kingdom's principal administrative centre.

It soon became one of the greatest cities of Africa, extending over an area of at least one square mile. It was surrounded by fertile grasslands, and blessed with annual summer rains – in stark contrast to areas of Nubia further north, which had to rely entirely on the Nile as a source of water. Large reservoirs were created around the city to store the rainwater; one required the removal of a quarter of a million cubic metres of soil. With the advantage of perennial irrigation, the fields around Meroë grew barley and millet, and supported large herds of cattle. The city itself housed flourishing industrial quarters, including a major iron foundry. Public buildings included a great temple to Amun, approached along an avenue of stone rams, and an extensive royal compound with palaces and government buildings.

The kings of Kush may have continued to worship Amun and to be buried in pyramids, but their court culture, severed from Egypt, showed a progressive move away from Egyptian influences and a reversion to more African modes of expression. Alongside Amun, the other popular cults were of Nubian origin: the lion god Apedemak, the creation god Sebiumeker and divine elephants. Kingly burials abandoned Egyptian-style servant statuettes in favour of the real thing, with retainer sacrifice readopted as a funerary custom. The ruling class comprised a small number of families who spoke a language unrelated to their Nubian subjects, and the kings seem to have ruled by force of arms; they were often depicted holding weapons and were customarily buried with spears and archery equipment. Yet women held high status and could rule alone.

In this remote part of Africa, more than a thousand miles up the Nile, foreign visitors were rare, yet the Meroïtic royal court embraced Hellenistic culture – the prestige of the exotic – in its art and architecture. Human statuary could combine the relaxed pose of Greek sculpture with the plumpness of local taste, while temple buildings might juxtapose Classical and Nubian elements. Manufactured goods, too, unearthed by archaeology, including bronzes, pottery and textiles, showed the inspiration of Mediterranean design. This receptiveness to Hellenistic influences underlined a more general accommodation between Ptolemaic Egypt and Kushite Nubia. Each needed the other to maintain its prosperity, and good relations seem to have existed between the two kingdoms for much of the Ptolemaic period. Kush ensured a steady flow of commodities from sub-Saharan Africa to Egypt – ivory, live elephants, spices and slaves – while grain and manufactured goods flowed in the other direction.

Macedon, Asia and Kush: to the north, east and south, Ptolemy I was faced by a ring of potentially hostile rivals. His strategic genius was to create a buffer zone inside this ring to protect his core possession, Egypt.

The first piece to be put in place was Kyrenaika (present-day coastal Libya), which Ptolemy secured in 321, early in his tenure as satrap of Egypt. It had the advantage of being already Hellenised, at least in the case of the main centre of population, Kyrene (close to present-day Shahhat). The fact that the city and its rural hinterland lay so far to the west – some 500 miles from Alexandria, beyond the Siwa oasis, beyond the furthest extent of Alexander's dreams of conquest – meant that it was never really in the sights of any of the other Hellenistic kingdoms.

Reflecting this relative lack of threat, the Ptolemaic attitude towards Kyrenaika seems to have been quite relaxed. Ptolemy founded a new city (named, inevitably, Ptolemais), and imposed on the city of Kyrene a new constitution, but many of this document's measures effectively confirmed the status quo. Likewise, civic institutions that had existed before Ptolemy's annexation were allowed to continue, or in some cases were even renewed. In the absence of intensive trading links between Kyrenaika and Egypt – for the former had little by way of resources that the latter coveted – the Ptolemaic government's main interest was to extract taxation. A monetary union with Egypt facilitated the flow of income eastwards to Alexandria. With the Ptolemaic administration interested primarily in the collection of revenue, central control was largely confined to the major cities; pre-existing relationships between Kyrenaika's settled urban elite and the rural nomadic population remained largely unaltered. Even in the cities, traditional local cults were left alone, albeit supplemented by the worship of the Ptolemaic ruler and the new god Sarapis. Kyrene also boasted two temples of Isis, a cult that had already been introduced long before Ptolemy's time when the city maintained links with Greek settlers in the Egyptian city of Naukratis. Thanks to these historic cultural ties and a relatively benign colonial administration, Kyrenaika, once secured for Egypt, would remain a core Ptolemaic possession, uncontested by any rival power, for over two centuries.

The next part of the defensive belt around Egypt was the Levantine littoral. This had formed part of an Egyptian empire back in the golden age of the pharaohs, and Ptolemy recognised early on the region's vital strategic and economic importance. He managed to secure control of the Phoenician coast and inland Lebanon as early as 320, but lost them again five years later. Undeterred, following the death of Antigonos the One-Eyed in 301, Ptolemy outmanoeuvred his rival Seleukos I to seize the coastal strip all the way north to the River Eleutheros. This new territory, known as Koile-Syria, not only brought greater security to Egypt, it also gave Ptolemy access to valuable natural resources: the famed cedars of Lebanon for shipbuilding; spices from Arabia; grain, oil and wine from Syria; and Jewish mercenaries and administrators from the formerly independent kingdom of Judaea. This last group would form an important part of the population of Alexandria, and of other Greek cities in Egypt, for centuries to come.

Ptolemy I had to wait a further decade before successfully wresting control of the commercial enclaves of Sidon and Tyre from the Seleukids – who were not willing to give up such valuable entrepots without a fight. Throughout the region, Ptolemaic administration was backed up by significant military force. Garrisons were established in all the main cities, their commanders hand-picked for their ability and loyalty by the king. To secure the surrounding countryside – or, at least, to make any native insurrection less likely to succeed – the Ptolemaic government settled military veterans on land outside the main urban areas. They seem to have been actively encouraged to take local wives to help secure native acquiescence. On occasion, members of prominent, local Levantine families might be taken into Ptolemaic service and entrusted with the oversight of military settlers. Every colonial occupation has its collaborators.

As in Kyrenaika so in Phoenicia and Koile-Syria: a major preoccupation of the Ptolemaic government was the collection of taxes. The administrative structures set up to achieve this aim seem to have been modelled on those already found in Egypt. From the rather sparse documentary evidence that survives, it appears that bureaucrats were stationed in the districts and villages to supervise the assessment and collection of a share of the harvest, and a census of livestock was carried out annually, with harsh penalties for non-compliance. People were encouraged to report suspected tax-evaders, with the promise of a share of any financial penalty or property confiscated from miscreants. With neighbour spying on neighbour, relations in rural communities must have been particularly strained at census time. Another source of tension was enslavement. Ownership of slaves was strictly controlled, although military settlers with native wives were free to keep slaves without having to register them. By contrast, the trade in slaves between Syria and Egypt was a flourishing business. Like later colonial regimes, the Ptolemaic administration clearly understood that enslaving a people in their own land was likely to lead to civil unrest, whereas sending them abroad was a good source of profit.

Relatively little is known about the cities of Phoenicia and Koile-Syria under Ptolemaic rule. Because they played less of a role in tax collection than their counterparts in Kyrenaika, they feature less in the documentary record. The local king of Sidon appears to have been allowed to retain his status, if not his authority, after the city's annexation by Ptolemy I, as shown by the sarcophagi from the royal necropolis of Sidon, currently displayed in the Istanbul Archaeological Museum. Other local bigwigs enthusiastically adopted Hellenistic customs to curry favour with their new overlords.

The third major component of the Ptolemaic possessions outside Egypt was Cyprus. Having won the island in 315, only to lose it again a decade later, Ptolemy lost no time in retaking it in 295, as soon as the opportunity presented itself. The Ptolemaic approach to its newest colony was very different – and very stark. Instead of tolerating or accommodating established economic or political structures, the new regime imposed total control. Local kingdoms, which had existed for centuries, were summarily abolished. Garrisons were installed in every city, including new urban foundations, and were placed under the control of a single, all-powerful military governor (Gr. *strategos*), appointed by Ptolemy himself. Not only was he the commander-in-chief, he was also the highest religious authority on the island. The local Cypriot script was suppressed; henceforth all official documents were to be written in Greek. Aspects of the indigenous culture survived in the countryside; but, within a few short years of Ptolemy's annexation, urban Cyprus had become completely Hellenised.

The overriding purpose of these administrative changes was to secure total control of the economy. In Cyprus, as in Kyrenaika and Koile-Syria, only Ptolemaic currency was permitted to circulate; and production, as well as exchange, became a royal monopoly. For generations, the Cypriot countryside had been controlled by the cities; and now, the cities were controlled by the Ptolemaic government. This ensured that all the island's natural resources – wood, wine and, especially, copper (after which the island was named) – went straight to the treasury in Alexandria. In effect, Cyprus became the personal possession of the Ptolemaic monarchy.[3]

Two developments illustrate this transformation particularly starkly. The first was in the area of religious practice. Outwardly, Cypriot temples retained their traditional architectural forms; but inside the sanctuaries, different gods had taken up residence. Foremost among them was Sarapis, Ptolemy's personal and dynastic deity. Almost as soon as Ptolemy took control of Cyprus, his patron god gained singular prominence at some of the island's most important shrines, not least in the capitals of two of its pre-Ptolemaic kingdoms, Soloi on the north coast and Salamis on the south-east coast. The second unequivocal expression of Ptolemaic colonial power was the establishment of a brand-new capital on the west coast, an act which replaced Soloi and Salamis and relegated them to mere provincial status. The city, called New Paphos – Old Paphos had been destroyed by Ptolemy during his first invasion of Cyprus – was strategically located to exploit the two commodities most desired by the island's new rulers: its stands of timber and its copper mines, both located in the Troodos Mountains of the western interior. Just as important, perhaps, New Paphos offered an easy maritime route to the Egyptian coast. Cyprus's abundant natural resources would now flow directly into Alexandria's harbours.

Alexandria stood at the epicentre of Ptolemy's empire. In the years following its foundation, 'the castle of Alexander by the Sea of the Greeks' grew rapidly, as the dreams of the city's founder were turned into reality. Not for nothing did native Egyptians refer to Alexandria as 'the building site': over a period of several decades, the whole area swarmed with construction workers, the streets resounding to the din of hammers, saws and chisels, the canals and wharves choked with building stone from across Egypt. An army of builders followed the master plan devised by Alexander himself. As fully realised under Ptolemy, the vision for Alexandria displayed a keen awareness of the city's natural features and unique location; it was laid out with a primary orientation northwards, towards the Mediterranean world, while maximising the potential of its links with the fertile Nile Valley.

Today, there are few visible remains of the ancient city; but, thanks to an extensive first-hand description by the Greek geographer Strabon (Strabo) in the late first century, we can reconstruct Ptolemaic Alexandria in great detail. Travellers arriving by sea would have caught their first sight of the city as they neared the shore. Although the coastline was flat and featureless, the local topography created the perfect conditions for safe anchorage, 'for the shore of the mainland forms a bay, since it thrusts two promontories into the open sea, and between these is situated the island which closes the bay, for it lies lengthwise parallel to the shore'. This was the island of Pharos, mentioned by Homer in the *Odyssey*, which had drawn visitors to the area for hundreds of years. Its eastern end lay very close to the headland of the eastern promontory (named Lochias), thus forming a narrow harbour mouth. The western approach was not quite as narrow, but still required caution and careful piloting by incoming vessels.

In a brilliant stroke of genius by Alexandria's planners, a causeway some 600 feet wide was built linking the mainland to Pharos. Not only did this give ready access to the island, it also conveniently divided the harbour into two, providing twice the opportunity for ships to moor and dock. The causeway was named the Heptastadion, 'seven stadia', denoting its length, which exceeded three-quarters of a mile. At its top and bottom it was cut and bridged, allowing ships to pass from one side of the harbour into the other. A further piece of ingenuity was to incorporate an aqueduct into the masonry of the causeway, in order to bring fresh water to Pharos.

To the east of the Heptastadion, the anchorage was named the Great Harbour, and it lived up to its billing. In Strabo's words, 'in addition to its being beautifully enclosed both by the embankment and by nature, it is ... so deep close to the shore that the largest ship can be moored at the steps'. Furthermore, in the south-eastern corner of the Great Harbour, close in to the shore, lay the tiny islet of Antirrhodos, which was Ptolemy's private property. It housed a royal palace and sheltered two innermost harbours, the Small Harbour and the Royal Harbour, the latter an artificial basin set aside for the king's exclusive use. Lining the walls of the Royal Harbour and extending up the Lochias promontory was the principal royal quarter of Alexandria, where Ptolemy had his palaces, interspersed with 'groves and numerous lodges painted in various colours'. It was a stunning location: to the west there were views of the Great Harbour, to the east lay the open sea, while, to the north, the island of Pharos shimmered in the distance.

On the western side of the Heptastadion, the harbour was named Eunostos, 'the port of good return'. (The ancient Egyptian port of Memphis bore a similar moniker, Perunefer, 'bon voyage'.) Although Eunostos did not have the cachet of the Great Harbour, it was by far the more practical for the export of goods from Egypt. For on its south side it joined a man-made harbour basin, Kibotos ('box'), that was connected by means of a canal with Lake Mareotis, which in turn gave access to the Nile and thence to the interior of the country. As Strabo noted, 'through these canals the imports are much larger than those from the sea'.

Lying between two great bodies of water, the Mediterranean Sea to the north and Lake Mareotis to the south, the isthmus of land on which the city itself was built was thought to resemble the Macedonian military cloak known as a *chlamys*. Extending some thirty stadia (nearly three and a half miles) from west to east, and between seven and eight stadia (0.8–1 mile) from north to south, it was divided into districts or quarters. At the westernmost end, in keeping with ancient Egyptian custom, lay the necropolis or city of the dead 'in which are many gardens and graves and halting-places fitted up for the embalming of corpses'. Next came the district of Rhakotis (the original 'building site') which straddled the canal linking Kibotos harbour with Lake Mareotis. This was the Egyptian quarter where the native population lived and worked, loading and unloading the ships going to and from the Egyptian interior. Rhakotis also supported a flourishing death industry connected with the nearby necropolis: the arts of mummification and coffin-making were sectors in which native Egyptians held all the experience and practised a virtual monopoly.

Moving eastwards beyond Rhakotis, the next district constituted the ceremonial heart of Alexandria where many of the public buildings were situated. According to Strabo, these comprised 'one-fourth or even one-third of the whole circuit of the city'. They reflected the Greek culture of the city's ruling class. On the south side, close to the lake shore, was the stadium (for races on foot), and next to it the city's main temple of Sarapis, the Sarapieion. On the north side, and a little further east, were the agora (market place), theatre (for dramatic performances) and gymnasium (for indoor sports, bathing and conversation). This last institution, regarded as an essential component of any civilised Greek city, was especially splendid; graced by shaded porticoes extending some 200 yards in length, it was regarded as the most beautiful of all Alexandria's public buildings. It also housed groves of trees and the city's principal court of justice. The other high point (quite literally) of the central district was the Paneion or temple to Pan. A man-made eminence, 'it has the shape of a fir-cone, resembles a rocky hill, and is ascended by a spiral road; and from the summit one can see the whole city lying below it on all sides'. All along the harbourside, to the west and east of the Heptastadion, were shipyards, wharves for loading and unloading, and warehouses for the storage of merchandise. Imported goods were taken to the nearby emporium for display and sale. Also at the water's edge, on a spit of land jutting out into the Great Harbour, was the temple of Poseidon. Ptolemy's dynastic seat and commercial capital was thus protected on its southern and northern flanks by the patron deities, respectively, of the royal family and the sea.

East of the ceremonial quarter was the main residential neighbourhood for Alexandria's Greek-speaking population. Known as the Brucheion, it abutted the royal quarter to the north. This juxtaposition conferred prestige on the city's Greeks – casting Alexandria, forever, as a Greek city in Egyptian eyes – but also gave them a sense of ownership and influence over the city's – and the dynasty's – affairs. The people of Alexandria gained a reputation for being febrile and prone to rioting, and the close proximity to the royal palace of an entitled, well-educated and politically engaged population would prove a persistent thorn in the Ptolemies' side. The final, easternmost district of the city was the Jewish quarter where administrators and military veterans from Ptolemaic-controlled Judaea settled in large numbers. Beyond the Jewish quarter, outside the walls of the city, lay the hippodrome (racetrack), and, close by, a network of canals that linked to the Canopic mouth of the Nile a few kilometres further east. These canals also brought fresh water to Alexandria, which was stored in great underground cisterns in the central city.

To any Egyptian from a ramshackle settlement in the Nile Valley, or visitor from a rambling Mediterranean town, one of the most striking features of Alexandria, besides its stunning natural location and impressive public buildings, was its layout. For the whole city was arranged on a grid plan: a simple but hugely innovative design, attributed originally to Hippodamos of Miletos and put into effect in

Alexandria by Dinokrates of Rhodes, which would influence town planning for ever after. Among the criss-cross of broad streets, 'practicable for horse-riding and chariot-driving', were two magnificent boulevards more than a hundred feet wide. Running directly west-east and cutting a broad swathe through the centre of the isthmus was the Canopic Way. At its western end was the Gate of the Necropolis, which gave access to the city's main cemetery; at its eastern end the Canopic Gate, which led to the nearby city of Kanopos. Intersecting with the Canopic Way at right angles was the equally impressive Street of the Soma, which connected the Royal Harbour with Lake Mareotis. Its northern and southern ends were likewise marked with gates, the Gate of the Moon on the harbourside and the Gate of the Sun on the lakeside. The Street of the Soma took its name from the nearby enclosure that formed part of the royal compound and which housed the body (Gr. *soma*) of Alexander the Great – the sacred talisman of Ptolemaic rule – in a magnificent mausoleum.[4]

With so many wonders, natural and artificial, Alexandria quickly became famous throughout the ancient world. One Greek commentator declared it 'the first city of the civilised world', ranking it 'far ahead of all the rest in elegance and extent and riches and luxury'.[5] Another averred that Ptolemy I had 'boldly achieved such grand schemes as no man but he could ever have thought of'.[6] Even three centuries after its construction, Alexandria attracted the praise of Roman visitors, one remarking that it could never be burned down because there was no wood to burn: the city was a mesmerising mixture of smooth limestone, polished granite and dazzling marble. With its direct shipping lanes to Cyprus and Rhodes, its canals connecting with the Nile and its safe anchorage for vessels from across the Mediterranean, Alexandria swiftly became the world's greatest entrepot, where copper ingots from Cyprus, cedar logs from Lebanon and amphorae of wine from Rhodes could be seen stacked up on the wharves alongside leopard skins from Nubia, sticks of cinnamon from India and incense trees from Arabia – not to mention vast bushels of grain from the fertile fields of Egypt.

Ptolemaic Alexandria was a magnet for ambitious people from across the ancient world, and a melting pot of races and tongues – the first universal city. It was a place where someone with energy and an entrepreneurial bent could make their fortune. But Ptolemy, steeped in

Greek history and tutored by Aristotle, believed that greatness could not simply be weighed in coinage or the balance of trade. A great city, to this philosopher king, had to be a city of learning. In the centuries before Alexander, Athens had gained its reputation as much for its philosophers as for its merchants or generals. If Alexandria were to replace Athens as the greatest city in the Greek-speaking world, it needed to shine intellectually as well as commercially. Fortunately for Ptolemy, one of Alexandria's early arrivals knew exactly what it would take to seize Athens' crown – for he had worn it himself. Demetrios of Phaleron (a port of Athens) had, like Ptolemy, been a pupil of Aristotle, and had gone on to achieve renown as a philosopher of the Peripatetic school. He had also been a successful Athenian statesman, ruling his home city for a decade, which was a period of peace and stability that was only brought to an end by a Macedonian invasion. Like many seeking a new life, Demetrios fled – first to Boeotian Thebes, then to Alexandria. He arrived in the city in 297 with a reputation as a fine thinker, writer and orator. One of his first helpful acts, if legend is to be believed, was to be struck blind and swiftly restored to sight by praying to the city's patron god, Sarapis. Such a miracle would certainly have helped cement the popularity of the Sarapis cult with Alexandria's Greek-speaking population, and would have made Demetrios equally popular with Ptolemy. That Demetrios lost no time in penning a paean to the god was an added bonus.

Encouraged, perhaps, by Demetrios, Ptolemy determined to make Alexandria a magnet for scholars as well as for traders. His solution was to found a temple of the Muses, a Mouseion, in which great thinkers would have the time, space and resources to codify existing learning and create new knowledge. As Strabo later described it:

> The Mouseion is also a part of the royal palaces; it has a public walk, an Exedra with seats, and a large house, in which is the common mess-hall of the men of learning who share the Mouseion. This group of men not only hold property in common, but also have a priest in charge of the Mouseion.[7]

Ptolemy I's foundation would go on to become the world's first great centre of learning, an institution where extraordinary feats of scholarship and invention would change the course of human history.

As Ptolemy grew old and sensed, perhaps, that his days on earth were numbered, he commissioned one last, extraordinary monument that would, quite literally, beam Alexandria's wonders to the wider world. Despite a perfect location for trade, the city was built on a flat stretch of coast with few prominent landmarks. This made it very difficult for incoming vessels to spot while they were still out at sea. When they did near the shoreline, dangerous shoals, sandbanks and reefs hidden beneath the surface made navigation difficult. To make matters worse, some of the most treacherous rocks lay in the narrow passage between Pharos and the Lochias promontory, the very entrance to the Great Harbour. What was needed was a visible landmark and a beacon.

Ptolemy's chosen entrepreneur, a man named Sostratos who came from Knidos in south-western Anatolia, came up with the plans for a great lighthouse, to be erected at the easternmost end of Pharos, overlooking the main shipping channel. The structure took twelve years to build (Ptolemy would not live to see it finished), at a colossal cost of 800 talents (the same amount as the entire Egyptian state treasury that had been handed over to Alexander in 332). It was a miracle of engineering the like of which the world had never seen before. Reaching at least 400 feet into the sky, the height of a 40-storey building, the lighthouse was built from huge blocks of limestone weighing an average of 75 tons – some of which have recently been found, lying beneath the waters of Abukir Bay – and was faced in dazzling white marble. The tower rose in three massive storeys, by turns square, octagonal and cylindrical. At the summit, topped by a gigantic statue of Zeus the Saviour (Gr. Zeus Soter), was the crowning glory: a beacon which burned day and night. Its light, magnified by mirrors, was visible thirty miles out to sea — to guide people, goods and ideas from across the Mediterranean into Ptolemy's thriving kingdom.[8] Its dedicatory inscription ran, 'Sostratos, son of Dexiphanes the Knidian, dedicated this to the Saviour Gods, on behalf of all those who sail the seas'. A practical landmark for shipping and a powerful symbol of royal and commercial power, the Pharos lighthouse epitomised the energy and ambition of Ptolemy the Saviour, ruler of Egypt, founder of a new dynasty and harbinger of a new age.

3
Grain, Gold and Glory

Over the course of his long and eventful reign, Ptolemy I righted the wrongs of the hated Persians, respected the traditions of his new homeland and played to the aspirations of Greek-speakers and immigrants from across the Hellenistic world. In his twilight years, he wrote his own history of Alexander, which became the principal source for the main surviving biography. Ptolemy thus ensured that posterity would remember his childhood friend – and of course himself – in the most favourable of lights. And just as he hoped to shape the narrative surrounding the rise of his dynasty, he also took steps to ensure its future. From his knowledge of history, as well as his own experience growing up in Macedon, he was all too aware of the threat that a disputed succession might pose to any ruling family. Moreover, Macedon's noble lineages seem to have had a particular penchant for internecine squabbles, and Ptolemy's own clan was no exception. His personal life had only added to the tensions, as he had been married three times: first, at Alexander's behest, to a Persian woman, Artakama, at the mass wedding in Susa in April 324; second to Eurydike, daughter of the Macedonian regent Antipatros; and third to Eurydike's cousin and lady-in-waiting, Berenike. From his second and third marriages, Ptolemy I had fathered a number of sons, any one of whom, in the absence of a tradition of strict primogeniture, might hope to follow in his father's footsteps and claim the throne of Egypt. As Ptolemy grew old, securing the royal succession became a pressing preoccupation.

Hopes had initially rested on his eldest son, from his marriage to Eurydike. The boy had been born in Alexandria around 319 and was named – with more emphasis on dynastic succession than originality – Ptolemy. But this younger Ptolemy was no chip off the old block. Indeed, he soon acquired a nickname that revealed his distinctive personality: Keraunos ('thunderbolt'). For, as he reached maturity, he displayed an increasingly impatient and impetuous, not to say destructive, character. It soon became apparent that he was entirely unfit to govern, especially over a kingdom that was both geographically extensive and culturally complex. If Ptolemy I had been looking for a safe pair of hands to succeed him as king of Egypt, he must have been bitterly disappointed. Relations between father and son seem to have reached their nadir around 287, when Ptolemy Keraunos left Alexandria to seek his fortune at the court of a rival monarch, Lysimachos of Thrace. Ptolemy I's doubts were soon justified, when Keraunos embroiled himself in Thracian dynastic politics, leading eventually to the kingdom's conquest by Seleukos I (whom Keraunos promptly murdered).

In place of the thunderbolt kid, Ptolemy I's attention came to rest on his son by his third wife. This prince, born on the island of Kos in 309 while his father was on campaign, was also named Ptolemy. Though a full-blooded Macedonian, he seems to have been less hot-headed than his half-brother, and offered the welcome prospect of securing, rather than destroying, his father's life's work. Time and again throughout his long career, Ptolemy I had shown himself to be an astute politician – too astute by far to leave the future of his dynasty to chance. So, in the spring of 285, when he had already outlived the vast majority of his contemporaries and must have sensed that his years on the throne were drawing to a close, he appointed Ptolemy son of Berenike as his formal co-ruler. Co-regency was a venerable institution in Egypt, and had been used on countless occasions over the centuries to ensure a smooth succession from father to son. Recognising the son as king while his father was still alive reduced the chances of a dispute when the throne fell vacant.

And so it proved. When Ptolemy son of Lagos died, well into his eighties (an astonishing age for the time), his heir as *basileus* and pharaoh acted quickly to prevent any challenge to his rule: one of Ptolemy II's first acts was to order the execution of his two remaining half-brothers, who belonged to Keraunos' branch of the family. Just as swift and decisive was the expulsion from Alexandria of the famous

Demetrios of Phaleron, the inspiration behind the establishment of the Mouseion, because the sage had dared to support the claims of Euridike's children (headed by Keraunos) against those of Berenike (headed by Ptolemy II).

Having secured his throne, Ptolemy II could now devote his energies to taking full advantage of his birthright. The Egyptians had long expected their kings to deliver prosperity. As for Greek rulers, their success and reputation was measured by the magnificence (Gr. *tryphē*) of their court. Mindful of both traditions, Ptolemy II embarked on a plan to transform Egypt into the wealthiest, most dazzling land in the entire world.

In the first four decades of Ptolemaic rule, Macedonian ingenuity had laid the foundations for Egypt to become the richest of all the Hellenistic kingdoms. Greek economic concepts were introduced to the Nile Valley, including a nationwide banking system and a monetary economy, with the state bank in Alexandria issuing coinage, backed up by bills of exchange. Out in the countryside, local bank branches acted as agencies of the central government by providing the seeds and tools required for intensive agriculture, especially the cultivation of cereal crops. Egypt's agricultural bounty was fabled, and had underpinned the civilisation of the pharaohs for thousands of years. But to produce the kinds of surpluses desired by Ptolemy II – enough to generate a healthy balance of trade and fund his foreign policy ambitions – a massive increase in production was required. Thanks to the chance discovery of hundreds of papyri on Egypt's desert margins, we have first-hand testimony from two of the men involved in bringing Ptolemy II's economic vision to reality.

Kleon was an engineer who came to Egypt as part of an early wave of immigrants in the early decades of the third century. Arriving in the great port city of Alexandria, he soon made his way to the provincial town of Shedyt, in the low-lying region of the Fayum, west of the Nile Valley. The town was famous throughout Egypt for its shrine to the local crocodile god, Sobek, where sacred reptiles were kept in a special enclosure; pilgrims came from far and wide to feed them. To Kleon and his fellow Greek speakers, therefore, Shedyt was known as Krokodilopolis, 'crocodile city'. As befitted a region presided over by an aquatic deity, the Fayum's main geographical feature was a huge body of fresh water, named by the Egyptians the 'Great Lake' (Eg.

Mer-wer), that was fed by a secondary branch of the Nile. As the level of water in the Nile rose and fell during the course of the year, so the lake waxed and waned. It had been thus for millennia – until the advent of the Ptolemaic dynasty. For Macedonians knew a thing or two about drainage and land reclamation. In the reign of Philip II, the marshy plains around his new city of Philippi in western Thrace had been drained to improve their agricultural productivity. Similar drainage work took place around the shores of Lake Kopais in Boeotia. So when Macedonian rulers and settlers arrived in the Nile Valley, they at once recognised the special potential of the Great Lake region. In order to turn it into the grain basket of Egypt, they needed a cadre of qualified hydraulic engineers. Kleon fitted the bill perfectly.

Shortly after arriving in Krokodilopolis, he was appointed by Ptolemy II to the post of chief engineer (Gr. *architekton*), with responsibility for all public works in the Fayum. It was an important role at the head of a large team, which consisted of a deputy, at least ten foremen and thousands of labourers. The lowly workers were all Egyptians, and earned just a fifteenth of Kleon's wages: wealth as well as culture divided the native and immigrant populations in Ptolemaic Egypt. Irrigation works – cutting and dredging canals, constructing and repairing dykes, and large-scale land reclamation – dominated Kleon's working life, as Ptolemy II's government set about increasing the acreage and productivity of agricultural land. Key elements of the overall plan included a new sluice at the entrance of the Fayum, a large embankment and dam that controlled the flow of water and diverted it to the region's western edge, and a series of new canals to manage drainage. These innovations, bringing together Macedonian and Egyptian expertise, succeeded in lowering the level of the Great Lake by as much as thirty feet, exposing a large tract of land for reclamation, irrigation and agriculture.

Kleon's surviving correspondence is full of references to the construction of bridges and jetties, sluices and floodgates, fascines and embankments: all the paraphernalia of large-scale irrigation projects. But creating the infrastructure was only part of the challenge: maintaining it was hard, unceasing work. If left untended, channels would clog with sand and silt, while dykes and embankments would develop breaches, leaving precious farmland prone to desiccation or flooding.

To keep the Fayum's complex irrigation network in good order, Kleon needed to supplement his core workforce with convicts and slaves. In emergency situations, he could also obtain special government authorisation to requisition labour and supplies from other projects, though this must have made him deeply unpopular with other officials, trying their hardest to meet their own targets. All in all, the lot of a chief engineer was a stressful job, not helped by the tendency of Egyptian workers to withdraw their labour if they thought they were being unfairly treated. The tone of Kleon's letters reveals a constant tension between meeting the expectations and demands of the government in Alexandria and working with the imperfect realities on the ground in the Fayum.

In this atmosphere, the announcement of a royal visit to the Fayum only added to the pressure. As the day of Ptolemy II's arrival drew ever closer, with the work he was due to inspect still unfinished, the stress on Kleon and his family began to tell. His wife Metrodora wrote to him, anxiously, 'I am frightened ... as I am wondering how things are going to turn out for you and for us.'[1] The only option open to Kleon to save his reputation, and perhaps his job, was all too familiar from workplaces throughout history: he went on sick leave. This removed him from the immediate line of fire – we may never know what Ptolemy II found when he visited – but led, in short order, to Kleon's permanent retirement or dismissal. Creating the infrastructure for the king's economic miracle came at a huge cost, in lives as well as money.

Men like Kleon were the footsoldiers of Ptolemy II's agricultural revolution. The ultimate beneficiaries, besides the royal court itself, were the members of the Greek-speaking elite who were granted the newly reclaimed land by the crown. Of course, they were required to farm these estates as productively as possible, in order to generate the maximum tax revenue for the central government; but, in the process, the landowners grew fabulously wealthy in their own right. A prime example was Ptolemy II's finance minister (Gr. *dioiketes*), a man named Apollonios. In return for his loyal service, the king granted him a 6,800-acre estate in the Fayum. Apollonios used his position as the biggest of the local bigwigs to advance his own private interests, while ensuring that he paid his taxes on time and in full to the state treasury. Agents working for Apollonios locked horns with Kleon on more than one occasion, demanding that labour and materials be diverted to their master's projects. It was hard, if not impossible, to resist such pressure when it came from the second most powerful man in the land. And it made Kleon's task even harder.

The second eyewitness to Ptolemy II's bold plans for the transformation of Egypt would have sympathised with Kleon's predicament. Zenon was Apollonios' estate manager, and had the hard – sometimes impossible – task of mediating between his boss's insatiable demands and the practical limitations of doing business in the Egyptian countryside. Thanks to the discovery of Zenon's personal archive, we know more about this one man than any other individual from Ptolemaic Egypt. His story shines a light on the inner workings of the economy under Ptolemy II, and reveals how the king's development programme changed the landscape and social fabric of the Nile Valley for ever.

Like Kleon, Zenon was an immigrant. He was born at Kaunos, a town on the south-western coast of Anatolia, in the province of Karia. The region had been settled by Greek-speakers as early as 1100 BC, and Kaunos was an early addition to Ptolemaic territory. The links between Karia and Egypt were already long-standing – Karians had been settling in the Nile Valley since the early sixth century – so Egypt would have been a natural destination for a man like Zenon, seeking to make his fortune. On arriving in Alexandria, he soon gained a position in the service of Apollonios, who just happened to be a fellow Karian: in the Hellenistic world, your family background and geographical origin mattered. For five years from 261, Zenon was Apollonios' commercial agent, representing his extensive private business interests in Egypt and abroad; these included vineyards by the Sea of Galilee. Apollonios even had his own ships, to transport goods from his various estates to the markets of the eastern Mediterranean. Then, in 256, Zenon moved to the Fayum as manager of Apollonios' landholdings.

The spur to Zenon's change of position may have been the promulgation of new laws in 259 to increase tax revenues, and a nationwide census of Egypt's agricultural wealth ordered by Ptolemy II the following year. By reviving an institution from pharaonic times, the king was determined to obtain an accurate assessment of national productive capacity. Returns had to be submitted by scribes and district officials in each province, and the whole operation was under the control of the finance minister himself. By the end of the exercise, Apollonios would have had a detailed picture of Egypt's water sources, the extent of temple and crown landholdings, as well as the location and potential of every plot of land, together with its current state of cultivation and a record of which crops were grown there.

The finance minister's own estate in the Fayum soon became something of a model farm, a showcase for the Ptolemies' superior techniques of reclamation, land management and agricultural production. The Fayum was visited by embassies from as far away as the Bosphoros and Argos, and seems to have gained a reputation as a good place for those seeking employment and opportunity. The centre of operations was a newly founded village named Philadelpheia. Indeed, one of Zenon's early tasks was to supervise the laying out of the settlement. Small details from Zenon's archive reveal aspects of life in Philadelpheia, and its hybrid Greek–Egyptian culture. The village had its own gymnasium, an essential institution in the life of (male) Greek-speakers, while a beer shop-cum-brewery catered largely for the tastes of the Egyptian population. The Greek settlers, on the other hand, preferred wine, and the village was a major centre of production, with a thriving pottery industry to supply amphorae. The central government actively encouraged the planting of vines in the Fayum, both to keep the settlers happy and to provide the state with a reliable source of tax income – levied at a rate of one-sixth of the harvest. Once a landowner like Apollonios had planted a vineyard, he was more likely to remain in the area and keep the land as productive as possible in order to recoup his investment. Other changes in land use included the introduction of crops better suited to marginal land and attuned to the dietary preferences of the Fayum's new settlers. In place of the emmer-wheat previously grown by the Egyptians, Apollonios planted durum-wheat. Olives, however, proved impossible to grow in the Egyptian climate; Zenon and his compatriots had to make do with sesame oil for cooking and castor oil for lighting.

Another key local activity was the rearing of livestock. Apollonios' estate raised a large number of pigs; in one year, a herd of 400 was rented out to a local pig breeder, who had to hand over some of the resulting piglets (211 per year, to be precise) by way of payment. Sheep and goats were also reared, again to cater to the tastes of the Greek settlers, who preferred woollen clothing to the linen garments of the Egyptians. Under Ptolemy II, new breeds of sheep and goats with superior fleeces were introduced to Egypt, in preference to the domestic breeds which were kept principally for milk and meat. Prize flocks were often tended by experienced shepherds from Arabia. As for Zenon, he seems to have had a fondness for rare hens, and was delighted on one occasion to receive a present of differently coloured fowl.

All this produce, of course, had to be transported to market. That meant an initial overland journey by donkey to the nearest inland port on the Nile, then downstream to Alexandria. Here, Apollonios kept a large fleet of his own barges for the onward shipment of goods to market; he thus controlled every part of the supply chain. One of Zenon's challenges as estate manager was to procure supplies of good quality timber for shipbuilding – no easy task in Egypt, with its predominantly scrubby vegetation. Yet he was not allowed to use his master's craft for his own travel: whenever he needed to visit Memphis or Alexandria, Zenon had to find, and pay for, a willing boat owner.

Zenon's life, however, was not entirely one of thankless drudgery. His personal archive reveals a man of learning, with educated tastes. He wrote in concise, correct Greek, and owned his own copies of Greek literature. When his favourite hunting dog Tauron ('bull') died of wounds sustained while saving his master from an attack by a wild boar, Zenon commissioned two epigrams in the hound's honour. Zenon's letters make no mention of a wife or children but he did foster a number of orphans, the sons of Greek mercenaries who had died in Ptolemy II's service. Zenon saw that they received all the elements of a respectable Hellenistic education, from reading and writing to music and gymnastics. (Even in the countryside, far from Alexandria, Greek culture remained strong among the Greek-speaking population.) True to his Greek background, Zenon seems to have operated, at home and at work, in a largely male-dominated society; of the 3,000 individuals named in his correspondence, only sixty are women, and most of these are named but once.

Through the eyes of a farm manager acting for a powerful official, the Zenon papyri illustrate the social and economic changes wrought by Ptolemy II's policy of agricultural intensification. Zenon was the leading figure in the life of one small village, yet the varied produce from Apollonios' estates and the networks by which it was traded underscore the internationalist outlook and commercial reach of the Ptolemaic empire.

Agricultural produce – grain in particular – was the mainstay of the Egyptian rural economy, and the foundation of Ptolemaic prosperity. But it was another commodity that made Ptolemy II not just rich but fabulously wealthy: gold.

Since the dawn of Egyptian history, the hills and dry valleys of the Eastern Desert, lying between the River Nile and the Red Sea, had yielded abundant supplies of gold. Egypt was famous throughout the ancient world for its reserves of the precious metal. As one envious foreign ruler had written to the pharaoh in the fourteenth century BC, 'in my brother's country gold is as plentiful as dirt'.[2] Ptolemy I restarted intensive and systematic exploitation, with activity concentrated around a site that combined the twin advantages of gold and water. The site, today known as Samut, housed a natural well that provided the means of life deep in the desert. Initially, mining took place some three miles north of the well, close to a vein of gold-bearing quartz. Next to the mine, a camp comprised living quarters for the miners and their overseer, communal cooking and dining facilities, storage rooms for equipment and a small shrine. But work took precedence over everything else: there were extensive areas for crushing the quartz and washing the powdered rocks to separate out the gold.

The Ptolemies brought with them from the Greek world efficient grinding mills and iron tools, both of which allowed for more intensive and efficient gold processing. This new technology is much in evidence at Samut, where two large circular mills, each thirty feet in diameter, were installed. Each mill was paved with large slabs of stone and surrounded by low walls made from local stones bound together with a clay mortar. At the centre of each mill, a post hole supported the axle of a mill stone, which was rotated by men or animals walking around the perimeter of the installation. Yet, despite all this investment, gold mining at the northern Samut site lasted no more than a decade. Before the end of Ptolemy I's reign, the ore-bearing rocks had been exhausted. When Ptolemy II came to the throne he needed to find other sources of gold to finance his ambitions.

Attention therefore shifted to areas further south. The 'gold of Kush', as the Egyptians called it, had always been the main reason for pharaonic interest in Nubia, and the spur to successive waves of Egyptian invasion and colonisation. By the fourth century, the pharaonic government had lost all control of the Nubian gold mines, and the Kingdom of Kush emerged as the main beneficiary. Twice, Kush pushed northwards from its Upper Nubian heartland to reassert control over Lower Nubia. While Egypt smarted under the Persian yoke, two successive Kushite rulers, Harsiyotef and Nastasen, extended their writ as far as the First and Second Cataracts, respectively. Ptolemy II made a concerted attempt to win back control of the Nubian gold mines. In 275, he led a well-planned military campaign into the southern regions. A decisive victory against the Kushite forces enabled him to annex a seventy-five-mile stretch of Lower Nubia (named in Greek the Dodekaschoinos, 'twelve-*schoinoi* territory'; the *schoinos* being a unit of length equal to forty *stades*). He symbolically donated the land to the temple of Isis at Philae, and had a list of subject Nubian territories carved on the walls of the temple.

Control of Lower Nubia gave Ptolemy II access to the most lucrative gold mines. He may even have stationed troops in the twelfth-dynasty fortresses of the Second Cataract – built some 1,700 years earlier, but still standing strong – to reinforce the Egyptian presence in the region. A secondary outcome of the campaign was that the Kingdom of Kush, cut off from its northern markets, effectively became a client state of the Ptolemaic empire, required to send 'tribute' to the government in Alexandria. And that tribute included regular supplies of gold.

To ensure unfettered access to the mines, Ptolemy II founded a new settlement. Located in the heart of gold country, it was named Berenike after the king's mother, but with the added epithet Panchrysos ('all-gold'). Archaeologists rediscovered All-Gold Berenike as recently as 1989, and their investigations have revealed the application of typically Ptolemaic strategy and efficiency to the exploitation of Nubia's gold resources.[3] The main village was strung out over a distance of one and a quarter miles, either side of a main road which followed the floor of the wadi. The extent of the housing suggests a sizeable resident population, perhaps as many as 10,000 people at its peak. Flanking the broad central thoroughfare, some twenty feet wide, were two narrower parallel streets, one running along the foot of the hills.

Intersecting streets enclosed a central square. Even here, in the midst of the inhospitable desert, the Macedonian preference for orthogonal town planning was in evidence. And this was not the only Hellenistic import at this remote site: the technology used for gold smelting most closely resembles that found in Greece at the same period.

All over the surface of the settlement there is evidence of gold-working, including mortars and pestles used to crush and pulverise the gold-bearing rock. Conditions in the gold mines were harsh and unforgiving, the miners working in intense heat in narrow trenches and at the bottom of shafts sunk into the rock to a depth of dozens of metres. A few everyday items found discarded in the village – small votive objects and dice – suggest that praying and gambling were among the few consolations available to the workers in this godforsaken spot. Overlooking the settlement and its associated mines were two rectangular forts of dry-stone construction, to keep marauders out or workers in, or both.

Extracting gold from the veins of quartz running deep into the mountainsides was only the first logistical hurdle. The resulting gold dust and granules then had to be transported hundreds of miles to the Nile Valley, for onward shipment to the treasury in Alexandria. Ptolemy II's programme for Nubia therefore included the construction of an extensive network of roads, way stations and watchtowers across the Eastern Desert, together with new port facilities on the Red Sea coast. A series of stone cairns marked the route all the way from the Second Cataract to the Wadi Allaqi. Known as the 'Way of Gold', it was protected at regular intervals by fortified guard posts.

Another more northerly route across the desert was reconditioned and fortified by Ptolemy II. It ran from the Nile Valley at Apollonopolis (present-day Edfu) to a newly established harbour on the Red Sea coast. This latter foundation, like the gold-miners' town, was named Berenike in honour of the king's mother, but with the epithet Troglodytika ('of the cave dwellers'), apparently referring to the local desert nomads. The town seems to have come into use within Ptolemy II's first decade on the throne, and it quickly became a bustling port and a flourishing community. The settlement was built from locally available materials: naturally occurring cobbles and boulders, supplemented by coral, gypsum and bricks of compressed sand. As befitted a Ptolemaic royal foundation, there was a temple to the god Sarapis. As well as gold from the Wadi Allaqi, the wharves and warehouses handled exotic commodities from far and wide. Imports included frankincense and myrrh from Arabia and the Horn of Africa, silk from China, pepper, cinnamon and cassia from India; exports from Egypt and the Mediterranean included Red Sea coral, glass, linen, wine and grain.

Goods arriving by sea at Berenike-of-the-Cave-Dwellers took twelve days to reach the Nile Valley by donkey caravan; but shorter routes to market were also available, owing to the construction of a series of port facilities all the way up the Red Sea coast of Egypt. More or less directly opposite Apollonopolis, Ptolemy II established a harbour at Nechesia. It had the added advantage of proximity to Egypt's only emerald mines. Further up the coast, there was another port at Myos Hormos (present-day Quseir), which was easily accessible from the Nile Valley via the Wadi Hammamat. Further north still, new harbours were created at Philotera and present-day Abu Shaʿar. In 270/69, Ptolemy II had the old canal from the Nile Valley to the Gulf of Suez, first dug under Persian domination, dredged and repaired, providing yet another access route from river to sea. He also established a garrison town at the head of the Gulf of Aqaba, which he named – predictably – Berenike. Together with a colony on the Arabian coast north of Jeddah, it was designed to protect the lucrative maritime trade in incense. Ports, roads, fortifications and a canal: all these installations represented a huge investment by Ptolemy II's administration, but they more than paid for themselves through the upsurge in economic activity they facilitated and the taxes that the state levied on imports.

There was another reason why Ptolemy II was so keen to secure access to Nubia, and why he went to such lengths to establish ports on the Red Sea coast and direct overland routes to the Nile Valley: elephants. The great pachyderms' effectiveness as instruments of war had first been brought home to Macedonian soldiers when fighting alongside Alexander the Great at the Battle of the Hydaspes in May 326. Large numbers of Indian elephants with their mahouts were subsequently acquired by the Seleukid kings in the carve-up of Alexander's empire, and some of these were captured by Ptolemy I during the Wars of the Successors. But by the reign of Ptolemy II, these beasts were either dead or too old to be of use in battle. As the son of a general, Ptolemy II knew that economic prosperity had to be backed up by military strength. What use was a flourishing Egypt if it could all too easily fall victim to a well-armed aggressor?

Indeed, only a decade into his reign, Ptolemy II experienced these threats at first-hand. In 274, Seleukos I's son and successor Antiochos I seized territories in coastal Syria and southern Anatolia. The Seleukid army was bolstered by Indian elephants from Bactria. Ptolemy II recaptured the losses and also extended Ptolemaic rule throughout southern coastal Anatolia as far as Karia. But as soon as the dust had settled on the so-called First Syrian War, he determined to secure a ready supply of war elephants to counter the ongoing Seleukid threat.

Since the market in Indian elephants was effectively cornered by his adversary, Ptolemy's only option was to seek to acquire their smaller cousins, the African forest elephants. At first, expeditions set off from Philotera; but it was a long journey from the northern Red Sea coast to the elephants' natural habitat above the Fifth Cataract. So, having secured control of the Eastern Desert of Nubia, Ptolemy II established a new base for elephant-hunting expeditions, south of Berenike-of-the-Cave-Dwellers. The settlement rejoiced in the name of Ptolemais-of-the-Hunts. According to later accounts, it was founded on the king's orders by a trusted official, who 'secretly enclosed a kind of peninsula with a ditch and a wall, and then, by courteous treatment of those who tried to hinder the work, actually won them over as friends instead of foes'.[4] This last oblique reference seems to hint at unrest among the local population caused by the upsurge of Egyptian activity. Indeed, the Nubians in the vicinity attempted to overthrow their philhellenic king Arqamani (Gr. Ergamenes), but with Ptolemaic support he retained his throne – and Ptolemy II retained control of Nubia's natural resources.

Ptolemais-of-the-Hunts was well situated, with enough fertile land in the vicinity to sustain it as a viable community without having to rely on imports from distant Egypt. It went on to serve as the major base for Ptolemaic elephant-hunting for some seven decades. As with gold-mining, so with elephant-hunting, procuring the desired commodity was only the start: getting it back to Egypt was an equal challenge. Transporting elephants hundreds of miles from coastal Nubia to the Nile Valley demanded particular ingenuity. They were an exceptionally heavy cargo, requiring specially designed transport vessels known as *elephantegos*-ships. Shipyards were built to maintain and repair the craft, and the animals themselves were offloaded at Berenike-of-the-Cave-Dwellers before being walked across the desert to the Nile Valley. There were special facilities near Luxor for housing the elephants, where the beasts could be fed and restored to health after their arduous sea journey and desert march.

The result of all this effort – 'perhaps the largest and most complex project ever undertaken by the Ptolemies'[5] – was that Ptolemy II succeeded in building up a sizeable corps of war elephants: according to the written sources, perhaps as many as a hundred animals.

With grain and gold filling his coffers, and a formidable corps of war elephants to deter any would-be aggressor, Ptolemy II presided over a golden era of international trade and established something approaching hegemonic power across the eastern Mediterranean. The First Syrian War (274–271) strengthened Ptolemaic control over the coasts of Syria and Anatolia, not least by the establishment of a garrison at Halikarnassos and a naval base on the island of Samos. At the same time, the League of Islanders gave Ptolemy II controlling influence in the central Aegean. Through the League's appointed governor (Gr. *nesiarch*), Ptolemy exercised de facto suzerainty over all the Cyclades, including Naxos, the holy island of Delos and Thera, with its excellent natural harbour. Ptolemy II was nothing if not a savvy self-promoter, and he saw to it that altars to the Ptolemaic dynasty were set up across the Aegean, while statues of himself and his queen were manufactured in Alexandria to be exported to the wider Mediterranean world. In the city of Thmuis, located in the central Nile Delta, a mosaic floor was commissioned from an artist named Sophilos showing Alexandria as a woman wearing a naval crown, with a ship's prow on her brow trailing long ribbons. Its symbolism was clear: Alexandria was queen of the seas, Ptolemy II their undoubted master.

The consolidation of Ptolemaic power also extended to mainland Greece. Here, rivalry with Macedon was the dominant driver of Ptolemy II's foreign policy. He concluded an anti-Macedonian treaty with Athens and Sparta, and joined them in attacking Macedon in the so-called Chremonidean War (267–261). Ptolemy was less concerned with the fortunes of Athens or Sparta than with weakening Macedon to advance his own hegemonic interests. Indeed, he held back from deploying his full military forces in the war, with the result that Athens was besieged and forced to surrender (never regaining its independence), and the Athenian general Chremonides fled to Egypt, bringing his considerable military talents. He subsequently served as commander of Ptolemy II's 400-strong fleet, the largest in the Hellenistic world.

While Ptolemy II was consolidating his power in the eastern Mediterranean, another war was raging far to the west, centred on the island of Sicily. Here the dominant power, the Carthaginian empire, was coming under pressure from an upstart neighbour, the Roman Republic. The naval conflict that erupted between Carthage and Rome in 264 for control of Sicily dragged on for nearly a quarter of a century (264–241), the longest continuous conflict in antiquity. (It is known today as the First Punic War.) It would end with Carthaginian defeat, the annexation of Sicily as a Roman province, and the emergence of Rome as the leading military power in the western Mediterranean. But for now, and for Ptolemy II, it was a quarrel in a faraway country between people of whom he knew nothing.

Ptolemy's own military exploits were funded by Egypt's rapid economic growth and the high levels of taxation. At the end of the Chremonidean War, he sought to recoup his losses by promulgating a wide-ranging series of revenue laws setting out the proportion of each crop to be handed over to the state treasury. A typical clause ran thus: 'If the cultivators do not comply with [any of] these regulations in accordance with the law, they shall pay double the quota.'[6] One of the measures imposed a royal monopoly on the cultivation and production of oil for cooking and lighting oil – essentials of daily life. The monopoly covered all varieties of native oil-bearing plant, and required every stage of production to be supervised by royal agents. The state even prescribed the acreage of land to be sown and the particular oil-seed crops to be grown in every field. Even more draconian was the imposition of a new tax on all adult inhabitants of Egypt. Dubbed the 'salt tax', it was the first time in Egypt's long history that a monetary tax had been levied on individuals.

Exorbitant duties were also levied at Egypt's ports. One of the papyri from Zenon's archive lists the charges that had to be paid on the cargoes of two ships that docked at Pelousion in 259. The commodities included honey from the Athens region, Karia and Rhodes; nuts and fish from Pontos on the southern Black Sea coast; and wines from the Aegean islands of Chios and Thasos. The import duty on olive oil was levied at 33 per cent, that on wine at 50 per cent – the highest rates known from the ancient Mediterranean world. And there was more: the shipowner also had to pay dues towards the maintenance of the Ptolemaic navy (which provided protection for merchant shipping), for transporting goods from Pelousion, and a 19 per cent harbour tax. It is a wonder that merchants used the Egyptian ports at all, but the rewards were still sufficient and, in truth, the Ptolemaic lands were still the best place in the Hellenistic world to get rich quick.

To boost international trade in the Mediterranean, Ptolemy II cultivated close diplomatic relations with the distant land of Bithynia and the port of Byzantion to gain preferential access to the fertile grain-producing lands around the shores of the Black Sea. He made a lavish gift to Rhodes of Egyptian coinage, notably bronze coins for day-to-day usage, in essence creating a parallel currency to the island's own. This was a remarkable gesture on the face of it – Egypt being otherwise a closed monetary zone – but it was carefully calculated to save Egyptian traders operating on Rhodes the extra expense of changing their money for local currency. It had the desired effect of incentivising continued trade between Rhodes and Egypt, to the benefit of both governments. And, at the other end of the maritime trade route, Alexandria became well known throughout the Hellenistic world as an exporter of high-value commodities like papyrus, linen, glassware, perfumes, jewellery, sculpture, mosaics and oil.

With unprecedented wealth and commercial dominance, Ptolemy II set about sealing his personal reputation as the greatest ruler of the age, and that of his dynasty as the most magnificent in the Hellenistic world. Conspicuous ostentation defined Ptolemy II's tenure of the throne, and set the bar impossibly high for his successors.

The unashamed self-promotion started with his own family. Right at the start of his reign, Ptolemy had married Arsinoe (I), the daughter of Lysimachos of Thrace. But within a decade she was sent into internal exile, supplanted by Ptolemy's own sister, Arsinoe II. Brother–sister marriage was uncommon in Egypt, but culturally acceptable, especially for royalty. A pragmatic way of keeping all the levers of power within the same family, it was also revered as a pattern established by the gods: Isis and Osiris were brother and sister as well as husband and wife. So Ptolemy II's marriage to Arsinoe II scarcely raised an eyebrow in the temples of the Nile Valley; the priests may even have been pleased to see a ruler of Macedonian heritage behaving like a traditional pharaoh. But to Ptolemy's Greek-speaking subjects, sibling marriage was anathema and broke a fundamental taboo. One of Alexandria's resident Greek poets, Sotades, composed an obscene, satirical poem attacking the incestuous marriage. It included the line, 'You're sticking your prick in an unholy hole'. Ptolemy II was furious and had the poet imprisoned. When he escaped, the king had him hunted down, captured, put in a lead casket and thrown into the sea. By contrast, Ptolemy II's court poet, Theokritos, did what was expected of him and celebrated the union of brother and sister by likening them to the gods. He thus became a royal favourite, celebrated throughout the Ptolemaic lands.

To mark his second marriage, Ptolemy II adopted the moniker Philadelphos ('sibling-loving'). He clearly came to believe his own rhetoric, and regarded himself as following divine precedent. He saw to it that his wife was jointly worshipped with him as part of the Ptolemaic ruler cult. Across the Hellenistic world, the founders of cities and other significant rulers, such as Alexander the Great, might become the focus of their own cults. Such deified individuals were rarely worshipped in shrines of their own (although Alexander was an exception), and instead had statues placed in the temples of other (Greek) gods. Ptolemy II was an avid exponent of the practice – for his own family. Together, he and his wife were Theoi Philadelphoi ('the sibling-loving gods') – and when Arsinoe II died in July 270, he had her formally deified in her own right. A commemorative stela was set up in the temple at Mendes in the Delta, showing Ptolemy II and his deceased wife jointly worshipping the local Egyptian god. The accompanying inscription declared that Arsinoe's image was to be placed in every Egyptian temple, as 'guest goddess' beside the main deity. And Arsinoe was not just a guest in other gods' shrines. Following Alexander's example, temples were built in her sole honour, including an 'Arsinoeion' at Memphis and another by the Bitter Lakes, its foundation rites carried out by Egyptian priests according to hallowed ancient tradition.

The Fayum district was renamed the Arsinoite province, with the deceased queen as its patron deity. The tax revenue from its vineyards was to be devoted to funding Arsinoe's cult. Any number of cities named after her were founded in Egypt and beyond, and she became the patron deity of sailors throughout the eastern Mediterranean. Even in Alexandria, where the population was most sceptical, people set up their own altars and held festivals in her honour (Gr. *Arsinoeia*). To cap it all, a shrine to the dead queen was built in a prominent location on the harbourside, adorned with an obelisk brought from the temple of the sun god at Heliopolis. The intended star attraction was a statue of the queen made of iron that hung inside the inner sanctum, suspended in mid-air by magnetism. Where Ptolemy I had introduced the cult of an invented god, Sarapis, to serve his dynastic purposes, his son succeeded in creating a focus of worship based on a member of his own family. The intention, no doubt, was to reinforce the prestige and power of the Ptolemaic royal house.

The magnificence of Ptolemy II's court culminated in a grand procession staged in Alexandria. Festivals were a recognised way of asserting identity in the Hellenistic world, and Ptolemy recognised the soft power of hosting participants and spectators from across the Greek-speaking world. His establishment of the Ptolemaieia festival, in honour of his parents, was a mechanism for celebrating and asserting both his family's and his own dynastic credentials.

An invitation to participate in the Ptolemaieia was met with enthusiasm across the Mediterranean. The League of Islanders, for example, issued a formal decree to record their acceptance. It noted with pride that Ptolemy I had been a blessing to the Islanders and other Greeks, and that Ptolemy II was now continuing in the same vein, offering in his father's honour 'a gymnastic, musical and equestrian contest to be equal in rank with the Olympic Games'.[7] The decree was set up on the sacred island of Delos, next to Ptolemy I's altar.

At the first Ptolemaieia, staged in 279/8, envoys from far and wide were welcomed in a pavilion topped with enormous gilded eagles, their wings spanning twenty-five feet. The eagle, traditionally the image of Zeus, was now being used by the Ptolemies as their own dynastic symbol, and the festival provided the perfect opportunity to deploy this new element of propaganda. The highlight was a grand procession through the streets of Alexandria. This made such an impression on all those who witnessed it that the event was talked and written about for years afterwards.

The start of the event saw three smaller processions make their way through the city, honouring the Morning Star, Ptolemy II's deified parents and all the gods of the Greek pantheon. This was only the warm-up act. The central part of the Grand Procession was dedicated to Dionysos, god of wine and pleasure – and both were offered in abundance. The participants lined up in Alexandria's city stadium before moving off into the surrounding streets. First came the heralds and marshals to keep order among the excited crowds. They were dressed as fauns clad in purple and crimson cloaks, and as satyrs carrying gilded torches decorated with ivy leaves. Accompanying them were women representing the goddess of victory, Nike, complete with golden wings, much gold jewellery and lavishly embroidered cloaks. Next came a group of actors, named the Guild of Artists of Dionysos, who performed tableaux around the city.

There followed a series of elaborate floats displaying scenes from the mythical life of Dionysos. A double altar nine feet long, covered with gilded ivy leaves and crowned with a beribboned diadem of vine leaves, was escorted by boys in purple cloaks bearing gifts of frankincense, myrrh and golden saffron on 120 golden plates. A four-wheeled cart, drawn by 180 men, bore a statue of Dionysos himself: fifteen feet high and dressed in a purple tunic, it poured wine from a golden goblet. In front were further gold vessels filled with wine, incense, cassia and saffron; and covering them all, an awning adorned with more ivy and vine leaves. Another float bore a seated statue of Nysa, personification of the place where Dionysos was raised. To the delight of the crowds, the statue was an automaton, and 'stood up mechanically without anyone laying a hand on it, and it sat back down again after pouring a libation of milk from a gold phiale'.

If the spellbound spectators had come in search of a good time, they were not to be disappointed. For along came another four-wheeled cart, even larger than the god's own float, pulled by 300 men. On it was set up 'a wine-press 36 feet long by 22½ feet wide, full of ripe grapes. Sixty Satyrs trampled them as they sang a vintage song to the flute.'[8] The following cart was drawn by 600 men, and carried a vast wineskin, made from leopards' pelts, which held 3,000 measures of wine. As it released its contents, the wine literally flowed in the streets. Next, a series of floats celebrated the bridal chamber of Dionysos' mother and the cave of the god himself. The latter was covered with ivy and yew, and two springs gushed forth from it, one of milk and one of wine, while pigeons and doves flew from the cave.

One of the reasons why Ptolemy II wished to emphasise the cult of Dionysos – besides the opportunity it presented for an orgy of ostentation and pleasure – was its resonance for the Ptolemaic monarchy. One of the key episodes in the god's life was his triumphal return from India; the parallels with the life of Alexander were not lost on the citizens of Alexandria. The elements of the Grand Procession symbolising Dionysos' return from India were thus among the most lavish of the entire spectacle. A figure of the god on the back of an elephant was followed by an enormous parade of chariots – drawn, not by horses, but by wild animals from every quarter of the known world. There were twenty-four chariots drawn by elephants, sixty by goats, twelve by saiga antelope from Central Asia, seven by Arabian oryx, fifteen by hartebeest and eight by ostriches (representing Africa), seven by wild asses and four by onagers (Asia), four by horses – how conventional! – and six by camels from Bactria. Next came human tribute from the furthest reaches of the Ptolemaic empire: mule-carts carrying Indian women, Ethiopian envoys bearing all the produce of Africa (600 ivory tusks, 2,000 ebony logs, 60 bowls of gold and silver and 2,400 hunting dogs), and 150 men carrying trees with birds and animals suspended from them. Finally, a parade of exotic animals from the royal menagerie featured parrots, peacocks, guinea fowl and pheasants; sheep from Ethiopia, Arabia and the Greek island of Euboea; cows from India and Ethiopia; a large, white bear (surely an albino rather than a polar bear, although the latter cannot be discounted entirely); fourteen leopards, sixteen cheetahs, four caracals, three cheetah cubs, a giraffe and a rhinoceros. Ptolemy II was a keen collector of wild animals, sourced both from hunters (who were amply rewarded for capturing live specimens) and as diplomatic gifts from overseas. But never before can the citizens of any town or city, anywhere in the world, have witnessed such an extraordinary collection of fauna as was paraded that winter's day in Alexandria.

As the procession approached its grand finale, the orgiastic, sexual nature of Dionysos was celebrated by a float bearing a 180-foot-long golden penis, wound around with golden ribbons and tipped with a gold star nine feet in circumference. More wild animals, including twenty-four extremely large lions and 2,000 identically coloured bulls, preceded the golden statue of Alexander the Great, carried on a chariot pulled by four elephants. Further statues followed, representing Ptolemy I, Arete (the personification of excellence), the city of Corinth and the god Priapus, followed by women dressed as more Greek cities, all accompanied by a band of musicians.

Just as the Grand Procession had begun with the Morning Star, so it now culminated with the appearance of the Evening Star. But, before this most extravagant of events reached its conclusion, there were two final spectacles. An unparalleled display of treasure, reflecting the wealth and magnificence of the Ptolemaic royal house, was consciously designed to overawe and astonish. It included a crown, said to have been made from 10,000 pieces of gold, displayed on the throne of Ptolemy I; seven gilded palm trees, each twelve feet high; gilded eagles – the Ptolemaic symbol – thirty feet high; 3,200 further golden crowns; twenty gold shields and sixty-four suits of golden armour; 400 cartloads of silver, twenty of gold and 800 of spices, including cinnamon, cassia and orris from India; and golden statues of Ptolemy II himself, some borne on chariots, others atop columns. All this opulence, symbolising his unimaginable wealth, was followed by a parade of 57,600 infantry and 23,200 cavalry to emphasise his military might. The point would not have been lost on the delegates from across the Hellenistic world, perhaps as many as 130 of them, watching from Ptolemy II's gilded tent set up within the walls of the royal citadel.

Altogether, the Grand Procession cost the staggering sum of 2,239 talents and 50 minae. But the cost was immaterial: the purpose of the whole extravaganza, of all that raw wealth and power, was to promote Ptolemy II as the greatest ruler of the age. By honouring the dynastic gods – especially Dionysos, Alexander and the first Ptolemaic royal couple – the king asserted the continuity of his reign and the legitimacy of his inheritance. By honouring Greek cities like Corinth, Ptolemy II presented himself as the champion of Panhellenic freedom.

But no amount of ostentation could hold at bay the forces that had been tearing the Mediterranean world apart since the death of

Alexander. Conflict with the Seleukid empire broke out again in 260. A new Seleukid king, Antiochos II, was determined to reverse the territorial losses suffered by his father. After forging an alliance with the king of Macedon, he launched an attack against Ptolemaic lands in Asia and succeeded in winning back the important cities of Miletos and Ephesos, as well as further territory along the western and southern coasts of Anatolia. The war only came to an end, in 253, when Ptolemy II offered his own daughter, Berenike, in marriage to Antiochos. The match was sealed, to the Seleukids' glee, with a massive dowry of silver and gold. For Ptolemy, it was a face-saving measure: better a dowry than war reparations, even if they cost the same.

So it was with a certain world-weariness that Ptolemy II contemplated his life and legacy in the years following the Second Syrian War. According to a later commentator, the king, confined to his palace with a painful attack of gout (the result of a life of luxury and licence), looked out from a window to the Alexandrian shore below, and envied the peasants eating their plain food and enjoying the simple pleasures of the sea. If this is true, it points to another aspect of the king's personality: his philosophical bent. And a fascination with the meaning of existence and the nature of the universe produced other glories in Ptolemaic Alexandria; not the transient success of territorial gain or the brief spectacle of a grand procession, but lasting insights that would change the world for ever.

4

The Life of the Mind

The Ptolemies were an unusually learned family, even by the high standards of the Hellenistic world. As a youth, Ptolemy I had been taught by Aristotle, the greatest philosopher-scholar of the age; Aristotle had been taught by Plato. Hence the first Ptolemy was the beneficiary of, and heir to, decades of scholarship and critical thinking about the natural world and humanity's place in it.

Partly to satisfy his own interest in learning, and partly to establish his dynastic capital as the new epicentre of science and culture, Ptolemy I set about establishing an academic infrastructure in Alexandria that would enable it to compete with, and indeed surpass, Athens. As we have seen, the first piece to be put in place was the Mouseion, an institution founded under the guidance, if not at the instigation, of the Athenian Demetrios of Phaleron. Since being exiled from Athens in 307, Demetrios had wandered the Mediterranean, finally arriving in Alexandria in 297, just a few years after Ptolemy I had assumed royal titles. The bond between the two men was clearly strong – they had both been pupils of Aristotle – and Ptolemy appointed Demetrios his counsellor for cultural affairs. Demetrios persuaded the king that an academy to rival that of Plato was what Alexandria – and Ptolemy – needed to seize Athens' crown.

From its inception, the Mouseion was intended to be an ivory tower, a place where intellectuals could seek sanctuary from the world outside and focus on their studies. The resident scholars, numbering perhaps thirty, had their stipends paid by the state, and were well provided for in other ways, too. There was a communal dining hall, a shaded portico and a tree-lined garden, all to provide convivial spaces for discussion and debate. Members of the Mouseion also held formal dinners and drinking parties (Gr. *symposia*), in which the king might himself participate; prizes were awarded to the most brilliant participants. All in all, it was a charmed life. And its growing reputation soon began to attract leading intellectuals from across the Greek-speaking world.

One of the earliest scholars to be drawn to Alexandria was the mathematician and logician Eukleides (Euclid). Remarkably little is known about the life of the man dubbed the 'father of geometry', but it is generally accepted that he resided in Alexandria from around 300 – in other words, at the same time as Demetrios – and that it was in the Ptolemaic capital that he carried out the core of his most important work. He may even have taught at the Mouseion. His best-known work, which is reputed to be the most translated, published and studied book in the Western canon after the Bible, was a treatise called the *Elements*. Arranged in thirteen separate books, it synthesised the theories of earlier Greek mathematicians and combined them with brilliant, original insights to establish the foundations of geometry as a distinct discipline. The first six books dealt with the geometry of planes, books seven to nine number theory, book ten irrational numbers, and the last three books solid geometry. At the heart of the *Elements* is a series of theorems, and Euclid broke new ground by providing proofs that were at once rigorous and elegant; his approach would become a defining characteristic of the theoretical sciences.

Although the *Elements* remains by far Euclid's most famous work, at least five more of his books have survived to the present day, and they illustrate the extraordinary scope of his geometrical research. *On Divisions* examines the division of geometrical figures into two or more equal parts, while the *Data* deals with the knowns and unknowns in various geometrical problems. Alongside these highly theoretical works are studies grounded in the observation of natural phenomena, in particular sight and vision. *Optics* is the earliest surviving treatise on perspective; *Catoptrics* investigates the mathematics of mirrors, and how images are formed in concave mirrors; and the *Phenomena* takes as its subject spherical astronomy – bringing the disciplines of geometry and mathematics to bear on the observation of celestial bodies. All five works adopt the same structure as his magnum opus, with propositions accompanied by elegant proofs. As if these remarkable contributions to scholarship were not enough, four other works, long since lost but referenced in the writings of other authors, are also attributed to Euclid. Again, they range from the highly theoretical to the practical, and include a study of geometrical reasoning (the *Fallacies*) and a four-book treatise on conic sections (the *Conics*).

In the research carried out and written up by Euclid during his time in Alexandria, theory and application were given equal attention, reflecting the productive blending of Greek and Egyptian approaches. (The land surveys, carried out by Egyptian officials since the foundation of the pharaonic state, must have given rise to a significant body of knowledge; some surviving documents include quite complex mathematical notations.) Within the cloisters of the Mouseion, scholars had the space and freedom, perhaps for the first time in history, to think about the fundamental laws of nature as well as the visible phenomena that they produced. This revolutionary combination of the theoretical and the applied was extended to other areas of knowledge besides mathematics.

The study of the human body and disease was a case in point. In the history of Western medicine, the name of Hippokrates resounds down the centuries; the Hippocratic oath remains a central tenet of the medical profession. The Hippocratic tradition of clinical observation was brought to Alexandria while Ptolemy I was still officially satrap, at the end of the fourth century, by one Praxagoras of Kos. But it was Praxagoras' pupil, Herophilos of Khalkedon, who took the subject in vital new directions. What attracted him to study in Alexandria was not only the support given to scholars in the Mouseion, but also the particular reputation of the Nile Valley for advanced medical knowledge. The age-old practice of mummification, involving the evisceration and embalming of the body, had enabled the Egyptians to build up an understanding of human anatomy unparalleled in the ancient world – a world where, for many cultures, interfering with the bodies of the dead was taboo. This intimacy with the functioning of the body, the internal organs and the causes of disease, is reflected in the surviving medical papyri.

One, the Edwin Smith Surgical Papyrus, may represent a later copy of a much earlier text dating back to the Pyramid Age, over 2,000 years before the Ptolemies. Yet it is remarkably modern in its approach, dealing systematically with trauma injuries, starting at the top of the head and working down to the spinal vertebrae. In total, forty-eight cases are considered, each summarising the symptoms, before indicating if they are treatable or not. If treatment of the condition is considered feasible, a description of the appropriate procedure follows. A second significant medical text is known today as the Ebers Papyrus. It focuses on internal diseases, and displays a level of medical knowledge on a par with that of pre-modern Europe. For example, there is some evidence that the properties of opium were known and applied. The ancient Egyptians also appear to have had a rudimentary understanding of the circulatory system, which they envisaged – not wholly erroneously – as a network of vessels centred on the heart and extending to the organs and other parts of the body.

Although many Greeks of the Hellenistic Age looked down their noses at pharaonic culture as exotic (at best) or downright barbarian, Egyptian science, and medical knowledge in particular, were widely admired. The Ptolemies had a policy, highly unusual at the time, of providing the cadavers of executed prisoners for dissection. (Some authors alleged that prisoners were supplied for vivisection while still alive.) For an aspiring physician like Herophilos of Khalkedon, there was no better place than Egypt to pursue his studies. With a steady supply of bodies, he was able to make dissection a regular practice, giving him an unprecedented and unrivalled understanding of human anatomy. His careful observation and recording transformed understanding of the brain, the eye, the liver, the intestines and the reproductive organs. Herophilos also used his insights to critique the established Hippocratic corpus (the collection of early Greek medical works attributed to Hippokrates) and to complete his own pioneering work in medical terminology.

His younger colleague, Erasistratos, with whom he worked in Alexandria, made even greater advances in the knowledge of the human body by studying whole systems – digestive, vascular and nervous – and attempting to understand how they worked. He described the valves of the heart, distinguished arteries and veins, and accurately concluded that the heart was not the seat of emotions (as the ancient Egyptians and Greeks had previously believed) but was primarily, and prosaically, a pump. Erasistratos was perhaps the first medic in history to deduce the role of nerves in controlling movement, to distinguish between motor and sensory nerves, and to link the nervous system with the brain. Indeed, he seems to have recognised that diseases of the nervous system were just that – diseases – and not the result of supernatural interference. He is regarded today as the founder of psychiatry and of neuroscience. Although regular dissection seems to have ended after the work of these pioneering scholars, the Alexandrian school of medicine they established became the most important in the ancient world, and would later foster such medical luminaries as Galen.

Ptolemy I evidently took a keen personal interest in the myriad advances in scholarship being made in his Mouseion. He also contributed to the upsurge in academic activity by deploying his own training and skills as an historian, dedicating the closing chapter of his reign, not to statecraft, but to writing an account of the life and campaigns of Alexander. In addition to being an academic exercise in biography, befitting a scholar-king, the work had a political purpose: to secure Alexander's reputation – and that of his loyal lieutenant, Ptolemy – for eternity.

The Mouseion was not Ptolemy I's only contribution to the life of the mind. It had a sister institution in Alexandria whose purpose was to collect not scholars but books. Founded in 284, in the last months of Ptolemy's reign, the Library of Alexandria was situated adjacent to the Mouseion, and seems likewise to have been created at the instigation of Demetrios of Phaleron. The Library was linked to the Mouseion by a colonnade of white marble. Inside, it was divided into halls with study spaces in each hall dedicated to a different branch of knowledge. Over the entrance was carved the inscription 'A Sanatorium for the Mind'. In time, the Library would surpass its neighbour in reputation.

Recognising that his fledgling Library would need inspirational leadership to establish itself and thrive, Ptolemy I appointed one of the leading philologists of the age, Zenodotos of Ephesos, as the first head librarian. Besides curating – and adding to – the collection of books, the librarian's other duty was to tutor the royal children: Ptolemy wanted his offspring to share the love of learning that Aristotle had given him. Zenodotos set about both tasks with alacrity. But, within two years of his arrival in Alexandria, his royal patron, Ptolemy I, was dead.

If his successor harboured any doubts about continuing his father's remarkable intellectual legacy, the arrival in Alexandria of another extraordinary scholar, soon after Ptolemy II's accession to the throne, seems to have convinced him that the path to fame and glory lay as much in academic achievement as in territorial conquests, grain exports, gold mines or grand processions. The latest newcomer – like Praxagoras, Herophilos and Erasistratos, an immigrant – was a man called Aristarchos. He hailed from the island of Samos, off the western coast of Anatolia, which was also – and propitiously – renowned as the birthplace of Pythagoras. Aristarchos followed in the footsteps of his island's most famous son and applied himself to the study of mathematics. Where he differed from Pythagoras (and indeed Euclid) was his interest, not so much in the theory of numbers, as in its application to the mysteries of the cosmos. By combining close observation of the heavens with a deep understanding of mathematical principles, Aristarchos made a series of extraordinary, revelatory deductions. For example, he recognised the relative sizes of the sun, earth and moon: earlier generations had regarded the two heavenly bodies as roughly equal in size, and considerably smaller than the earth. Most revolutionary of all was Aristarchos' proposition that 'the earth revolves around the sun on the circumference of a circle, the sun lying in the middle of the orbit'.[1]

Never before had anyone seriously posited a heliocentric model of the universe. Aristarchos' conjecture threatened to undermine the very foundations of philosophy and established religion, and other scholars were aghast. One, the Stoic philosopher, Kleanthes of Assos, wrote a counterblast entitled *Against Aristarchos*. As a result of such trenchant opposition, the heliocentric model came to be regarded as heretical and found no adherents in Aristarchos' time or subsequent generations. When advanced by Copernicus, some nineteen centuries later, it would meet similar resistance from the religious authorities.

While Aristarchos was thinking his revolutionary thoughts in the Mouseion, next door in the Library Zenodotos was making fundamental breakthroughs of his own. He lectured on the poets Hesiod and Pindar, but his particular passion was the greatest of all Greek poets, Homer. So, while Zenodotos' two assistants, Alexander of Aetolia and Lycophron of Khalkis,[2] set to work editing the Library's tragic and comic writers, respectively, Zenodotos embarked on producing the first critical editions of Homer's collected works. For this, he collated all the different Homeric manuscripts already in the

Library, deleting any verses he considered out of place, transposing lines and introducing new readings. He also divided Homer's poems into twenty-four books.

This aptitude for literary categorisation served Zenodotos well in his greatest professional undertaking: the classification of the Library's entire holdings. It was a vast task, but his methodical approach brought order to the diverse and sprawling collection. The details of his system remain sketchy, but may have included categorisation by subject matter and then alphabetically by the name of the author (a system of library classification used down to the present day). Zenodotos also understood the needs of his readers. In order to track down a particular text, scholars were used to laboriously unrolling countless papyri to find the one they were looking for. Zenodotos had his staff attach a small docket to the end of each scroll giving the author's name and other essential bibliographical information. For the scholars from the Mouseion, who seem to have constituted the Library's main users, this brilliant idea saved hours of their precious time – time that could more profitably be spent pondering and unravelling the secrets of the universe.

Zenodotos' enthusiasm clearly reassured Ptolemy II that the Library was well worth preserving. Indeed, he greatly expanded the collection, and may even have commissioned the first Greek translation of the Torah, the first five books of the Jewish scriptures. The Mouseion also benefited from Ptolemy II's patronage, being extensively – and expensively – rebuilt on the waterfront adjacent to Alexandria's palace quarter. Finished in white marble, the resplendent new academy boasted lecture theatres, assembly halls, and – much to Aristarchos' delight, no doubt – its own observatory.

By the time Ptolemy II died in early 246, Alexandria was firmly established as one of the greatest centres of learning in the Hellenistic world – very much the equal of Athens or Pergamon. The next king, Ptolemy III, tutored by the great Zenodotos, was keen to pick up where his father had left off, and make the Mouseion and the Library institutions of unrivalled intellectual distinction. But before he could turn his attention to books or learning, troubles from without and within impinged on the scholarly hush of the royal palace.

Once again, the external source of tension was the Seleukid empire. Ptolemy II's great rival, Antiochos II, had also died in 246; but the succession to the Seleukid throne was fiercely contested between his son from his first marriage (to Laodike, a noblewoman from Anatolia) and his son from his second marriage (to Ptolemy II's daughter, Princess Berenike). As part of the marriage agreement which settled the Second Syrian War, Antiochos II had promised that any son of his by Berenike would inherit the Seleukid throne. However, as soon as Antiochos II was dead, Laodike set forth from her exile at Antiokheia proclaiming her son, Seleukos (II), as the rightful king. She even claimed that Antiochos II had experienced a deathbed conversion and had renounced his earlier promise. Ptolemy III, for his part, felt compelled to intervene in support of his sister and infant nephew. Leading his troops into Syria, he learned that both Berenike and her baby son had been murdered at Laodike's behest. Furious, he prosecuted the campaign – the Third Syrian War – as far as Mesopotamia, until the entire heartland of the Seleukid empire had been subjugated. In the spring of 245, having put in place his own governors in the conquered territories, and with a vast haul of booty, Ptolemy III returned to Egypt in victory, and was acclaimed as Euergetes ('benefactor').

But his triumph was shortlived. What should have been a glorious homecoming was almost immediately overshadowed by domestic troubles. (Indeed, he may have returned to Egypt to deal with an unfolding crisis.) A low Nile flood led to crop failure throughout Egypt, compounding the misery of the rural population who had already suffered from the swingeing taxes levied to fund the war effort. The result was the first native revolt in Ptolemaic history. Putting down the insurrection was relatively easy for Ptolemy III's battle-hardened troops, but preventing large-scale starvation required a Herculean effort. The government was forced to import grain, at huge expense, from Koile-Syria and Cyprus. Egypt, renowned for its agricultural productivity, was now having to buy in food to avert famine. While the king was preoccupied with restoring stability to his Egyptian realm, western Asia quickly reverted to Seleukid control, swiftly followed by Mesopotamia. Seleukos II was recognised as king in Babylon by July 245.

Ptolemy III's gains in Anatolia and Thrace proved more loyal. Ephesos, in particular, became a key Ptolemaic possession for the next half-century. In 241, hostilities with the Seleukid empire were formally brought to an end with the signing of a peace treaty. By its terms, Ptolemy was recognised as ruler of virtually the whole of coastal Anatolia, including Ionia, the Dardanelles and Thrace, and a strategic enclave on the coast of Syria (named, with not a little irony, Seleukeia). The Ptolemaic kingdom was now the most powerful state in the eastern Mediterranean.

Ptolemy built on this success by shoring up the southern and western parts of his empire. He strengthened his existing Red Sea bases and founded a new one, Adulis, on the island of Massawa (in present-day Eritrea); while Kyrenaika, recently returned to full Ptolemaic control after some forty years of de facto independence, was thoroughly reorganised to secure royal control. This involved the foundation of three pristine cities, to replace the old centres of Kyrenaikan power: a new capital, named Ptolemais, and two new ports, Berenike and Arsinoe. Together with Kyrene itself, they formed a city league, and were given theoretical autonomy, but in reality they were under direct Ptolemaic authority.

Having extended Egypt's boundaries abroad and secured its stability at home, Ptolemy III saw to it that the extraordinary events of his early reign were commemorated in an unprecedented manner. In late February 238, to coincide with his birthday, he summoned all the priests of Egypt together in synod. Such priestly gatherings – invariably called to pass decrees in praise of the ruler – were not unknown in Greek tradition, but the synod of 238 represented something utterly new in the long history of Egyptian religion. The outcome of the convocation was a decree, dated 7 March, the primary purpose of which was to laud Ptolemy III and his wife Berenike II as Theoi Euergetai ('beneficent gods'). Where pharaonic inscriptions generally praised the king for preserving cosmic order, this Ptolemaic decree honoured the royal couple for conferring material benefits on their realm.

No fewer than six copies of the decree have survived: such was its importance, it was ordered to be set up in major temples the length and breadth of Egypt. After the usual recitation of royal names and titles, the inscription recounts the royal couple's praiseworthy achievements:

> Ptolemy ... and Berenike ... the two Benefactor Gods, are performing many great and benevolent deeds for the temples of the Egyptians, and are on every occasion sanctifying the honour of the gods, and at all seasons provide for the needs of Apis and Mnevis and all the other sacred animals that reside in shrines and are venerated in Egypt; and they supply everything that is needed in large quantities, and provisions in overflowing abundance in order to ensure the performance of the proper service.

Ptolemy was especially lauded for restoring Egypt's dignity and security:

> In the matter of the divine images which the vile Persians carried off from Egypt, His Majesty set out on an expedition to the lands of Asia, and he recaptured the images and brought them back to Egypt and set them upon their thrones in the temples wherein they had stood originally, and he has made Egypt very safe and secure by fighting beyond its borders, in the valley and on the plain, and in many foreign lands and against many foreign rulers; and has made safe and secure all the people of Egypt and all the inhabitants of all the subject territories.

Last but not least, the royal couple had shown exemplary care for their subjects:

> When a year came with a very low Nile, and the hearts of all men and women in Egypt were afflicted with grief ... His Majesty and his sister took great care for those who lived in the temples and for the people of Egypt, showing much foresight and giving up large amounts of revenue to keep the people alive; and they had grain imported from Syria, Phoenicia and Cyprus, and from other foreign lands, and they spent vast quantities of gold to buy the grain at a high price, being anxious only to protect the people of Egypt.[3]

The synod's reward for these acts of temporal munificence was a host of spiritual honours. First, statues of the royal couple's recently deceased and newly deified daughter, another Princess Berenike, were to be erected in all the major temples of the land, and her cult integrated into the existing Egyptian pantheon. This marked a decisive shift in Ptolemaic theology: deification no longer required brave deeds, but could be achieved, and promulgated, by mere royal fiat. Princess Berenike had earned her divinity by virtue of her royal blood, and because her parents had wished it. This set a precedent that subsequent rulers would enthusiastically embrace. Second, the king's control over the clergy was strengthened and codified. To the four traditional 'tribes' (Gr. *phylai*) of priests, which had served every Egyptian temple since time immemorial, a new, fifth group was added, to be appointed exclusively by the ruler. It incorporated all the priests appointed thus far in Ptolemy III's reign, and all the incepting clergy. Third, Ptolemy III and his wife themselves received honours, in the form of a festival to be held annually on the first day of the year.

This was not as straightforward as it might have been. By long tradition, the Egyptian New Year was marked by the rising of the Dog Star, Sirius, above the horizon, just before dawn. Back in the mists of time, when a nascent Egyptian kingdom had found it necessary to adopt a formal calendar, the heliacal rising of Sirius coincided with the start of the annual inundation of the Nile when the river, swollen by summer rains, burst its banks and brought life-giving water and fresh silt to the fields of Egypt. This seemed a propitious coincidence and an appropriate moment to mark the beginning of the agricultural year. But the official calendar, comprising twelve months of thirty days each, plus five additional ('epagomenal') days at the end of the year, failed to take account of the true length of a solar year (365¼ days). Over the centuries, the lack of a leap year caused the civil calendar to fall progressively out of synchronisation with astronomical observations. After some 730 years, New Year's Day fell exactly six months after the rising of Sirius. Another 730 years later, the two coincided once again. And so it went on, through the millennia of pharaonic rule. Until the reign of Ptolemy III. The observations and calculations of scholars like Aristarchos revealed the true workings of the solar system, and the regularity of astronomical phenomena. Suddenly it became clear that the calendar itself was at fault, and needed adjusting. Ptolemy III's decree of 238 recognised this fact: 'festivals which are [properly] celebrated in winter are observed in summer, because of the change of the New Year festival one day every four years, while other festivals that are [properly] celebrated in summer are observed in winter'.[4] To put matters right, and ensure that the festival of Ptolemy III and his queen would be celebrated on the correct day every year, the decree resolved:

> from this day onward, one day, a festival of the Benefactor Gods, shall be added every four years to the five additional days at the beginning of the new year, so that all men shall know that the [former] arrangement of the seasons was somewhat defective, and that the year itself, and the rules and beliefs concerning the order of the universe, have been set right by the two Benefactor Gods.[5]

It was a striking instance of Hellenistic scholarship being brought to bear on an age-old problem. An added bonus was that the Benefactor Gods would henceforth – and for eternity – be associated with the inundation, guarantor of Egypt's prosperity. But neither Ptolemy III nor the brightest minds of the Mouseion had fully reckoned with the innate conservatism of Egyptian society. The clergy might have been willing to accept the deification of a princess and the imposition of a fifth tribe of priests, but messing with the great rhythm of the universe was a step too far – no matter how evidence-based the proposition. So Ptolemy III's attempted reform of the Egyptian calendar failed, and the addition of a leap day only gained official acceptance on 29 August AD 22, 260 years after it was first suggested. Not for the first nor for the last time in history, faith won the day over fact.

The synod and decree of 238 marked the stabilisation of Ptolemy III's reign. The trials and tribulations of his early years behind him, he was now able to indulge his passion for learning – and especially for books. According to a later commentator, the king wrote a letter, 'To All the World's Sovereigns', in which he declared his wish, no less than to acquire a copy of every book ever written. By the end of Ptolemy III's life, he had more or less achieved his goal: at its zenith, the Library of Alexandria contained perhaps three-quarters of a million volumes. This remarkable feat of collecting was achieved by a variety of means, not all of them reputable. For example, ships docking in Alexandria's harbours were systematically searched by government agents, looking for manuscripts. Any that were found were immediately confiscated and taken to the Library for copying. The copy, not the original, was then returned to the owners. Ptolemy III was so desperate to acquire original editions of Greek literary classics that he even resorted to outright theft. His ruse was to borrow manuscripts from the great libraries of Athens, in return for a hefty deposit of fifteen talents of silver. As soon as the documents arrived in Alexandria, the king sent his thanks to the Athenians: they could keep the deposit, he was keeping the books. So passionate – nay, obsessive – a bibliophile was Ptolemy III that he founded a branch of the main Library next to the temple of Sarapis in Alexandria. Temple libraries were a longstanding Egyptian tradition, but this one was no rarefied resource for theologians. It seems to have been open for use by schoolteachers, perhaps even members of the general public.

Across the city at the main Library, the first director, Zenodotos of Ephesos, had been succeeded by Apollonios of Rhodes. His main claim to subsequent fame was his authorship of the poem *Argonautica*, which told the story of Jason and his quest for the Golden Fleece. It was a bold exercise in reimagining Homeric epic poetry for the Hellenistic Age, and it would prove influential for generations of later poets. While Apollonios was describing the exploits of Jason and the Argonauts, his down-to-earth assistant, Kallimachos of Kyrene, had been given the task of re-cataloguing the entire Library: updating Zenodotos' work for a greatly expanded collection. The result was a 120-volume work, entitled the *List of Those who Distinguished Themselves in All Branches of Learning, and Their Writings*, or *Lists* (Gr. *Pinakes*) for short. Its name was falsely modest. For Kallimachos' catalogue was no mere list of books. It was a comprehensive survey of the Library's holdings, accompanied by biographical and bibliographical details of every author. So weighty was it, in every sense, that one of Kallimachos' own pupils, Aristophanes of Byzantion, published a sarcastic riposte, *Against Kallimachos's Library Lists*. Like academic communities through the ages, there was never any shortage of rivalry or cattiness in the Library of Alexandria.

Undeterred, Kallimachos continued with his work, also publishing poetry inspired by the classics, and epigrams which were noted for their concision and finely turned phrase. (Another reason, no doubt, for rivals to resent him.) His major work was the *Causes* or *Origins* (Gr. *Aetia*). This was a collection of origin stories, written in couplets and extending originally to some 4,000 lines, organised into four books. Written in Kallimachos' own distinctive voice, it collected myths and legends spanning the whole of the Hellenistic world.

Perhaps Ptolemy III's greatest contribution to the intellectual life of his age was to appoint (as Apollonios' successor) an even more brilliant scholar as the third director of the Library and tutor to the royal children. Eratosthenes of Kyrene was the ideal candidate. His home city was, if not exactly a rival to Alexandria, then certainly a centre of considerable academic endeavour and achievement. Under the liberal constitution granted to the city by Ptolemy I, its scholars had developed a reputation for free thinking and challenging received wisdom. From Kyrene, Eratosthenes had moved to Athens. There, he came into contact with, and was heavily influenced by, the Sceptics, a school of philosophers who sought to understand the nature of the universe by 'searching' (Gr. *skeptomai*) for the truth. So, when Eratosthenes arrived in Alexandria at Ptolemy III's invitation, he brought with him a keen understanding of the main intellectual currents of the time, a deep knowledge of the Greek philosophy and a yearning to discover.

At his instigation, the Library expanded its collections of authors such as Aiskhylos (Aeschylus), Sophokles and Euripides. Eratosthenes himself wrote short epic poems and a twelve-volume work *On Ancient Comedy*. But his scholarship was not confined to literature. A true polymath, his interests ranged widely, and he applied himself to a dizzying range of challenges. In the field of astronomy, he wrote books on the constellations and compiled a catalogue of 675 major stars. In the field of history, he made the first concerted attempt to fix all the principal dates of Greek political and literary history from the siege of Troy down to his own time; the result was a work, *Chronology*, that effectively spawned a whole new area of study. In mathematics, he summarised the entire subject and devised a method for calculating prime numbers that is still used today, called 'Eratosthenes' sieve'. He also produced a solution to the longstanding 'Delian problem', one of three puzzles that preoccupied mathematicians of the time. Eratosthenes composed an epigram explaining his solution and had it inscribed on a column erected in Alexandria. (The Delian problem has since been proven to be insoluble.)

But it was in the study of the earth that he made his most remarkable, and lasting, breakthroughs, in the process coining a new term for the subject: geography. Eratosthenes wanted to understand, and to measure, every aspect of the planet. He realised that the earth was tilted on its axis, calculated the angle of the tilt as 23°51' – just one-twelfth of a degree out (it is actually 23°46') – and created the armillary sphere to explain his insights; one was set up in the portico of the Mouseion. At a stroke, his discovery provided a scientific explanation for the seasons. He revised the existing map of the known world, greatly improving its cartography, and using lines of latitude and longitude. (The prime meridian, naturally, ran through Alexandria.) He also created a detailed map of Egypt, as far south as the Fifth Cataract.

Eratosthenes' greatest achievement, and the one for which he is still remembered today, was to calculate with astonishing accuracy the circumference of the earth. By the standards of any time, this was a remarkable feat of both science and imagination. To start with, in the third century it was by no means universally accepted that the earth was spherical. Practical scientist that he was, Eratosthenes may well have climbed to the top of the Pharos lighthouse, and observed the curvature of the horizon. Certainly, the later Greek geographer Strabo (who quoted extensively from Eratosthenes) noted, 'It is obviously the curvature of the sea.'[6] Having thus proved that the earth was not flat, the next step was to attempt to measure its size. In this endeavour, Eratosthenes displayed the sheer brilliance of his reasoning. Having noticed – or had drawn to his attention – the fact that, at Syene (present-day Aswan) at midday on the summer solstice, the sun was directly overhead, shining straight down to the bottom of a well, at the next summer solstice he measured the shadow cast by a vertical stick at Alexandria. Then, using a royal pacer, he measured the distance between the two locations. By means of simple geometry, these measurements told him the circumference of the earth, which Eratosthenes calculated as 252,000 *stadia*, or 24,662 miles. We now know that, measured around the poles, the earth's circumference is in fact 24,860 miles. Eratosthenes was less than 1 per cent out. He brought together all his findings in an epoch-making work, *Geographika*. And from that moment on, Egyptian priests began to write the name of Syene with the hieroglyphic signs of a protractor and a plumb line.

Eratosthenes would survive his royal patron, living into his eighties. When age and infirmity started to take their toll, and he realised he was losing his sight and would soon be unable to read, he chose instead to starve himself to death. He simply could not bear to live a life without books. His fellow academics had given him the nickname Pentathlos ('pentathlete'); but his epitaph simply recorded him as dying 'after pondering over high matters'.[7]

Among such a galaxy of intellectual stars, two further scholars active in Alexandria during the reign of Ptolemy III deserve special mention. Their achievements lay not so much in understanding the workings of the universe, as in applying science to the workings of practical devices here on earth. The first was Ktesibios, who was said to have started his career as a barber, until his invention of an adjustable mirror led him away from cutting hair to a life as an impecunious inventor. One of his most lasting inventions, and the one for which he is perhaps best known today, was a water organ, the precursor of the modern pipe organ; both Ktesibios and his wife Thais are said to have excelled at playing the novel instrument. Alongside such diversions, his fascination with hydraulics led him to ponder more practical challenges, too. One was timekeeping. Until the reign of Ptolemy III, the most accurate means of keeping time was the water clock (Gr. *klepsydra*). This device had been invented in Egypt as early as the sixteenth century BC, and by the time of Alexander had adopted its classical form of a stone (often basalt) vessel with a small hole near the bottom that allowed water to drip out. As the water level inside the vessel fell, it marked the passage of the hours. The problem, to which Ktesibios applied himself, was the rate of the drips. For, as the volume of water inside the vessel decreased, so did the pressure, thus slowing the rate of dripping. The challenge was to find a way of regulating the clock so that the vessel did not have to be continuously topped up. Ktesibios' ingenious solution was to devise a three-tier mechanism in which a cistern emptied into the clock-vessel to ensure it remained full, while a third container bore a float and pointer to indicate the elapsed time. Ktesibios' clepsydra remained the most accurate clock in the world for the next fifteen centuries. As a basic design, it would eventually be bettered only by the invention of the pendulum clock in AD 1656.

Ktesibios was equally fascinated by the properties and uses of compressed air, and his lost work, *On Pneumatics*, broke new ground in describing the elasticity of air. Ptolemaic Alexandria was not only fertile ground for scholars to develop new theories, it was also a playground for inventors to put them to the test. The city's Greek shrines and temples employed all sorts of gadgets to amaze worshippers, from iron statues suspended in mid-air by magnetism to hidden lights shining out of statues' eyes. Ktesibios' ingenuity in the fields of hydraulics and pneumatics was applied to produce a range of dazzling special effects: temple doors that opened as if by magic, propelled by the hot air from pilgrims' burnt offerings; statues that seemed to move by themselves; trumpet fanfares and sudden bursts of fire on the altar powered by hidden hydraulic bellows. A visitor to an Alexandrian temple must have felt like Dorothy in the Emerald City.

In a more practical vein, by bringing two areas of study – water and air – together, Ktesibios may have been the first to describe the principle of the siphon and is credited with inventing one of the first pumps for lifting water from wells. This was no mere inventor's whimsy: raising water from a well, or the Nile, to irrigate the fields many feet above the river level was of immense practical importance in Egypt. For thousands of years, the Egyptians had relied on manual labour to perform this essential task. In the fourteenth century BC, the introduction of the *shaduf* had made life easier, but water could still only be raised one bucket at a time. By the third century, the Ptolemies' focus on boosting agricultural production made the invention of a more efficient water-lifting device a pressing priority. Ktesibios' pump was a first step. But the real breakthrough came at the hands of a second engineer-scholar active in Alexandria under Ptolemy III. Unlike Ktesibios, his name resounds down the centuries: Archimedes.

The son of an astronomer, Archimedes was born in the Greek colony of Syracuse on the island of Sicily in about 287. Although there is no concrete proof that he came to Alexandria, he became a close friend and correspondent of Eratosthenes, and also of Ptolemy III's court astronomer Konon of Samos (most famous today for naming the constellation 'Berenike's Lock', in honour of the king's wife), and this can only have come about by meeting them in person. Konon and Archimedes both worked on the problem of conic sections, but it was the latter who made the more important advances. In his work on solid geometry, he surpassed even Euclid, and his book *The Sand-Reckoner* displayed an understanding of numbers more advanced than that of any other ancient mathematician. A mere list of some of his other surviving works hints at the breadth of his scholarship: *On*

Spirals, *On Conoids and Spheroids*, *On the Sphere and Cylinder* and *Quadrature of the Parabola*. In these treatises, he demonstrated and proved the formulae for measuring the area of a circle, the surface area and volume of a sphere, the area of an ellipse, and the area under a parabola. In another early book, *Measurement of a Circle*, Archimedes came up with an accurate approximation of the value of pi, showing that it is greater than $\frac{223}{71}$ and less than $\frac{22}{7}$. Also in the field of pure mathematics, he anticipated modern calculus and devised a system for expressing very large numbers.

But it is perhaps in the field of applied mathematics that Archimedes made his best-known breakthroughs. By applying fundamental principles to practical problems, he became the foremost engineer of his time. For example, the principles of mechanics outlined in his *On the Equilibrium of Planes*, in which he proved the law of the lever, were applied to calculate the centres of gravity of various geometrical figures and thereby to invent ingenious war machines for defending his native city of Syracuse from invaders. He is quoted as saying, 'Give me but one firm spot of land on which to stand, and I will move the earth.'[8] He was also adept at formulating theories to explain natural phenomena: he invented the whole field of hydrostatics by observing how the mass of his body displaced the water in his bath – prompting his famous (if apocryphal) exclamation, '*Eureka!*' ('I have found it out!'). For Egypt, the most useful demonstration of a fundamental principle was the invention of a device to raise water. By turning a screw inside a close-fitting pipe, water could easily be raised from the Nile onto the fields. Although a similar device may already have been developed in Egypt before the Ptolemaic period, it was Archimedes who first described it – and understood the science behind it – and with whom it has been associated ever since.

A contemporary critic may have derided the scholars of the Mouseion and Library as 'cloistered papyrus-warblers quarrelling endlessly in the Muses' bird-cage',[9] but it was in Ptolemaic Alexandria that the whole literary and intellectual heritage of the ancient Greek world was collected and edited, blended with the best of Egyptian and Babylonian science, and – crucially – written down so that it could be transmitted to later generations, including our own. The Mouseion and the Library of Alexandria comprised the first integrated multidisciplinary research complex in history, and was the world's greatest repository of knowledge – the first true university. In its first seven decades, it hosted the greatest thinkers and inventors in every conceivable sphere of human enquiry, from geography and astronomy to bibliography and philosophy, from mathematics and medicine to engineering and exegesis. Never before, and never again, would a relatively small group of scholars have such familiarity with the whole of Greek literature. Euclid's pioneering geometry and Aristarchos' lonely view of the universe, Erasistratos' understanding of the human mind and body, and Eratosthenes' measurement of the earth: that these fundamental breakthroughs in the history of science all occurred in a few short decades in a single city is remarkable, but no coincidence. For Ptolemy I's vision, nurtured and expanded under his two successors, was to assert his authority, and that of his dynasty, as scholar-kings.

The success of the first three Ptolemies also lay in their understanding that their position – at home and abroad – depended as much on fulfilling the role of Egyptian pharaoh as on meeting the expectations associated with a Greek *basileus*. So Ptolemy III continued the policies of his grandfather, appointing indigenous leaders to important positions in his government. One example was a man named Djedhor, who served as a nomarch (provincial governor), combining a variety of administrative, priestly and military offices.

Perhaps influenced by such men, Ptolemy III sponsored a large-scale construction programme at some of Egypt's holiest sites. He built a birth house and a new sanctuary for Isis and the infant Horus at the temple of Philae, and a new temple of Isis in nearby Syene. At the great religious complex of Karnak, he added a gate to the temple of Khonsu, while nearby he ordered the construction of a sacred lake and sanctuary for the Theban war god Montu. At Kanopos, where one of the copies of the priestly decree of 238 was set up, he founded a new temple dedicated to Osiris, lord of the dead and god of resurrection; while in the distant Kharga Oasis, he decorated a temple begun by the Persian king Darius I some 250 years earlier.

All these acts of benefaction would have been recognised by the Egyptian population as commensurate with the traditional duties of a pharaoh, and helped to secure Ptolemy III's acceptance and reputation as a legitimate ruler. But he went one step further in his efforts to buy the support of his native priests and people: he founded a spectacular new temple in southern Upper Egypt, heartland of traditional pharaonic civilisation. Indeed, the chosen site, Apollonopolis, was sacred to none other than the patron deity of Egyptian kingship, the falcon god Horus (whom the Greeks identified with their god Apollo). A temple had first been founded there by Nakhtnebef, first king of the thirtieth dynasty, but had progressed little beyond a monumental gateway. Now, Ptolemy III decided to bring Nakhtnebef's dream to fruition. The foundation ceremony took place on 23 August 237, just a year after the Kanopos Decree. Construction would continue, with interruptions, for 167 years until the temple was finally ready to be consecrated. The temple of Horus remains to this day the best preserved, most harmonious, most complete example of a traditional pharaonic temple – yet it was conceived and founded, not by an Amenhotep or a Ramesses, but by a Ptolemy. Inside its sanctuary, Ptolemy III revived another Egyptian tradition – that of ancestor worship as an explicit element in the royal cult. This facet of pharaonic religion chimed perfectly with the Hellenistic custom of the ruler cult; it was therefore especially attractive to Ptolemy as he sought to reinforce his dynasty's divine credentials in the eyes of all his subjects.

By extending his kingdom's borders, securing its prosperity, fostering its scholars and honouring its deities, Ptolemy III more than matched the greatness of his two forebears. Winning two decades of peace by his brilliance on the battlefield, he presided over a glittering court in Alexandria and a renaissance in temple building in the countryside. The dynasty of the Ptolemies, founded by the grandfather and strengthened by the father, had been solidified and secured by the son.

Or so it appeared.

In fact, the seeds of instability had already been sown and were lurking in Egypt's fertile soil, ready to germinate as soon as conditions changed. Just when the Ptolemies had seemed to reach an apotheosis, crisis was waiting in the wings.

PART II

CRISIS (221–145 BC)

5
Fragile State

When Ptolemy III died in the winter of 222/1, after a reign of twenty-four largely peaceful years, the storm clouds were already gathering. Once again, the rivalry between the Hellenistic kingdoms, and internecine squabbles within their borders, were provoking instability in the wider eastern Mediterranean. In Ptolemy's final years, events in mainland Greece had prompted him to defend against further Macedonian expansion, not least by strengthening his alliance with Athens which was always keen to manoeuvre against its hated overlord. He also supplied mercenaries to Sparta, which was facing its own war against Macedon. However, when Macedonian forces prevailed over the Spartan army to advance across the Isthmus of Corinth, the king of Macedon, Antigonos III, played a trump card to capitalise on his success: he offered to cede some territory in Anatolia to Ptolemy if the latter would withdraw his support for Sparta. For Ptolemy III, the chance of enlarging his empire yet further was too good an opportunity to resist. In any case, Sparta was too costly to defend in the long term, and of no great strategic value to Egypt. So Ptolemy abandoned Sparta to its fate. The Spartan army was comprehensively defeated at the Battle of Sellasia in 222, forcing its leader, Kleomenes III, into exile. He fled to Alexandria, hoping that his erstwhile friend would once again rally to his side and help him regain his throne. He was sorely disappointed. For Ptolemy III had other, more pressing problems to attend to, in the shape of a fresh, young Seleukid monarch, Antiochos III, newly acceded to the throne just a few months earlier. Ptolemy renounced any future intervention in Greece in order to focus on the resurgent threat to his Syrian territories.

Hence, on becoming pharaoh and *basileus* at the turn of the year, Ptolemy IV, still only in his late teens, inherited a geopolitical situation fraught with danger: a victorious Macedon in Greece, and a determined new rival on the Seleukid throne. Putting on a brave face, he took the cult title Philopator ('father-loving'), trying, no doubt, to channel some of his late father's reputation. In a similar vein, he promoted the cult of Dionysos which had strong connotations with the glorious reign of his grandfather and, even further back, with Alexander; and erected a shrine, within the Sarapieion at Alexandria, dedicated to 'Horus the child, son of Sarapis and Isis', identifying himself with the heir of the Ptolemaic dynasty's patron deities. But he was an inexperienced new monarch, grappling with issues that threatened his very inheritance. For advice and guidance, therefore, he turned to his chief minister, Sosibios of Alexandria, an intelligent and powerful courtier who had first won renown as an athlete before being appointed priest of Alexander by Ptolemy III. But Sosibios was also manipulative and deceitful. If later commentators are to be believed, Ptolemy IV effectively abrogated responsibility for foreign and domestic affairs, leaving all the tricky decisions in Sosibios' capable and calculating hands.

On picking up the reins of power, the courtier showed no mercy. Before Ptolemy III's body was even cold in its tomb, Sosibios had every potential rival for the throne murdered. The victims included the new king's uncle, Lysimachos; his younger brother, Magas; and even his mother, Berenike II, despite the fact that she had helped to advance Sosibios' career. At a stroke, all of Ptolemy IV's would-be challengers were removed. Next, Sosibios had the exiled Spartan king Kleomenes placed under house arrest; he would eventually escape and attempt to incite the Alexandrian population to revolt, but, receiving no support, took his own life to avoid capture and an even worse fate.

Sosibios' actions served to secure his own position as the power behind the throne, but they had an unsettling effect on the court at Alexandria. Intrigue and fear stalked the corridors of the royal palace, paralysing the efficient operation of government. In distant Syria, Antiochos III sought to take advantage of this instability at the heart of his rival's kingdom. Within a year of coming to the throne, the new Seleukid monarch had already reconquered his own rebellious provinces of Media (present-day north-western Iran) and Persia. He then turned his eyes towards the Ptolemaic land of Koile-Syria. In 221, he launched an abortive invasion, followed two years later by a full-scale assault. With the swift capture of cities in Phoenicia, including the strategic port of Tyre, a Fourth Syrian War had begun.

Faced with this serious threat – not only to Ptolemaic prestige on the international stage, but to the very security of Egypt itself – Sosibios is reported to have held a council with his trusted lieutenant Agathokles. Ptolemy IV seems to have been notable by his absence. True to form, the two chief ministers decided on a strategy of deception: they would send embassies to Ptolemaic allies, including Rhodes and Byzantion, encouraging them to send delegates to discuss a negotiated settlement to the conflict. This would give Antiochos the impression that Ptolemy's friends were trying to persuade him to cede Koile-Syria without a fight. All the while, under this cover of frenzied diplomatic activity, preparations for a full-scale war could proceed apace within Egypt.

According to a later account, Sosibius and Agathokles established themselves at Memphis, Egypt's traditional capital, where they received Antiochos III's envoys with 'every sign of courtesy'. At the same time, they summoned to Alexandria – out of view of the Seleukid diplomats – mercenaries from Ptolemy's overseas possessions and allies, and started amassing a war chest to pay the gathering army. Throughout these preparations, each of the chief ministers took turns to visit Alexandria, 'to see that none of the supplies required for their purpose were wanting'.[1]

Just as vital as the procurement of foreign mercenaries was the despatch of recruiting officers into the Egyptian countryside to draft domestic troops. In this hour of need, a long-standing Ptolemaic policy showed its merits. From the moment Alexander the Great's empire had been divided among his generals, each of the Hellenistic rulers had needed to build their own army to defend their newly acquired territories, given that Alexander's forces owed their allegiance, first and foremost, to Macedon. Employing mercenaries was a costly undertaking, so a large force of reservists was the preferred option. The challenge was one of recruitment. Ptolemy I's solution had been radically different from that adopted by the Seleukids.

Instead of founding communities of soldiers, he attracted fighting men to Egypt with the promise of individual grants of land. The extra economic security that this gave the settlers effectively tied them to their new homeland, greatly reducing the risk of desertion or emigration. (And while Egypt had an open-door policy towards immigrants, leaving the country required an exit permit.) The policy showed its merits early on. When, in 307, the Ptolemaic army was defeated by Demetrios on Cyprus, most of those captured as prisoners of war defied custom by refusing to enter Demetrios' service, explaining that their means of subsistence lay back in Egypt.

Migrants who came to Egypt to serve in the Ptolemaic army, mostly from impoverished villages in Macedon and rural Greece, were processed on arrival in Alexandria by crown agents. Each was allotted a plot of land by the state – fifty to a hundred *arouras* (up to sixty-eight acres) for a member of the royal guard or cavalryman, twenty-five or thirty *arouras* (up to twenty acres) for an infantryman – before being despatched up the Nile to their new landholding. Initially, land grants were tied to the performance of military duties; the grantees, known as cleruchs (from the Greek *klerouchos*, 'lot-holder'), were expected to answer the call-up whenever the state needed soldiers. When a settler died, his land reverted to the crown. A papyrus from the reign of Ptolemy II, dated to December 239 or January 238, records the instructions to a district official to take back the landholdings of recently deceased cavalrymen. However, within a generation or two, and certainly by the reign of Ptolemy IV, cleruchs had come to regard their plots as private land, to be leased or sold, or passed down to the next generation, without any official permission. In time, this would fundamentally change the structure of the rural economy, and weaken later Ptolemies' ability to levy armed troops.

Besides tying military settlers to the land and thus to the Ptolemaic crown, another significant advantage of the cleruch policy was that it helped to bring waste or marginal land into production. The all-out drive to expand the agricultural economy, pursued most vigorously under Ptolemy II, needed willing hands to prepare and farm previously unproductive land. Cleruchs provided a vital component of an expanded rural workforce. Those who cultivated less favourable plots paid lower taxes. Nonetheless, competition for the best land was intense, and newly arrived military settlers used every connection at their disposal to win a favourable allocation. Zenon, the finance minister's estate manager in the Fayum, was accustomed to receiving begging letters asking for special favours in the allocation of land and billets.

Such correspondence touches on another contentious aspect of military settlement: the temporary billeting of newly arrived immigrants with local Egyptian families. This was not entirely welcomed by many hosts. Local households had little, if any, say in whether they received an uninvited lodger; tensions between arrogant, condescending Greek-speaking cleruchs and bitter, resentful Egyptian hosts often led to friction. Some of the earliest surviving Ptolemaic royal edicts deal with abuses perpetrated by billeted soldiers.

In 221, shortly after Ptolemy IV's accession, one cleruch, assigned lodgings in a rural village, simply evicted the owner of another house that he liked better. There was little point, and considerable danger, in fighting back against a trained soldier, moreover one sent at the will of the government. In desperation, some houseowners resorted to ruses to deter unwanted lodgers, blocking up doorways, pulling down roofs, even building altars against the entrances to spare rooms to make them look like household sanctuaries. But the authorities soon got wind of these subterfuges, one officer in charge of billeting writing to his superior, 'So please, as we are pinched for billets, give orders to compel owners of houses to remove the altars.'[2] Lodgers, for their part, might attempt to protect their own tenancy and privacy by building an internal wall to divide their section from the homeowner's. Such semi-detached dwellings – or, rather, houses in multiple occupation – soon became common practice in the Egyptian countryside.

By drafting cleruchs from the Egyptian countryside and recruiting mercenaries from across the eastern Mediterranean, Ptolemy IV's ministers managed, in the space of a year or two, to amass the largest army since the days of Alexander the Great. There were 25,000 regular soldiers and 8,000 mercenaries in the Greek-speaking phalanx, including 3,000 Cretans and 3,000 Libyans from Kyrenaika. The cavalry comprised 700 elite Macedonians, 3,000 Libyans and 2,000 mercenaries. Six thousand Thracians and Galatians were joined by 4,000 cleruchs and their descendants. And, most significant of all for the later trajectory of Ptolemaic history, a separate phalanx of native Egyptian soldiers was recruited, totalling 20,000 men under the direct command of Sosibios himself. It was the first time since the demise of Egypt's last native dynasty in 343 that Egyptians had been drafted to serve in their own national army.

Antiochos III, meanwhile, had been basking in his conquest of Koile-Syria and interpreted the lack of response on the Egyptian side as evidence of Ptolemaic capitulation. He could not have been more wrong. Finally, in the summer of 217, the Ptolemaic army was ready and assembled. On 13 June, Ptolemy IV, with his wife Arsinoe II at his side, marched out from Pelousion at the head of his forces – the last time a pharaoh would personally lead his troops into battle in Asia. On the eve of battle the king addressed his army, acting the part of a traditional pharaoh, but the pretence fooled nobody, especially as he had to use an interpreter to translate from Greek into Egyptian.

The Ptolemaic and Seleukid armies met just outside the small Syrian town of Raphia (present-day Rafah, near Gaza). After a few days of minor skirmishes, the decisive battle took place on 22 June. The forces ranged against each other were massive: Ptolemy (aged about twenty-four) commanded 70,000 infantry, 5,000 cavalry and 73 African war elephants; Antiochos III (just a year older than his rival) led 62,000 infantry, their numbers bolstered by Medes and Persians from the recently recaptured territories, 6,000 cavalry and 102 Indian war elephants. It was the only military encounter in history to pit African pachyderms against their Indian cousins, and indeed the behaviour of both of the armies' elephants proved decisive to the course of the battle. In the heat of the first charge, the African elephants panicked, turned tail and fled into their own ranks, causing chaos and confusion. But the young Ptolemy, who had 'retired under shelter of the phalanx suddenly came forward and showing himself to his troops caused consternation among the enemy and inspired his own men with increased alacrity and spirit'.[3]

Buoyed by this display of royal leadership, the Ptolemaic army prevailed. Antiochos retreated to his dynastic capital, Antioch, and sued for peace. Ptolemy, sensing that the momentum was now with him, sent the wily Sosibios to negotiate on his behalf. As a result, Koile-Syria in its entirety was returned to Ptolemy, and the king was able to return in triumph to Egypt, a conquering hero in the mould of his forebears. His homecoming also brought vast quantities of booty, seized from the battlefield: prisoners of war, elephants, gold and silver. The king rewarded his army with 300,000 pieces of gold, fulfilling what was expected of a victorious leader in the ancient world.

Despite winning a decisive victory at Raphia, Ptolemy did not exact punitive terms against the Seleukids. Rather, the treaty signed with Antiochos III in the aftermath of the battle sought to restore the status quo ante. Ptolemy and his advisers no doubt realised that they could never defeat the Seleukid kingdom entirely; statecraft required a restoration of the balance of power in the Levant.

Like every pharaoh before him, Ptolemy IV exploited his victory for every ounce of propaganda value. He timed his return to Egypt to coincide with the festival celebrating the birth of the god Horus, thus subtly equating his success against Antiochos with the mythical victory of Horus, god of kingship, over Seth, god of confusion. To reinforce the point, orders were given that a statue of the king, named 'Ptolemy Horus who protects his father and whose victory is beautiful', should be set up in every temple in the land. At a stroke, his 'father-loving' epithet resonated with his Egyptian subjects. The victory celebrations – held at Memphis, not Alexandria – culminated in a great synod of the Egyptian priests, gathered from across the country. In time-honoured fashion, they issued a decree, dated 15 November 217.[4] Inscribed, following Ptolemaic precedent, in Egyptian and Greek, only the Egyptian (demotic) text survives in large part. It expresses, in traditional pharaonic language, the personal prowess of the king in defending Egypt and protecting its native religion.

The decree placed a deliberate emphasis on the restitution of sacred statues pilfered from Egyptian temples during the time of the Persian occupation, in the decades before Alexander. In the words of the text, Ptolemy IV had ordered a search for the missing pieces, returning those that were found to their original settings. In the eyes of Ptolemy's Egyptian subjects, this was exactly the behaviour expected of a legitimate pharaoh; while, to his Greek-speaking countrymen, the king was following in the footsteps of his father Ptolemy the Benefactor, and by repeating his deeds he was demonstrating his 'father-loving' nature. The same inscription thus spoke, in subtly different ways, to both audiences.

To seal his reputation as a great benefactor, once the celebrations at Memphis were concluded, Ptolemy IV embarked on a victory tour of Egypt, taking the opportunity to visit all the major temples, make offerings to their gods, and beautify their shrines – even though he had already expended a vast sum on the military campaign itself. And therein lay the sting in the tail. For the victory of Raphia had come at a high price, and the taxes levied to fund the war – taxes that fell heaviest on Egypt's rural population – alongside the arming of Egyptians to serve in the Ptolemaic army, would very soon give rise to a host of unintended consequences.

In the aftermath of Raphia, the Ptolemaic government explicitly recognised the role played by Egyptian soldiers, and later made it possible for them to be allocated their own plots of land as cleruchs – even though the typical allocation, of just five to ten *arouras* (up to seven acres), underscored their second-class status. Nonetheless, at a stroke, impoverished peasants were provided with opportunities for economic betterment and social advancement that they had not enjoyed for generations. There were, however, restrictions. When drafted, Egyptian cleruchs were excluded from serving in the higher ranks of the army; when at home in their villages, they were barred from joining the local club for officers and enlisted men (Gr. *politeuma*). Egypt was very much a country of two classes, divided by language and ethnicity.

The uneasy relationship between a Greek-speaking elite and a largely Egyptian-speaking populace is reflected in the surviving documents. Numerous letters and memoranda on papyrus reveal the workings of the machinery of government in small communities up and down the Nile. To appreciate how the system operated, and how it was experienced on the ground, it is first necessary to understand the structure of local government in Ptolemaic Egypt.

The administrative division of the Nile Valley and Delta into provinces dated back to the foundation of the pharaonic state in the early third millennium. When Ptolemy became satrap of Egypt in 323, he inherited a system that worked remarkably well, especially in a country as geographically extensive as Egypt. Provincial governors exercised authority in their localities on behalf of the central government and ensured that taxes were paid to the royal treasury. The provinces themselves were based on natural irrigation basins, reflecting the fact that the efficient exploitation of the Nile's agricultural bounty lay at the heart of the Egyptian state from the very beginning.

As satrap and then king, Ptolemy I left the basic structure in place,[5] although each province, or nome, was now named after its administrative capital: so, for example, the Hare-province became the Hermopolite nome, after the town of Hermopolis. This reflected the historic importance of towns and cities in the Greek-speaking world, and in the Greek view of government. Ptolemy likewise retained the office of nomarch, although provincial governors now reported to the finance minister in Alexandria. The nomarch was still responsible for overseeing agricultural production in his province, and was assisted at the local level by district and village governors (Gr. *toparch* and *komarch*, respectively). Royal scribes continued to keep detailed records, especially concerning land ownership and use, just as they had done since time immemorial; they too had locally based assistants, the district and village scribes. In each province, the governor's official deputy was termed the 'household manager' (Gr. *oikonomos*): as the title suggests, he was responsible for supervising finances and ensuring that the state's economic interests, always paramount, were safeguarded.

One of the most revealing documents to have survived from the time of Ptolemy IV is a memorandum from the finance minister to an anonymous *oikonomos* instructing him how to carry out his duties. Although such works on the proper exercise of administrative authority had a long tradition in ancient Egypt, this particular missive highlights the extreme attention to detail expected from an *oikonomos*. The first section of instructions deals with grain production, the backbone of the Egyptian economy, and starts with irrigation, which was fundamental to the whole agricultural system. The *oikonomos* was required to inspect the water ducts which ran through the fields, taking careful note 'whether the intakes into them have the prescribed depth and whether there is sufficient space in them'. Canals were to be checked regularly to assess 'whether they are solidly made and whether the entries from the river are kept as clean as possible'.

The *oikonomos* was required to conduct a tour of inspection of his province to ensure the land was being used to maximum efficiency, since the state's tax take depended on the size of the harvest. In the centrally planned Ptolemaic economy, even the crops to be grown in each field were prescribed by the government; and the *oikonomos* was reminded, 'You must consider it one of your most imperative duties to make sure that the nome is sown with the crops specified in the sowing schedule.' At the end of the agricultural year, proper oversight of the collection and transport of the harvest was a vital task. The state's imperative was to ensure 'that the prescribed cargoes of corn … are brought down to Alexandria at the right time'.

Alongside grain, the government's other main sources of wealth and taxation were cattle – of which an annual census was mandated – and the manufacture of secondary products. Textile production was a state-controlled enterprise, and it was the responsibility of an *oikonomos* to oversee the weaving-houses in his province, ensuring a regular supply of flax to feed the looms. Oil production was similarly regulated, and a royal monopoly to boot. In exercising oversight of the oil factories, the *oikonomos* was urged to ensure that 'the amounts measured out to the oil-workers are not greater than what is going to be used in the oil presses', to guard against illicit or black-market activities. A further, lengthy section of the instructions deals with the planting of native trees on river and canal embankments, to provide much-needed timber in a country where it was always in short supply.

The role of an *oikonomos* was thus wide-ranging and demanding. As the finance minister explained, 'it is not easy to include everything and to convey it to you through memoranda'. The overriding duty of the 'household manager' was to audit the accounts of government revenue within his province – ideally village by village, but, if this was not possible, district by district – to ensure that all sums due to the government were paid in full and on time. Like similar instruction texts from earlier periods of pharaonic history, the missive reminded the *oikonomos* of the need to exercise power with justice: 'Take especial care that no act of extortion or any other misdeed is committed. For everyone who lives in the country must clearly know and believe that all such acts have come to an end and that they have been delivered from the previous bad state of affairs.'[6] The 'household manager' was additionally urged: 'During your tour of inspection try as you [go] about to encourage everybody and make them feel happier'[7] – a tough call for a tax inspector.

Economic considerations were always to the fore, as they had been throughout Egyptian history; but quite early in the Ptolemaic period, the settlement of large numbers of cleruchs necessitated a change to the structure of local government. Because the whole purpose of the military settlers was to provide the king with a reserve force to serve in foreign campaigns but also to quell any domestic unrest, it was not sensible for cleruchs to be answerable to a nomarch, then to a minister, and only then to the pharaoh. The Ptolemies wanted much closer control over their army reservists. The solution was to appoint a military commander in each province, who reported directly to the monarch. All the cleruchs in a nome – infantry and cavalry of all ranks – would fall under the commander's personal authority, and the commanders were appointed by the king. This new system had the effect of diminishing the authority of the nomarchs. Since the beginning of Egyptian history, they had wielded power in their localities. Now, their writ was largely confined to the native population, while the commander was unquestionably the first-ranking official in each province. Moreover, the military settlers and their commanders effectively constituted a state within a state. It was a case of one power structure for indigenous Egyptians, another for Greek-speaking immigrants.

As part of this system, Ptolemy IV appointed a series of new military commanders on acceding to the throne in 221. One such was Diophanes, whose bailiwick was the Fayum. His archive of correspondence, covering the first four years of Ptolemy IV's reign, reveals the tightrope that a Greek-speaking commander had to walk to maintain peace and prosperity in his region.

All the documents in Diophanes' extensive collection concern private grievances. They were lodged with the commander as one might today write to one's Member of Parliament or congressional representative. Most of the complaints sought to recover money or property that the complainant believed had been wrongly or unfairly extracted. In accordance with longstanding Egyptian custom, any citizen could in theory petition the king directly, seeking redress in any matter. In practice, the business of replying to these tedious, often petty complaints was delegated to the state's principal representative in each region – in other words, the commander.

Such was the volume of documents delivered to Diophanes that he quickly developed an efficient system for dealing with them. A clerk read the complaint aloud to Diophanes, who dictated a brief response, which the clerk then noted on the petition before moving on to the next one. After being processed, the original document was filed in Diophanes' office and a copy, recording both the complaint and the approved redress, was handed back to the petitioner to deliver to the appropriate official tasked with the follow-up action. (In most cases this was the chief of police of the village in which the accused lived.) It was a bureaucratic process, but a relatively streamlined one.

Diophanes' modus operandi was to seek the line of least resistance. His preference was to find a settlement that would reconcile the opposing parties: anything for a quiet life. Hence, his most frequent instruction, scribbled by the attendant clerk at the bottom of the document, was 'If at all possible, reconcile them. But if not, send him/her/them to me so I can look into it.' Another favourite response was 'Look into the law and make them do what's right.' For more complex cases that required a little extra information, the clerk was frequently instructed, 'Fill me in on what this is about.'[8] These instructions were so familiar that the clerks developed their own form of shorthand – a few brief squiggles to denote the commander's response. Only if such measures failed to resolve a dispute did Diophanes have to burden himself with taking a decision, or referring the matter to the appropriate tribunal.

The archive reveals all the tensions of rural village life, where extended families lived cheek by jowl and petty rivalries were magnified by the claustrophobic atmosphere. Such tensions are all too familiar in villages today. In cramped conditions, domestic disputes were particularly common. One petition, dated 27 February 221, involved a father, a prodigal son and a prostitute – all the characters required for a Greek comedy. Overdue payments and unpaid bills were also frequent causes for complaint. The previous day, 26 February, Diophanes received a petition from an Arab barber named Parates, who lived in a settlement called Ptolemais-of-the-Arabs. Its precise location is unknown, but it had clearly attracted a large number of Arab settlers and developed its own distinctive character. One of Parates' customers, a Syrian named Malichos, had failed to pay his barber's bill. That a military commander tasked with administering an entire province should have had to deal with such petty cases may seem inefficient; but the escalation of every complaint, no matter how minor, up to the very top is still a feature of life in many traditional societies today. The outcome of the case is not known, but Malichos was playing with fire: under the Ptolemaic legal code, failure to pay a debt on time attracted a 50 per cent penalty charge and could ultimately lead to debtors' prison.

In a province like the Fayum, which had witnessed a particular influx of military settlers, disputes between the native inhabitants and the incomers were frequent. Complaints (more often than not by an Egyptian against a Greek) ranged from damage to property and quarrels over lodgings to defaults on loans, theft and assault. In another petition dated 26 February 221, an Egyptian farmer complained he had been thrown out of his own house by a local Greek landowner, even though the latter already had lodgings in the village. To add insult to injury, the farmer's cattle had been deliberately let loose. Diophanes' weary response – for he must have received countless complaints along the same lines – was to instruct the chief of police to reconcile the parties, or, if that was not possible, send them to be judged by the 'mixed tribunal' (a court for resolving matters involving Egyptians and Greeks).⁹ On another occasion an Egyptian woman, Tetosiris, who had filed a lawsuit against a Greek, Apollodoros, was visited by a thug hired by him to intimidate her and her witnesses.

Faced with arbitrary persecution, poor Egyptian farmers had little expectation of justice, especially in a land where the Greek-speaking settlers had the ear of the authorities. Sometimes, therefore, Egyptians found other ways of kicking against the system. In one case, a Greek farmer complained that his Egyptian neighbours had interfered with the irrigation system, causing his field – which he had just sown with crops – to be flooded.

Even though Diophanes acted as the king's personal representative and exercised the state's full authority, his instructions did not always succeed in resolving a dispute. When a case involving rival farmers had been referred to the local police chief, the policeman wrote back that he had duly summoned the parties, but they had rejected his attempts at conciliation – so he had sent them to Diophanes. The commander's heart must have sunk when he received the note.

As tensions in the countryside simmered, Ptolemy IV singularly failed to exercise effective leadership. After the decisive victory at Raphia, the young king might have been expected to assert his personal authority, engage actively with foreign and domestic affairs, and continue the glorious rule of his three predecessors. Instead, in the withering judgement of a later commentator, he 'abandoned entirely the path of virtue and took to a life of dissipation'.[10] In truth, Ptolemy IV was not a total disaster. He continued royal patronage of the Mouseion, and founded a whole branch of the Library dedicated to collecting, collating, editing and revising the complete works of Homer. It was the first time in history that a single author had been singled out for scholarly attention. Ptolemy even built a temple and established a cult to Homer in Alexandria. He also composed a play of his own (the tragedy *Adonis*) and sponsored a Festival of the Muses – a celebration of music, poetry and drama – in the Ptolemaic capital.

But such intellectual pursuits had always been conducted *alongside* the affairs of state. In Ptolemy IV's case, they seem to have replaced any interest in politics or government. Secure in his own position after Raphia, he is said to have become increasingly 'inattentive to business and difficult of access as regards the members of his court and the officials who administered Egypt', treating those responsible for foreign affairs in particular 'with entire negligence and indifference'.[11] It is not difficult to imagine a young man, fabulously wealthy and confident of his own authority, delegating the difficult decisions to others and abandoning himself to a life of enjoyment – in the words of a later critic, 'shameful amours and senseless and constant drunkenness'.[12]

A striking example of this decadence was the royal yacht commissioned by Ptolemy IV. In the Hellenistic world, a ship was an important symbol of a monarch's wealth and authority, a very visible demonstration of the concept of *tryphé* (magnificence). A royal yacht might double as a naval flagship, and Hellenistic rulers competed with each other to build the most impressive craft. Yet, even by the standards of the time, Ptolemy IV's ship was outrageous in its size and ostentation. Half a *stade* or 200 cubits (350 feet) in length and 30 cubits (52 feet) wide, it required a special dock at Alexandria to build and launch it. It is likely to have been kept in the royal harbour at Alexandria for most of the time: a venue for diplomatic meetings or royal parties that was designed to impress.

The ship itself, a catamaran, was entered at the stern. An enfilade of pillared halls led to a central sitting room panelled with costly cedar and cypress from Koile-Syria, and surrounded with cypress columns, their Corinthian capitals inlaid with ivory and sheathed in gold leaf. Inside this opulent room were couches for twenty people. Doors made of citron wood and decorated with yet more ivory led out to the main deck, which also accommodated the women's quarters, a dining room and a state bedroom. A staircase led to the upper deck, which revealed even greater spectacles: a miniature temple to Aphrodite complete with a marble statue of the goddess, and a sitting room dedicated to Dionysos, decked out with a replica of the god's cave. This upper sitting room had external walls inlaid with gold and precious stones, while inside there were translucent statues of Ptolemy IV and other members of the royal family. Much of the central part of the upper deck was open to the sky, but could be covered with an immense purple awning. The ship's 70-cubit (122-feet) mast carried an immense topsail of the same imperial hue. Towards the aft of the top deck was a third sitting room decorated in 'pharaonic' style, with papyriform columns and alabaster panels inlaid with floral motifs. Down in the bowels of the ship were the stores, kitchens and crew's quarters. A floating palace required a vast staff to service it.

But magnificence was not enough for a Hellenistic ruler of the third century: you also had to be prepared to engage in power politics, and fight, if necessary, to retain your throne. Early battles with Antiochos III should have taught Ptolemy this lesson; but instead, while he whiled away his time with lavish waterborne entertainments, the Mediterranean world was entering one of the most dangerous periods in its turbulent history.

In the aftermath of the battle at Raphia, Antiochos had not been idle. If he could not – yet – take back control of Koile-Syria, he could try to consolidate his other territories and return the Seleukid empire to its former glory. In 216, he marched his forces into Anatolia to suppress a local rebellion. Ptolemy IV sought to assist his enemy's domestic opponents but, within two years, the rebels had been expelled and executed. The city of Sardis in western Anatolia held out against Antiochos for a few more months, but eventually surrendered. With much of the central Anatolian peninsula now back under Seleukid control, Antiochos turned his attention to its northern and eastern reaches. In 212, the King of Armenia was besieged and forced to capitulate. Three years later, it was the turn of Parthia (present-day north-eastern Iran) to be invaded, occupied and subjugated. And still Antiochos pressed on.

Fresh from his victory in Parthia, he led his army into Bactria, which he brought back into the fold, and continued in the footsteps of Alexander by crossing the Caucasus mountains and descending into Indian lands, to parley with the ruler of the Kabul valley. The result of the diplomatic meeting – an outcome that every Hellenistic monarch would have dreamed of – was a gift of Indian elephants, bolstering the total Seleukid force to 150 beasts. After personally leading the animals back to the dynastic city of Seleukeia-on-the-Tigris, Antiochos led a short expedition down the Arabian coast of the Gulf to secure his southern flank. As a result of these remarkable victories, which restored Seleukid control in the east, he adopted the title of the Persian rulers of yore, 'Great King', and styled himself Antiochos the Great.

A resurgent Seleukid empire to the north and east should have been warning enough to Ptolemy IV. But the lands to the west, too, were in turmoil. A generation earlier, the First Punic War between Rome and Carthage had ended – after twenty-three years and heavy losses on both sides – with a Roman victory. Licking their wounds, the Carthaginians had turned their attention to Iberia, expanding their territory on the peninsula. In 219, their leader Hannibal had besieged and captured the Roman client city of Saguntum, provoking a declaration of war by Rome a few months later. The Second Punic War would rage for the next seventeen years. In its early stages, the momentum was with the Carthaginians. Hannibal surprised his enemies by marching an army overland from Iberia, through Gaul and over the Alps into northern Italy, winning decisive victories, before continuing southwards and defeating the largest Roman army assembled to that date (at the Battle of Cannae). The extent of Rome's losses – more than 120,000 troops in less than three years – persuaded its allies, in southern Italy and further afield, to defect to the Carthaginian side. These new players in the conflict included the Greek city of Syracuse and the Kingdom of Macedon. As a result, by 215, virtually the whole of the central Mediterranean was embroiled in conflict.

War begot war. The young Philip V of Macedon, sensing Rome's weakness, decided to try to expand his influence westwards into Illyria, which lay within the Roman orbit. On hearing news of Hannibal's initial victories in northern Italy, Philip assembled the largest fleet Macedon had known since the days of Alexander: some 100 newly constructed warships, together with trained sailors to man them. After Cannae, Philip sent ambassadors to Hannibal to negotiate a formal alliance between Macedon and Carthage. The result was a treaty in which both sides promised support for each other in their common fight against Rome. News of the alliance caused consternation in Rome, which despatched additional ships to bolster its Adriatic fleet, fearing a seaborne invasion of the Italian peninsula.

Rome, now fighting for its life on two fronts, took drastic steps to increase the forces under its command. Working men of fighting age who did not meet the usual property qualification, slaves, even convicted criminals: all were drafted. In Sicily and Sardinia, the Roman army held off assaults by the Carthaginians and, by 211, was able to launch a counter-offensive in Iberia. In the east, it sought an alliance against Macedon with the Aetolian League (an anti-Macedonian confederation of central Greek states) and the independent ruler of Pergamon. Rome even sent an embassy to Egypt to renew friendly ties and, crucially, ask for shipments of grain to feed its army and its hard-pressed population. Ptolemy IV's response was to sit on the fence, neither actively supporting Rome nor answering a similar plea for assistance from Syracuse. Ptolemy may have believed he was protecting his interests by distancing himself from the spreading conflict, hunkering down in his gilded chambers as the wider Mediterranean burned. But although he succeeded in keeping Egypt out of the war, it came at the price of fatally weakening Ptolemaic influence in the peace that followed.

Eventually, the Roman army started to make gains against the Carthaginians, capturing their main base in Iberia in 209 and conquering the whole peninsula three years later. In Greece, they successfully pinned Philip V down, preventing him from sending military assistance to Hannibal. From a position of strength, Rome sued for peace. Egypt, as a neutral power, was one of the states, alongside Rhodes, that sent representatives to the peace conference. Eventually, in 205, after nearly two years of shuttle diplomacy, a treaty was drawn up at Phoenike (Finiq in present-day Albania), bringing the so-called First Macedonian War to an end.

But such kudos as Egypt might have garnered from the deal soon evaporated. Within a few months of the peace treaty, Ptolemy IV was dead, aged just forty, his legacy not one of strength and prestige but of weakness and increasing irrelevance. How things had changed since his great-grandfather had been acclaimed as *basileus* and pharaoh exactly a century before! Beset by crises abroad, Ptolemy IV had opted for neutrality where Ptolemy I had campaigned to defend and expand his interests. Alexandria, once the jewel in the Ptolemaic crown, was now a tawdry gem, a city of luxury and licence. The wider Egyptian countryside, having absorbed generations of Greek-speaking immigrants and military settlers, now seethed with ethnic tension. And where earlier Ptolemies had enriched their treasury with copious amounts of grain and gold, Ptolemy IV had spent vast sums on raising and rewarding his army, while foreign conflicts disrupted the trade on which Egypt's wealth ultimately depended.

Most damaging of all for the long-term stability and security of his kingdom, Ptolemy IV had spent the better part of his reign focused obsessively on his Hellenistic rivals, determined to outdo and outshine both Macedon and the Seleukid empire. In doing so, he had ignored two growing threats, one from without, the other from within. Beyond Egypt's borders, it was not in Greece or the East that the main geopolitical threat now lay, but in the Italian peninsula. The upstart power that was challenging Carthage for hegemony in the central and western Mediterranean was an army on the march. All too soon, it would be knocking at the gates of Egypt. Inside the country, dissatisfaction and dissent were growing among the native population, weighed down by years of oppressive taxation and consigned to the status of second-class citizens in their own land. Yet had not thousands of Egyptian men fought – and won – at Raphia? After they were demobilised and sent back to their villages, it was only a matter of time before things came to a head.

At the start of Ptolemy IV's reign, a storm was approaching. At the end, the tempest burst with cataclysmic force.

6
Rebellion and Retrenchment

Within days of Ptolemy IV's demise, all hell broke loose.
The king had been just forty years old at his death, in the late summer of 204. His son and heir, Ptolemy V (who had been proclaimed co-regent shortly after his birth), was not yet six, and in no position to wield effective power. So different factions at court immediately began jostling for position, knowing that whoever emerged as the young boy's official guardian would have carte blanche to run the kingdom. His mother, Arsinoe III, had the most obvious claim to the regency, but others had different ideas.

Ptolemy IV's Machiavellian adviser, Sosibios, moved quickly to secure his own position – which might have been seriously threatened had Arsinoe gained power – by allying himself with his fellow courtier, Agathokles. The latter's rise to power under Ptolemy IV, as well as the manner of his advancement, had made him one of the most hated figures in Alexandria. He could claim a tenuous kinship with the Ptolemaic royal house – his great-grandmother was the half-sister of Ptolemy II – and some of his relatives had been in royal service. But Agathokles owed his own position to lust, not blood: his sister, Agathoklea, had been Ptolemy IV's mistress. Brother and sister alike had been introduced to the late king early in his reign by their ambitious mother; Ptolemy IV favoured both, taking the sister into his bed, the brother into his court. Agathokles had even served for a year as the priest of the cult of Alexander, one of the most prestigious positions in the king's gift. Even after Ptolemy IV had married, Agathoklea had remained his favourite.

The widowed Arsinoe III was thus no fan of brother or sister, and Agathokles had everything to lose. He and Sosibios hushed up the king's demise long enough to enable them to plunder the royal treasury and murder Arsinoe III. According to a later account, they then

> summoned a meeting of the bodyguard and household troops as well as the officers of the infantry and cavalry. When all these had collected, Agathokles and Sosibios mounted the dais, and in the first place acknowledged the death of the king and queen and enjoined the populace to go into mourning as was their usual practice. After this they crowned the boy [Ptolemy V] and proclaimed him king, and then read out a forged will, in which it was written that the late king had appointed Agathokles and Sosibios guardians of his son. They begged the officers to remain well disposed and maintain the boy on his throne; and afterwards brought in two silver urns, the one said to contain the bones of the king and the other those of Arsinoe. In fact, the one did contain the king's bones, but the other was full of spices. Hereupon they at once celebrated the funeral.[1]

The truth of Arsinoe's fate slowly dawned on the assembled company, and news soon spread to the wider population of Alexandria. It is said that they 'fell into such a state of distraction and affliction that the city was full of groans, tears and ceaseless lamentation'.[2] Whether this reflected genuine love for the murdered queen or hatred of Agathokles was hard to tell.

Sosibios seems to have died soon after his moment of triumph. His passing left the welfare of Ptolemy V to Agathoklea and the affairs of state in the sole hands of her brother. With public sentiment running dangerously high, Agathokles sought to buy the support of the army – always a vital power broker in such situations – by giving the troops two months' pay. As for their officers, he despatched them on urgent state business – negotiations over the proposed marriage of the infant Ptolemy V to the daughter of Philip V of Macedon – to get them out of the way. He then brought in new recruits to staff the household division and the palace guard, and similarly replaced the detachments of soldiers stationed in Alexandria. By such means, he calculated, 'the men he himself had enlisted and whom he paid, as they had no political sympathies regarding past events of which they were ignorant, and as they reposed their hopes of preservation and advancement on himself, would readily support him and join heartily in executing all his orders'.³ It is the modus operandi of coup leaders throughout history.

But such ruses eventually ran out of road. The population of Alexandria became increasingly exasperated by Agathokles' barefaced outrages, and within a year of his coup d'état, the citizens rose against him. Surrounding the palace at night, they forced their way in. Agathokles begged for his life, but to no avail. He was killed by his friends as an act of mercy, to spare him from being torn limb from limb by the bloodthirsty mob. Such a fate awaited Agathoklea and her sisters when the rioters discovered them hiding in a nearby temple. They were dragged out and taken to the stadium of Alexandria, where their frenzied killing was staged as a public spectacle. Every other member of the Agathokles clan who was implicated in the murder of Arsinoe III was likewise hunted down and killed. As their blood ran through the streets of Alexandria, Ptolemy V's throne, just a year old, teetered on the brink.

And there was worse news to come. The officers sent by Agathokles to negotiate a diplomatic marriage between the kingdoms of Egypt and Macedon had instead discovered a plot, hatched by the Macedonian and Seleukid rulers, to dismember the Ptolemaic realm and divide it between them. For a century, the Ptolemies' Hellenistic rivals had looked on Egypt and its dominions with jealous eyes. Now, with the accession of an infant pharaoh and a court in turmoil, the Ptolemaic kingdom had never looked so weak. Under the terms of the pact, Philip V would receive Kyrenaika and territories around the Aegean, while Antiochos III would add Cyprus and the Nile Valley to his already sprawling empire.⁴

Despite its travails, Egypt was not going down without a fight. When news reached Alexandria, the pharaoh's army prepared for war. The resulting conflict, which raged for seven years between 202 and 195, is termed the Fifth Syrian War. At the outset, Antiochos III launched a lightning offensive against the Ptolemaic province of Koile-Syria. Meeting only light resistance, he succeeded in seizing the strategic port cities of the Phoenician coast, including Sidon and Gaza, disrupting the Ptolemaic trading networks. The Ptolemaic governor of Syria promptly defected to the Seleukid side. Meanwhile,

Philip V opened up a second front in the Aegean, as he attempted to impose Macedonian hegemony on the whole region. The unintended consequence of this was to bring Rome into the fray, which was determined to prevent such an outcome. When Philip rejected a Roman ultimatum to cease hostilities, conflict with the rising power of the Mediterranean became inevitable. The Second Macedonian War (200–197), fought between Rome and Macedon, occupied all of Philip's energies, preventing him from realising his wider strategic objectives.

But if the Egyptian army thought that Rome would now swing to its side, it was sorely mistaken. A Roman embassy did indeed make its way to Alexandria in 200, but showed no interest in actively supporting the government of Ptolemy V. Rather, its intention seems to have been to ensure that the Fifth Syrian War would continue to rage, occupying Seleukid energies and thereby preventing an alliance of Antiochos III and Philip V against Rome.

Rome got its wish, and the war dragged on. A Ptolemaic counter-offensive had won back some territory in the winter of 201. Then, the following summer, the opposing forces met in a decisive encounter near Mount Hermon, at a riverside location famed for a cave sacred to the god Pan (Gr. Paneion). The army of Antiochos III numbered some 70,000 men – even larger than the army deployed at Raphia seventeen years earlier. There were battalions of infantry, heavy cavalry, an elite cavalry regiment and, of course, the fabled Seleukid war elephants. Facing them was the 50,000-strong Ptolemaic army, strung out over a front line four kilometres wide. It included an elite regiment of 30,000 Macedonian soldiers, a battalion of African war elephants and a force of 6,500 mercenaries from Aetolia, a mountainous region of north-central Greece, led by their countryman Scopas, who also held supreme command of the Ptolemaic army. In the end, the Battle of Paneion was swift and conclusive. The Seleukid heavy cavalry opened the offensive by attacking and routing the Ptolemaic cavalry. When the Ptolemaic forces made gains at the centre, they were stopped in their tracks by a charge of Seleukid elephants. Seleukid cavalry then attacked the Ptolemaic troops from the rear, leaving them no means of escape. The elite Macedonian force commanded by Ptolemaios was annihilated where it stood. Scopas fled the field, taking some 10,000 troops with him, and seeking refuge at Sidon. Other survivors of the erstwhile Ptolemaic war machine beat a disorganised retreat to Jerusalem and Samaria. All were forced to surrender by the end of 198, when Antiochos III emerged as the undoubted ruler of all Koile-Syria and Judaea.

The era of Ptolemaic power in the Levant had come to an inglorious end. Three years later, Ptolemy V was compelled to sign a peace treaty which recognised the Seleukid victory. This bitter pill was sweetened just a little by the offer of Antiochos' daughter's hand in marriage – along with her considerable dowry.

No earlier Ptolemy would have taken such a military defeat lying down, never mind conceded hard-fought territory to the Seleukids. But no earlier Ptolemy had faced quite the combination of pressures that now assailed the government in Alexandria. For, even as enemies abroad were seeking to divide and conquer, enemies at home were trying to deprive Ptolemy V of his very throne.

The troubles in Egypt that ran in parallel with the demise of Ptolemy IV and the Fifth Syrian War had their origin some years earlier. The root cause was economic mismanagement. The conscription of Egyptian peasants, though it helped win the Battle of Raphia, had had the unintended consequence of reducing agricultural production in the countryside. This in turn had led to a steep rise in food prices. In response, the finance minister had introduced a radical change in the relative value of silver and bronze, devaluing the bronze coinage that was the everyday currency in towns and villages throughout Egypt. The price of commodities denominated in bronze then rose sharply, unleashing a spiral of inflation that ruined countless rural households when their savings became increasingly worthless. An increase in taxation to fund the war effort merely added insult to injury. Egyptians who had accommodated themselves to rule by a Greek-speaking elite now began to question the legitimacy of a government that could no longer look after their basic needs.

When Ptolemy IV's health had started to deteriorate, it looked to many as if things would go from bad to worse. Simmering resentment in the countryside quickly erupted into full-scale revolt, as thousands of Egyptian soldiers, demobilised after Raphia, used their military training to advance their own interests. One of the first areas to rebel was the Delta settlement of Lykopolis ('wolf city', present-day Segin al-Kom) which was close to the inland port of Naukratis. According to a contemporary account, 'Egyptian bandits attacked a military post and a temple precinct; the attackers came from an area outside the village.'5 Insurrection in the vicinity of a free *polis* – and one of the cornerstones of the Ptolemies' international trading network – was a serious threat to royal authority. Reconquering Lykopolis thus became an immediate and pressing priority for the government.

With the state distracted by rebellion in the north, threats from abroad and disarray in its own ranks, Egyptians in the far south of the country, where Ptolemaic rule had always been most heavily resented, seized the moment. An insurgency that had started in 206 now became a full-scale revolt, and its leaders proclaimed one of their own as king. This represented the gravest challenge to the political order since Alexander's conquest 120 years earlier. The new claimant, named Horwennefer, started issuing his own decrees, while sympathetic communities and organisations – including some of the native priesthoods – gave him their formal recognition by dating documents to the new 'reign'. The construction of temples ground to a halt as priests hurried to sever links with the Ptolemaic government. At Apollonopolis, for example, the massive main doors of the temple were ready for hanging but would have to wait another thirty years before they were put in place. Greeks living outside the temple walls had to flee their houses as local Egyptians sought to 'cleanse' the town of its non-native inhabitants.

In the autumn of 205, the rebel forces seized control of the holy city of Thebes (present-day Luxor), the heartland of Egyptian religion and culture. Horwennefer duly assumed the traditional title of 'pharaoh', together with the epithet 'beloved of Amun-Ra, king of the gods'. Now it was the turn of Theban Greeks to abandon their homes, while work on local temples came to an abrupt stop. The Theban clergy disassociated themselves from their erstwhile overlords: not a single document mentioning the Ptolemaic ruler has been found anywhere in southern Upper Egypt (Thebaid, from the Greek *Thebais*) from the six years after Horwennefer's arrival. Moreover, no taxes were paid in at the state bank of Thebes. Even in the remote eastern desert, soldiers abandoned the fortress guarding the gold mines of Samut, unwilling, it seems, to rely on vulnerable supply lines now that the Ptolemaic state was fighting for its survival. The base would never again be garrisoned on a permanent basis.

Horwennefer's new regime seems to have taken concerted steps to establish itself as a fully functioning alternative government. A new chancellery was set up to administer the collection of taxes. People continued to marry, buy and sell land, and essentially carry on life as usual, but the legal contracts were now drawn up under the new pharaoh's authority. The rebels were keen to portray themselves, not as insurgents, but as a proper government acting accordingly.

They also turned to religion to challenge Ptolemaic authority and assert their own legitimacy. The very name of their leader, Horwennefer, included a well-known epithet (Wennefer) of Osiris, the god whose mythical rule had come to be seen as the model of divine kingship. The Ptolemaic dynasty had itself sought to establish close theological links with the cult of Osiris, dedicating buildings to the god throughout Egypt. Ptolemy IV had even juxtaposed his name with that of Osiris, as if god and king were reigning together. The rebels were now throwing theology back in the government's face.

The government's initial response to this unprecedented challenge seems to have been to bypass Thebes and concentrate the counter-offensive further south, perhaps to prevent the rebels from joining forces with Kush. Horwennefer's regime was thus able to extend its authority beyond Thebes. By the autumn of 204 the rebel leader was mentioned in a document from Pathyris (present-day Gebelein); two years later he gained recognition in the Coptite nome, and the following year he won over the holy site of Abydos. By then, however, the Ptolemaic government had marshalled its forces in the northern Nile Valley and was ready to launch the fight-back in earnest. The first major settlement to return to the Ptolemaic fold was the royal foundation of Ptolemais, a bastion of Greek-speaking loyalists. It was publicly recognising the rule of Ptolemy V by the sixth year of his reign (200/199).

Then something odd happened. As soon as the rebellion started to come under sustained pressure, Horwennefer disappeared from the record. In his place, a new king appeared, named Ankhwennefer. It has generally been assumed that the latter was Horwennefer's successor, but there are problems with this interpretation. First and most striking,

Ankhwennefer continued the regnal years of Horwennefer. There was no precedent for this in pharaonic history, and the rebel leaders were nothing if not sticklers for pharaonic tradition. Second, a later Ptolemaic decree referred to Ankhwennefer as the 'rebel against the gods ... who began the fight within Egypt' – suggesting that he had led the rebellion from its inception. Third, the similarity in the names Horwennefer and Ankhwennefer may indicate different phases of a single reign, rather than two separate reigns. There *were* pharaonic precedents for this, especially in time of conflict.

Whether a new pharaoh or an old one defiantly declaring a new lease of life (Eg. *ankh*), the transition from Horwennefer to Ankhwennefer marked an escalation in the conflict between rebels and government forces. In August 199, the Ptolemaic army besieged Abydos, and the rebels' other strongholds started to crumble. In the province of southern Lykopolis (present-day Asyut), there were massacres and famine. Thebes returned to Ptolemaic control before the end of 199. Rather than fleeing south to confront government troops, the rebels made a daring northward move, perhaps using the desert routes to the west of Thebes. This brilliant tactical manoeuvre, accompanied by fierce fighting, succeeded in cutting the state's supply lines to Alexandria. Ptolemaic troops in Thebes found themselves isolated, their comrades further south cut off. By the autumn of 198, the rebels had managed to retake Thebes. They would hold it for the next seven years, allowing contracts across the Thebaid to be dated to the reign of 'pharaoh Ankhwennefer'. A new lease of life indeed.

Ptolemy V's government responded to the loss of Thebes by enacting extraordinary punitive measures. A royal decree dated 12 November 198 legalised, for the first time, the enslavement of any native Egyptians seized by government soldiers in the course of anti-insurgency operations. And there were external factors, too, far beyond the rebels' control, that now upended their calculations. The shifting plates of geopolitics moved decisively in Ptolemy V's favour with the end of the Fifth Syrian War. The resulting peace allowed the king to concentrate on winning back control of the Nile Valley. Marshalling his forces and turning them southwards, he recaptured the district of southern Lykopolis, ravaging the land, before retaking Thebes – for good. Ptolemaic supply lines between Alexandria and

Upper Egypt were restored, and the Thebaid sent grain southwards to Syene to feed the Greek troops stationed there.

The rebels' options were narrowing fast. With no escape to the north, Ankhwennefer and his followers fled south, hoping to secure Kushite support. There is scant evidence for this final phase of the Great Southern Rebellion until the last battle, fought at an unidentified location in southern Upper Egypt on 27 August 186. Kushite troops did indeed fight alongside the rebel pharaoh, but they were no match for the well-trained and well-armed Ptolemaic forces. Ankhwennefer was defeated and taken prisoner; his son and would-be heir was killed in action. It took ten full days for the news to reach Alexandria. According to Ptolemy V's subsequent victory inscription, the rebel leader – branded 'the enemy of the gods' – was taken 'in copper chains to the place where Pharaoh was'.[6]

Following an intervention by the priests, Ankhwennefer seems to have been spared execution – not out of any show of Ptolemaic mercy, but to avoid him becoming a martyr. As for his followers, an amnesty decree issued shortly after the victory, on 9 October 186, seems to have spared them as long as they pledged undying loyalty to Ptolemy and returned at once to their homes and fields. The decree reduced debts and pardoned all crimes (except murder and theft from the temples) committed up to that date, a sure sign of the government's desperation to see a return to normality. Even in Thebes, there is no evidence for any retribution having been exacted once the city returned to the Ptolemaic fold. Nonetheless, to try to prevent any future rebellions, Greek soldiers were settled in Egyptian communities throughout Upper Egypt and the office of supreme military commander (Gr. *epistrategos*) was created with its headquarters in the loyal Greek *polis* of Ptolemais.

For two decades, the flame of Egyptian nationalism had burned brighter than at any point since the defeat of Nakhthorheb by the Persians in the 340s. In the end, Ptolemaic military superiority prevailed, and the Great Rebellion was snuffed out. Never again would a native resistance movement mount an effective challenge to the state's authority.

The priests of Isis at Philae, who had remained loyal to the Ptolemaic government throughout, were happy to issue a decree giving the official version of events:

> The rebel against the gods, he who had made war in Egypt, gathering insolent people from all districts on account of their crimes, they did terrible things to the governors of the nomes, they desecrated the temples, they damaged the divine statues, they molested the priests and suppressed the offerings on the altars and in the shrines. They sacked the towns and their population, women and children included, committing all kinds of crimes in the time of anarchy. They stole the taxes of the provinces, and they damaged the irrigation works.
>
> [Whereas] the king of Upper and Lower Egypt Ptolemy, beloved of Ptah, has given many orders and showed considerable care for protecting the temples… His Majesty caused that great quantities of silver and gold came to the land to bring troops to Egypt, money from the taxes of the provinces, in order to protect the temples of Egypt against the impious men who violated them.[7]

Despite the confident tone, however, the shock of the experience had been profound. The civil war had claimed many casualties on both sides, and large numbers of people had fled their homes; the damage to Ptolemaic prestige was lasting. Nor had the underlying causes of the revolt – disenfranchisement of the native population combined with punitive taxes to fund disastrous foreign wars – been addressed.

Moreover, the uprising in the Delta continued to flare. Ptolemy V's army had made some headway a decade earlier, besieging Lykopolis, blocking the surrounding canals to cut off the water supply, storming the city and taking the ringleaders to Memphis to be executed. But the marshy terrain of the Delta, crisscrossed by numerous Nile branches and irrigation channels, made it perfect for low-level guerrilla warfare.[8] Calculating that an all-out military assault was impractical, Ptolemy V turned instead to subterfuge. In 185, on the pretext of seeking a negotiated settlement, he lured some of the insurgents to Sais in the north-western Delta. The city had been a symbolic centre of Lower Egyptian identity and resistance for centuries. Too late, the rebels realised it was a trap. On the king's orders, they were stripped naked, harnessed to carts like oxen, and forced to pull them through the city streets – watched by the terrified inhabitants – before being tortured to death.

Final victory for the government came soon afterwards. In March 184, Ptolemy V led his troops against the last of the insurgents in the central and north-eastern Delta. Naval battles on the Nile's branches brought the rebellion to an end.

A decade earlier, with his kingship challenged on every side, Ptolemy V had desperately needed opportunities to assert his legitimacy and authority. After the end of the Fifth Syrian War, his advisers decided to stage a spectacular coronation, not in Alexandria but in the traditional seat of pharaonic power, Memphis. The ceremony was personally conducted by the high priest of Ptah, who placed the double crown on the thirteen-year-old monarch's head on 27 March 196. The main entertainment at the coronation banquet was the public execution of the rebels from Lykopolis.

The following day, priests from around the country gathered in synod to pay homage to the king and issue a decree. It began in customary fashion, by lauding the monarch in traditional terms. A reference to the king conquering his enemies, though a stock phrase in such inscriptions, would have struck a particular chord with the audience, given the insurgency in Lower Egypt and the rebellion in Upper Egypt. The bulk of the decree comprised a lengthy recitation of the king's acts of munificence towards the temples, especially those of Memphis. Particular praise was heaped upon Ptolemy V for his piety towards the sacred bull Apis. The text also recalled the recent siege of Lykopolis and how the king punished the ringleaders 'in a fitting way'.[9]

In recognition of Ptolemy's pious deeds, the priests ordered that a statue of the king should be installed in every major temple in the land; each statue would depict Ptolemy being handed the sword of victory by the temple's resident deity. More royal statues would be placed in temple sanctuaries. The shrines containing the statues of the king would be decorated with ten gold crowns, each bearing the rearing cobra (Gr. *uraeus*) that symbolised pharaonic authority; and private citizens would be encouraged to have replicas of this shrine in their homes, as a sign of their loyalty. The king's birthday and coronation day would henceforth be celebrated as religious festivals; and every priest in the land would, in addition to their main role, become a priest of Ptolemy V, with a hieroglyphic inscription to this effect engraved on their ring of office.

Finally, the inscription stated that a copy of the decree itself would be placed in every temple 'of the first, second and third division' – in other words, not just the major temples, but even relatively small shrines – with the text set down in 'the writing of the divine words, the writing of documents, and the writing of the Ionians': hieroglyphic, demotic and Greek. Despite these provisions, only one substantially complete copy of the Decree of Memphis survived, to be discovered in AD 1799 by Napoleon's soldiers while fortifying a citadel to the east of Alexandria. Today, the Decree of Memphis is better known as the Rosetta Stone – the key to the decipherment of hieroglyphics and the founding document of Egyptology.

The priests who gathered at Memphis for the coronation and synod would have encountered a place still steeped in pharaonic tradition but with a distinct Hellenistic overlay. Most visitors arrived by river. On an island in the Nile there was an army camp – to maintain government control – while the riverbank was dominated by the royal dockyards and the port of Memphis, complete with its customs house. Nearby, the Nilometer of Memphis was of national significance, serving as the official measure of the height of the annual inundation, the datum from which agricultural yields were predicted and tax calculations were made. Near the water's edge there was a bustling marketplace where wares from across Egypt were bought and sold.

Behind the wharves and quays, the city occupied a series of hillocks, with views over the surrounding plain. In the bustling residential areas, markets and street-food vendors brought noise and colour, and the air would have been pungent with the smell rising from rubbish dumps and open sewers. As a break from the grittier realities of life, Memphis' wealthier, Greek-speaking inhabitants could enjoy trips to the theatre or gymnasium before retreating to their comfortable villas behind sturdy bronze gates to keep out *hoi polloi*.

Dominating the city to the north was the palace quarter, some of its crumbling buildings dating back a thousand years to the reign of Ramesses II. A later pharaoh had built his own spectacular residence in a particularly commanding position, but this too had seen better days. So the Ptolemies had constructed their own palace where Ptolemy V's coronation was held; a nearby garrison ensured the king's safety.

Beyond the palaces, on the well-watered plain, there were royal gardens, orchards and vineyards.

If north Memphis was reserved for royalty, south Memphis was for the gods. Indeed, to the casual visitor, Memphis was overwhelmingly a city of temples. Dominating the southern sector was the sacred precinct of Ptah. Covering an area of fifty acres, with monumental gateways in each of its four walls, it comprised an array of pylons, courts, ceremonial halls and sanctuaries, together with stalls, exercise yard and embalming house for the Apis bull and its divine mother. There were also special areas for rearing sacred animals, and others for bullfights; in one enclosure grew a special tree under which sat a sacred baboon. The temple of Ptah was the largest place of worship in Memphis, but by no means the only one. Other deities with their own sanctuaries included Astarte (an Asiatic war goddess) and the Greek gods Herakles and Zeus. Multi-faith provision for a multicultural city.

Indeed, the different residential quarters were characterised by different ethnic groups, and were often walled for protection. The immigrant community with the deepest roots was from Karia in south-western Anatolia. Because the Karomemphites had been in Egypt longer than any other group, they were especially valued by later migrants as a source of local knowledge. Familiar with the strange customs and mores of the Nile Valley, Karians played a key role as interpreters of Egypt to its Greek-speaking Macedonian conquerors and their allies. With a privileged position among the capital city's different communities, the Karomemphites prospered under the early Ptolemies; their quarter was to the north of the city, surrounded by verdant parks and gardens.

A second group, which could likewise trace its origins back to the sixth century, was that of the Hellenomemphites, descendants of the Ionian merchants who had first established the trading colony at Naukratis. The Hellenomemphite quarter was centrally located and had its own shrine, the Hellenion, dedicated to 'Zeus the king' (Gr. *Zeus basileus*).

The early Karian and Ionian settlers assimilated relatively quickly, marrying Egyptian women and adopting some Egyptian customs. By contrast, migrants from coastal Phoenicia retained their distinctive identity, which was constantly reinforced by waves of new immigrants from Koile-Syria. Known as Phoenico-Egyptians, they lived in a southern quarter of Memphis, adjacent to the temple of Astarte. Like other immigrant groups, their religion helped reinforce their sense of community. The year before Ptolemy V's coronation, a Syrian resin seller was recorded living up on the necropolis: providing unguents to the 'death industry' was probably his main livelihood. Phoenicians, for their part, seem to have maintained their connections with shipping and commerce. Also from the Levant, Jews had served as garrison troops in Egypt for over a century. At Memphis they had their own synagogue and cemetery.

While Egypt's traditional capital was thus a melting pot of peoples and cultures, the tensions between the country's rulers and its native inhabitants remained – no matter how much effort and treasure the court expended on lavish ceremonies, royal statues and annual festivals honouring the king.

At his accession, Ptolemy V had followed family tradition by adopting a cult title. His father had been 'father-loving', his grandfather 'the benefactor'. The young king's advisers, more in hope than expectation, chose for him Epiphanes ('manifest'). The title sought to appeal to the monarch's Greek-speaking supporters while also resonating with his Egyptians subjects, for whom the notion of the king as god incarnate was as old as pharaonic civilisation itself. The problem was, from the very start of Ptolemy V's reign, the only thing that was manifest was the disintegration of royal authority, at home and abroad.

The plain truth was that the Ptolemaic empire had overreached itself. Territories beyond Egypt had been hard-won; but they required an enormous effort, a strong military and vast amounts of money to keep them within the Ptolemaic ambit. When times were good and the monarch capable, the empire could be held together. But without economic prosperity or dynastic stability at home, it was an impossible task. The pharaohs of old had discovered the same harsh truth, and an Egyptian empire had waxed and waned over the centuries. The Ptolemies faced the added challenge of complex geopolitics in the eastern Mediterranean: three Hellenistic kingdoms (Ptolemaic, Seleukid and Macedonian) vying for supremacy, and a fourth power, Rome, aiming for world domination.

The Second Macedonian War ended with a peace treaty which dealt a mortal blow to Macedon's designs for territorial expansion and confirmed Roman power in the Aegean. After the Battle of Paneion, when it was clear that Ptolemaic forces had lost all hope of regaining Koile-Syria, Rome intervened to prevent an over-mighty Seleukid empire. In the very year of Ptolemy V's coronation, the Roman senate sent an envoy, Lucius Cornelius Lentulus, to Syria to mediate between the Egyptian and Seleukid monarchs. The ancient rites at Memphis were thus exposed as hollow theatre, for the pharaoh was now being represented in diplomatic negotiations by a foreign power. Slowly but surely, Egypt was being drawn into Rome's suffocating embrace.

As we have seen, Antiochos asserted his independence by giving his daughter in marriage to Ptolemy V, thus cementing relations between the two rival kingdoms and leaving Rome out in the cold. Emboldened, the Seleukid ruler turned his eyes to the Aegean and, declaring himself the 'champion of Greek freedom against Roman domination', waged a four-year war against Rome to win back control of mainland Greece for the heirs of Alexander. Ptolemy V sought to take advantage of the situation and sent his own embassy to Rome, offering Ptolemaic support for an all-out war against Antiochos III – hoping, no doubt, to recover some of the territories lost in the Fifth Syrian War. But Rome was supremely uninterested. The Republic could fight its own battles, and had no wish to see the Ptolemaic kingdom in the ascendant.

The eventual Roman victory ended Seleukid domination in Anatolia for good, and the Ptolemaic claims in the region were not even raised for discussion. The former Ptolemaic possessions of Ephesos, Lykia and Karia were awarded to Rome's supporters, and Rome itself became the ultimate arbiter of Hellenistic fortunes.

The remainder of Ptolemy V's reign was a story of managed decline. Cleaving to pharaonic traditions seems to have become his policy of last resort. A second proclamation was issued at Memphis to celebrate the enthronement of a new Apis bull. Predictably, the text confirmed the income of the temples and reduced their taxes; but the most striking aspect was the prominence given to Ptolemy V's wife. Her name was a new one to the Ptolemaic royal family: Cleopatra (Gr. *kleopatra*, 'glory of her father'). The wedding took place at Raphia, on the border of the Ptolemaic and Seleukid kingdoms whose royal houses were being united by the match. For Ptolemy V, the location must have been bittersweet: the site of his father's great victory over the Seleukids was now playing host to a ceremony marking his own defeat. Nonetheless, he took his new queen into the bosom of the royal house, granting her the status that earlier Ptolemaic consorts had enjoyed. For example, a proclamation of 185 lauded her in appropriate terms: 'The queen, Lady of the Two Lands, Cleopatra ... gave presents of silver, gold and precious stones in great quantity for the other statues of the goddesses of Egypt, making sacrifices and pouring libations, and the rest of the ceremonies performed in the temples of the gods and goddesses of Egypt.' As always, there was an expectation of a quid pro quo:

> In return for these things, all the gods and goddesses of Egypt have granted many years of might, strength, life, welfare and health to the King of Upper and Lower Egypt, the Son of Ra, Ptolemy (may he live for ever, beloved of Ptah), and to ... Cleopatra: the two Gods Manifest establishing their kingdom in the whole land, with their dignity consolidated for them and their children for ever.[10]

It was a vain hope; but Cleopatra, at least, would fulfil the weight of expectation placed upon her. And her name would be adopted as a talisman by future Ptolemaic queens – right down to the last.

7

The Hinge of Fate

Ptolemy V was a singularly ill-fated monarch. From his troubled accession to his untimely death – in the spring of 180, aged just thirty – his time on the throne was marred by revolution and intrigue. Fate followed him to the last, his grisly end brought about by a poisoner's cup. His army generals, it was rumoured, had acted to stop him carrying out a threat to sequester the assets of his wealthier subjects to finance a hare-brained scheme to regain Koile-Syria. The loss of the Ptolemaic territories in Asia had overshadowed the whole of his reign; it was perhaps inevitable that a desperate bid to reclaim them should have cost him his life. As a result, Egypt found itself, for the second time in two decades, with a boy pharaoh. The new monarch, Ptolemy VI, was a mere six-year-old – the same age as his father when *he* had acceded to the throne. The court at Alexandria, and the country at large, braced itself for another bout of dynastic turmoil.

The difference this time around lay in the personality of the dowager queen. Where Arsinoe III had succumbed to an assassin's dagger within hours of her husband's demise, Cleopatra I was sufficiently popular – and wily – to survive and prevail. She quickly emerged as the unchallenged regent for her young son, though aged just twenty-four herself. She exercised sole power on behalf of the crown, the first Ptolemaic queen to do so. To reinforce her authority, she had coins minted bearing her own name and image. She also forged her own foreign policy, ending hostilities with the Seleukid kingdom (now ruled by her half-brother, Seleukos IV) to bring about a period of relative calm and stability after decades of conflict. Cleopatra's hand may likewise be detected in the appointment of a new military governor of Cyprus. With the recent loss of Koile-Syria, Thrace and the Ptolemaic territories in Anatolia, Cyprus had gained a new importance as the dynasty's sole significant possession in the eastern Mediterranean. Its strategic, economic and commercial value rose accordingly, and there was an imperative to maximise Cypriot revenues flowing into the coffers at Alexandria. According to a later commentator, the new governor 'was gifted with good sense and ability. For having taken charge of the island when the king [Ptolemy VI] was still an infant, he applied himself diligently to the collection of revenue'.[1]

Cleopatra I set a precedent, establishing the right and qualifications of female members of the Ptolemaic dynasty to rule in their own right. But her prominence did not come out of the blue. Almost from the start, the Ptolemies promoted their wives and daughters, unlike the other Hellenistic monarchs whose kingdoms remained resolutely male-dominated (although Antiochos III was accompanied by his wife, Laodike, at the Battle of Raphia). Berenike I, the third wife of Ptolemy I, was formally incorporated into her late husband's dynastic cult upon her own death, and was granted her own shrine in Alexandria, the Berenikeion. Ptolemy II lavished similar attention on his mistresses. Statues of one were placed in the temples of Alexandria, while his favourite mistress, Belistiche, was formally identified with Aphrodite and given her own sanctuaries. He went even further for his sister-wife, Arsinoe II. Her posthumous honours included her own throne name (the official regnal name adopted by a sovereign upon their accession) and her own priesthood, held at times by the High Priest of Ptah at Memphis. In the reign of Ptolemy III, the queen consort, Berenike II, became the first Ptolemaic spouse to receive a royal titulary in her own lifetime. In demotic documents, she was accordingly described as 'the female pharaoh' (Eg. *ta peraat*). Her daughter, meanwhile, was posthumously deified and, like her grandmother, installed in every place of worship throughout the land as a 'temple-sharing goddess'.

Both the Greek and Egyptian religions found it easy to accommodate female deities. Arsinoe II, for example, was identified by Greeks with Hera, Demeter and Aphrodite, and by Egyptians as Isis. In other ways, too, the two cultures of Ptolemaic Egypt were accustomed to honouring prominent royal women: in the Hellenistic tradition by founding eponymous cities and festivals; in the Egyptian by emulating royal nomenclature (the Egyptian priestly families of Memphis frequently named their daughters Arsinoe or Berenike). But the distinctive prominence of Ptolemaic women, in the political as well as the cultic realm, reflected above all the native Egyptian milieu.

Pharaonic Egypt had been ruled by its first queen regent as far back as the beginning of the third millennium, and by its first queen regnant in the middle of the second.[2] Female pharaohs may have been the exception, but the eighteenth dynasty in particular, at the height of Egypt's golden age, had been characterised by a series of powerful royal wives who exercised considerable political and religious authority alongside their husbands. The concept of a powerful 'king's great wife' was thus both familiar and reassuring to the Ptolemies' Egyptian subjects. So too was a prominent role for women in daily life. Since the dawn of history, Egyptian women had held temple offices, dominated certain industries (notably the manufacture of linen) and run their households. An Egyptian didactic text from the eighteenth dynasty had advised its (male) readers, 'Do not control your wife in her house... Let your eye observe in silence and you will see her skill.'[3] Egyptian women likewise enjoyed greater legal equality than their counterparts in any other civilisation of the ancient world. They retained control of their own property even after marriage, could divorce or testify against their husbands, and could dispose of their wealth as they saw fit.

These long-held freedoms survived Macedonian domination unscathed, helped by the fact that Macedonian tradition imposed fewer restrictions on women than other Greek cultures. Egyptian women continued to serve in the temples of their native deities. In the cult of the cat goddess Bastet, for example, a particular office reserved for a woman was that of 'cat's wet-nurse', responsible for feeding the sacred cats with bread and milk. A third-century papyrus from the Arsinoite nome (the Fayum) refers to associations formed by local women to help share the costs of mummification and participating in religious activities. Women served as necropolis attendants and mortuary priests, and could buy, sell, inherit and bequeath these lucrative offices. So sure were Egyptian women of their rights, they did not hesitate to assert them, even in the face of a male-dominated, Greek-speaking bureaucracy. A papyrus dated July 256 records the complaint – terse and angry – of an Egyptian widow complaining to the local Greek bigwig (Zenon) that another Greek official had confiscated her donkey, preventing her from transporting her beehives to the best meadowland. The widow pointed out to Zenon that, if the donkey were not returned forthwith, the royal treasury, and therefore the king himself, would suffer. This was not the sort of behaviour associated with Greek women, but it was ingrained in the Egyptian character. And, slowly but surely, it began to infiltrate the whole of Ptolemaic society.

The change revealed itself most clearly in the arena of marriage. Nuptial contracts drawn up in demotic, between native Egyptians, maintained the pharaonic legal tradition. Thus, in one such document inscribed at Thebes in 226, the husband promised, in the event of a divorce, to hand back to his wife all the belongings she had brought into the marriage (a shawl, a coat and a cloak, several bronze and silver items, some jewellery and two beds) – and a third of all *his* property as well. By contrast, a marriage contract from Elephantine, dated to 311, written in Greek and drawn up between two Greek-speaking immigrants, followed the practice current in the Greek world, giving a dominant role to the bride's father. True, the old Greek inhibitions preventing a man marrying a woman from another city had been forced to give way (the husband in question was from Temnos in Anatolia, his wife from the island of Kos), yet none of the contract's clauses showed any sign of Egyptian influence.[4] Within a few generations, however, local mores had started to spread through the settler population. In a marriage contract from Krokodilopolis, drawn up in the reign of Ptolemy VI, a Macedonian woman asserted her right to give herself away, instead of being given away by her father. Slowly but surely, greater legal independence of women over their own and their children's affairs spread among the non-native population.

The political power exercised by Cleopatra I was thus a distinctive and quintessential characteristic of Ptolemaic society, reflecting the enduring influence (and conscious exploitation) of pharaonic traditions and setting Egypt apart from other Hellenistic kingdoms. The Romans would later characterise the authority wielded by successive queens as symbolic of the Ptolemies' oriental decadence. But in reality, affording such agency to kings' mothers, wives and sisters represented a pragmatic response to political necessity – occasioned by the habit of Ptolemaic rulers of dying young – while also bolstering the Macedonian dynasty's credentials in the eyes of its Egyptian subjects. From the start, the Ptolemies were adept at using and modifying traditions to construct an identity that would legitimise them in the eyes of their multicultural and multi-ethnic subjects. In the case of queenly authority, pharaonic precedent was enthusiastically embraced.

By deploying ideology in support of political expediency, Cleopatra I succeeded in stabilising the Ptolemaic kingdom at a moment of great peril. At the accession of an underage sovereign, she averted another bout of internecine bloodletting. But her regency – her steadying hand – was to last just four years. Her death in the spring of 176 robbed the kingdom of its steadying influence. Ptolemaic history had a habit of repeating itself, and, true to form, two courtiers emerged as Ptolemy VI's new guardians. Neither was particularly prepossessing, or likely to deliver strong and stable government. Lenaios was a former slave; he had come to Alexandria from Syria, probably as part of Cleopatra I's retinue on her marriage to Ptolemy V. He took charge of the government's finances. His colleague, Eulaios, was a eunuch who had served as tutor to the young Ptolemy VI. As the more senior of the two co-regents, he lost no time in putting his own name on the copper and silver coinage.

Eunuch and former slave: the unlikely pair now running the country knew they had to take steps to establish and enhance their power. The easiest way to do this was to bolster the profile of their young charge, Ptolemy VI. So, early in 175, they announced the marriage of the ten-year-old king to his young sister, named Cleopatra after their mother. The regents hoped, no doubt, that this brother–sister union would remind Egyptians of the glory days of Ptolemy II and Arsinoe II. The new royal couple were formally incorporated into the Ptolemaic dynastic cult and given the joint title Theoi Philometores ('the mother-loving gods') in honour of the recently deceased Cleopatra I. When translated into ancient Egyptian, this title immediately recalled the archetypal mother–son relationship between Isis and Horus. The fact that Isis was perhaps the most popular native deity in Egypt – with increasing adherence among the Greek-speaking population, too – while Horus was the god of kingship, gave the metaphor an especially powerful resonance.

Lenaios and Eunaios had made a good start. But, as so often in Ptolemaic history, events beyond Egypt's borders soon threw the carefully laid plans into utter disarray. The cause of instability was, once again, the Seleukid kingdom. Ptolemy VI's uncle, Seleukos IV, had respected the entente with his sister, Cleopatra I, and for a while the two Hellenistic states were at peace. However, in September 175 he was murdered in a court conspiracy, plunging the empire into chaos. His eldest son and heir was in Rome as a hostage of the Republic, while his younger son, Antiochos, was a boy of five. Sensing an opportunity, the boys' uncle made haste to Syria and had himself proclaimed king as Antiochos IV. There followed months of conflict between the opposing camps, with Antiochos IV eventually emerging as the winner.

The turmoil in Syria prompted the hawks in the Ptolemaic administration to urge all-out war with the intention of regaining Koile-Syria, the loss of which still smarted. The regents were either complicit or powerless to resist these calls. By 172, preparations for military action were well under way. Meanwhile, the third Hellenistic kingdom, Macedon, was embroiled in a simmering conflict of its own. Its ruler, Perseus, harboured similar ambitions to restore his forefathers' territories; in Macedon's case, Rome was the main obstacle. Perseus set about stoking anti-Roman sentiment, in an attempt to win friends and allies for his cause. But Rome had no intention of allowing mainland Greece to turn against it. Before Perseus could muster an effective coalition, Rome declared war on Macedon in 171. The ensuing conflict, dubbed the Third Macedonian War (171–168), raged mostly in Macedon itself and neighbouring Thessaly. An early battle, fought near the Thessalian capital, saw the two rival armies, their cavalries matched almost man for man, fight to a stalemate. With Rome thus preoccupied defending its Greek interests, and unlikely to intervene in any wider conflict, the Ptolemaic government decided that the time was ripe to launch an attack on the Seleukid kingdom.

The Ptolemaic regents were no military strategists, but they were adept when it came to propaganda. As they readied the country for a costly foreign war, they implemented a series of extraordinary measures to reinforce their legitimacy and prepare the public mood.

First, in September 170, they promoted Ptolemy VI's younger brother and namesake to the status of co-monarch with his two siblings. The kingdom was now under the joint reign of 'Ptolemy, Ptolemy the brother, and Cleopatra the sister'. Such a move was unprecedented, even in the strange world of Ptolemaic dynastic politics, and may hint at an attempt to reconcile opposing court factions. If so, it did not convince everybody: a petition by the priests of Isis at Aswan, dated 17 September 170, promised offerings for 'the pharaoh, his sister and his brother';[5] the word 'sister' is accompanied by the hieroglyphic sign for a deity, the word 'brother' is not. The regents' next move was to announce a new era, to recognise both the triple monarchy and Egypt's claim to Koile-Syria. A legal contract from the village of Philadelpheia in the Arsinoite nome, drawn up on 12 November, used the prescribed new dating formula, referencing Year 1 of the triple monarchy instead of Year 12 of Ptolemy VI. Finally, Ptolemy VI himself, now sixteen, was declared an adult and celebrated his formal coming-of-age. In theory, he was now ruling in his own right; in practice, Lenaios and Eunaios continued to exercise control. They would lead the Ptolemaic kingdom, not to past glories, but to the brink of extinction.

In the second half of November 170, the Egyptian army set out for Syria; but the enemy was ready, its position better defended and its supply lines better prepared. The two forces met in the shadow of Mount Kasion, near Pelousion on Egypt's north-eastern border. In a swift and decisive encounter, the Ptolemaic forces were utterly defeated, their rout so comprehensive that further military engagement was considered futile. A ceasefire was declared, and Antiochos IV took possession of Pelousion – a key port and entrepot as well as a frontier fortress. This gave him and his army unfettered access to Egypt, and they swiftly occupied much of the Delta.

The repercussions in Alexandria were serious and immediate. Eunaios was said to have attempted to send Ptolemy VI into exile on the Greek island of Samothrace, together with the contents of the royal treasury. But, if true, the plot failed. The hapless Lenaios and Eunaios were dismissed from the government, and were heard of no more. Their places were taken by two distinguished citizens of Alexandria named Komanos and Kineas, who, recognising the weakness of their hand, opened negotiations with the invaders. One immediate step was to drop the charade of a new era, reverting to the dates of Ptolemy VI's reign. This is likely to have been a signal of goodwill towards the Seleukids, for whom any implicit claim to Koile-Syria amounted to a declaration of war. Meanwhile, Antiochos IV sought to strengthen his position within Egypt by winning over the Greek-speaking city of Naukratis. By early 169, Seleukid forces were advancing towards Alexandria itself.

Ptolemy VI, perhaps in an attempt to assert his independence, left the city to meet Antiochos IV. The two rulers – uncle and nephew – negotiated an agreement which proclaimed their mutual friendship. In practice, however, the arrangement reduced Ptolemy to little more than a puppet ruler. The ambiguity of his position is demonstrated by a papyrus document from the time which records an order for the delivery of barley. The destination of the supplies is given as 'the camp with the King' rather than the usual 'the King's camp'. Was Ptolemy VI king or not? Nobody seemed quite sure.

When news of the pact filtered back to Alexandria, its citizens did what they did best, and rioted. Komanos and Kineas rejected Ptolemy VI's settlement outright, and declared his younger brother and co-ruler to be the sole king (with Cleopatra II still at his side). Antiochos, masquerading as Ptolemy VI's protector, responded by placing Alexandria under siege. However, the city was well provisioned and able to hold out for many months.

In the summer of 169, the government sent an embassy to Rome asking it to intervene. Rome vacillated, preoccupied with the fight against Perseus of Macedon. In September, Antiochos was forced to return to Syria to deal with his own domestic issues, and his army withdrew back to Pelousion. In the ensuing peace, Ptolemy VI and his brother were briefly reconciled, and the triple monarchy restored. Egypt was calm once more; but it was the calm before the storm.

With Antiochos gone from their midst, the reunited government in Alexandria repudiated the agreement that Ptolemy VI had made, and started to recruit new troops from Greece. Instead of piling the pressure on Antiochos, this merely enraged him further. The following spring, the Seleukid army captured Cyprus and invaded Egypt for a second time, occupying much of the Delta and the rich farmlands of the Fayum. Now, there was no pretence of defending the interests of Ptolemy VI: Antiochos made straight for Memphis, where he was crowned pharaoh. He then marched on Alexandria. Nothing, it seemed, would now stand in the way of uniting the Seleukid and Ptolemaic realms under his crown.

The move galvanised Rome into action. The Republic's policy towards the Ptolemaic and Seleukid kingdoms was one of divide and rule. Unification, whether by diplomacy or conquest, was unconscionable. When the Roman army defeated Perseus at the Battle of Pydna, bringing Macedonian independence to an end, it was able to turn its attention fully to events unfolding in Egypt.

If Antiochos believed that his neutrality in the Third Macedonian War would win him favour with Rome, he could not have been more wrong. At the start of July, as he crossed the Nile branch at Eleusis, about four miles east of Alexandria, he was met by an envoy from the Roman senate, Caius Popilius Laenas. The Seleukid monarch held out his hand in friendly greeting; in response, Popilius extended not his own hand but the tablets bearing the senate's decree. He told Antiochos to read it. The king, seeing which way the wind was blowing, stalled for time, saying that he would summon his council and consider his answer. But Popilius, stern and imperious as ever, made an astonishing move: with the stick he was carrying, he drew a circle around the king and said, 'Before you step out of that circle give me a reply to lay before the senate.' Antiochos, astounded by such peremptory behaviour, is said to have hesitated for a few moments, before conceding, 'I will do what the senate thinks right.'[6] Only then did Popilius extend his hand to the king. Antiochos evacuated his forces from Egypt on 30 July 168. At Popilius' command, Ptolemy VI and his brother were formally reconciled. The Roman embassy then went to Cyprus to oversee the removal of the Seleukid army and restore Ptolemaic authority.

Breathing a huge sigh of relief, the government in Alexandria sent its own envoy, Numenios, to Rome to thank the senate for its decisive intervention. The report of his trip, written ten years later in demotic, has the distinction of being the oldest surviving reference to the city of Rome in an Egyptian text. But, in reality, the Ptolemies had little to be thankful for: the 'Day of Eleusis', as it came to be known, was an utter humiliation for a once-great kingdom. Where Ptolemaic armies had failed to save their country from foreign annexation, a mere Roman envoy had succeeded. To make matters worse, Antiochos' invasion had sparked a native revolt, as Egyptian nationalists once again saw a chance to overthrow the rule of a Greek-speaking, culturally Greek dynasty. This resulted in large areas of productive land being abandoned, weakening Egypt's agricultural economy and rendering the government ever more dependent on foreign support. A private letter dated 29 August 168, less than a month after Antiochos' departure from Egypt, refers to 'times like these': for the population at large, the invasion and its aftermath ushered in a period of profound unease.[7]

The Day of Eleusis represented a decisive shift in the geopolitics of the entire ancient world. By brokering the end of the Ptolemaic-Seleukid dispute, a rivalry that dated back to the death of Alexander, Rome had asserted its right to intervene in the future of both kingdoms, and to arbitrate in internal dynastic matters as well. The core of Alexander's empire, Macedon, had ceased to exist, divided into four client republics subservient to Rome. The two remaining Hellenistic kingdoms had been humbled and would never again try to assert hegemony in the eastern Mediterranean. Each of the first five Syrian Wars had ended to the advantage of either the Ptolemies or the Seleukids. The sixth and last ended to the detriment of both.

Antiochos IV's invasion and subsequent proclamation as pharaoh dealt a massive blow to the Ptolemaic institution of kingship. Ever since Ptolemy I had elevated himself from satrap to sovereign, the ruler's legitimacy had depended on satisfying two different concepts of monarchy. For native Egyptians, the time-honoured role of the pharaoh was to protect the people, honour the gods, and act as interlocutor between humanity and divinity. For the Ptolemies' Greek-speaking subjects, kingship drew its status from feats of arms and displays of magnificence. The events of 168 robbed Ptolemy VI of his credibility on both fronts: his pharaonic status had been openly challenged while his military weakness was made clear for all to see. To make matters worse, the resulting socio-economic dislocation depleted the Treasury's reserves, severely restricting the king's ability to put on elaborate shows of wealth. The court's response was to seek other ways of projecting the king's status, looking back over the previous century and a half of Macedonian rule for inspiration.

Alexander the Great had created a personal kingship – to the horror of some of his Greek subjects, for whom monarchy was a throwback to a barbarian past – by the sheer magnitude of his military conquests. He projected a 'charismatic invincibility' and his spear-won territory, stretching from North Africa to India, gave him the right to bear the title *basileus*. His royal status depended upon success as 'saviour, liberator, protector, begetter and guarantor of fertility and abundance',[8] qualities that were consciously adopted and promoted by the first two Ptolemies. They protected and enlarged their realm, defended their allies, and made very public donations to Greek cities and shrines. Their adoption of Dionysiac iconography equated the monarch with the god of wine, fertility and abundance. In Greek eyes, a king's wealth was the basis and demonstration of his success. Ptolemy III even adopted the epithet Tryphon ('the magnificent') to emphasise the point.

The dawn of the Hellenistic Age ushered in a growing scepticism about the old Olympian gods. In their place, people turned to human heroes. The fourth century witnessed a proliferation of ruler cults, with a particular focus on the founders of cities. Not for nothing did Alexander give his name to his new port city on the north coast of Egypt, and to a host of other foundations across his empire. Ptolemy I followed suit, most notably with the city of Ptolemais in Upper Egypt, which was intended from the outset to replace Thebes as the regional capital. In due course, the Fayum was renamed the Arsinoite nome, while any number of settlements named after Berenike were established, not least in the eastern desert.

Ptolemy I succeeded in having his cult established in locations throughout the eastern Mediterranean, from Rhodes to Delos; Byzantion would subsequently pay a similar honour to Ptolemy II, and Athens to Ptolemy III. But the Ptolemies' primary mechanism for securing divine status in the eyes of their Greek-speaking subjects was to associate themselves with Alexander. The removal of Alexander's body from Memphis to Alexandria sought to suffuse the entire Ptolemaic capital with the divine hero's aura; another innovation was to elevate Alexander to a state god and his eponymous priest to pre-eminence among the clergy. The priesthood of Alexander was reserved for Macedonians and Greeks of high social status; one of the first holders of the office was Ptolemy I's own brother, Menelaos.

The ruler cult would, in time, be transformed into the central element in the Ptolemaic conception of Greek kingship. It elevated the institution of *basileus* to a theological plane, strengthening the legitimacy of each successive king by associating him with his illustrious forebears. Ptolemy II saw the potency of the institution, adding the living royal couple (himself and his sister-wife Arsinoe II) to the cult of Alexander. The priest of Alexander was henceforth known as 'the priest of Alexander and the brother–sister gods'. In the following reign Ptolemy III and his wife Berenike II had themselves incorporated into the cult, and the priestly title was further extended in recognition. Private individuals now started to make donations to the ruling couple, alongside established deities such as Isis and Sarapis. Ptolemy IV completed the set-up by adding Ptolemy I and Berenike I, so that all the ruling couples since the birth of the dynasty were now formally part of the ruler cult, starting with Alexander and ending with the current king and queen.

It is no coincidence that Ptolemy IV should have sought to assert the legitimacy and continuity of his dynasty just as its political power was starting to wane. Even though subsequent sovereigns and their spouses were added to the ruler cult, the dynastic gods were invoked less often by private individuals, who detected declining levels of divinity in an increasingly powerless and pathetic series of monarchs. Ptolemy V added himself to the ruler cult in 199/8, and Cleopatra I shortly after their marriage. But without military victories or displays of wealth, the credibility of the ruler suffered irreparable damage.

A different approach, also pioneered by Ptolemy IV in the face of political decline, was to emphasise his dynasty's direct link with Alexander by reburying the hero (for the third time) in a new mausoleum (the Soma), erected within the palace precinct at Alexandria. The building was also intended to serve as the final resting place of the Ptolemaic monarchs. Rather tellingly, the mausoleum was given a superstructure in the shape of a pyramid. The Battle of Raphia and its aftermath marked a decisive shift in the balance between the two Ptolemaic concepts of kingship: as the king's role as *basileus* started to wane, so his position as pharaoh was deliberately promoted.

The invention and promulgation of the cult of Sarapis (Osiris-Apis) had been intended to bridge the theological gap between

Greek-speaking and native Egyptian subjects. In practice, the new deity proved more popular with the former group. The indigenous inhabitants of the Nile Valley had enough gods of their own, with distinctly longer pedigrees, and showed little interest in the Greek gods. Alexander had instinctively recognised the power of pharaonic religion, and had gone out of his way to honour the traditional cults, from Apis of Memphis to Amun of Luxor. The Ptolemies regularly made donations to Egyptian deities. The restitution to the native temples of lands and statues confiscated or plundered by the Persians was a particular cause célèbre. Ptolemy III claimed to have returned up to 2,500 cult images from his foreign expedition, while the fourth Ptolemy asserted that he had concluded the search for stolen sacred statues and had brought back to Egypt any he could still find. Not only did such actions resonate with the powerful Egyptian priesthood, they also reminded the native population that the Macedonians had delivered the Nile Valley from the hated Persians.

Thus did the Ptolemies start to present themselves, not merely as guardians of the Egyptian pantheon, but as fully paid-up members. By the reign of Ptolemy V, the continued prestige of the monarchy had come to rely on the blessings of the native priesthoods, not victory in war. So, while earlier gatherings of priests had taken place at the Greek foundations of Alexandria (in 243) and Kanopos (in 238), Ptolemy V called his clergy together at Egypt's ancient capital. The Decree of Memphis (Rosetta Stone) represented not so much a transcendent, authoritative monarchy but a bargain struck by two parties who each needed the other. From now on, synods would be summoned to ratify all important royal decisions.

Ptolemy VI may have been honoured by the citizens of Athens with a bronze equestrian statue on the Acropolis; but closer to home, in the aftermath of foreign invasion, native insurrection and diplomatic humiliation, he turned to Egyptian rather than Hellenistic ideology to repair his tattered royal credentials. He and his sister Cleopatra II made annual visits to Memphis to coincide with the New Year festival, during which Ptolemy would personally carry out the rituals expected of a pharaoh. The iconography of his reign similarly drew on pharaonic precedent, albeit in a peculiarly Ptolemaic fashion. One of the most famous surviving images of Ptolemy VI is on a gold signet ring, currently in the Louvre. The carefully engraved royal portrait shows him in profile with the prominent nose and jutting chin so characteristic of his dynasty. He sports the sideburns and curly locks of a Greek hero and the double crown of an Egyptian king, while the twin streamers of Macedonian royalty flutter around his shoulders. This conscious blending of attributes reflects the complex, fluid relationship between a Ptolemaic king and his subjects. Balancing two very different conceptions of kingship was a constant challenge.

After the withdrawal of Seleukid forces in July 168, Egypt returned to a fragile peace. The Day of Eleusis brought two unexpected developments, one of immediate benefit to the Ptolemaic regime, the other of lasting significance for the history of Egypt.

Ptolemy VI was able to reassert control over the northern stretch of the Nubian Nile Valley, the Dodekaschoinos, between the First and Second Cataracts. This brought tribute from local Nubian leaders, providing a welcome boost to the royal treasury. Some of the additional revenue was subsequently granted to the temples on Philae, to keep them loyal. To secure Ptolemaic control, two new military colonies, named Philometris and Cleopatra in honour of Ptolemy VI and his sister, were founded in Lower Nubia, and the region as a whole was placed under the control of the military commander of Upper Egypt. It is even possible that elephant-hunting expeditions resumed, to replenish the Ptolemaic army after recent heavy losses. For a time, a restoration of rule south of the First Cataract promised a return to happier, more prosperous times.

A second development likewise benefited the military establishment. Antiochos IV, returning to his homeland after the humiliation at Eleusis, vented his fury against his domestic opponents. In particular, he launched a sustained campaign against the Jews, suspecting them of disloyalty. But an attack on their temple in Jerusalem only succeeded in provoking a major uprising. The Maccabean Revolt (167–160) prompted a wave of emigration, as Jews fled persecution and unrest; many of them headed for Egypt, where their kin had long served in the army. The leader of the main group of refugees was a man named Onias IV, son of the high priest whom Antiochos IV had deposed. On arrival in Egypt, Onias and his sons were given important positions in the military and became influential figures at court. His followers were allowed to settle in the Delta city of Leontopolis, and to build a temple to Yahweh there, with Onias as its high priest. (Leontopolis is still known today as Tell el-Yahudiya, 'mound of the Jews'.) In Alexandria, Jewish inhabitants had their own quarter, complete with synagogues, and Ptolemy VI granted them their own self-governing community. Indeed, the king seems to have taken a particular interest in Jewish literature: an exegesis of the book of Moses by the philosopher Aristoboulos was dedicated to Ptolemy VI. The Jews of Alexandria would remain a significant and influential group right down to modern times.

But even such advantageous developments merely papered over the cracks. The temporary truce between Ptolemy VI and his brother soon broke down, leading to renewed infighting at court. The appointment of Egyptians to high office, for the first time in several generations, was perhaps an attempt to bolster national unity, but it backfired spectacularly. In 165, one of this new cohort of Egyptian officials, a man named Dionysios Petosarapis, launched an attempted coup. In the main stadium of Alexandria, he announced to the crowd that Ptolemy VI was planning to assassinate his troublesome brother. Realising that this was an existential threat to their dynasty, the siblings put on a show of unity, appearing together in the stadium to reassure the populace. Dionysios fled Alexandria (to Eleusis, of all places), but not before he had persuaded some military units to mutiny.

The rebellion was snuffed out relatively quickly, but the unrest and uncertainty only exacerbated a calamitous situation in the countryside. Through years of conflict, faced with the possibility of conscription and the certainty of punitive taxation, farmers had abandoned their land in droves, often seeking sanctuary and employment in the temples as casual labourers. This flight from the countryside (Gr. *anachoresis*) had a major impact on government revenue; if left unchecked, it might lead to complete economic collapse. The state's response, in the late summer of 165 – before the start of the new sowing season – was to issue a royal decree. Entitled *On Agriculture*, it mandated the compulsory cultivation of abandoned land. Any field not voluntarily taken back into cultivation was simply assigned to a local inhabitant with the expectation of production. There was no right of refusal, and even soldiers were not exempt. A new branch of government, called the Special Account (Gr. *idios logos*), was set up to administer the estates that had automatically reverted to crown ownership due to abandonment.

These measures, though economically necessary, proved deeply unpopular. Native Egyptian soldiers complained bitterly, and the finance minister responded by watering down the regulations. But it was too little, too late. A rebellion broke out in the Thebaid, always the epicentre of native Egyptian sentiment; priests and Greek settlers were targeted as government collaborators. Rebels even looted a temple and burned the property deeds. Ptolemy VI's forces recaptured Thebes with little difficulty, but Panopolis further north only surrendered after a protracted siege.

Another symptom of the unrest and general lawlessness in the Nile Valley was an increase in attacks on river traffic by bands of outlaws. Egypt depended on shipping for transporting harvests from provincial depots to the state granaries, so no government could afford to ignore threats to riverine commerce. Ptolemy VI's response was to constitute groups of cleruchs as marines who patrolled the Nile in police boats. They were supplemented by river guards stationed at regular intervals along the Nile.

The native revolt and its aftermath seriously rattled the regime, and the simmering tensions between the king and his brother boiled over. The moment Ptolemy VI returned to Alexandria from Upper Egypt, his sibling made a decisive move against him. The details of exactly what happened remain murky, but the result was dramatic. Ptolemy VI fled the city, accompanied only by three slaves and a eunuch. He travelled first to Rome, but the Day of Eleusis would not be repeated: instead of assistance, Ptolemy received the cold shoulder. So he then travelled to the loyal province of Cyprus where he was soon joined by his sister. Their brother, the younger Ptolemy, ruled Egypt alone. (Somewhat confusingly, historians refer to him as Ptolemy VIII, because the individual once identified as Ptolemy VII has subsequently been revealed as a scholarly misunderstanding.)

The citizens of Alexandria were a powerful force for political change, but they were fickle friends. In the summer of 163, after barely a year of the new dispensation, they rioted against Ptolemy VIII. Now it was his turn to go into exile. Ptolemy VI was recalled from Cyprus and restored to power. To try to patch up the sibling rivalry within the royal family, and possibly under pressure from Rome, he awarded his brother Kyrenaika, and Cleopatra II was recognised as official joint monarch. The sibling sovereigns, now ruling as 'the pharaohs Ptolemy and Cleopatra', made their annual visit to Memphis at the new year. But there was still nervousness. Before setting off, Ptolemy sent a letter to the military commander of the city making it clear that he did not want to receive any legal complaints during his stay; moreover, fearing possible attacks, the commander ordered a search of the sacred precinct close to the royal palace.

To win native support, Ptolemy VI followed established precedent by holding a synod of priests and issuing a wide-ranging amnesty decree. But further instability was never far away. Ptolemy VIII was not content with Kyrenaika: he wanted Cyprus as well. He travelled to Rome to plead his case. This played into the senate's hands. As a later commentator tersely remarked, 'the Senate… wishing to make an effective partition of the kingdom for themselves, acceded to the request of the younger brother, which coincided with their own interests'.[9] It was the old tactic of divide and rule: 'availing themselves of the mistakes of others they effectively increase and build up their own power, at the same time doing a favour and appearing to confer a benefit'.[10]

Two Roman ambassadors were dispatched to accompany Ptolemy VIII – now officially a 'friend and ally' (Latin *amicus et socius*) of Rome – to Cyprus and enforce the transfer of power. Ptolemy VI, however, stalled for time and refused to concede. He knew full well that Rome was preoccupied with another imminent war against the Carthaginians, and unlikely to provide any practical assistance to his brother. The ambassadors, frustrated by the king's intransigence, returned to Rome. Cyprus remained loyal to Ptolemy VI.

Having gained the upper hand, he might have used his authority to restore stability and prosperity to Egypt; but that was not the Ptolemaic way. Instead, Ptolemy VI decided to involve himself in a scheme to destabilise the Seleukid kingdom. Antiochos IV had recently died on campaign, leaving the throne to his underage son, Antiochos V. The accession of a minor soon had Ptolemy VI facilitating the escape from captivity of his first cousin, Demetrios (eldest son and heir of Seleukos IV), who immediately returned to Syria to claim his throne. The boy-king Antiochos V was deposed, and for a brief moment it looked as if Ptolemy VI might benefit from his role as kingmaker. But once Demetrios had won recognition as sovereign, he soon reverted to type and began preparations for war – against his Ptolemaic backer.

As officials positioned themselves for the inevitable conflagration, the governor of Cyprus tried to sell the island to Demetrios for 500 talents. But his plot was uncovered and he hanged himself to avoid execution for treason.

The situation in the eastern Mediterranean was unravelling fast, and Rome was becoming increasingly anxious about its own interests. So, when Ptolemy VIII appealed once again to the senate in 154, having survived an assassination attempt which he blamed on his brother's agents, the Republic's politicians agreed to send troops, and five quinquiremes, to help Ptolemy VIII take Cyprus by force. The brothers' opposing forces met on the north coast of the island. The younger Ptolemy was captured and forced to accept terms of surrender: abandonment of his claim to Cyprus, exile in Kyrenaika and an annual payment of grain into the Alexandrian treasury.

Meanwhile, the Seleukid dynastic crisis, fomented by Ptolemy VI, had entered a new phase with the appearance of a third claimant to the throne, Alexander Balas. His origins are mysterious. While he purported to be a son of Antiochos IV, it is perhaps more likely that he was plucked from an obscure background and used as a puppet by forces opposed to Demetrios. It suited Ptolemy VI to support any destabilising influence, so he married his teenage daughter (Cleopatra Thea) to the pretender. Strengthened by the alliance, Alexander Balas succeeded in killing Demetrios, and consolidating his own position as monarch. As for Ptolemy VI, having strengthened his right to interfere in Seleukid affairs, he launched a full-scale invasion of Syria in 145. His troops met no resistance, the army of Alexander Balas believing they were friendly. Within a few months, Ptolemy VI succeeded in realising his life's ambition: to take back control of coastal Koile-Syria.

Things then turned messy. Alexander Balas, furious at Ptolemy's treachery, hatched a plan to kill him. The plot was discovered before it could be carried out, prompting Ptolemy to switch sides and back Demetrios' young son and namesake (Demetrios II). Ptolemy had Cleopatra Thea remarried to the new claimant and continued his northward march. After receiving the backing of several important cities, he was formally crowned king of Asia. A double dating system for royal documents equated Year 36 of Ptolemy's reign in Egypt with Year 1 of his reign in Asia. But he knew that Rome would not stand for such a public assertion of unification. Reluctantly, he dropped the title 'King of Egypt and King of Syria', and pledged to serve as a loyal tutor to the young Demetrios II.

After all the vicissitudes of the previous three decades, Ptolemy VI had restored his dynasty's fortunes, and, like his grandfather, could claim legitimacy as a *basileus*, as well as a pharaoh. But his moment of glory was short lived. A final, decisive battle against Alexander Balas resulted in the total defeat of the Seleukid claimant, but Ptolemy was wounded in the fight after falling from his horse. He died three days later.

The reigns of the fourth, fifth and sixth Ptolemies had been marred by a succession of crises. There would be more to come.

8

One Country, Two Cultures

The attempts by successive Ptolemies to appease Egyptian sentiment, set alongside the periodic native rebellions, served as a stark reminder that the Nile Valley was a country riven by ethnic and cultural divisions. In Alexandria and the two other Greek cities (Gr. *poleis*), Naukratis and Ptolemais, the population predominantly spoke Greek. In the countryside, by contrast, most people were Egyptian. The two communities lived side by side, but without much mixing. Each held resolutely to its own culture, its own religion, its own language. Greeks remained unequivocally Greek, even after several generations in Egypt. And most Egyptians remained unaffected by Hellenism – even if they now paid their taxes to foreign pharaohs. The overwhelming sense of Ptolemaic Egypt is of a country characterised by 'coexistence, not coalescence'.[1]

Alexander's conquest of Egypt in 323 had prompted an initial wave of migration from the Greek-speaking world into the Nile Valley. Under the early Ptolemies, this wave turned into a flood. People from impoverished communities throughout the Aegean and Anatolia made haste to Egypt in search of a better life. Settlers arrived from over 200 locations across the Mediterranean, and it was not difficult to understand why. In the early third century, a Hellenistic poet, Herondas, lauded the kingdom of Ptolemy II as a land overflowing with milk and honey: 'In Egypt they have everything that exists or is made anywhere in the wide world: wealth, sports, power, excellent climate, fame, sights, philosophers, gold, young men, a shrine of the sibling gods, an enlightened king, the Museum, wine ... and women!'[2]

Writing a few years later, Ptolemy II's own court poet, Theokritos (himself originally from Syracuse, but now settled in Alexandria) penned the following advice to young men seeking their fortune: 'If you are ready to clasp the military cloak on your right shoulder, if you have the courage to plant your legs firmly to withstand the attack of the bold warrior, get you quickly to Egypt'.[3]

Alexander had founded his eponymous city on the coast, with its back to Egypt, facing the Mediterranean: there could have been no clearer indication that it was intended, from the outset, to be part of the Greek world. The Egyptians took note, and referred to the city in official inscriptions as 'the fort of Alexander by the Sea of the Greeks'. It was the first port of call, the natural destination, for migrants. Yet, with ever increasing numbers of Greek-speakers arriving in the city, not all could find a permanent home in the immediate vicinity. Military settlers and other migrants were therefore dispersed across the countryside, establishing new communities the length and breadth of the Nile Valley: islands of Hellenism in a sea of native Egyptian culture.

One province that witnessed a particular, and lasting, influx of immigrants was the Fayum (the Arsinoite nome). Rather than living side by side with native Egyptians, settlers established their own communities where they could maintain their own cherished cultural traditions. The village of Philadelpheia was one such settlement. To any Egyptian visitor, accustomed to the higgledy-piggledy layout of a native village, Philadelpheia would have presented an entirely alien appearance. It was laid out on the grid system typical of planned Greek settlements. Streets at right angles divided the built-up area into blocks, each measuring 100 by 200 cubits (165 by 330 feet) and comprising twenty dwellings apiece, with narrow alleys running between the houses. The public buildings, too, were of a kind entirely unfamiliar in the Nile Valley: temples to various Greek deities, and a gymnasium, a vital institution in Greek culture where young men received their education (academic as well as physical) and from which the community as a whole derived its sense of identity. Even in quite small Greek settlements, a gymnasium was considered essential, and such buildings were often funded by the community as a whole or by individual benefactors.

By such means, Greek-speakers in Egypt were able to adapt to their new homeland without any diminution of their own identity; even after several generations in the Nile Valley, descendants of settlers would have customarily described themselves as 'Greeks born in Egypt', not 'Egyptians'.[4] Their privileged position as part of a ruling class allowed them to take a condescending and exploitative attitude towards Egypt and its native population. The Egyptians, for their part, resented – as they always had – ill-treatment by foreign overlords. It was a recipe for mistrust, misunderstanding and simmering resentment.

Among the thousands of papyrus documents to have survived from Ptolemaic Egypt, a number provide first-hand testimony of the fractious relations between the immigrant and native communities. In many parts of the country, the elite and the underclass seem to have lived in an atmosphere of permanent, mutual hostility. For example, in a letter from the reign of Ptolemy III, an Egyptian priest complained that the Greek settler billeted in his home looked down his nose at him 'because he is an Egyptian'.[5] In another document, a Greek woman complained of being deliberately scalded by an Egyptian attendant when she visited the communal baths (a quintessentially Greek institution, albeit staffed by poorly paid natives): 'While I was bathing in the bath of the aforesaid village... and had stepped out to soap myself, when he brought in the jugs of hot water, he emptied one [?] over me and scalded my belly and my left thigh down to the knee.'[6]

A third case reveals how quickly tensions could turn violent. A Greek man called Herakleides, now residing in the capital of the Arsinoite nome, alleged that when he was visiting a nearby (Egyptian) village, a local woman named Pasetenbast (rendered in Greek as Psenobastis) leaned out of her window and

> emptied a chamber pot of urine over my clothes, so that I was completed drenched. When I angrily reproached her, she hurled abuse at me. When I responded in kind, Psenobastis with her own right hand pulled the fold of my cloak ... tore it and ripped it off me, so that my chest was laid quite bare. She also spat in my face ... When some of the bystanders reproached her for what she had done, she simply left me and went back into the house.[7]

Appalled and incensed at his treatment, Herakleides was moved to write to the king in Alexandria. The sense of injustice felt by a

Greek man having been assaulted by an Egyptian woman reveals the interracial sensitivities that permeated Ptolemaic communities large and small.

Ethnicity was not merely a matter of identity or social standing: it also had legal ramifications. From at least the reign of Ptolemy II onwards, all male citizens in Egypt required an official ethnicity in legal settings. Cases involving Egyptians followed the traditional body of pharaonic precedent, known as the 'laws of the land', unless superseded by Ptolemaic royal edict; whereas cases involving Greeks referred to written laws. The two types of cases were even heard in two different types of court. *Dikasteria* were established in the provincial capitals to cater to the needs of Greek-speaking settlers, and were overseen by the chief justice (Gr. *archidikastes*) of Alexandria, answerable directly to the king. In the countryside, tribunals of Greek judges (Gr. *chrematistai*) heard cases between Greeks (or arising from contracts written in Greek), while tribunals of Egyptian judges (Gr. *laokritai*) heard cases involving Egyptians. Contracts between Greek parties, written in Greek, were subject to 'Greek' law; those between Egyptians, written in demotic, to native law. It all seemed fair and equitable; but in cases involving members of both communities, Greek judges were grossly biased against Egyptians, reinforcing the grievances of the native population towards its imperialist overlord.

Such rigid distinctions seem however to have gradually broken down as Greeks and Egyptians became accustomed to each other and to each other's way of life. For example, at Taposiris Magna, situated twenty-eight miles west of Alexandria, a largely immigrant population established a town with its own Greek bath-house complex. Yet, alongside the baths and a series of wealthy villas was a sacred animal necropolis full of mummified ibis and falcons. By the end of the third century, as a result of such cultural interpenetration, ethnic identity had become partly a matter of self-definition. From the reign of Ptolemy VI onwards, the same individual was apparently able to adopt both Greek and Egyptian identities and draw on both legal traditions as desired. There are numerous examples of people bearing both Greek and Egyptian names: the former was generally used in official contexts, the latter in the private sphere. Thus, a notary might bear a Greek name when drawing up legal documents, but be referred to by his Egyptian name in family settings. Conversely, a village scribe used his Egyptian name (Menkhes) in his official capacity and his Greek name (Asklepiades son of Ammonios) only occasionally, despite referring to himself as a 'Greek born in Egypt'.

It is impossible to tell for certain if such dual names belonged to hellenised Egyptians or egyptianised Greeks; but, in practice, it was extremely rare for Greeks to learn Egyptian – the native script (demotic) was notoriously difficult for an outsider to pick up – or to borrow Egyptian customs, whereas an upwardly mobile Egyptian had an incentive to learn Greek, the language of the ruling class, and to adopt a Greek persona for professional advancement. Indeed, Egyptians with a fluency in Greek were much in demand in local government from the beginning of Ptolemaic history. As state functions were progressively opened up to Egypt's autochthonous inhabitants, knowledge of Greek became a passport to high office. From the mid-third century, the roles of royal secretary and finance officer were occasionally held by Egyptians; a century later, it was possible for an Egyptian to become commander; by the end of the second century, an Egyptian was appointed supreme commander of the Thebaid region, an office that – somewhat ironically – came with the rank of 'king's cousin'. Some Egyptians seem to have adopted dual names without holding an official position, perhaps reflecting their social aspirations. By the reign of Ptolemy VI, neither someone's name nor their official designation revealed much about their ethnic origins.

The complex relationship between Egyptian- and Greek-speakers, between the country's native inhabitants and the descendants of immigrants, is well illustrated by the story of one particular individual who lived in Upper Egypt, and whose career spanned the reigns of Ptolemy VI and his two successors. Dryton was born around 195, the year of Ptolemy V's humiliating peace treaty with Antiochos III. Despite the loss of Koile-Syria and the defeats suffered by the Egyptian forces, a life in the military still offered opportunities for ambitious young men. Dryton was one such man, and he enlisted in the army; he would go on to spend the whole of his adult life as a solider, stationed in garrisons or manning police posts in the vicinity of Thebes.

Upper Egypt was the heartland of pharaonic culture, Thebes its religious capital. But Dryton's early experience was in an altogether different milieu, for he was born in the Greek city of Ptolemais. A preexisting Egyptian village, Nesyt, was subsumed into a substantial city, destined to become the largest in Upper Egypt. Ptolemais was entirely Greek in character. Nesyt became a quarter reserved for Egyptians, but the rest of the metropolis was a place of foreign customs and architecture. It had temples to Zeus and Dionysos, although chief among its cults was that of its royal founder, Ptolemy I. The city's privileged Greek inhabitants elected their own magistrates and judges, had their own city council and assembly; citizens of Ptolemais, like their counterparts throughout the Greek-speaking world, were organised into tribes and *demes*. Ptolemais maintained active diplomatic and trading relations with locations across the eastern Mediterranean. Amphorae found at the site include imports from Rhodes and Knidos in south-western Anatolia.

The young Dryton, of Cretan heritage, with his Greek name in a Greek city, must have appeared to Egyptians as 'one of them' not 'one of us'. His early military service, in the garrison of Diospolis Parva, would have consolidated his status and identity. All the more unsettling, therefore, when he was transferred in his early thirties to the town of Pathyris, south of Thebes. For Pathyris was almost entirely Egyptian; Greek was heard only rarely in its narrow, winding, dusty streets. Dryton's transfer to Pathyris seems to have been part of a plan by the government of Ptolemy VI to guard against insurrection. But the soldiers did not always behave as expected. Sometimes they went native. Dryton, for one, started to live more and more like an Egyptian, adopting local customs and even writing in demotic. This gradual acculturation was particularly striking for a cavalry officer – as Dryton had now become – because the cavalry was generally reserved for men of pure Greek descent. Very few Greeks learned to read or write in demotic, regarding it as the language of the underclass, with no career benefits attached.

Dryton's transformation from member of the Greek-speaking elite to pillar of society in a largely Egyptian town was cemented by his marriage to a local – Egyptian – woman. Intermarriage had begun about a century earlier, first in rural areas among the poorer sections of both populations, then gradually spreading to military settlements, especially those isolated from centres of urban Greek culture. The marriage of a Greek officer to a native woman marked the culmination of this process. All documented cases involved a Greek man marrying an Egyptian woman, never the other way round. For the husband, marriage to a local girl may have been the only choice. For the wife, marriage into the ruling class conferred huge social benefits. Dryton's wife Setenmontu – a good Theban name – certainly seems to have relished her move up in the world. She largely dispensed with her Egyptian name, more often using a Greek one instead: Apollonia. As the documents show, Apollonia knew she had made a good match, and she was determined to exploit her new status to advance her own career and the fortunes of her children.

Native Egyptians rarely gained wholesale admission into the Greek-speaking elite.[8] Fighting against this tide, Apollonia no doubt sought to emphasise the Greek identify of her children. Her son, Esthladas, followed in his father's footsteps by joining the army. His sisters no doubt thought of themselves as Greek, and enjoyed the superior legal status that went with it; yet even they could not remain impervious to the predominant Egyptian culture of Pathyris – especially after three of their own marriages ended in divorce. Later in their lives, they reverted to using their Egyptian names.

The reality of life in rural Upper Egypt is brought into sharp focus by Dryton's last will and testament, signed and dated in Pathyris on 29 June 126. Here was a successful man of pure-Greek descent, drawing up the document that would determine the distribution of his estate after his death. Dryton's will was written in Greek; but, after the names and occupations of the witnesses, the following statement was added for clarification: 'These four signed in native script because there aren't enough Greeks in this area.'[9] Beyond Alexandria and Ptolemais, Egypt was still overwhelmingly a country of Egyptians.

Dryton died around 111, well into his eighties – more than twice the average life expectancy in Ptolemaic Egypt. His career had served him well. His wife, too, had prospered following her marriage to the dashing cavalry officer. Turning her back on the barter economy of her own culture, she embraced the monetary economy of Egypt's Greek-speaking rulers and became a moneylender herself. The surviving documents show her to have been hard-headed, tight-fisted and cold-hearted in equal measure. She often charged exorbitant rates of interest – up to 5 per cent per month, despite the legal maximum being just 2 per cent – and regularly flouted the law prohibiting the total amount of interest from exceeding the value of the principal. Apollonia must have been a deeply unpopular figure in the local community. Esthladas maintained this new family business alongside his military career.

The adoption of Hellenistic economic practices by aspiring members of the native Egyptian population illustrates the essentially one-way pressure of acculturation. It benefited an aspiring Egyptian to learn Greek, and to acquire a veneer of Greek culture. For the vast majority, however, the strange ways of the 'Ionians' and their ilk remained utterly alien. Egyptian culture retained its innate chauvinism and conservatism.

One exception to this rule was Apollonia's chosen profession, moneylending. The widespread use of coinage and the introduction of a monetary economy into Egypt were some of the most fundamental changes wrought by the early Ptolemies. Papyri from the early third century, before the changes had bedded down, demonstrate just how bewildering these novelties were for the mass of the Egyptian peasantry.

At first, there was just one type of bank, the 'royal bank'. This was an arm of central government, run by civil servants for the benefit of the Treasury. There was a branch in every provincial capital, with subsidiary branches in the larger villages. Most Egyptians referred to them as 'tax offices', which is what they were. Although individuals could open accounts, make deposits and take out loans, most people's experience of the royal bank was the annual demand for payment of taxes.

Then, under Ptolemy II, a second type of bank was introduced, known as a 'concessionary bank'. This represented something quite different and novel as far as the Egyptians were concerned. For a start, the right to run a concessionary bank, of which there were relatively few, was leased by the state to the highest bidder. This brought an element of private enterprise into the realm of financial management, a concept familiar in the Hellenistic world but utterly alien to the Egyptian economy, which had been centrally planned and directed for millennia. Concessionary banks focused on private banking, including currency exchange and pawnbroking.

All bankers were Greeks. Upon appointment, each had to swear and sign an oath of office. The first clause of the oath was the most important: 'I will duly and truly deposit all payments to the Treasury.' The main preoccupation of a banker was the government funds kept at his branch. This is confirmed by a dossier of documents collected by a banker named Nikanor, who ran a provincial branch of the royal bank in northern Upper Egypt during the reigns of Ptolemy II and III. He kept meticulous receipts for all money paid out, and copies of official notes authorising payment. In one instance, he paid out a sum to the local police force from the revenues of the police tax levied the previous year. On another occasion, he received a sum from the Treasury for the grain-purchase account of a neighbouring province, and carefully recorded both the sum 'fifteen copper talents' and the completion of the transaction.

Government business took priority, but Nikanor also had a few private clients – wealthy landowners and officials. (Zenon, for example, kept a private account at Memphis, and another at Athribis in the Delta.) For this side of the business, a smattering of Egyptian was helpful; a banker was therefore allowed to hire an Egyptian as an assistant, as long as they had a sufficient knowledge of Greek.

By the time Apollonia embarked upon her moneylending career, therefore, the functioning and structure of the Egyptian economy had been fundamentally altered by over a century of Greek practice.

These changes to millennial ways of working were felt not just in the cities or larger provincial towns like Pathyris but also in the wider countryside. Throughout Egyptian history, the peasants had paid taxes – levied as a proportion of the harvest – to the state. Under the Ptolemies, tax collection was radically reformed to increase its efficiency and guarantee that the state would receive its expected revenue, come feast or famine. The government achieved this by contracting out tax collection to private operators. Known as 'tax-farmers', they were wealthy entrepreneurs who were able to pay, up front, the tax due on a specific parcel of land. If a plot's actual yield fell short of the guaranteed sum, the tax-farmer would bear the loss himself. If there was a surplus, he would keep a large proportion of it as profit. The contracts with the government were sold at annual auctions, and there was spirited bidding for the most lucrative ones. A fertile plot of land was almost certain to produce a surplus, even if the tax was quite high, and represented a good investment. A more marginal field might attract a lower level of tax, but be a riskier proposition. So tax-farmers often operated as a consortium, to spread the risk and share the reward. To protect their own interests, tax-farmers kept a close eye on every stage of tax collection. This in turn benefited the state, which could count on lots more pairs of ears and eyes to root out any cheating. By introducing private reward as an incentive, the Ptolemaic government ensured its own coffers were filled, reliably, year after year.

For the most part, the tax-farmers were businessmen, investors who never dirtied their hands with agriculture. They would generally lease their plots to actual farmers, or even to middlemen who then subleased to landless Egyptian peasants at exorbitant rents. Under the Ptolemies' system of land management, the government and the moneyed settler class prospered, but little benefit trickled down to the native population.

The pattern of private enterprise was replicated in other areas of the economy as well. Many industries – from glass-making and metal-working to textiles and perfumes; from the brewing of beer to the manufacture of bricks – were operated as government concessions. The right to run a particular business in a particular area for a given period of time was sold to the highest bidder at auction. The state benefited not just from the sale of the concession but also from the taxes levied on the finished products. Oil production, mainly from castor and sesame, was especially closely regulated, the profits from this lucrative industry being channelled directly to the state. And there was no possibility of avoiding the oil tax through cheap imports: imported oil was taxed at 50 per cent, and had to be sold to the government at a fixed (low) price, making it uneconomic.

Some government revenue was earmarked to support specific areas of government expenditure, including a dyke tax (for the maintenance and repair of the irrigation system), a police tax and a medical tax; but most went straight into the royal coffers in Alexandria. Much of the Treasury's income was in kind – principally grain, but also fruit, livestock, linen and other manufactured goods – but monetary taxes were also levied on specific activities. There was a tax on salt production, a tax on the use of land as pasture and a tax on commerce. Customs dues were levied on cargo carried up and down the Nile; Memphis was one of the main customs posts, supported by a string of checkpoints along the nearby stretch of river, and Memphite harbour tolls are well recorded.[10]

Wherever there are dues to be paid there is the opportunity for corruption, and customs officials were notorious for taking backhanders. An account of business expenses incurred by a ship owner travelling from Memphis to Alexandria lists the quantities of wine and beer given to inspectors as facilitation payments (bribes). Not even the grain ships bringing the harvest to Alexandria for export were exempt from interference, as a letter of complaint from a ship-owner to the finance minister, dated December 258, attests. Customs officers were not averse to confiscating items to sell for their own profit; if these included parts of a vessel's equipment then the owner might be left not only out of pocket but also unable to continue his journey at all. Imports and exports were heavily taxed, unless they were royal monopolies. The spice trade was so valuable that the workers employed in the factories of Alexandria were strip-searched before leaving for home each evening.

Sometimes increasing levels of government regulation and taxation spelled economic ruin. The small village of Plinthine, on the north coast of the Delta, offers an example. The community, which was made up of Greek-speaking immigrants, seems to have been entirely geared around wine production. They experimented with different grape varieties to find those best suited to the local sandy soils, and built a communal vat and treading platform which could produce 176 gallons of juice in a single pressing. The resulting high-quality wine may have been sold to customers at nearby Taposiris Magna, and perhaps as far afield as Alexandria. But wine production came to an abrupt halt in the second century and the associated structures were abandoned. Various factors may have been to blame, but the loss of markets or rising taxes are likely to have played a role.

Through concessions, taxes and dues, Ptolemaic control of the economy was thorough, far-reaching and carefully calculated to maximise government revenue. As Apollonios, finance minister for more than two decades under Ptolemy II, observed laconically, 'everything is regulated for the best'.[11] The state benefited most, exporting millions of bushels of grain every year via international distribution centres on the islands of Rhodes and Delos. Wealthy Greek settlers, who constituted most of the business class, made healthy profits, boosting Egypt's reputation as a place to prosper. And, always at the bottom of the economic pile, the ordinary population bore the brunt. Hence, while Ptolemaic Egypt was the wealthiest of the Hellenistic kingdoms, its economic policy contributed to periodic bouts of instability and insurrection.

The different strands of the Ptolemaic economy wove a complex fabric. This is well illustrated at Memphis – the old pharaonic capital but also a major industrial and commercial centre. Grain production was the basis of Egypt's prosperity, but Memphis was a net consumer. The fields surrounding the city grew wheat, barley and emmer, but not in sufficient quantities to feed the urban population. At some point in the reign of Ptolemy IV or V, the government in Alexandria felt compelled to appoint a crown official to oversee the distribution of grain in Memphis and ensure that the population of such an important city did not go hungry. Agriculture within the city limits seems to have catered largely for immigrant tastes. Memphite olives were not the wild Egyptian type, but a Mediterranean variety introduced by early Ionian settlers, highly prized by the local Greek inhabitants. The vineyards of Memphis produced a sweet wine much favoured by Greek palates. The same was true for the pomegranates, figs, walnuts and mulberries which were grown in the city's market gardens. The palace grounds in the north of Memphis contained a nursery for seedlings, including walnut trees.

What Memphis lacked in primary agricultural production, it made up for in manufacturing capacity. Sesame and castor-oil seeds were brought into the city from the Fayum, to be turned into oil for cooking and lighting. The government inspectors kept a watchful eye on production, but were less concerned with working conditions. A second-century document records how an unfortunate labourer fell to his death in a vat of castor oil.

The city had a particular reputation as a centre of the textile and garment industry. Flocks of sheep and goats were kept on scrubby land along the desert edge, their fleeces and hides taken to a large wool factory. There was little tradition of woollen clothing in Egypt, but such garments were popular among immigrant communities. In the early third century, new types of sheep, bred for their fleeces, were introduced from the Mediterranean. Milesian sheep, for example, were said to wear 'fleeces protected beneath leather jackets'[12] that had to be plucked rather than sheared.

Flax, grown in the nearby Arsinoite and Herakleopolitan provinces, was brought to Memphis for bleaching. This process required natron and castor oil. Since both products were state controlled, obtaining reliable supplies could prove challenging. The weaving of wool and linen into cloth, traditionally a cottage industry carried out by women at home, was semi-industrialised under the Ptolemies. Memphis played host to a number of large weaving-sheds, one of them owned by the finance minister, Apollonios. He would have been well placed to win the concession for such an establishment. In some factories, the workers engaged in collective bargaining for better wages. But Apollonios faced no such demands: his employees – girls to spin, men to weave – were slaves. The products of the textile industry were traded locally, but also further afield.

Other Memphite industries likewise reflected the priorities of the Ptolemaic administration. The city's bronze-workers manufactured weapons for the army, and the supply of materiel for the Fourth Syrian War was organised from Memphis. The foundries also churned out moulds for the terracotta models so beloved of Egypt's Greek inhabitants. Many such moulds and models have been found during archaeological excavations at Memphis. The faience industry, a feature of the Nile Valley economy for millennia, adapted rapidly to Hellenistic taste, replacing the classic aquamarine of pharaonic faience with the green or peacock blue favoured by the Ptolemies. The items themselves also catered to Greek preferences: in place of votive figurines the workshops now produced medallions, portrait heads and jugs adorned with the images of Ptolemaic queens.

Even the native temples, bastions of traditional culture that covered a third of the city and employed large numbers of Egyptians, were forced to adapt to foreign rule and foreign ways. To be sure, sacred ibis were still bred along the city dykes and in the nearby Lake of Pharaoh, and the Apis bull continued to pound its stall, but the sacred infrastructure had fundamentally altered. Under the pharaohs, the temple of Ptah had served as a branch of the state, guaranteeing the weights used in transactions; now it guaranteed the purity of the silver used in Ptolemaic coinage. In the olden days, the temples had derived huge wealth from their extensive landholdings. Now, much of this land had been appropriated by the government, and temples instead received a block grant (Gr. *syntaxis*) from the Treasury, supplemented by income from pilgrims and tourists.

Under the Ptolemies, Memphis relinquished its status as national capital in favour of Alexandria. It ceased to be the seat of government, and played only a supporting role in the affairs of state. At the same time, the major expansion of agriculture in the Fayum boosted the city's fortunes as a marketplace and entrepot. Virtually all of Egypt's grain passed through the port of Memphis. Shipping and shipbuilding boomed. Vineyards and olive groves switched production to suit their new buyers' tastes; craftsmen found new outlets for their wares; and new commodities appeared in the city's markets.

Egypt's indigenous population was vital to the Ptolemies' mission of creating the wealthiest state in the Hellenistic world. Yet native resentment periodically boiled over, fuelling a succession of revolts. In the early second century, oppressive levels of taxation, exacerbated by costly foreign wars and the loss of overseas markets, hit the economy hard, forcing countless impoverished and desperate peasants to abandon their land. As a papyrus letter from the period put it, 'We are worn out, we will run away.'[13] But for the vast majority of the population, there was nowhere else to go.

PART III

NEUROSIS (145–80 BC)

9
Out of Joint

Kings throughout history have had two overriding concerns: to hang onto their throne, and to bequeath it in an orderly fashion. Ptolemy VI was a failure on both counts. When he died in the summer of 145, there was no son and heir to succeed him. Some seven years earlier, the king had appointed his eldest son, Ptolemy Eupator, co-regent, but the teenager had died within months. Later, Ptolemy VI had established an eponymous cult for his second daughter, Cleopatra (III), effectively identifying her as his chosen successor. But when the time came, the people of Alexandria opted for a measure of continuity and stability, and recalled the late monarch's younger brother, Ptolemy VIII, from his banishment in Kyrene. After a mere three-week interregnum, he was back in the capital to be acclaimed as ruler.

This was the moment Ptolemy VIII had been waiting for all his adult life. A quarter of a century earlier, he had first been elevated to the kingship, but as part of a shared arrangement with his older brother and sister. For a few brief months in 164/3, he had ousted his brother to rule as sole pharaoh. But then the fickle Alexandrians had turned against him, forcing him into exile. For the next eighteen years, he had had to content himself with ruling Kyrenaika. There he had acted every inch the Hellenistic monarch, giving spectacular feasts, making lavish donations to the temple of Apollo and sponsoring impressive construction projects, including a royal mausoleum. But Kyrenaika was a consolation prize. Ptolemy VIII considered the Nile Valley his rightful kingdom, and his triumphant return to Alexandria in 145 represented the fulfilment of his ambitions.

Some two decades before, in the aftermath of Dionysios Petosarapis' failed coup, Ptolemy VIII had adopted the cult title Euergetes ('benefactor'), in deliberate emulation of Ptolemy III. But the moniker now rang hollow: once back in Egypt, the new king displayed a cruel streak, purging anyone who had opposed him. According to one report, he let his soldiers rampage through the streets of Alexandria, murdering indiscriminately, until he 'found himself a king, not of men, but of empty houses'.[1] Ptolemy the Benefactor could give, but he could also take away.

With his political opponents removed from the scene, there was still the matter of his sister (and late brother's widow), Cleopatra II. She remained official co-regent, a status she had held for much of Ptolemy VI's reign. To prevent her becoming a rival or focus of dissent, Ptolemy VIII promptly married her. The following year, she bore him a son. Predictably, they named him Ptolemy. His birth, around the same time as the royal couple's coronation at Memphis, caused him to be given the epithet Memphites. In a temple inscription he was identified as 'the king's successor', in other words crown prince. Little did the lad know what fate had in store for him.

In Alexandria the purge gathered pace. Next in the king's sights were the city's intellectuals, whom he accused of showing insufficient loyalty (or, worse, of publicly opposing him). The targets included no less a scholar than Aristarchos of Samothrake, director of the Library of Alexandria. He fled to Cyprus before the king's henchmen could arrest him. However, the trauma of leaving his beloved city and Library proved too much, and he died within a few months, robbing the Hellenistic world of one of its leading thinkers. The exodus of academics dealt Alexandria a terminal blow as a centre of learning; it would never recover its status as the pre-eminent city of scholarship.

The people of Alexandria reacted by branding Ptolemy VIII not as a benefactor but its opposite, Kakergetes, a malefactor. They also gave him the nickname Physkon ('fatty'), in reference to his ample figure (the result of all those lavish banquets during his years in Kyrene). When the coercive power of the state was ranged against you, there was always satire to fall back on.

A failed insurrection in May 141 merely strengthened Ptolemy's position still further, and he emerged as undisputed master of Egypt and its overseas possessions. But there was no masking the sad diminution of the Ptolemaic realm since the days of the king's childhood. The gains from the Sixth Syrian War had been lost almost immediately upon the death of Ptolemy VI, and Koile-Syria remained under Seleukid control. An acknowledgement of the new reality was the decision to recall Ptolemaic troops from the last three bases left in the Aegean: Methana off the north-eastern coast of the Peloponese, Itanos on the eastern tip of Crete and the island of Thera in the Cyclades. The empire forged by the first three Ptolemies was now reduced to its core components: Egypt, Cyprus and Kyrenaika.

This decline in fortunes, combined with ongoing dynastic strife in the Seleukid kingdom, had not gone unnoticed. In 139, a Roman embassy arrived in Alexandria with the intention of settling the situation in the east to Rome's permanent advantage. The head of the delegation was one Scipio Aemilianus, victorious general in the third and last Punic War (149–146) and destroyer of Carthage. The signal should have been clear. But Ptolemy VIII nonetheless took pains to welcome the visitors personally at the harbour and accompany them to the royal palace. However, rather than impressing the Romans, this royal gesture backfired spectacularly. It was said that 'Fatty' struggled to keep up with his muscular visitors, due to his 'girth and effeteness', while his attire, a diaphanous, see-through robe, scandalised his guests. To add insult to injury, the luxury and licence of the royal quarters appalled the Roman visitors, and confirmed their dim view of Ptolemy. (They were much more taken with a visit to Memphis, the fertility of the Nile making a lasting impression.)

Pride, wrath and gluttony were not Ptolemy VIII's only vices: he also had a tendency towards lust. Soon after the birth of Ptolemy Memphites, when Cleopatra II had fulfilled her role as king's wife by providing an heir, the king began a relationship with his niece, Cleopatra III. He wed her while he was still married to her mother, Cleopatra II – and elevated her to the rank of queen. Bigamy, especially with the daughter of a wife still living, was anathema to Greek mores, and Ptolemy's Greek-speaking subjects were scandalised. Competition for the king's favour drove a wedge between mother ('Cleopatra the sister') and daughter ('Cleopatra the wife') and they became the bitterest of enemies. The marriage also divided public opinion along ethnic lines. Greeks were aghast, while Egyptians couldn't understand what all the fuss was about: pharaohs had been marrying their sisters and daughters for millennia.

Towards the end of 132, the toxic double marriage erupted into civil war, with Ptolemy VIII and his new wife on one side, the jilted older wife on the other. At first, the king's command of the armed forces enabled him to retain control of the major cities. But within a year, the citizens of Alexandria, weary of Ptolemy's excesses, set fire to the royal palace. Ptolemy, Cleopatra III and their children were forced to escape the burning city by boat and head for the relative safety of Cyprus.

Cleopatra II remained in Alexandria and had herself crowned as sole queen. It was the first time in Ptolemaic history that a woman had ruled alone – not as regent, but in her own right. To mark this momentous occasion, Cleopatra II started a new era, counting 132/1 as 'Year 1', and assumed a new cult title, Thea Philometor Soteira ('mother-loving saviour goddess'), which explicitly connected her both to her late husband Ptolemy VI (Philometor) and to the founder of the dynasty, Ptolemy I (Soter).

Both the royal factions in Alexandria (Cleopatra II on one side, Ptolemy VIII and Cleopatra III on the other) sought to portray themselves as national saviours. First out of the blocks was the army of Cleopatra II, which captured key sites in Upper Egypt. Ptolemy VIII, however, knew that he enjoyed the backing of many of his Egyptian subjects, and sought to use this support to his advantage. Where earlier Ptolemies might have mustered a loyal army of Greek-speaking cleruchs and mercenaries, Ptolemy VIII appointed an Egyptian named Paos as commander of the Thebaid. It was a brilliant move. The population of Thebes recognised Paos as one of their own, and lent him their support. Paos, for his part, knew how to fight like an Egyptian and understood the Nile Valley instinctively, far better than any foreign mercenary or Macedonian officer. By 15 January 130, Paos was in full control of Thebes. The forces loyal to Cleopatra II retreated southwards to the garrison at Hermonthis. At the end of the following July, Paos' army marched northwards and routed any remaining opposition. His reward was to be promoted to commander-in-chief with the courtly rank of 'blood relation'. The Nile Valley's indigenous inhabitants were back in the seats of power.

Even by the standards of the second century, the reign of Ptolemy VIII was an uncommonly unpredictable and uneasy time. A contemporary work of literature, the *Oracle of the Potter* – written in demotic for an Egyptian audience but preserved, ironically, in a Greek translation – spoke of the country's predicament in apocalyptic terms: 'The country will be made unstable and not a few of those who inhabit Egypt will abandon their home... Men will perish at the hands of each other.' But at the same time as lamenting Egypt's fate, the text expressed the hope, fond though it might have been, of a saviour king coming to the rescue and restoring the old ways. The *Oracle* imagined, gleefully, the end of Alexandria:

> the city of foreigners which was founded will be deserted. This will happen at the end of the period of evils, when a crowd of foreigners like fallen leaves came to Egypt ... The city by the sea will be a drying place for fishermen.[2]

Brave words. But not everyone could take comfort in an imaginary future. Some people were so overwhelmed by the troubled times that they sought escape from society as a whole: stop the world, I want to get off. A remarkable archive of correspondence documents the life and inner thoughts of one such recluse. And he was a Greek, not an Egyptian.

Ptolemaios – named in honour of the king – was born around the year 200, at the height of Horwennefer's rebellion. His father, Glaukias, was a Macedonian soldier who had settled in the village of Psichis south of Memphis, built a house and prospered: the story of countless military settlers in Ptolemaic Egypt. Glaukias and his four sons were proud of their Greek identity, calling themselves 'Macedonian by descent'. But there are indications of an Egyptian connection, too. Ptolemaios' youngest brother, Apollonios, learned to write demotic – an extremely unusual accomplishment for a pure-blooded Macedonian – and was evidently more confident in the script than in Greek. Moreover, his spelling of Greek words indicates that he spoke the language with an Egyptian accent. Perhaps Glaukias, like Dryton the cavalry officer, had married an Egyptian woman, with the result that their children grew up bilingual. Certainly, Glaukias' sons had friends and associates from both communities.

When he reached his late twenties, Ptolemaios suddenly turned his back on his comfortable, provincial existence, and became a recluse in the Sarapieion of Memphis. Perhaps he wanted to avoid being drafted into the army. Perhaps he had just had enough of life in Ptolemaic Egypt, with the ever-present threat of war, the febrile tension between different communities, the rampant corruption and official indifference. Appropriately for someone seeking an escape from life, the Sarapieion was located in the realm of the dead. Among the numerous tombs, shrines and catacombs that dotted the necropolis of Memphis, on the western escarpment overlooking the city, the enclosure of Sarapis stood out as one of the largest and most impressive buildings. Here, in great underground vaults, the embalmed bodies of the Apis bulls were laid to rest. Above ground, the cult complex comprised a series of courts, ritual spaces and smaller shrines. In Ptolemaios' time, the sacred enclosure was entered through a great gateway, built in the thirtieth dynasty, while the temple to Sarapis, dedicated by the last native pharaoh, stood within. Evidence of more recent royal patronage included a chapel in Corinthian style next to an Egyptian chapel that housed a painted limestone statue of Apis. It was an amalgam of different statues, buildings, religious and cultural traditions. Although the enclosure was dedicated first and foremost to Sarapis, it also housed smaller temples to three of the principal female deities of Egyptian religion: Isis, wife of Osiris; Sekhmet, goddess of pestilence; and Astarte, goddess of love and war. It was in a cell in the temple of Astarte that Ptolemaios found refuge.

Life on the inside, as a sacred detainee, was basic but not uncomfortable. Ptolemaios got himself added to the temple payroll, and was eligible for a regular allowance of water, oil and grain – although deliveries were not always predictable. To supplement his income, he was permitted to sell porridge at a small profit to the countless pilgrims who visited the Sarapieion. He also dealt in linen, buying lengths of cloth from the weavers of Memphis to resell at a profit to supply the local 'death industry' (the mummification of humans and sacred animals). Finally, Ptolemaios' family members – first his father, then, after his death, his three younger brothers – provided food to supplement the basic temple rations.

More irksome than the spartan conditions was the persistence, even in the confines of a temple, of the ethnic tensions that beset society at large. The liturgical language of the Astarte cult was Phoenician (reflecting the goddess's Levantine origins), but most of the temple staff were Egyptian. As a Greek, albeit one of mixed parentage, Ptolemaios was resented as an interloper by many of his fellow residents. He was periodically assaulted, both verbally and physically, by Egyptian temple staff, and complained that, 'People here abuse me ... because I am Greek.'[3] On one occasion, he reported that a group of temple cleaners, armed with stones and rods, had come to the Astarte shrine intent upon plundering it, and killing him if he got in the way. Two years later, the same group – which included a clothing-seller, two porters, a baker and a grain-seller – launched further attacks, throwing stones through Ptolemaios' window. Desperate, he wrote to the king and queen to seek royal redress. Beyond the temple walls, too, there was the ever-present threat of interracial violence. Ptolemaios' three younger brothers complained of harassment by their neighbours and community leaders, after their father and protector died.

In an attempt to escape such persecution, the youngest brother, Apollonios, decided to follow in Ptolemaios' footsteps and live as a recluse in the temple of Astarte. But, unable to bear the restrictions, he left again after a few months. Perhaps Ptolemaios encouraged him to seek betterment on the outside, rather than suffer discrimination in silence. Ptolemaios took up the baton on behalf of his brother, petitioning the king and queen on one of their periodic visits to Memphis, and asking them to enrol Apollonios in the Macedonian military corps stationed in the city. This would provide a stable career, a regular income and some measure of social standing. The petition explained how their father, Glaukias, had died, and asked the royal couple to do the right thing by one of their loyal compatriots. The petition, like all of Ptolemaios' correspondence, was written for him by Apollonios. Its passage through the bureaucracy of government reveals the hoops through which a Ptolemaic subject, be they Greek or Egyptian, had to jump in order to receive an official response.

Having sent the petition to the monarch, Apollonios received it back and was told to deliver it, sealed, to the correct person – in this case, the king's chief bodyguard and chief of commissariat. His office promptly returned it to the complainant with instructions to take it to the secretary in the accountant's office (because there were financial implications to the request). From the accountant's office it was passed to two further officials in turn: nobody, apparently, having the authority (or the inclination) to respond with a definitive answer. Eventually, the petition was presented at court, four months after it had first been lodged.

In response, two royal orders were forthcoming, one addressed to the chief of commissariat and one to the accountant's secretary. The chief of commissariat responded by issuing Apollonios with four letters, for him to take to the commander of the province, the paymaster-general, a government secretary and the finance minister. The letters were duly delivered, and an order, authorised by the finance minister, was issued in reply by his secretary and the head of his correspondence bureau. Apollonios brought this order, first to the independent auditor, then to a minor official in the correspondence bureau, then to two other named individuals, before, finally, a copy of the order was made. The original and the copy were then submitted, via the correspondence bureau official, to the finance minister for his formal review. (Official requests, it seemed, had to be considered in duplicate, or not at all.)

Apollonios received a reply and submitted it to another official, who in turn wrote to a colleague to request that two further letters be sent, one to an official at the treasury and the other to the provincial commander. Because Apollonios' appointment had both fiscal and military implications, it had to be approved by both treasury and army officials. The fact that the petition (concerning a fairly minor matter) had to go twice to the finance minister (one of the most senior members of the government) illustrates the extraordinarily bureaucratic mindset of Ptolemaic officialdom, an attitude they had inherited from their pharaonic forebears. The passing of Apollonios' petition from official to official, and from one administrative department to another, also points to the labyrinthine nature of the government machine, a fair degree of individual incompetence, and supreme institutional indifference towards the individual making the request – all characteristics of state bureaucracies throughout history. Eventually, however, Apollonios secured his appointment in the Macedonian regiment, with its pay and status.

Weighed down by concerns for his brothers and himself, it is hardly surprising that Ptolemaios suffered from bad dreams. His accounts of these nightmares reveal a range of concerns: his own childlessness (in a society where children provided the only support for aged parents); his longing for release (psychological as much as physical); and disturbing, complex feelings of sexual frustration.

The last were prompted by the twin girls, Taous and Tawê, whom Ptolemaios had taken under his wing. Their story provides another illustration of the vicissitudes of life in second-century Egypt. Their Egyptian mother left their father for a Greek soldier, and persuaded him to murder the twins' father. The latter escaped by jumping into the Nile, swimming to an island, and taking a passing boat to the neighbouring province where, the twins said, he 'died of grief'. His body was brought back to Memphis for burial, but the mother appropriated his property, sold the matrimonial home and evicted her own daughters. Their friend Ptolemaios took them in at the temple of Astarte, and secured for them roles as official mourners at the funeral of a recently deceased Apis. But they, too, experienced nightmares. For many ordinary people in late Ptolemaic Egypt, life was one long, bad dream.

Ptolemaios spent over twenty years holed up in the Sarapieion enclosure. After a decade and a half inside, he had grey hair. Seven years later his letters came to an end, presumably at his death. For individuals like Ptolemaios – and the twins – a lack of liberty was a small price to pay to escape the trials of life on the outside.

Back in the febrile world of dynastic politics, the civil war between Ptolemy VIII and Cleopatra II entered a new and vicious phase. The king realised that Cleopatra II was not the only threat to his rule: his son by her, Ptolemy Memphites, might also attract support, especially as the boy had been publicly hailed as the heir apparent. To neutralise this source of potential opposition, the king displayed his ruthless streak once more. According to later accounts, he had Ptolemy Memphites brought to him and murdered before his eyes. So much for the lad acclaimed in the temple of Apollonopolis as 'heir of the king, given birth by the queen, who takes over from the sole lord, the king's eldest son, the king's beloved'. Ptolemy VIII then had his son's body dismembered and the parts delivered to Cleopatra II in Alexandria, timed to arrive the night before her birthday celebrations. But the queen was every bit as calculating as her brother-husband, and equally politically astute: she had the mutilated remains of her son put on public display to arouse the wrath and sympathy of the citizens.

By early 130, the king and his niece-wife Cleopatra III had returned to Egypt from their temporary exile in Cyprus, and by spring of that year were back in control of Memphis. Esthladas, son of the cavalry officer Dryton and his Egyptian wife Apollonia, saw active service in the civil war; he wrote to his parents, 'Keep your spirits up and take good care of yourself until things settle down.'[4] The fight between rival factions of the royal family affected ordinary families the length and breadth of Egypt.

Paos' success in putting down the native insurrection and his subsequent promotion to commander-in-chief gave the king's forces new momentum, and they soon turned their attention to Alexandria, epicentre of Ptolemaic power. The city was besieged, but its defences were strong and its maritime supply lines secure. Cleopatra II refused to surrender. Frustrated by his inability to regain the capital, Ptolemy VIII resorted to psychological warfare. He installed a rival priest of Alexander – the most important role in the dynastic cult – with the result that there were two such priests, each claiming legitimacy, for the next three years. Ptolemy also elevated Cleopatra III, equating her with the living Isis. For Cleopatra II, acutely conscious of her royal status, this barb must have hurt.

News of the protracted civil war spread across the Mediterranean world and, that same year, Roman senators debated the fate of Egypt. With the Ptolemaic empire tearing itself apart, there was no need for Rome to risk political or military intervention. The senators sat on their hands. With no prospect of assistance from outside Egypt, Cleopatra II had few options left. In desperation, with her son Ptolemy Memphites dead, she offered joint rule to her son-in-law, the Seleukid king Demetrios II, who had just been restored to his own throne after a period of captivity in Parthia. The tactic worked. In 128 Demetrios launched an invasion of Egypt to claim his prize. His army made straight for Pelousion and was in the midst of laying siege to the city when news arrived of trouble back home. In Demetrios' absence, his wife (Cleopatra Thea, daughter of Cleopatra II and Ptolemy VI) had taken the opportunity to install her son as king, with herself as the power behind the throne. On hearing this news, Demetrios' troops mutinied, and he was forced to return to Syria without an inch of Egyptian territory to his name.

With a dynastic conflict of its own to deal with, the Seleukid kingdom offered no more assistance to Cleopatra II. She realised the game was up. She took the contents of the state treasury and fled Alexandria, making her way to join her embattled son-in-law in Syria. With her gone, the capital finally succumbed to Ptolemy VIII. Fully restored to his realm, he turned victory into a rout. This time, a purge of opponents was not enough: those who had backed his sister were rounded up and taken to the city's gymnasium, and the building was set on fire with many still inside. It was a grim warning to any future rebels. For good measure, Ptolemy sent his agents to Syria to murder Demetrios II.

From a position of strength, Ptolemy opened peace negotiations with his exiled sister and her hosts. He agreed to recognise Demetrios' son, Antiochos VIII, as king of Asia, and sealed the agreement by sending his daughter by Cleopatra III, Tryphaina, as a royal bride. For a second generation, the Ptolemaic and Seleukid royal houses were joined in matrimony. Cleopatra II was allowed to return to Egypt and – in a remarkable show of family unity – resume her erstwhile status as co-regent. From 124 onwards, official inscriptions referred once again to the triple monarchy of Ptolemy the king, Cleopatra the sister and Cleopatra the wife. The people of Egypt must have wondered what the previous eight years of suffering had achieved.

To underscore the dynastic reconciliation, the murdered Ptolemy Memphites was added to the dynastic cult, under the name Theos Neos Philopator ('the new father-loving god') – apparently without a hint of irony. Then, family squabbles set aside, the three joint sovereigns issued a wide-ranging decree in April 118. In overall structure, it followed in the tradition of earlier royal decrees, but this time the clauses were much more pointed. Nearly a century of insurrection and civil strife had created desperate, lawless conditions in much of the Egyptian countryside. Large numbers of farmers had fled their fields, leading to a disastrous drop in food production and tax revenue. Restoring order and prosperity were key objectives. A good way to start, to bring the people onside, was to promise a general amnesty. The decree therefore began with a royal pardon for all offences, except murder and sacrilege, and restored to fugitives their sequestered property on condition that they return to their homes and resume their former occupations.

Further popular measures included the remission of tax arrears, certain exemptions from having to put up soldiers, the reduction of import duties and a crackdown on official corruption. Under the latter heading, the list of activities to be prohibited gives a clear picture of the abuses of power that had become endemic under the Ptolemies: the illegal seizure of goods by customs officials, even when the proper dues had been paid; the forcible removal of people from recognised places of asylum; preventing home owners from rebuilding burned or damaged properties; and, most tellingly, military commanders pressurising local people to carry out personal services, requisitioning their livestock, compelling them to feed sacred animals, or to make gifts of livestock to keep their jobs, and forcing them to work without payment. The decree also forbade commanders and other officials from making spurious arrests to settle private grievances; henceforth, all disputes were to be settled according to the proper laws and regulations.

Many of the measures contained in the decree were aimed at restoring agricultural productivity as swiftly as possible. One of the effects of *anachoresis* (the flight from the countryside) had been the illegal occupation of 'relinquished land'. To reverse this practice, the decree stipulated that 'all the cleruchs and all the holders of sacred land or other relinquished land ... shall evacuate all the excess land they hold, declare themselves and pay a year's rent'. Vineyards and orchards were granted tax exemptions if they were brought back into cultivation.

In an important gesture to the two different sections of the population – and mindful that the Greeks had largely supported Cleopatra II; the Egyptians, Ptolemy VIII – the decree reconfirmed the application of two different legal systems:

> Egyptians who have made contracts in Greek with Greeks shall give and receive satisfaction before the *chrematistai*, while the Greeks who have concluded contracts in Egyptian shall give satisfaction before the *laokritai* ... The suits of Egyptians against Egyptians

shall ... be decided before the *laokritai* in accordance with the laws of the country.⁵

Alongside these instruments designed to restore the smooth functioning of the economy and society, the decree paid particular attention to the rights and perquisites of the Egyptian temples and their priesthoods. Native sentiment ran deep, and history had shown that any perceived neglect of a pharaoh's most basic task – to honour the gods and beautify their shrines – could spark indigenous dissent. So the decree confirmed the immunity of temple lands from taxation and the rights of temples to grant asylum. Priestly emoluments were renewed and – in a measure harking back to Alexander and Ptolemy I – the sacred animal cults, especially the expenses related to the burials of Apis and Mnevis bulls, were guaranteed from the royal treasury.

In its choice of topics, the decree revealed the dependency of the state on two critical factors: tax revenue from agriculture and the support of the native population.

With peace, and a degree of prosperity and a semblance of order restored, Ptolemy VIII set about consolidating his support. Since the very beginning of the dynasty, successive rulers had engaged in temple building. Ptolemy I had focused on completing the edifices of the last native pharaohs, to signify continuity and legitimacy. Ptolemy II had inaugurated the temple of Isis at Philae to demonstrate his conquest of Lower Nubia, and a new shrine at Heroonpolis in the eastern Delta to signify his authority over the whole of Egypt. Ptolemy III had built at many sites, and founded the great temple of Horus at Apollonopolis to defuse a tense political situation in Upper Egypt.

By contrast, the crisis years of the fourth, fifth and sixth Ptolemies had witnessed a decline in major projects, and a focus instead on adorning and enlarging existing structures. At Apollonopolis, for example, Ptolemy IV had added new decoration that named himself, modestly, as 'ruler of Phoenicia and ruler of the whole world' – before building work was halted for five decades. Ptolemy V, thwarted from carrying out any significant work in Upper Egypt, had decided instead to focus his attention on Memphis. Here he sponsored new decoration in the temple of Apis and new construction at the Anoubieion. The intention was to bolster the profile of the capital as a counterweight to rebellious Thebes.

The unrest under Ptolemy VI and VIII had demonstrated, once again, that native acquiescence could not be taken for granted. The result was an upsurge in construction of temples to Egyptian gods throughout the Nile Valley. The sites where building took place stretched from Tanis in the eastern Delta and Xois in the western Delta, via Antaeopolis in Middle Egypt, to Hermonthis in the Thebaid, Elephantine and Philae at the First Cataract, even Berenike on the Red Sea coast and Kalabsha in Lower Nubia. Upper Egypt in general, and the stretch south of Thebes and Syene in particular, were focus areas for royal patronage: regions that had proved especially vulnerable for the Ptolemaic state.

Ptolemy VIII was determined to live up to his chosen cult title, benefactor. He lavished attention on the Thebaid, as if to prove himself a worthy successor of the pharaohs of old. To the north and south of Thebes, he expanded the temples of Montu, Theban god of war. To the west, he enlarged a sacred sanatorium dedicated to the healing gods Imhotep and Amenhotep son of Hapu, and built a small temple dedicated to the same two deities. The god of war to the north and south, the gods of healing in the west: together they spoke to Ptolemy VIII's priorities. At Karnak, meanwhile, the king decorated the small temples of Khonsu (divine child) and Opet (mother goddess). These same themes would recur in many of his other schemes.

Among the projects he undertook in southern Upper Egypt, three sites stand out as particularly significant, and reveal much about the king's politico-religious programme. The first was the island of Philae, sacred to Isis and intimately linked with the Osiris story, one of the founding myths of ancient Egyptian religion. Some forty years earlier, Ptolemy VI had recaptured the Dodekaschoinos, establishing military colonies at the foot of the Second Cataract. Now Ptolemy VIII set the seal on his overlordship of Lower Nubia by beautifying sacred structures that had been patronised by earlier Kushite kings – at Dakka (enlarged by Arqamani) and Dabod (begun by Adikhalamani). But Philae, dedicated to the goddess whose cult had the widest adherence throughout Egypt, was the object of special veneration. To the existing temple, Ptolemy VIII added a plethora of new structures: an extension of the birth house, an elaborate colonnade and a pair of obelisks in front of the first pylon. He also expanded a temple dedicated to the Nubian deity Arensnuphis, reinforcing the message that he was king of Lower Nubia as well as Egypt.

The second site singled out for royal patronage was Ombos (present-day Kom Ombo). It had been recently established as the administrative capital of the first province of Upper Egypt. To celebrate the town's elevation, Ptolemy VI had founded a new temple, dedicated to the twin gods Horwerra (an aspect of Horus) and Sobek (the crocodile deity worshipped in the local area). Inscriptions on the temple walls identified these deities with figures from the creation myth. Horwerra was equated with the god of light and air, Shu, while Sobek was associated with the earth god, Geb. This new theology was reinforced by an account of the creation of Osiris by Shu and Geb. Since the Ptolemies associated themselves with Dionysos, and the Greeks identified Dionysos with Osiris, the texts at Ombos linked the king's divine birth with the very process of creation. Asserting that the pharaoh was part of the divine order was at the core of traditional Egyptian religious thought. Ptolemy VIII tapped into this ancient strand of belief to underscore his legitimacy in Egyptian eyes. The king's divine origins were likewise celebrated in the birth house at Ombos, where different mother goddesses and child gods from the Egyptian pantheon converged on the figure of a single mother and child: to be read as Ptolemy VIII and his mother. Throughout the temple of Ombos, some fifty inscriptions described in great detail the cultic rites, the mythology of the site itself, legends of the gods and the very nature of heaven. Together they constitute an unprecedented, unparalleled treasury of ancient Egyptian religious belief and practice – and all thanks to a Macedonian monarch sitting on an uneasy throne.

The third key site was Apollonopolis. The fact that building work on this most ambitious of Ptolemaic projects had been halted by civil war more than once would not have been lost on Ptolemy VIII. In a lavish ceremony, ninety-five years after his hero Ptolemy III had presided at the foundation ritual, he dedicated the entire temple complex to Horus, god of kingship and protector of the Egyptian monarchy. In texts carved within the temple itself, the dedication was described as a 'great popular celebration which was enthusiastically attended by the people living in the city and the surrounding regions'.[6] The magnificent inner hypostyle hall was decorated with scenes of Ptolemy VIII's coronation, and a birth house was built in front of the main temple. The king's penchant for birth houses reflected an uncomfortable truth: as the earthly power of the pharaoh continued to decline, the transcendent aspects of kingship had to be foregrounded instead.

The cult of Isis and the mystery of Osiris at Philae; the creation of kingship at Ombos; the institution of monarchy and the divine birth at Apollonopolis: each of Ptolemy VIII's projects consciously projected a venerable, unchanging concept of pharaonic power that every native Egyptian would have recognised. Yet not even this lavish programme of temple building could avert mortality. On 28 June 116, Ptolemy VIII died – not in battle, not from an assassin's dagger, but from natural causes. His reign, reckoned (somewhat creatively) at fifty-two years, was the longest of any Ptolemy. Despite his brutality, he had shown himself to be a shrewd politician. Despite his purge of Alexandria's intellectuals, he was a noted philologist himself, a Homeric scholar and the author of twenty-four books on topics as diverse as the mistresses of Ptolemy II and the fauna of Libya.[7] Though despised by many of his Greek-speaking subjects, he gained widespread popularity among the native population, and made it possible for Egyptians once again to hold the highest offices in their own land. He gave away the Ptolemies' last remaining Aegean bases, but sponsored a maritime expedition to India. Ptolemy VIII was a conflicted, controversial and contradictory monarch, even by the standards of his dynasty.

Perhaps the most consequential aspect of his multifaceted, tumultuous reign was his legacy. In March 155, following an attempt on his life by supporters of his older brother, he had drawn up a will. Designed to frighten his domestic opponents, it recorded his wishes should he die without an heir:

> Should any mortal fate befall me before I can leave behind heirs to the throne, I bequeath the kingdom that belongs to me to the Romans ... To them also I entrust the task of protecting my interests.[8]

At the time, the gesture was ignored. But by carving it in stone and setting it up in the temple of Apollo at Kyrene, Ptolemy was commending it to posterity.

Posterity would take note.

10

Mother's Ruin

The long reign of Ptolemy VIII could have provided the opportunity both to boost the status of the monarchy through lavish temple building, and also to reset its foundations and ensure a more stable succession in the future. But perhaps that was too much to expect of a king who had schemed and murdered his way to the throne; a king to whom close family members were rivals and enemies. After the killing of Ptolemy Memphites, Ptolemy VIII had proclaimed as crown prince the older of his two sons by Cleopatra III. But Cleopatra herself preferred her younger son. As Ptolemy VIII lay dying, the queen conspired to have her elder son appointed resident military governor of Cyprus, to get him out of the way. This cleared the way for her younger son when the moment arrived.

Cleopatra III, however, was not the sole arbiter of the royal succession. Within the court, a good deal of store was set by the expressed preferences of the previous monarch. And Ptolemy VIII had spelled out his wishes: Kyrene was to be left to Ptolemy Apion, his son by a minor consort; his intentions for Cyprus were left unhelpfully unclear; and the throne of Egypt he bequeathed to Cleopatra III and 'whomever of the two sons she would choose'.[1] It was a recipe for disaster. By setting aside the normal rules of primogeniture, Ptolemy VIII had ensured that the chaos and conflict of his reign would continue long after his death.

In the summer of 116, Cleopatra III manoeuvred to elevate her younger son to rule alongside her. But she had reckoned without the interference and determination of her own mother, Cleopatra II, who favoured the elder son (more, one suspects, out of lasting enmity towards her daughter than out of any sentiment for her late husband's wishes). The older Cleopatra won the day, with the support of the army and the people of Alexandria; by October that year, the elder son had been duly installed as co-ruler (Ptolemy IX) in a new triple monarchy with his mother and grandmother. His younger brother had to accept the consolation prize of Cyprus – where, within twenty-four months, he would proclaim himself monarch.

In Alexandria, the new king of Egypt, recognising the source of his power, took the masculine version of Cleopatra II's own cult title, announcing himself as Philometor Soter ('mother-loving saviour'). But the old queen died within months of Ptolemy IX's accession, leaving just two co-monarchs: himself and Cleopatra III. They continued as the 'mother-loving saviour gods', counting their years from the death of Ptolemy VIII.

From the outset, Ptolemy IX's dependence on his mother's continued goodwill severely dented his own authority. A pharaoh's titles were supposed to project an air of royal supremacy and invulnerability. But Ptolemy IX's epithets were explicit about the manner of his accession, calling him 'the one whose mother placed him upon the throne of his father', before adding, with a little more customary chutzpah, 'who has seized the inheritance of the Two Lands in justification'. The citizens of Alexandria, always quick to make fun of their rulers, nicknamed him Lathyros ('chickpea').

Nonetheless, this mummy's boy asserted his rule over both Egypt and Kyrenaika, and stepped up to fulfil the traditional duties expected of a pharaoh.

An early example was his participation in person in the annual celebrations marking the start of the inundation. For these rites, commencing at the end of August 115, Ptolemy travelled all the way upstream to the island of Elephantine at the foot of the First Cataract – a journey of nearly 700 miles from the royal palace in Alexandria. According to legend, the inundation had its source in a cavern deep below the rocks of Elephantine, and the island's Nilometer provided an early, crucial indication of the height of the coming flood, with major implications for the following year's harvest and the amount of tax revenue the state could expect. No doubt the economic as well as the religious connotations of the celebrations were in Ptolemy's mind, but Elephantine also had geopolitical significance: since the foundation of the Egyptian state, it had acted as a border control point and a forward base for pharaonic campaigns into Nubia. The Dodekaschoinos remained vulnerable to the Meroitic kings of Kush, so keeping Elephantine, and the First Cataract region as a whole, loyal to the Egyptian state was of the utmost strategic importance. This combination of factors helps to explain Ptolemy IX's personal participation in the inundation festival and his granting of privileges to the priesthood of Khnum, which had its headquarters on Elephantine.

The inscription commemorating the royal visit was carved in (clumsy) Greek on a monumental slab of pink granite set up in the temple of Khnum. The text claimed, somewhat unbelievably, that the reason for the largesse shown by Ptolemy and his mother was because 'our public affairs are going well'. That must have raised a few eyebrows when it was dictated to the stonemason.

The inscription as a whole, though traditional in much of its phraseology, underlined the political significance of the occasion. Ptolemy arrived at Elephantine with an entourage of his closest advisers and a military escort: travelling so far from the capital, and so deep into native territory, was not without security risks. Waiting to greet him were not only the priests of Khnum but also clergy from a host of other Upper Egyptian temples. A royal visit to the deep south was a rare and important occasion, and worth some inconvenience to attend. As was expected of a pharaoh, the first thing Ptolemy did on arrival was to perform the proper sacrifices and libations to Khnum, Lord of Elephantine and the other local deities. The niceties accomplished, the priests were keen to show him the sacred sites under their jurisdiction: the cataract itself and the islands in the stream which were believed to be the source of the Nile. At each location the king performed the appropriate rites. Significantly, he and his entourage did not hurry back to Alexandria, but stayed for two days, entertaining his hosts with a lavish banquet. Even when acting the part of an Egyptian pharaoh, there was still room for a little Hellenistic *tryphé*.

The privileges granted to the Khnum priesthood occupied most of the inscription: the clergy's chief concern was securing their own perks and emoluments, not bolstering the king's authority. After an introduction setting out the rationale for the royal decree – 'desirous to be as far as possible gracious to all people … and having towards divinity the most pious attitude' – came the quid pro quo: a wish (but no promise) that Ptolemy IX and Cleopatra III would be remembered for ever, and reign over the whole earth. So much hot air. By comparison, the benefits set out by the priests were specific and concrete: precise amounts of wheat and barley from the royal treasury, tax free.

At other sites besides Elephantine, the king took pains to honour the local deities. At Athribis in the central Nile Valley he founded and built a new temple to the lioness-headed Repyt (Gr. Triphis). She was an ancient goddess, with origins lost in the mists of time, who had a connection with the portable carrying-shrine that bore the image of a deity. Her cult thus lay at the very heart of ancient Egyptian religious practice. Ptolemy IX also established a small temple to Isis, the most popular goddess of his own era, at Contra-Latopolis.

At Karnak he continued work begun over a century earlier, under Ptolemy III. The new work, in the small temple of Khonsu situated within the enclosure of Amun-Ra, was designed to demonstrate Ptolemy's reverence for the traditional gods of Thebes; but it also revealed much about the character of his early reign. At the edge of the scene, the king was shown wearing the crown of Upper Egypt in the presence of a host of deities, perhaps a reference to his recent visit. But, at the centre of the tableau, he was shown standing *behind* Cleopatra III. The accompanying texts followed suit: mother, not son, was given pre-eminence. Theology reflected the political reality.

Perhaps the most telling instance of royal veneration of Egypt's native gods was Ptolemy IX's promotion of the cult of Apis. The king, born in the early 140s, seems to have linked his conception with the discovery of a new sacred bull: his Horus-name (the oldest and most prestigious of a pharaoh's royal titles) began 'holy of birth with the living Apis'.[2] To strengthen the connection still further, he appointed a priest of Sarapis to officiate in the dynastic cult of himself and his mother Cleopatra III.

But Ptolemy IX, like so many of his forebears, would soon discover that honouring the traditional gods of Egypt was not enough to keep the indigenous population quiescent and obedient. Nor was honouring his mother with public displays of affection and subservience enough to keep her on side.

Much of the drama of Ptolemaic politics was played out against the backdrop of Egypt's two big cities, Memphis and Alexandria. Consequently, it is easy to forget that the ancient Nile Valley was predominantly rural in character. The old and new capitals acted as magnets for wealth and labour, attracting those seeking preferment or merely a better life, but the economic engine of the Ptolemies' sprawling realm was the Egyptian countryside (Gr. *chora*). While politicians jockeyed for position in the corridors of power in Alexandria, and priests negotiated with the king in synod at Memphis, the vast bulk of the population carried on, as they always had, tilling the fields, sowing and reaping, repairing dykes and field boundaries, bringing in the harvest – and paying a goodly portion in taxes to the government of the day. Egypt's agricultural bounty, collected from towns and villages the length and breadth of the Nile Valley, to be shipped, stored and traded in Alexandria, gave the Ptolemies their economic, political and diplomatic clout. Rural communities may have been quiet backwaters, remote from the statecraft and intrigue of the court, but they were the backbone of the country.

The most detailed first-hand account of life in the *chora* is provided by an archive of documents compiled by the village scribe Menkhes between the years 120 and 111. His correspondence reveals the everyday concerns and struggles of Egypt's rural population in the early part of Ptolemy IX's reign. Menkhes worked in the village of Kerkeosiris (Eg. Gerge-usir, 'settlement of Osiris'), a small community of some 1,500 souls in the south-western part of the Fayum. The low-lying Fayum was a major centre of agriculture, where extensive land reclamation under the early Ptolemies had significantly boosted production.[3] But Kerkeosiris must have felt remote from the action: it was located neither on the Nile, nor on a navigable waterway; it was some fifteen miles from Lake Fayum and an equal distance from the provincial capital of Krokodilopolis – a long journey on the back of a donkey.

The surrounding region had been a magnet for immigration since the earliest days of Macedonian rule. As a result, by the time of Ptolemy IX, it was perhaps more ethnically diverse than any other part of Egypt. Of the 114 Fayum villages attested in the Ptolemaic period, over half had Greek names, while several had Jewish names, reflecting the dominant background of the local population. Even a small, remote community like Kerkeosiris reflected this cultural mix. The personal names recorded in Menkhes' documents are mostly Greek and Egyptian, with theophoric names popular among both groups – Apollo and Sarapis were the gods favoured by the Greek-speaking community; Horus, Sobek and Osiris by the Egyptians. (A few Egyptians named their sons Inaros, 'the eye of Horus is turned against them': a patriotic dig directed at the Greek incomers.) There are also a few names suggesting immigrants from more distant parts of the Hellenistic world: Iran, Thrace, Assyria and Ethiopia. As for Menkhes himself, his name – used in his official capacity as village scribe – was Egyptian. But he also had a Greek name (Asklepiades), and described himself as a 'Greek born in this land', indicating that he could trace his ancestry in the male line to at least one settler from the Greek world.

The multi-ethnic character of Kerkeosiris was apparent in its local cults. Although the village was named after Osiris, its chief deity was the crocodile god of the Fayum. He was worshipped, under a variety of names, in two separate shrines, while in the nearby town of Tebtunis he had a more significant temple that had been refounded by Ptolemy I. In the countryside around Kerkeosiris, along the banks of the irrigation channels, sacred crocodiles were bred to be mummified as votive offerings. The village also had minor shrines dedicated to other native deities, reflecting the polytheistic nature of ancient Egyptian religion. There were chapels dedicated to Horus son of Isis, Amun and the cat goddess Bastet; to Thoth, Arensnuphis (Orsenouphis in Greek) and Anubis, god of mummification; to Taweret, goddess of childbirth, and of course to the great mother and healer of the sick, Isis. Each of these shrines was a small, low building of mudbrick, not a showy stone temple endowed by royal patronage. Alongside native places of worship, there was a chapel dedicated to the divine twins (Gr. Dioskouroi) of Greek mythology. But in general, the Greek-speaking population of Kerkeosiris seem to have gravitated towards the Egyptian cults. By contrast, there is little evidence for the reverse: the Egyptians' own religious traditions were simply too venerable, too ingrained.

In its domestic buildings, Kerkeosiris presented a typical picture of a rural Egyptian village. Most dwellings were built from mudbrick,

Alexander the Great: victor against the Nile Valley's Persian rulers, welcomed by the Egyptians as a conquering hero

An imaginative eighteenth-century reconstruction of the Pharos of Alexandria: lighthouse and miracle of engineering, beaming Ptolemaic civilisation to the wider world

Ptolemy I, founder of the dynasty

Ptolemy II, depicted as a Greek hero

Eratosthenes, polymath and director of the Library of Alexandria under Ptolemy III

Preserving pharaonic traditions for a Greek-speaking monarch in the face of Roman aggression: the Egyptian royal crowns, on a relief from the rear wall of the temple of Hathor at Tentyris (Dendera), reign of Cleopatra VII

Mixing Egyptian and Hellenistic styles: harvest scene from the tomb of Padiusir/Petosiris at Hermopolis (Tuna el-Gebel), early Ptolemaic

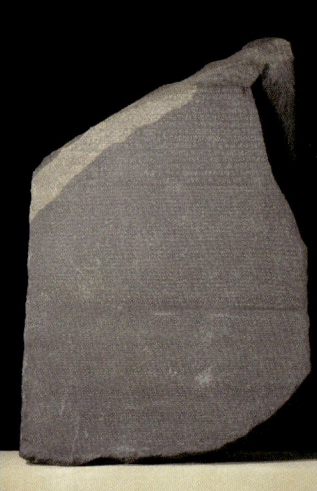

The Decree of Memphis (Rosetta Stone), key to the decipherment of hieroglyphics and the founding document of Egyptology, reign of Ptolemy V

Furniture inlay of gold and glass depicting the Egyptian goddess of truth, Maat

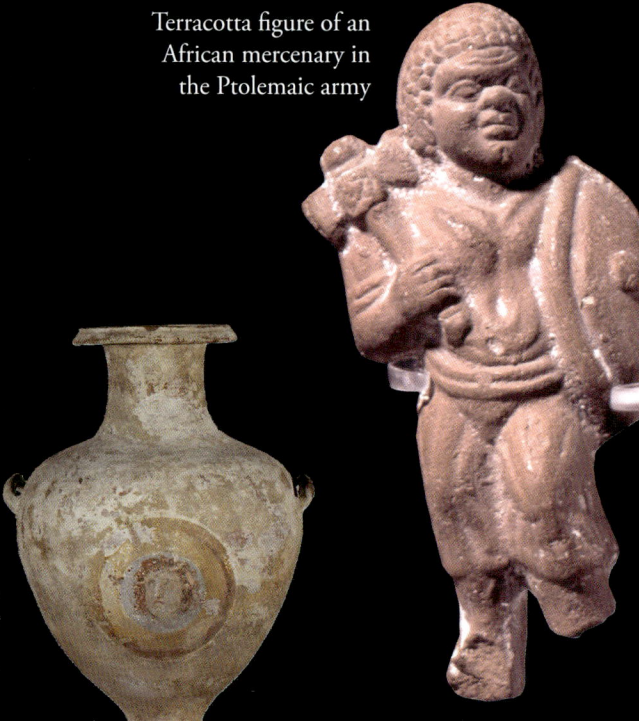

Terracotta figure of an African mercenary in the Ptolemaic army

Egyptian terracotta water jar decorated with the head of the Greek gorgon Medusa

Stela showing Ptolemy V offering to Buchis, the sacred bull of Hermonthis (Armant)

Bust of Serapis, the Ptolemies' invented god

Limestone offering table with representations of the Egyptian deities Osiris, Isis and Min

The Palestrina mosaic: a late Hellenistic imagining of the Nile Valley

Pharaonic religion in all its glory: the painted Hypostyle Hall of the temple of Hathor at Tentyris (Dendera)

A Ptolemaic king and queen before Horus, the Egyptian god of kingship; temple of Sobek and Horus, Ombos (Kom Ombo)

The back of a gold amulet in the shape of *ba*-bird, representing one of the parts of the human soul in Egyptian belief

Underwater archaeology at Thonis-Herakleion; exploration revealed a sunken city on the shore of the 'Sea of the Greeks', twenty miles from Alexandria, with a complex of temples dedicated to one of the most important group of deities in the Egyptian pantheon, the Theban triad of Amun, Mut and Khonsu

The temple of Horus at Apollonopolis (Edfu)

The temple of Isis on the island of Philae

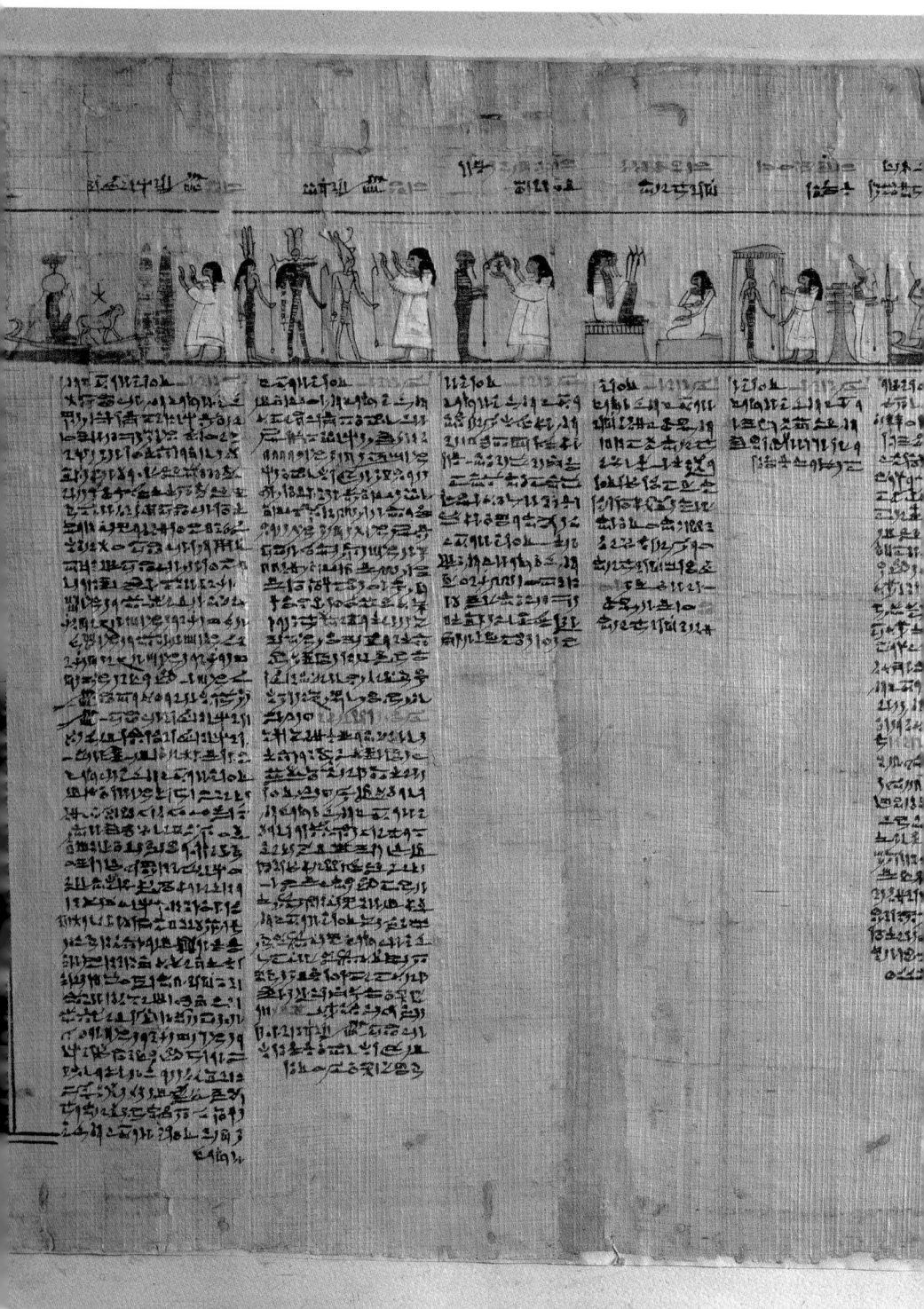

A traditional Egyptian *Book of the Dead* papyrus, prepared for a high-status individual under Ptolemaic rule. These texts included prayers and magical spells to guide and protect a dead person through their journey into the afterlife.

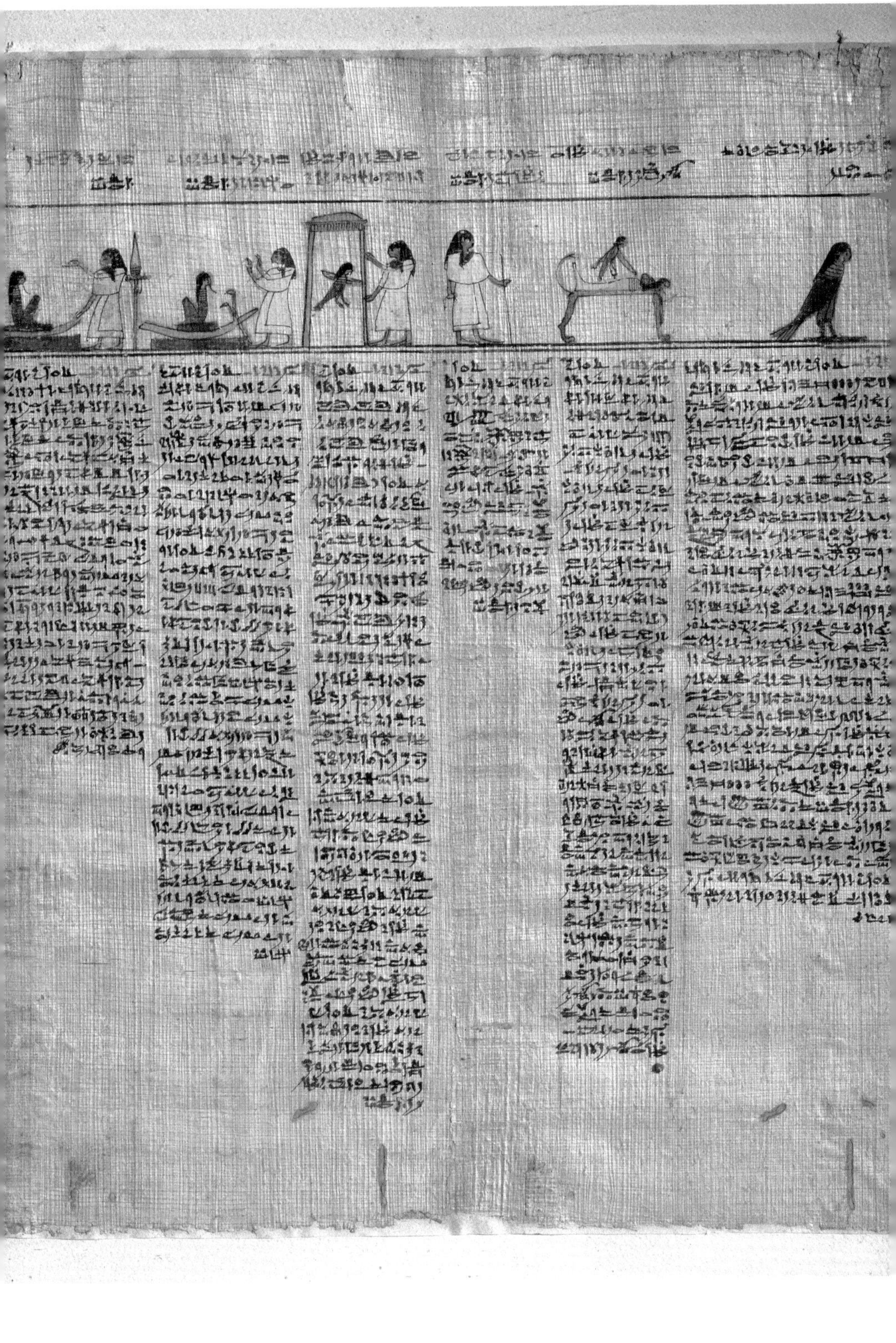

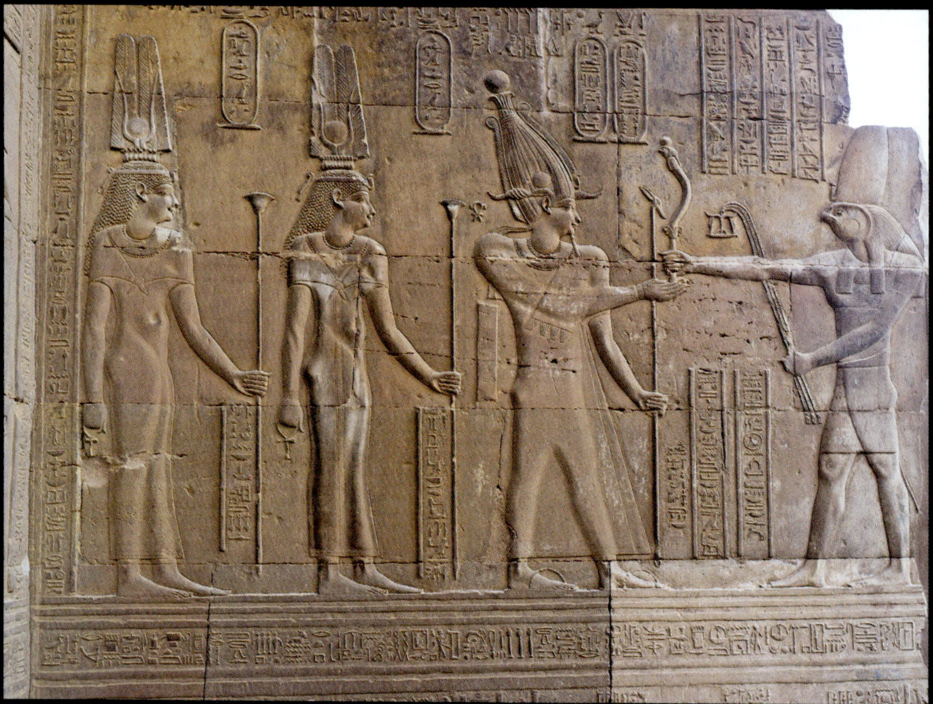

A rare display of dynastic unity: Cleopatra III, Cleopatra II and Ptolemy VIII before the god Horus, temple of Sobek and Horus, Ombos (Kom Ombo)

Gold coin of Ptolemy V as a radiant Greek god

Gold plaque of Ptolemy VI: a Greek king wearing an Egyptian crown

Marble bust of Ptolemy IX

Emperor Augustus (Octavian)

Mark Antony

Coin of Cleopatra VII

Marble bust of Cleopatra VII

Coin issued by Augustus, Emperor of Rome, 'on the capture of Egypt'; the ruler's head is on the obverse, a chained crocodile (representing Egypt) with the legend AEGVPTO CAPTA on the reverse

The end of the dynastic line: Cleopatra VII and her son Ptolemy XV (Caesarion) offering to the Egyptian gods on the back wall of the temple of Hathor at Tentyris (Dendera)

with wooden windows and doors, and roofs of palm branches or straw. Windows were placed on the north side, to take advantage of cooling breezes, while the main entrance to a house might be on an upper floor, reached by an external staircase or an internal courtyard. This was for the protection of the family, since relations with neighbouring villages seem to have been fraught and attacks by marauding gangs not infrequent. Set among the houses were pigeon lofts, to provide regular supplies of manure and meat. The birds would have provided a valuable supplement to people's diets, which were otherwise heavily dependent on lentils and grain. Estimates of the population of Kerkeosiris, the acreage under cultivation, and the average crop yield suggest that local cereal production would have been sufficient to provide every man, woman and child with a daily intake of around 2,175 calories: enough to survive on, but a meagre diet all the same for a farm labourer. Nonetheless, the main economic activity in the village – as throughout Egypt – was the production of grain for the royal treasury. An area of rough land just outside Kerkeosiris housed the community's threshing floor, where the harvest was taken each year for assessment and taxation – with the levy stored temporarily in the village grain depot – before any produce was released back to the farmers.

Menkhes' archive reflects this fundamental rhythm of Egypt's rural economy. The main duty of a village scribe was to keep records related to agriculture, and the vast majority of his correspondence was concerned with land tenure, crop production and taxation. The Ptolemies perfected an agricultural system inherited from the pharaohs; every aspect was centrally dictated, and designed to maximise government revenue. As a third-century finance minister told his subordinate, 'Consider it one of your most important duties that the nome is sown with crops according to the crop schedule.'[4] Reflecting the interests of the state rather than the needs of the farmers, the main crops were cereals – predominantly wheat (representing over half of all the sown land in Kerkeosiris), with smaller amounts of barley and spelt – supplemented with other edibles such as lentils and beans, and fodder crops including wild chickling, grass and fenugreek. A three-year rotation was used, with wheat sown for two years in a row followed by legumes in the third year to rejuvenate the soil. Everything was geared to maximising the wheat harvest that underpinned the entire Ptolemaic economy.

As village scribe, Menkhes answered to the provincial scribe who in turn worked under the royal scribe. The work was both bureaucratic and unrelenting. Each new season, field boundaries had to be re-established, land ownership confirmed, soil fertility assessed, yields calculated, taxes predicted, crops guarded, harvests received, levies deducted, grain stored and, finally, revenues taken to the provincial capital for onward delivery to Alexandria. The paperwork in a typical village scribe's office must have been voluminous.

Despite a semblance of order and due process, the system was by no means watertight. Documents were often carried over from one year to the next, without any further checks; as a result, mistakes could be perpetuated for years without anyone noticing – until government income was affected and an audit was carried out. Human error was ever present, and Menkhes' documents are full of copying mistakes, inconsistencies and inaccurate calculations. The task of managing every aspect of a village's agricultural production was simply too large for one man; shortcuts and workarounds were inevitable.

What made the process particularly complicated was the pattern of land ownership, with different rules and regulations applying to different types of landholding. The total area of land belonging to Kerkeosiris amounted to some 3,149 acres, of which the village itself occupied just 1.5 per cent and waste land another 3.5 per cent. Of the land under cultivation, a little over half belonged to the crown and 6 per cent to temples, a third was farmed by cleruchs, and the remaining 9 per cent was classed as miscellaneous. Crown land was generally leased, in plots of varying sizes, to local farmers, who tended to regard them as their own; they could sublet crown land, or even transfer possession if they registered the transaction with the village scribe. Given that the state's main interest was to maximise revenue, it is surprising that, in Kerkeosiris, less than half the available crown land was actually sown with crops. The reason seems to have been that rents were unattractively high. Periodically, the government had to resort to compulsory cultivation to bring crown land back into production.

In some parts of Egypt, the temples controlled a third of the available land, but in the Fayum the proportion was much smaller, reflecting the state's overriding interest in the region. Like crown land, sacred land was farmed under long-term leases, by individual farmers or local cooperatives. Lessees might also be given offices (both lay and clerical) in the local cult, providing them with additional perquisites. From time to time, the king might donate crown land to a temple, to curry favour with an important priesthood or win the support of the native population. Behind any such official pronouncement, carved in stone, there must have been a mountain of paperwork, archived in local government bureaux.

The final category of land around Kerkeosiris was cleruchic land, granted to settlers in return for their military service. Often it was a way of bringing marginal land into production. No ground rent was payable on such allotments, although tax was levied on the harvest. When a cleruch was mobilised to fight abroad or put down a domestic insurrection, his land might be taken back by the state or rented out to other local farmers: more paperwork for the village scribe. The pattern of cleruchic settlement reflected the political situation in the country at large. After the Battle of Raphia, for example, Egyptian veterans became eligible for allotments, although at Kerkeosiris it was ninety years after the battle that the first native troops were given plots of land. In the troubled times between 180 and 150, there was almost no settlement of new cleruchs: reservists were on almost continuous call-up, and the government was too preoccupied with the security situation to worry about installing new settlers in the countryside. Towards the end of Ptolemy VIII's reign, a new round of cleruchic grants marked the end of the civil war between the king and his sister. Plots of land granted to immigrant mercenaries or native Egyptian soldiers might be farmed by local labourers, contracted on one-year leases. Such hired hands probably also had to farm parcels of crown or temple land to make a living. Despite Egypt's famed wealth, ordinary families still struggled to make ends meet.

The life of a village scribe was not just one of paperwork and drudgery. Although keeping agricultural records was the main responsibility, the role also encompassed investigating and even settling minor disputes, such as the demarcation of field boundaries, and keeping records of infractions and offences. All this Menkhes did with great diligence, even if it made him enemies. On one occasion, both Menkhes and his brother were arrested on a trumped-up charge of poisoning, kept in prison overnight, then brought to trial and summarily released when it transpired there was no case to answer. Incidents of theft, burglary and assault occur throughout Menkhes' archive. So do disputes between cleruchs and local Egyptians. Reservists seem to have regarded peasants with disdain, even two centuries after the first Greek-speaking settlers had come to Egypt. On a single day in August 113, five separate complaints were addressed to Menkhes by five different farmers; all complained about a violent gang, headed by a Greek cavalry officer, that had gone on the rampage, breaking down doors and stealing at will. One hard-pressed farmer lost two items of women's clothing and a jar containing 1,600 copper drachmas, probably his entire accumulated wealth.

The background to such incidents was a general economic decline during the last years of the second century. Even in stable times, land could easily be lost to cultivation – through drying out, increased salinity or flooding – if the irrigation system was not properly maintained. The civil unrest and armed conflict that marred the reigns of Ptolemy VIII and his successor merely exacerbated the problem. In times of uncertainty or instability, embankments, dykes, sluices and regular dredging – all the paraphernalia necessary to sustain irrigation agriculture – tended to be neglected, with dire consequences. In the year 120, the number of farmers abandoning their land and fleeing for their own safety reached a peak. Even the amnesty decree of 118, with its five-year tax holiday for those bringing land back into cultivation, failed to stop the rot. Over the course of just twelve months, between 116 and 115, the amount of land around Kerkeosiris sown with wheat declined dramatically, while the area of derelict land increased. The yield on crown land plummeted by 12 per cent over a ten-year period.

The government's attempts to reclaim abandoned land met with mixed results: little more than one-third of wasteland was successfully reclaimed in the years after the amnesty, while losses from uncultivated land outstripped the yields from cultivated land. And Kerkeosiris seems to have mirrored the picture in the country at large: a dearth of coins from Ptolemy IX's reign may indicate a partial return to the barter economy, as the entire economic system came under increasing pressure.

As for Menkhes himself, at least his role as village scribe provided steady employment; his lot was considerably better than his neighbours'. When he applied for reappointment, his request was granted, but only on condition that he take on a parcel of unproductive land, work it at his own expense and pay rent on it to boot. In Ptolemaic Egypt, every perk had its price tag.

The uneasy truce between Ptolemy IX and Cleopatra III did not last long. Within eighteen months of coming to the throne, the king was forced by his mother to divorce his sister-wife Cleopatra IV in favour of his younger sister, Cleopatra Selene. The prospects for a divorced queen, anywhere in the Hellenistic world, were not bright; so Cleopatra IV headed for Cyprus where she married the Seleukid king Antiochos IX, even though he was caught up in a bitter dispute for power with his brother Antiochos VIII. Seleukid dynastic politics were notoriously fractious; but what made this family dispute more intractable than most was that the two rival kings (Antiochos VIII and IX) were married to two Ptolemaic sisters (Tryphaina and Cleopatra IV). Sibling rivalry in the Ptolemaic royal house was something of a tradition, and true to form Tryphaina had Cleopatra IV put to death in the sanctuary at Antiokheia in 112. Ptolemy IX's beloved sister and wife, and the mother of his two eldest sons, had been driven from her home, forced into exile and murdered – all by members of his own family.

In the royal palace at Alexandria, the last vestige of domestic harmony vanished completely five years later, when Cleopatra III accused Ptolemy IX of trying to kill her. (And who could have blamed him?) Rousing the city's populace, she had him driven from Egypt; in his haste to save his own life, he left behind his new wife and sons. Ptolemy made first for Cyprus, which he knew well. Cleopatra III sent her troops there to hunt him down, and he fled once more, this time across the sea to the port city of Seleukeia-in-Pieria. There he finally prevailed against his attackers. Cleopatra III had her commander promptly executed for failing to capture and kill her son, and Ptolemy IX returned to Cyprus to conquer the island and rule it as king.

With her elder son gone from Alexandria, Cleopatra III summoned her younger son, Alexander, whom she had always preferred, from Cyprus. She met him at Pelousion before escorting him to the capital and appointing him to rule alongside her as Ptolemy X. Conscious of his birth name, he hoped no doubt to usher in a return to the glorious days of Macedonian hegemony. (In this spirit, he defiantly issued his own coins for Cyprus, minted in Alexandria.) But the situation in 107 was a far cry from what it had been two centuries earlier. For a start, the institution of kingship that the Ptolemies had inherited from Alexander the Great was sadly diminished: never before had a female ruler banished one son and appointed another. Cleopatra III, now with her favourite son by her side and under her thumb, made no pretence of being the junior partner. Her word counted for everything. She forced Ptolemy X to marry his brother's wife (and his own sister), Cleopatra Selene, to keep the princess within the inner circle. Cleopatra III's name was always mentioned first in royal inscriptions, and she had herself appointed priest of Alexander in the dynastic cult. The most prestigious religious office in Hellenistic Egypt had hitherto been reserved exclusively for men. It was a bold and provocative move, flouting long-held traditions and social mores. The citizens of Alexandria responded characteristically, with caustic wit, giving Ptolemy X a variety of disrespectful nicknames. The most polite was Pareisaktos ('smuggled in'). Another was ho Kokke ('son of the cuckoo', or perhaps 'son of the cunt'). But for Cleopatra III this was all water off a duck's back. Her own position was unassailable.

Not that the deposed Ptolemy IX had given up hope of regaining his lost crown. From his exile in Cyprus, he initially held on to Kyrenaika as well, but the territory eventually declared independence under his half-brother, Ptolemy Apion, and was thereafter lost to the Ptolemaic realm. To shore up his position, Apion did what his father, Ptolemy VIII, had done in similar circumstances: he published a will which stated that, in the event of his death without an heir, he bequeathed his kingdom to Rome. This time around, the Romans invoked the document and took control of the north African territory – the oldest of all the Ptolemaic overseas possessions – after Apion's death. Without Kyrenaika, Ptolemy IX knew he had to regain Egypt if he were to restore his status as a major player.

In 103, renewed turmoil in the Seleukid kingdom presented an opportunity. The Phoenician port city of Ptolemais Ake (present-day Acre) was being besieged by the Judaeans, and appealed to Ptolemy IX for assistance. He sailed from Cyprus and helped to lift the siege, before invading Galilee, defeating the Judaeans and plundering their territory. These developments caused alarm in Alexandria, where Cleopatra III and Ptolemy X (rightly) feared that Ptolemy IX would use Judaea as a springboard to invade Egypt. The Egyptian government therefore launched a pre-emptive invasion of Judaea, with Ptolemy X attacking by sea from the Phoenician coast, while Cleopatra's forces attacked Ake. Somehow, Ptolemy IX managed to slip past the encircling armies and head for Egypt. Ptolemy X had to regroup quickly in order to repel his brother's attempted invasion of the Nile Valley. Ptolemy IX camped for the winter at Gaza – almost within sight of the Egyptian border; so near yet so far – before sailing back to exile in Cyprus early in 102. There he remained, bowed but still determined, biding his time. Cleopatra III, meanwhile, saw an opportunity to strengthen her own influence in Asia by marrying off Cleopatra Selene to one of the rival Seleukid claimaints, Antiochos VIII. The fact that this required Ptolemy X to divorce Selene first was of no consequence to their mother. Power play trumped family relationships every time.

A year later, everything changed in Alexandria. It was perhaps inevitable that Cleopatra III and Ptolemy X should eventually come to blows. The son must have grown tired of his mother's domineering personality, of doing her bidding whatever the personal cost, and playing second fiddle in the royal hierarchy. On this occasion, however, the mother–son dispute ended not in the son's banishment, but in the mother's murder. In the late summer of 101, Ptolemy had Cleopatra III killed – the woman who had towered over Ptolemaic dynastic politics for more than forty years. Free at last from his mother's shackles, Ptolemy X chose his own wife (his brother's daughter, Berenike III) and made her his co-regent. At the same time, to make a very public point, he changed his dynastic cult title from Philometor Soter ('mother-loving saviour') to Philadelphos ('sibling-loving'). No one could be in any doubt that the mother was finally gone from the equation.

After all the turmoil and factionalism, the Egyptian economy was in a parlous state. The limited amount of work carried out on native temples under Ptolemy X – just a small amount of decoration at Tentyris and Thebes, with no new commissions – reflects the political uncertainty and the weakness of the public finances. The result of royal neglect was yet another native insurrection in Upper Egypt. Attacks on Latopolis and the Ptolemaic garrison of Pathyris were followed by the secession of Thebes. The conflict dragged on for years, communities pitted against each other, with no resolution in sight. Ptolemy IX, watching events closely from his Cypriot bunker, decided to take advantage of the situation and make his move. In 88, with the support of the demoralised army and the weary citizens of Alexandria, he ousted his younger brother from the palace and the throne. All sorts of rumours started to spread about the reasons for Ptolemy X's downfall: he had shown too much support for Egypt's Jewish population, to the anger of the notoriously anti-Semitic Alexandrian mob; he had melted down the gold sarcophagus of Alexander the Great and replaced it with a glass one. In truth, the Alexandrians had grown tired of his regime's excesses. Driven into exile, he managed to raise a naval force and attempted to invade Egypt, but was repulsed. He then fled to Anatolia where, with borrowed Roman money, he recruited mercenaries and launched a second armada towards Cyprus. But this adventure, too, ended in defeat, and Ptolemy X was killed in battle. So ended one of the strangest reigns in the history of the Ptolemaic dynasty.

Ptolemy IX's re-entry into Egypt was not exactly a moment of triumph. He may have retaken the capital with relative ease, but much of the rest of the country was in revolt. A series of letters, written between March and November 88, provides dramatic first-hand testimony of the conflict. The correspondence was sent by the supreme military commander of the Thebaid, Platon, to the native Egyptian commander of besieged Pathyris, Nakhthor. In the first missive, still dated to the reign of Ptolemy X – either the news from Alexandria had not reached Upper Egypt or Platon was hedging his bets – the commander urged the inhabitants of Pathyris 'to be of good courage and rally to Nakhthor who has been given command over you, until I come to your district with what haste I can'.[5] The same day, Platon wrote to Nakhthor himself, to brief him on the situation and encourage him to stand firm: 'You will do well to hold the place and to exercise your command.'[6] Two days later, Platon wrote again, this time about provisions, indicating perhaps that a siege of Pathyris was being contemplated. The fourth letter, to the priests and people of the town, urged them to stand fast, and promised them, 'For if you do so, and maintain your loyalty to the realm … your superiors will respond with fitting gratitude'.⁷ The final letter in the sequence, written on 1 November, was dated to the reign of Ptolemy IX: his restoration was now recognised throughout the country. The communiqué, addressed to the priests and inhabitants of Pathyris, updated them on the national situation: 'King [Ptolemy IX] Soter has come to Memphis and Hierax has been appointed to subjugate the Thebaid with very large forces.'⁸ Platon added that he hoped this positive news would serve to keep up spirits in beleaguered Pathyris.

Nothing more is known about general Hierax, referenced in the last of Platon's letters, but his 'very large forces' evidently accomplished their mission. The rebellion in Upper Egypt was quelled, although most of Lower Nubia was lost, with the Ptolemaic writ reduced to a mere ten-mile stretch south of Philae. The reconquest of the Thebaid, epicentre of the uprising, seems to have been carried out with particular ruthlessness. (Thebes would not rebel again for another sixty years.) A later author reported that the inhabitants of Thebes were shown no mercy, and were left with 'not even a memorial of their former prosperity'.⁹ By contrast, new cult buildings, including a temple to the goddess Isis, were dedicated at Ptolemais to celebrate the restoration of Ptolemaic rule in Upper Egypt. As for Pathyris, despite its plucky resistance to the rebels, it seems to have been reduced to a shadow of its former self, and effectively disappeared from the map. It was replaced as provincial capital by Hermonthis, and the province as a whole was renamed accordingly. But there was no escaping the fact that royal authority in Upper Egypt had been gravely weakened. It never fully recovered. Henceforth, the government delegated day-to-day control of the region to a dynasty of native governors. They recognised Ptolemaic suzerainty in public while quietly running their own affairs.

Battered and bruised by recent events, the state was anxious to avoid further antagonising the native population. The policy response was to invest in small-scale, selective reconstructions of the holiest sites of Thebes. At Karnak, new decoration was added in the small temple of Ptah, showing the king worshipping the Theban triad (beloved of the priesthood) and the healing deities (revered by the local people). On the west bank of the Nile, royal largesse was directed towards the legendary burial place of Egypt's creator gods (present-day Medinet Habu). Here, Ptolemy IX renovated the second pylon and added an even more impressive outer gateway. In the hieroglyphic writings of his name, Ptolemy the Saviour added the epithet 'eldest heir of the beneficent gods' to remind people of his pre-eminent claim to the kingship, in stark contrast to his interloper younger brother.

By regaining his throne, defeating his brother's forces, putting down the Upper Egyptian rebellion and renewing the temples of the gods (or at least the most important ones), Ptolemy IX had fulfilled the most important duty of a pharaoh: to destroy chaos and restore order. In his second reign, he could assert his title of 'Saviour' with some justification. To set the seal on this new beginning, he staged a second coronation at Memphis in 86. Because this date also coincided with his thirtieth year as king (since his first accession in 116), he chose to mark the occasion with the traditional pharaonic jubilee rites. He thus became the first – and only – Ptolemaic ruler to celebrate such a festival.

The last five years of Ptolemy IX's reign were relatively quiescent, with no major crises at home or abroad. But the appearance of calm was a veneer. Beneath the surface, Egypt's economic and social travails continued unabated. Despite government incentives aimed at the cultivation of agricultural land, *anachoresis* escalated. A document from 83/2 reported that one village in the Herakleopolite province south of Memphis had lost the majority of its population. Egypt seemed to be stuck in a permanent downward spiral. It was a damning indictment of Ptolemaic rule. Dynastic politics had reduced Egypt from the wealthiest land in the ancient world to a weak and vulnerable state.

The vultures were beginning to circle.

Back at the start of Ptolemy IX's reign, just weeks after his accession, a group of tourists had visited Philae. Like countless sightseers since, they left graffiti, their names and a short text carved into the temple walls. What makes these particular scribblings noteworthy is that they are the earliest datable examples of Latin yet discovered in Egypt. The four travellers, C. Acutius, M. Claudius Varus, Sp. Varaeus and M. Titrius(?),[10] are likely to have come to Philae (as Ptolemy IX did himself, the following year) to witness and participate in the festivities marking the beginning of the annual Nile inundation (a phenomenon which the Egyptians believed originated in the region of the First

Cataract). Tourism may have been combined with pilgrimage – carving their names being an act of piety as well as of self-commemoration – and perhaps with business interests as well.

Acutius claimed to have been 'the first' to visit Philae. Whether by this he meant the first Roman, the first Roman trader or the first Latin-speaker is uncertain. In any case, Rome's contacts with the Ptolemaic empire were nothing new. The first recorded contact between the two states was in 273, when Ptolemy II sent an embassy to Rome to establish friendly relations. The context for this diplomatic initiative was a three-way struggle between the Roman Republic, the Carthaginians and King Pyrrhus of Epirus. In 275, after a long struggle, Pyrrhus had ended his campaign in Italy, leaving the way clear for Rome to consolidate its control of the entire peninsula. The moment must have seemed opportune for the great power of the eastern Mediterranean, the Ptolemaic empire, to cosy up to the emerging power of the western Mediterranean, Rome. Flattered by the gesture, Rome reciprocated the same year, sending a delegation of two senior statesmen, C. Fabius and Q. Ogulnius, to Alexandria.

A diplomatic entente may not have been the only outcome of this exchange: when the two Roman envoys became consuls four years later, silver coinage, bearing identical lettering to Ptolemaic Egyptian currency, was introduced for the first time in Rome. A financial agreement, if this is to be inferred, would have benefited both parties: Rome securing for itself a friendly lender to help finance its wars; Egypt finding a receptive new market for its grain. The friendship between the Ptolemaic kingdom and Rome seems to have fostered security ties, too: the earliest known Roman attested living in Egypt (Dinnos, residing in the Arsinoite nome) served as a mercenary in Ptolemy II's army. A couple of decades later, settlers from the Roman heartland of Campania are attested in Egypt.

The Ptolemies became the first of the Hellenistic dynasties formally to recognise Rome as a rising power. For its part, Rome gained valuable knowledge about a potential future rival and its legendary wealth. When Fabius and Ogulnius returned to Rome from Alexandria, they were said to have been so embarrassed by the extravagant gifts they had received in Egypt that they felt obliged to offer them to the public treasury. The senate, delighted with the outcome of the mission, allowed the ambassadors to keep the treasures for themselves.

Egypt's diplomatic recognition certainly worked to Rome's advantage. As we have seen, although Egypt had enjoyed friendly relations with Carthage for some years, Ptolemy II and III remained neutral during the First Punic War, declining the Carthaginians' request for a loan. A Roman embassy visited Alexandria at the end of the war to thank the Egyptians for their tacit support. Because of Kyrenaika, the Ptolemaic realm had stronger interests in the western Mediterranean and north Africa than any of its Hellenistic rivals. It could not afford to back the wrong side in the conflict between Rome and Carthage, so studied neutrality was a prudent policy.

During the Second Punic War, a Roman request for military assistance was met with a friendly but similarly non-committal response. Undaunted, Rome continued its diplomatic charm offensive. In 210, an embassy travelled to Alexandria to beg for grain supplies – Rome is said to have been 'suffering from a great scarcity'.[11] The ambassadors presented gifts, including a toga, to Ptolemy IV, and a Roman soldier was put at the king's disposal to command the Ptolemaic garrison at Itanos on Crete. When Hannibal was finally defeated, nine years later, at the end of the Second Punic War, Rome sent another embassy to Alexandria to thank the new monarch, Ptolemy V, 'for his steadfast friendship which had remained unshaken at a time when Rome's closest allies had deserted her'.[12] The truth was perhaps a little different, but the Romans had every interest in cosying up to the king. For, with Carthage humbled, a new offensive was to be directed further east, against Philip V of Macedon; the Romans knew only too well how the Hellenistic monarchies could turn in an instant from bitter rivals to firm allies when faced with an external threat. In preparation for an attack on Macedon, Rome wanted to ensure that 'Ptolemy would remain the loyal friend which he had been heretofore'.[13] Ptolemy V declared that he would not come to Philip V's aid, but would only intervene if asked to do so by the Romans. Within a couple of generations, Egypt's attitude towards Rome had changed from aloof to deferential. It was a harbinger of things to come.

One of the reasons behind the shift was Ptolemy V's own precarious position. His accession, at the age of six, had led his Hellenistic rivals to launch opportunistic invasions of the remaining Ptolemaic possessions in Koile-Syria and the Aegean. Ptolemy's supporters needed a strong backer: to rein in Seleukid and Macedonian ambitions and dissuade any potential domestic rivals from challenging the king's authority. Rome was invited to place Ptolemy V and his dominions under the Republic's formal protection. The senate readily accepted, and sent Marcus Lepidus to become one of the king's official guardians. From this moment on, Rome felt it had official justification to intervene in the internal affairs of the Ptolemaic dynasty. The infamous Day of Eleusis, in the following reign, epitomised this new world order. Before Eleusis, Egypt treated Rome as an equal; afterwards, the Ptolemaic kingdom felt increasingly like the junior partner in the relationship.

The stage was set for Ptolemy VIII's incendiary will. The tourists who scratched their names into the temple of Philae within weeks of his death paved the way for an intensification of contacts between Rome and the Nile Valley. In the early spring of 112, a Roman senator, Lucius Memmius, paid an official visit to Egypt. The government was anxious to ensure that the trip was a success, so an official in Alexandria sent a letter to a junior colleague in the Fayum to check that everything was in place ahead of Memmius' arrival: accommodation of an appropriate standard; suitable gifts for the honoured guest; and an itinerary that would include some of the famous sights of the Arsinoite nome, notably a visit to the Labyrinth (the ruined pyramid temple of Amenemhat III, already 1,700 years old) and an opportunity to feed the sacred crocodile.

Three decades later, when Ptolemy IX had seen off his brother and celebrated his jubilee, another senior Roman, the proquaestor Lucullus, paid a visit to Alexandria to celebrate the abiding bonds of friendship between the Roman Republic and the Ptolemaic kingdom. Needless to say, there was an ulterior motive: Rome was embroiled in the first of its wars against King Mithridates VI of Pontos (bordering the Black Sea), and was seeking military and financial assistance from its allies. Ptolemy IX showed his important visitor lavish hospitality, but Rome's request was fraught with difficulties. On the one hand, Ptolemy X had signed a will bequeathing his territories to Rome; Rome had not pressed its claim, but the arrangement hung over the Ptolemaic state like the sword of Damocles. On the other hand, the whole prosecution of the First Mithridatic War was mired in confusion and controversy: the Roman army was being led by the general Sulla, but he had been declared an outlaw by the government in Rome. Ptolemy had no wish to back the wrong side in an internal Roman dispute. Of even more concern, Ptolemy IX's two sons, who had been sent to the island of Kos with their half-brother in 103 for their own safety, had been captured by Mithridates fifteen years later and promptly engaged to his daughters. Antagonising the man who held his sons captive was not a wise move for Ptolemy, especially with the threat of Roman rule in the event the Ptolemaic dynasty failed. Weighing up all these considerations, Ptolemy IX declined Rome's request for support, and the proquaestor left Alexandria empty-handed.

A postscript to this encounter added yet another twist to the evolving relationship between Egypt and Rome. The war against Mithridates continued, without Egyptian support, and during the fighting one of the Ptolemaic princes managed to escape his captor and join Sulla. He was taken by the general to Rome, where he provided Sulla and his colleagues with unparalleled insight into the inner workings of the ever-fractious Ptolemaic dynasty.

Rome, with its unstoppable military might, had eliminated or absorbed every significant rival around its borders, and was extending its writ deep into Hellenistic territory. It now began to contemplate a decisive intervention in Egypt. Ptolemy IX was an old man. Perhaps his impending death might provide the perfect opportunity.

11

Keeping the Faith

Any ruler of the Nile Valley, be he a native pharaoh, a Macedonian monarch or a foreign invader, had to placate the temples. These ancient institutions were not only economically wealthy and politically influential, they also came to regard themselves as the custodians of pharaonic culture, torch-bearers of thirty centuries of tradition. From the shore of the Mediterranean to the First Cataract, the cults of Egypt's myriad deities were stitched into the fabric of society at every level, with a special place in the collective consciousness of the country's indigenous inhabitants. Unless the ruler paid due homage to the temples, confirmed (or preferably enhanced) their historic rights and privileges, and maintained (or preferably beautified) their buildings, the priests could choose to withhold their public support – or, worse still, actively foment dissatisfaction and revolt.

With the help of native advisers – men like Manetho of Sebennytos and Padiusir of Hermopolis – the first Macedonian monarchs quickly grasped this interdependence. They took very active, and public, steps to shore up their support among the major cults of the land. Within weeks of conquering Egypt in 332, Alexander the Great had personally paid his respects to the sacred bull of Memphis and ordered his general, Peukestas, to ensure the occupying forces respected the sanctity of the city's necropolis. While still officially only satrap, the first Ptolemy had restored temple property confiscated by the Persians. He seems to have been keen to learn what was expected of a pharaoh, and the native priests were just as keen to teach him. There developed a relationship between monarch and clergy that was mutually beneficial and carefully cultivated.

Throughout the Ptolemaic period, the interplay between 'church and state' manifested itself most clearly at Memphis. The city was the traditional capital of Egypt, a status it had enjoyed since the foundation of the state, nearly three millennia before Alexander's invasion. By contrast, Thebes in Upper Egypt had emerged as the religious capital of the country. Despite or because of this, the priests of Memphis saw an opportunity with the advent of the Ptolemaic dynasty to burnish their own credentials, advance their interests and get one up on their Theban counterparts. Even after Ptolemy I moved the capital to Alexandria, Memphis remained the unofficial headquarters of the native clergy until the very end. The priests of Ptah legitimised successive Ptolemaic monarchs, and basked in the reflected glory. Whatever the latest outrage in Alexandria or uprising in Thebes, Memphis remained steadfastly loyal to the crown.

The cult of Apis was a singular beneficiary of this connection. The sacred bull of Memphis was never one of the leading members of the native pantheon, despite the great antiquity of its cult. The lavish burial of an Apis bull seems to have become an event of national importance only during the reign of Ramesses II (1279–1213), who hailed from a parvenu dynasty with provincial, plebeian origins and was thus keen to present himself as a legitimate pharaoh. Other sacred bull cults came to prominence in the thirtieth dynasty (which had similar concerns), including the Buchis at Hermonthis and the Mnevis at Heliopolis.

It was Herodotus, as much as anyone, who propelled Apis to international fame. For the fifth-century historian and ethnographer, the animal cults of pharaonic Egypt were one of the country's most exotic and bizarre features. He seized on the worship of the sacred bull of Memphis as an exemplar of this strangeness; readers all over the Greek-speaking world were fascinated and appalled in equal measure. A description of the rituals surrounding the Apis became a standard ingredient in subsequent classical accounts of Egypt.

Certainly, to Greek eyes, the whole panoply of sacraments associated with the discovery, life and death of Apis seemed unbelievably esoteric. A new Apis bull might be found anywhere in the Nile Valley;

identification depended on the presence of certain distinguishing marks on the beast's body. According to Herodotus,

> The marks on this calf called Apis are these: he is black, and has on his forehead a three-cornered white spot, and the likeness of an eagle on his back; the hairs of the tail are double, and there is a knot under the tongue.[1]

Even the Persian rulers of Egypt before Alexander, not known for revering the traditional pharaonic cults, had come under the peculiar spell of Apis. Darius I had offered a reward for anyone discovering the new incarnation. Under the Ptolemies, the bulls came largely from the Delta, the main area of cattle rearing in Egypt, but at least one was found at Oxyrhynchos in Middle Egypt and another in the Thebaid. One of the bulls identified during the long reign of Ptolemy VIII was conveniently born in the temple of Memphis itself.

Upon discovery, each new Apis spent forty days at Nilopolis (present-day Delas) where local women, recognising the creature as a powerful symbol of fertility, would raise their skirts before it. (The bull's reaction is not recorded.) These rites accomplished, the beast was brought to Memphis to be crowned amid great celebration, before being installed in special quarters in the southern part of the precinct of Ptah. Fed, watered, bathed and generally pampered, the bulls usually lived long lives. In the three centuries of Hellenistic rule, Egypt saw fifteen Ptolemies come and go but only thirteen Apis bulls.

If the discovery and coronation of an Apis were occasions for rejoicing, the burial of one was an even more lavish and costly affair. In the sixth year of his reign as pharaoh, Ptolemy I had personally loaned fifty talents of silver for the burial of an Apis, perhaps the very same beast that Alexander had worshipped. Eleven further bulls would be buried under the Ptolemaic dynasty, each a spectacle that drew visitors from far and wide.[2]

Because of the relative rarity of an Apis burial, occurring only once in a generation, written instructions were essential: a priest was unlikely to live long enough to preside at two consecutive burials. Like a pharaoh, an Apis was embalmed after death, and the process – which took seventy days in total – was essentially the same.

A Ptolemaic papyrus, found among the archive of a family of Memphite undertakers, provides a detailed description. The preparation of the body was carried out in a special embalming house, located close to the Apis' stall in the temple of Ptah. First, in a process lasting four days – time was of the essence, if the body were not to putrefy – the bull's carcass had to be cleansed and prepared. It was laid out on a huge alabaster table, drained of its fluids and thoroughly cleaned – all using special, ritual instruments. Then the brain and other internal organs were removed. During this crucial first phase, members of the Memphite priesthood would participate in ritual fasting. Over the next forty-eight days, the body was cured by packing it in natron. Once mummification was complete, the bull was carefully wrapped in linen bandages to restore its lifelike appearance, a lengthy process taking sixteen days.

The final stage of the whole ceremony was the funeral procession to the burial vault. For this very public, four-day spectacle, huge crowds of pious mourners and curious tourists lined the route. The bull's embalmed body – placed in a special barque-shrine on wheels – was taken from the embalming house to the 'Lake of Pharaoh', north-east of Memphis. In the cortège, priests played the roles of major Egyptian gods, while two local girls acted the parts of Isis and her sister Nephthys, the chief mourners. Once the procession arrived at the lake, further rituals were enacted, before the bull was taken into a special tented pavilion set up on the shore. Here the most sacred of all the funerary rituals, the Opening of the Mouth, was performed on the corpse to bring it magically back to life. The body entered the pavilion from the west (the direction of sunset) and emerged from the east (sunrise), symbolising its rebirth. From the lake shore, the cortège wound its way up the escarpment to the necropolis of Memphis where lay the catacombs of Apis, the Sarapieion.

The oldest part of the complex lay deep underground, where a rock-hewn corridor gave access to a series of individual burial vaults (rediscovered by archaeologists in the 1850s). The laborious work of carving a vault from the living rock was carried out by teams of lowly labourers, usually a dozen men working at a time, and might begin as early as the third year after a new bull's installation. Although this was mundane employment, it was nonetheless a source of pride: a contribution towards the upkeep of a centuries-old tradition. A mason who worked at the Sarapieion in 96 could trace his occupation back twelve generations within the same family, to before Alexander's conquest.

Making the granite sarcophagus to house the embalmed body of the Apis represented another mammoth undertaking. A block of stone of suitable size was first extracted from the granite quarries of Aswan, then carved into shape with dolerite pounders, before being shipped northwards by barge, offloaded at the quay of Memphis and, finally, dragged to the Sarapieion, where it was lowered into the prepared vault. The last stage alone might take as long as eighteen days, with five days' rest; the men who performed the back-breaking task were paid extra rations. Once an embalmed Apis had been placed in its sarcophagus, it was sealed in its vault and left to rest in peace for eternity. The main doors to the whole gallery might be opened on special religious occasions, but otherwise all was dark and quiet – until excavation began of another new vault.

If the bull catacombs were impressive, so too were the associated cult buildings on the surface. The Ptolemaic necropolis of Memphis was indeed a city of the dead, with temples, shrines and avenues, and all the paraphernalia of a major tourist destination – from booths selling votive offerings and hawkers selling street food to interpreters of dreams and other mountebanks plying their dubious trades. A canal, named Phchêt, lined with houses and gardens, divided the city of Memphis from the necropolis zone. On its eastern side, a quay connected with the temple of Ptah. On the opposite bank, a ceremonial avenue, paved with stone and lined with sphinxes, led up the escarpment.

The first buildings it passed, on the very edge of the cliffs, were two massive enclosures sacred to the cat goddess Bastet and the jackal god Anubis, known as the Boubastieion and Anoubieion respectively. The first comprised two or three major temples, a host of smaller shrines and a scattering of priestly dwellings; the 'dancers of Bastet', officiants in her cult, played a key role in mummification rituals. To the south of the Boubastieion, a third, smaller enclosure, the Asklepieion, was dedicated to Imhotep (Gr. Asklepios), god of medicine. It had its own access up the escarpment, an avenue lined with stalls selling food, mementoes and other visitor services. The best pitches were eagerly sought after, and the revenue from these booths provided the temples inside the enclosure with a steady income stream. The cults of the

Memphite necropolis, though steeped in ancient Egyptian religion, were equally popular with Greek-speaking settlers. The Asklepieion, for example, was a popular destination for those seeking cures. A potential supplicant, having run the gauntlet of the hawkers, had to pay a fee to gain entry to the inner sanctum; if they were lucky enough to receive the god's message in a dream, a visit to the dream-interpreter would be the next outlay. Seeking divine assistance in Ptolemaic Egypt was an expensive business.

The Anoubieion was likewise a jumble of sacred and secular spaces. Alongside temples and shrines were administrative offices serving the whole necropolis. Those based here included a notary to register documents and a representative of the provincial governor. A police station provided security, and a prison held those convicted of crimes committed in the city of the dead. Humbler dwellings served a sizeable resident population – priests and embalmers, water carriers and porridge sellers, tailors and barbers, doctors and potters.

All around, the underground galleries of the sacred animal necropolis contained millions of mummified ibis, falcons, baboons, cats, jackals and cows (the latter regarded as the 'mothers of Apis'). The annual opening of the ibis and falcon galleries for mass burials – each bird donated by a visiting pilgrim – was a popular spectacle. One denizen of this strange world, a man named Hor (a close contemporary of Ptolemaios the recluse), recorded a nightmare in which he had to feed 60,000 ibis being farmed for future mummification. This was not far short of the strange reality: in the Ptolemaic period, as many as 10,000 birds were reared, mummified and buried in the Memphite necropolis every year. Hor also recorded that keeping the windblown sand out of the various chapels was a never-ending task, while chapels were fetid with the smell of decaying animals.

Beyond the animal necropolis, deep into the desert, at the end of the sphinx-lined avenue, lay the Sarapieion itself. The original temple had been built in the fourth century by the last native pharaoh, Nakhthorheb, who had sought to encourage the popularity of animal cults as an expression of indigenous tradition and a bulwark against increasing foreign influence. Ironically, under the Ptolemies the Sarapieion enclosure could not have looked more un-Egyptian, at least from the outside. In the first decade of Ptolemy II's reign, a chapel in Greek style had been built next to the thirtieth-dynasty temple, and some time later a portico was added, decorated with a semicircle of eleven marble statues of Greek poets and philosophers, including Pindar and Hesiod, Homer and Plato; they may originally have guarded a shrine – perhaps even the Memphite tomb of Alexander before its relocation to Alexandria. Alongside them were sculptures connected with the cult of Dionysos: a panther and peacocks, a child riding the hound Kerberos, and a singing Siren.

Above ground the country's foreign rulers could hold sway: in the underworld, the old gods continued to watch over the land of Egypt.

The stonemasons who excavated the Apis vaults were not the only members of the Memphite community to take pride in passing their office down from father to son. From undertakers and mummification specialists to official mourners and funerary priests, the Memphite 'death industry' was probably the biggest economic sector in the city. It remained steadfastly the preserve of Egyptians, and while its practitioners are not as well attested as Greek-speaking bureaucrats, a few scattered papyri provide glimpses into their lives and livelihoods. One family held the offices of overseer and undertaker of the necropolis for eleven consecutive generations. Other households monopolised the lucrative business of embalming, with each family enjoying the rights to service specific streets or even entire villages; a family's wealth was denominated in the number of prospective corpses among its client base. Sometimes, two or more families would band together to form a trade association, a 'closed shop' designed to exclude outsiders.

One particular family of Memphite undertakers seems to have kept every contract and memo relating to marriage and property. Native law, 'the law of the land' that applied to Egyptian-speakers, required documentary evidence to be produced to uphold a claim, so retaining every scrap of evidence was hardwired into the Egyptian psyche – a boon for archaeologists and historians millennia later. The undertakers' documents chart the mixed fortunes of a single family over the course of the Ptolemaic period. In the autumn of 146, for instance, Ptolemy VI ordered that all documents prepared in demotic (in other words, by and for native Egyptians) in the necropolis of Memphis had to be summarised and labelled in Greek before they could be deposited in the official archives, which were housed in the Anoubieion. This royal decree burdened ordinary Egyptians with yet more expense and inconvenience, and must have added further to native resentment.

There was no point, however, in complaining to the authorities (in this case the Memphite priesthood), because the high priests were complicit in the arrangement. Alexander the Great's decision, followed in turn by Ptolemy I, to be crowned at Memphis had sealed the bond between Macedonian monarchs and the city's priests. The high priest of Ptah became the mouthpiece of the crown, and the office was held in turn by thirteen members of the same family, spanning nine generations.

Like any aristocracy jealously guarding its privileges, the holders of high office in all the most important cults married into each other's families. The high priests of Memphis were closely related to their counterparts at Letopolis (the capital of the neighbouring province), and monopolised virtually all religious positions in and around the capital. The high status enjoyed by the 'first family' of Memphis is underscored by their surviving artefacts: beautifully crafted stelae, statuary, stone sarcophagi and illustrated funerary papyri. In emulation of royal practice, members of the family sometimes adopted double names. And to an ordinary citizen of Memphis, the high priest of Ptah – the man who crowned the Apis and the pharaoh alike – must have seemed closer to the gods than to humanity. The high priests of Ptah gave the Ptolemies the imprimatur of divine favour, and, in a public show of reciprocity, many of the Ptolemies took names incorporating that of Ptah. As Upper Egypt slipped progressively from the government's grasp, the god of Memphis seemed a better guarantor of royal legitimacy than Theban Amun or the traditional gods of kingship, Ra and Horus.[3]

To the same end, later Ptolemies paid increasingly regular visits to Memphis, especially at times of crisis or national celebration. Ptolemy IV visited both before and after the Battle of Raphia, while Ptolemy V's Memphite coronation in 197 was designed to secure his shaky grip on power. When Antiochos IV invaded Egypt three decades later, he took pains to visit Memphis for his formal proclamation as king. His ousting, at the Day of Eleusis, prompted the restored and reconciled Ptolemaic siblings – Ptolemy VI and Ptolemy VIII – to pay their own visit, and this was followed by a further royal sojourn in the city on the occasion of the New Year festival. This subsequently became a fixture in the royal calendar.

Ptolemy VI and Cleopatra II travelled to Memphis again in 163, while Ptolemy VIII came for his coronation as sole monarch in 145. His son Ptolemy IX was crowned twice in the temple of Ptah. While Memphis in general benefited from such attention, and the lavish spending it occasioned, none benefited more than the high priests of Ptah. Rulers in their own little kingdom, they revelled in their role as interlocutors between Egypt's traditional religion and its Macedonian monarchs.

The very first high priest attested in the Ptolemaic period, Nesisty Padibastet, was appointed by the king as 'first priest' in the cult of the deified Arsinoe II. It suited the monarch to stitch his own dynasty into the venerable fabric of pharaonic religion. The priesthood of Ptah, for its part, was a willing collaborator. Nesisty's son, Anemhor, received even greater royal favours when Ptolemy III made him 'overseer of priests of all the gods and goddesses of Upper and Lower Egypt' – in other words, primate of all the native clergy. Once again, there were benefits to the king from such an arrangement. The creation of this new post gave the monarch a clear, direct line of communication with priests the length and breadth of the country. Another of Anemhor's offices was priest of the cult of Nakhthorheb, the last native pharaoh. Through this careful web of associations, the high priests of Memphis and the Ptolemaic dynasty shored up each other's credibility. It was a cosy relationship. Anemhor's son and successor, Djedhor, boasted how he 'entered the king's house before all the priests and prophets of the temples of Upper and Lower Egypt' and was 'the first to be summoned among the great dignitaries of Egypt'.[4]

A later high priest, Padibastet IV, was invested by the king himself, in a ceremony conducted in the royal palace at Alexandria. An inscription recounted how,

> He came to the 'building site' [Alexandria] and drank in the presence of the king. He was given the gold sceptre of authority, vestments from the Southern Store, and the bouquet fitting for Ptah at festivals and processions. He had placed on his head the great

golden diadem, in keeping with the custom of his forefathers, in his seventeenth year.[5]

He went on to hold office for over a quarter of a century.

In addition to exercising theological authority over all the cults of Memphis, the high priest of Ptah also oversaw all building projects in the city's temples. His status gave him unparalleled convening power. Ptolemy III seems to have been the first monarch to summon a synod of priests. Under Ptolemy V, Memphis became the chosen setting for these synods, which drew priests from all over the country. The practice soon evolved into something of a tradition: at least fifteen synods took place during the third and second centuries. The formal resolutions of these conclaves, issued as decrees and carved in tablets of stone, focused on temple and cult matters – royal benefactions, amendments to priestly rosters, the emoluments of the clergy – but the discussions which took place must have covered a wider range of religious and political matters.

Over time, the decrees reveal a subtle change in the way the Macedonian monarchs presented themselves – or were presented by the native priests. With each successive synod, each set of resolutions, the king came across as less Hellenistic, more pharaonic. The tensions between government and clergy were no doubt lively, but an accommodation benefited both sides. For all that the native temples were bastions of indigenous culture, many priests were happy to collaborate with the Ptolemaic regime.

A vivid snapshot of Egyptian religion under the Ptolemies is provided by a drowned landscape recently uncovered beneath the waters of Abukir Bay. At the heart of this now-sunken land was the city of Thonis-Herakleion, located close to Kanopos at the mouth of one of the Nile branches, some twenty miles from Alexandria. Royal patronage of the new capital benefited the neighbouring region, too, and Thonis (Eg. Ta-henet) enjoyed its fair share of investment.

Though located on the shore of the 'Sea of the Greeks' and endowed by Greek-speaking kings, the temples of Thonis were unequivocally Egyptian in style, and dedicated to the most important group of deities in the entire Egyptian pantheon, the Theban triad of Amun, Mut and

Khonsu. The main temple honoured a local form of Amun, Lord of Gereb. His particular theological role (*gereb* is the Egyptian word for 'inheritance') was to hand over to each successive king the deeds to Egypt, thus conferring both sovereignty and legitimacy. As at Thebes, Amun was joined in the temple of Thonis by his wife and son, Mut and Khonsu, both of whom played important parts in the legitimation of Egyptian royalty – Mut represented the queen, Khonsu the heir to the throne. The Greeks latched on to the last, recognising in Khonsu their own youthful god Herakles, and gave the city its Greek name, Herakleion.[6] The fact that the Ptolemaic dynasty claimed descent from Herakles gave the city added appeal. Numerous private votive statuettes and amulets dedicated to Khonsu/Herakles have been found in the ruins of Thonis, not just in the temple enclosure but also in the surrounding settlement.

As befitted its coastal location, Thonis was a city of islands and canals – the Venice of Ptolemaic Egypt. One waterway connected to the Canopic branch of the Nile, providing access to the country's interior. The canals were not just used for practical purposes, however. The Grand Canal, which ran between the temple of Amun and a neighbouring island, was used for sacred processions, especially during the holy month of Khoiak (early December to early January). This was the fourth month of the season of inundation when the floodwaters of the Nile were at their peak. The sacred association between Thonis and the annual Nile flood was emphasised by the huge statues that dominated the façade of the main temple. Carved in traditional pharaonic style from red granite from the First Cataract region, the colossi represented the king, queen and Hapy (god of the inundation) as joint guarantors of Egypt's fertility.

The festivities during Khoiak included a flotilla on the twenty-second of the month and a procession by Osiris (from Thonis to Kanopos) on the twenty-ninth. This featured a cult image of the god which travelled in a special ceremonial barque of sycamore wood, as onlookers threw votive offerings into the canal. Just as the Greeks identified Khonsu with Herakles, so they regarded Osiris as an alter-ego of Dionysos. The Ptolemaic dynasty claimed descent from Dionysos, too.

The Khoiak ceremonies were observed nationwide. Hundreds of miles south of Thonis, at Tentyris and Apollonopolis, inscriptions tell how, each year, two figures were created for the annual Mysteries of Osiris. The details are as abstruse and esoteric as any religious mystery. On the twelfth day of the month, priests began to fashion a large corn mummy – a representation of the mummified Osiris filled with grain to symbolise his regenerative power – known to Egyptologists as *Osiris vegetans*. At the same time, they prepared a statue of the god in his chthonic aspect (*Osiris-Sokar*). This was made from a special blend of soil, minerals, resins and spices, stirred with a special spatula, and placed in fourteen receptacles; water from the temple's sacred lake was then added, and the resulting mixture formed into an egg shape and put in a silver vase covered with branches of sycamore.[7] Four days later, on the sixteenth of the month, the paste was pressed into the two halves of a golden mould which was placed on a golden bed, facing north. On the nineteen of the month, the two halves were put together and set on a golden pedestal to dry in the sun. On the twenty-third or twenty-fourth, the finished statue was painted – black for the skin, yellow for the face, blue for the wig and eyes – wrapped in linen bandages and anointed with unguents.

In the meantime, on the twenty-first, the *Osiris vegetans* figure was removed from its mould, glued and bound together with four bands of papyrus, left to dry in the sun for the day, then wrapped in strips of cloth. The following afternoon, at two o'clock precisely, *Osiris vegetans* took part in the sacred procession. At Thonis, this took place on the Grand Canal; at Apollonopolis (Djeba to its native inhabitants, present-day Edfu) on the temple's sacred lake. The procession featured thirty-four boats illuminated by 365 small lamps, one for each day of the year. At the end of the festivities, both statues of Osiris were put in special sycamore coffins and buried.

The Mysteries of Osiris were popular with Greek and Egyptian devotees alike. Greeks worshipped the god as Dionysos, honouring him with fertility rites, sexually explicit statuettes and much drinking; Egyptians revered Osiris as the archetypal king, lord of the underworld and guarantor of the Nile's bounty. Each group was essentially following its own beliefs and cultural practices, albeit projected onto one and the same deity, one and the same festival. It was a powerful illustration of the role of faith in uniting a divided country, and helps to explain the Ptolemies' interest in maintaining and promoting the native cults – or, at least, those that chimed with the instincts of

Egypt's Greek-speaking population and the royal family's own dynastic propaganda.

The closely aligned interests of monarchy and religion attested at Thonis-Herakleion and Memphis were not replicated everywhere. In Upper Egypt, the relationship between administration and clergy was more strained. As early as the reign of Ptolemy II, the government had appointed officials to supervise the finances of the Theban temples, which were some of the wealthiest landowners in the country. Under Ptolemy VIII, the number of such crown officials snowballed. They held honorary religious offices, but their principal responsibilities were secular: to run the temple finances and ensure the collection of taxes on behalf of the state. The king might no longer enjoy the same reverence, but his coffers still needed filling.

Furthest from the centres of Ptolemaic power, local cults in southern Upper Egypt developed in an increasingly independent way. Occasionally, a priesthood might seek to gain influence by currying favour with the monarch, like the clergy of Khnum during Ptolemy IX's visit to Elephantine in 115. But most of the large temples – though founded and sustained by royal benefaction – followed their own theological path. Even the influence of the Theban clergy may have been largely theoretical. In each temple, the priesthood functioned as a collegiate body: a largely closed society that interpreted its responsibilities according to local custom and precedent, albeit within a deeply traditional set of parameters. The result could easily have been a descent towards ever greater introspection. Instead, freed from the shackles of central control, Upper Egyptian temples of the later Ptolemaic period were crucibles for extraordinary innovation. Independence unleashed a pent-up creativity.

The temple of Horus at Apollonopolis was a case in point. Its foundation stone was laid by Ptolemy III in 237, and the main cult buildings were completed in less than a hundred years – even allowing for a seventy-year hiatus in construction work under Ptolemy V. The *pronaos* (portico) was added by Ptolemy VIII, and the final elements under Ptolemy IX and his immediate successors. The whole vast edifice took 180 years from start to finish. The temple was covered in texts and images, designed to convey and enhance its primary role as the house of the god. There seems to have been an accepted 'temple grammar', a set of rules or expectations governing which themes were suitable for which parts of a building. A novel element was the wholesale copying of sacred texts and orders of service onto the walls. Religious texts were generally kept in the temple on leather rolls, papyrus scrolls and metal tablets. The temple scriptorium would have held its own working copies. Until the Ptolemaic period, these texts were regarded as secret knowledge, to be passed down from one generation of priests to the next, interpreted and edited, but always out of view. The Ptolemaic priests of Apollonopolis clearly wanted such documents to be carved in stone for all eternity, even if that meant making them a little more public. While the clergy could not have foreseen the eventual extinction of pharaonic culture, they may have sensed that the Hellenisation of Egypt was unstoppable, and that the country's future was more likely than not to be determined by foreigners from beyond its borders. Whatever the motivation, the priests' decision ensured the preservation of the ancient rites and changed the decorative scheme of Egyptian temples for ever.

Equally noteworthy was the level of individual choice exercised by the priest-scribes responsible for adorning a temple's walls. By the time of Ptolemy IX and X, native priesthoods had inherited a vast array of religious texts and rites, some of relatively recent composition, others dating back to the age of the pyramids. The most common were available as 'pattern books', ready to be transcribed whenever the situation demanded. Rarer texts had to be consulted in the temple library or scriptorium. In each case, the priest had the freedom to make editorial choices: which sections to include, which to quote verbatim and which to shorten or amend. Choices might be dictated by practicality – the amount of space available on the walls – as much as by theology.

At Apollonopolis, most of the images and texts chosen related to the daily temple cult and the annual cycle of religious festivals. Particular prominence was given to the mythology of the resident deity. So a large area was devoted to a tableau depicting the mythical struggle between Horus and his malevolent uncle Seth (depicted as a hippopotamus). The accompanying texts were composed in the classical language of the second millennium, which nobody had actually spoken for the best part of a thousand years; certain instances of vocabulary suggest that the priests had consulted an edition dating to the eighth century. Very few people in the late Ptolemaic period would have been able to read these dead languages, yet the priests of Apollonopolis (and other Upper Egyptian temples) not only understood the texts, they played with them. Puns, alliteration, cryptic writings: all sorts of devices were employed to add further metaphorical and allegorical richness to already complex allusions, to enhance the content of the texts and elevate their interpretation. The priests were indulging in 'an intellectual game'.

Tellingly, even after two centuries of Ptolemaic rule, only a single Greek word made it onto the temple walls: *aqur*, representing Greek *arguros*, 'silver'. This illustrates the overwhelming conservatism of Egyptian theology (and the Greek emphasis on a monetary economy). While the government of the Nile Valley was dominated by Hellenophone officials, and fluency in Greek was necessary for social and professional advancement, the higher echelons of the clergy were closed to non-Egyptians. Within the temple sanctuaries, age-old customs and rites remained defiantly nationalistic.

What was true of religious texts was also true of art. In the pharaonic tradition, art never existed for its own sake, but was created to honour the gods and glorify the king. Under the Ptolemies, art in the Greek style followed the traditions set in the Aegean, with recognised artists and sculptors producing dazzling works of creative genius. The temple workshops, by contrast, continued to produce two- and three-dimensional art of the highest quality, but always guided by the conventions of Egyptian representation. Apart from a few early attempts at a hybrid style, there was no mixing of the two artistic traditions: they were simply too far apart in concept and execution. Thus, while the coins minted in Alexandria bore distinctive portraits of successive Ptolemaic rulers, the statues carved for display in Egyptian temples were idealistic, timeless and essentially anonymous. Even though the odd Hellenistic curl might be shown escaping from underneath an Egyptian headdress, pharaonic statues gained their identity from their attributes (crowns, robes, regalia) rather than any attempt to represent individuality.

On temple walls and sacred statuary, continuity was the overriding concern. The identity or cultural background of the reigning king was less important than the fact of his kingship. According to Egyptian belief, the maintenance of creation depended upon sustaining the contract between the monarchy and the gods – a contract in which the king, the gods' representative on earth, beautified their shrines and enlarged their endowments in return for a long and prosperous reign. In such a faith tradition, individuality had little or no part to play; custom and practice were everything. Indeed, empty cartouches became something of a feature on the walls of Ptolemaic temples: politically unstable times made it safer to leave a royal name blank than to risk honouring the losing side. In the face of such uncertainty, temples forged their own paths. At Apollonopolis, the resident god Horus was called 'son of Ra', effectively usurping the king's role, and was even crowned each year as divine monarch.

Alongside stock scenes of the king offering to the gods, new details were represented on temple walls for the first time: medical equipment in the temple sanatorium at Ombos, a complete set of royal crowns and a circular zodiac at Tentyris. The colour scheme adopted for temple reliefs was also novel, with bright blue, white and buff dominating. Colonnades and hypostyle halls remained stock features, but the Ptolemaic temple builders experimented with a wide range of new plant forms for the column shafts and capitals, bringing a fresh vitality to an established architectural vocabulary. In the eastern colonnade at Philae, built under Ptolemy VIII, no two columns are the same.

Remote from the centres of political power, the priest-scribes and architects of Upper Egypt were able to indulge their theological and creative energies while all the time maintaining the hallowed traditions of pharaonic religion. Sometimes, the local Greek-speaking population sought to engage with this exotic culture – some Egyptian reliefs have explanatory texts in Greek – but eventually the lack of state interest began to tell. The vitality of Egyptian temple culture had always depended on royal patronage, even if the kings only showed up in person on rare occasions. As the Ptolemaic period progressed, the initial royal enthusiasm for pharaonic religious traditions started to wane. There were other more pressing problems to attend to.

Delegating all communications with the clergy to the High Priests of Ptah was but one symptom of a wider malaise. A failing economy combined with dwindling royal interest took their toll on the programme of temple building and decoration. At Philae, high-quality raised relief was gradually replaced by quicker, cruder sunk relief. At

Apollonopolis, both the quality of the carving and the texts themselves deteriorated, with those added under Ptolemy IX and his successors showing progressively more errors as priests departed further and further from the pattern books.

Without a strong, stable and prosperous government, keeping the faith became increasingly difficult.

PART IV

NEMESIS (80–30 BC)

12

Fight for Survival

Since the dawn of history, Egypt's stability and prosperity – and its sense of itself as a nation – had depended upon a smooth transition of power from one reign to the next. The king lists inscribed on temple walls presented an unbroken line of succession stretching all the way back to Menes, the semi-mythical founder of the Egyptian state, or even to the gods and demigods who were believed to have ruled over the Nile Valley before him. It was, of course, a complete fiction – every era witnessed its dynastic struggles, palace coups, even civil wars – but it was a fiction that the court had a strong interest in maintaining.

The reality was altogether messier. Short life expectancy in the ancient world often meant that kings died young, before an heir had come of age. As early as the twentieth century BC, rulers had come up with the institution of co-regency – crowning a successor in his father's lifetime – to ensure an uncontested succession. The first Ptolemy, with the advice, perhaps, of his trusted Egyptian officials, embraced time-honoured precedent to strengthen his new dynasty's grip on power. His son and designated successor (Ptolemy II) ruled as co-regent for some eighteen months before commencing his sole reign. But as the dynasty gained legitimacy and security of tenure, it abandoned the norms of pharaonic inheritance and reverted to something more Macedonian and a good deal more chaotic. In the second and early first centuries, a seemingly unending series of family squabbles – the conflict between Ptolemies VI and VIII, the political machinations and manoeuvrings of Cleopatras II and III, and the all-out war between Ptolemies IX and X – were manifestations of a dynastic model that would have had the pharaohs of old spinning in their graves. It wasn't just that turmoil within the royal family undermined the very foundations of royal authority: dynastic strife also begat wider civil unrest, economic decline and a diminution of Egypt's international standing. The fortunes of an entire nation could be transformed, for better or worse, by the behaviour of its ruler.

When Ptolemy IX died at the end of December 81, the royal succession, already contested at the start of his reign, was left in utter confusion. A few months before his demise, he had appointed his daughter (and his brother's ex-wife) Berenike III as his co-regent. Pharaonic precedent, as well as centuries of Ptolemaic practice, made the idea of a woman holding regal status entirely natural in Egypt, even if it would have been unthinkable in other parts of the Hellenistic world. She therefore assumed the throne as sole ruler, taking the cult title Thea Philopator ('father-loving goddess') to emphasise her legitimate claim. She seems to have been a popular figure, at least among the notoriously febrile citizens of Alexandria. But Ptolemaic custom and precedent required a male member of the family to reign alongside a queen. The spotlight fell on Berenike III's half-brother, then in exile in Rome. The lad was duly recalled to Alexandria in the late spring of 80 to assume the kingship as Ptolemy XI Alexander II. Later commentators detected the hand of the Roman dictator Sulla in the decision: a young man accustomed to Roman ways might prove a useful puppet ruler of Egypt. To bolster his claim to the throne, Ptolemy XI immediately married Berenike III (his half-sister, stepmother and cousin!). But he seems to have had longer-term ambitions that left no room for a co-ruler. Within three weeks of his marriage, in the best Ptolemaic tradition, he had his wife murdered. It was an audacious but fatal step. The city's inhabitants were outraged, dragged the king from his palace and killed him in the gymnasium. His reign, of just eighteen or nineteen days, was the shortest of any Ptolemy, and his name was subsequently expunged from the official record in an act of *damnatio memoriae*.

With both Berenike III and her husband dead, the government and citizenry of Alexandria knew they had to act fast to find a legitimate successor or face the consequences, already spelled out in Ptolemy X's will: annexation by Rome. The most senior surviving member of the royal family was Cleopatra Selene, daughter of Ptolemy VIII, sister and ex-wife of both Ptolemy IX and Ptolemy X. Her dynastic credentials were impeccable, but she was now also the widow of three successive Seleukid monarchs (Antiochos VIII, IX and X) and living in Kilikia. She tried to assert the rights of her sons to both the Ptolemaic and Seleukid thrones, but it was a claim too far for both kingdoms. Passing over the sons of Cleopatra Selene left the two sons of Ptolemy IX from his marriage to Cleopatra IV. The boys had been born while their parents were in Cyprus, shortly before Ptolemy IX's accession. In the decades since, they had led adventurous lives. As babies, they had moved to Alexandria with their father in 116, and the elder of the two boys had in due course been given some prominence at court, being appointed for a year to the prestigious priesthood of Alexander. When Ptolemy IX was forced into exile in 107, the boys stayed behind with their grandmother, Cleopatra III, only to be sent four years later to the Greek island of Kos at the outbreak of hostilities within the royal family. What should have been a place of safety became a trap: both boys were captured at the outbreak of the First Mithridatic War by King Mithridates VI. He took them back to his homeland on the southern shore of the Black Sea as valuable political hostages. The two brothers spent the next seven or eight years as 'guests' of the Pontic monarch and became engaged to his daughters.

Complex their lives and relationships may have been, but the siblings, both named Ptolemy, were now their dynasty's only hope of retaining its sovereignty. In the summer of 80, they were recalled to fulfil their destinies: the younger brother as king of Cyprus, the elder as king of Egypt. It was the first time in Ptolemaic history that the two parts of the realm had been legally separated. The government was hedging its bets: Rome was more likely to accept continuing Egyptian independence if Cyprus were hived off. Political diminution was an acceptable price to pay for continued freedom.

So began the hapless reign of Ptolemy XII, his inheritance a realm financially challenged, diplomatically and militarily weak, and acutely vulnerable to foreign interference. He took what steps he could to secure his position, dating the start of his reign to the death of his father and ditching his Pontic fiancée in favour of his own relative Tryphaina.[1] She was appointed co-regent and adopted the regal name Cleopatra, and the royal couple were incorporated into the dynastic cult as Theoi Philopatores kai Philadelphoi ('father-loving and sibling-loving gods').[2] The title reinforced their joint claim to the throne as the children of Ptolemy IX – more than a mere convention in this case, as there were widespread rumours, fostered by Roman interests, about Ptolemy XII's legitimacy. The people of Alexandria, always quick to lampoon their monarchs, came up with their own nickname: they called Ptolemy XII Auletes ('flautist'), in reference to his reputed fondness for accompanying choruses on the flute. He is said to have held musical contests in the royal palace, taking part himself against his courtiers; these occasions are likely to have been Dionysiac rites rather than chamber recitals. A century later, the Roman emperor Nero fiddled while his city burned; Ptolemy XII played his flute while Rome plotted.

From the outset of the new reign, the overriding objective was simply one of survival. The government in Alexandria was ever conscious of the Roman threat, and the king was forced to curry favour with Rome and its various political factions to preserve his own throne. The challenges came thick and fast. In 75, after barely five years on the throne, Ptolemy XII's position was challenged by his own aunt, Cleopatra Selene. She travelled to Rome to advocate for her sons by Antiochos X. The senate took little notice, probably because it was too preoccupied by the formal annexation of Kyrenaika. For the oldest of the Ptolemaic territories outside Egypt, willed to Rome by its last king, Ptolemy Apion, some twenty years earlier, was now being formally incorporated as a Roman province. The spur may have been the region's agricultural productivity and a growing need to secure the Republic's grain supplies.

Of course, Kyrenaika was not the only potential breadbasket in Rome's sphere of influence: the Nile Valley's fertility and bounty were legendary. Within a decade of Kyrenaika's incorporation, a leading Roman statesman and an elected censor (the magistrate with responsibility for the census) for the year 65, Marcus Licinius Crassus, was publicly advocating for the annexation of Egypt. There was spirited opposition from the likes of Cicero, who recognised the potential dangers of becoming embroiled in a risky foreign venture, and the proposal was defeated. But Egypt's future status and its relationship with Rome were now openly debated. Ambitious Roman politicians began to see the conquest of the Nile Valley as a wonderful opportunity for career advancement. One of them, who in 65 held the office of aedile (an elected official responsible for maintaining public buildings and regulating festivals), was a certain Gaius Julius Caesar.

Ptolemy XII responded to this threat in the only way he could, lobbying furiously and offering lavish bribes to secure support for continued Egyptian independence. The alternative did not bear thinking about, yet it was brought sharply into focus just two years later when the once-great Seleukid empire, lately reduced to the city of Antiokheia and a few Syrian towns, fell to the Roman general Gnaius Pompeius Magnus (Pompey the Great). The last of the Seleukid monarchs, Antiochos XIII, was the son of Antiochos X by Cleopatra Selene and hence Ptolemy XII's own first cousin. But ties of blood and dynastic inheritance meant nothing to a rapacious Roman Republic.

First, Macedon had been gobbled up by Rome; now the Seleukid empire had gone the same way. Of the three Hellenistic kingdoms founded by Alexander the Great's successors, only the Ptolemaic realm remained. The only way to survive was by paying protection money – and lots of it. As a victorious Pompey set about reorganising the administration of Rome's new eastern provinces (he had also just won the Third Mithridatic War, conquering the Kingdom of Pontos and most of Anatolia with it), he received a lavish present of congratulations from Ptolemy XII: a golden crown. The republican general was unmoved. Ptolemy's next present, funding for 8,000 cavalry for Pompey's campaign against Judaea, was received rather more appreciatively. But Pompey still refused to come to Ptolemy's aid when Alexandria experienced one of its periodic bouts of civil disturbance. This was not a relationship of partners, still less of equals. Egypt was the supplicant, Rome the playground bully.

Despite Ptolemy XII's very public and expensive show of support for Pompey, that same year the Roman senate debated new proposals to take over control of Egypt's economy. Nothing, it seemed, could halt the juggernaut of Roman expansion. Once again, Cicero spoke against the proposal, his strong republican principles leading him to fear that a Roman placeman in Egypt might use the country as a power base to threaten or even destroy the Roman Republic. (In time, of course, he would be proved right.) The tectonic plates were shifting, not only across the old Hellenistic world, but also within Rome itself. The traditional checks and balances that had sustained the republican constitution were being increasingly overridden by individual ambition. At home, the influence of the senate was diminished; overseas, and especially in the east, Rome's relationships with its client kingdoms were hijacked for personal aggrandisement.

Ptolemy XII could not avoid being drawn into Rome's internal politics, but neither could he easily judge whom to back. The only solution was to continue casting bread – or rather gold – upon the waters. To finance Egypt's policy of appeasement, government spending was cut and taxes raised sharply. One new law, introduced in 63, provided that if someone died intestate, two-thirds of their estate would pass automatically to the Privy Purse. Such measures prompted widespread unrest, especially in the countryside where hard-pressed farmers struggled to survive. Even the cultivators of crown land felt the pinch. Those in the Herakleopolitan province resorted to going on strike in 61/60. With state revenues exhausted, Ptolemy XII had to turn to moneylenders – and the leading ones, like Caius Rabirius Postumus, were Roman. The more Ptolemy spent on buying Roman support, the more he became indebted to Rome. It was a death spiral.

In 60, in a brave move to change the dynamic, he travelled cap in hand to Rome, to negotiate official recognition of his kingship and his country's independence. It was a far cry from the days when visiting Roman delegates had been given lavish hospitality in the royal palace at Alexandria. Now, the shoe was on the other foot. Pharaohs had never been accustomed to pleading their case with a foreign power. But it worked. In return for a payment of 6,000 talents – equal to Egypt's entire annual revenue – the three triumvirs (Crassus, Pompey and Caesar) persuaded the senate to recognise Ptolemy XII as king, and he was added to the official list of 'friends and allies of the Roman people'. Cicero, who might have been expected to object, was bribed with the offer of an ambassadorship to Egypt. Although he confessed that he had long wanted to see the country, and Alexandria in particular, he turned down the offer, 'as it was against his principles and considered it deleterious to his reputation'.[3]

Ptolemy returned to Egypt relieved, his authority bolstered. He even felt confident enough to issue an amnesty decree. But in his desperation to win Rome's recognition, he had overlooked the status of Cyprus. Within a year, the senate had passed another law, the *Lex Clodia*, which annexed the island. Ptolemy dared not object. Its last king, Ptolemy's brother, took his own life rather than become a Roman puppet.

First Kyrenaika, then Cyprus. The policy of bribery was hardly a triumph, despite the privations it had visited upon Egypt's population. Played for a fool abroad and resented at home, Ptolemy XII was running out of options.

The economic travails of the time are illustrated by two apparently innocuous documents. Both are legal contracts, cessions of land, one dated to October 73, the other to August 57. In both cases, cleruchs who had inherited their plots decided to hand them over to others to cultivate, an indication, perhaps, that life as a farmer was becoming increasingly unattractive. These two small fragments of papyrus form part of a collection of half a million documents recovered at the end of the nineteenth century AD from the rubbish dumps of a Ptolemaic provincial town, Oxyrhynchos ('city of the sharp-nosed fish'), in Middle Egypt. Although most of the texts are of a workaday nature – sales and leases like those referred to above, census and tax returns, petitions and court records, bills and accounts, inventories and wills, horoscopes and private letters – there are also works of literature. Indeed, among the papyri, discarded by the inhabitants of Oxyrhynchos (present-day Bahnasa) are writings by some of the most famous authors of antiquity. They include the oldest and most complete set of diagrams from Euclid's *Elements*, and a treatise attributed to Aristotle on *The Constitution of the Athenians*. Plays by Menander and Euripides, a previously unknown play by Sophocles, poems by Pindar and Sappho, and passages from the *Iliad* all ended up on the town rubbish dump, worn out or simply no longer wanted. The reading tastes of Ptolemaic Egypt's Greek-speaking inhabitants were broad, and, even in the depths of countryside, remarkably sophisticated.

The range of literary and scholarly texts available to the general population highlights an important aspect of Ptolemaic society: the influence of Alexandria as a centre of learning. The ripples of scholarship and literacy reached beyond the city's library and museum. The early Ptolemies had sought to establish their reputation as scholar kings, and their patronage of Alexandria's intellectuals yielded key breakthroughs in every field of enquiry. After a long period of decline during the second and early first centuries, Ptolemy XII presided over something of a renaissance, nurturing the development of new schools of philosophy and encouraging scholars to push the boundaries of learning once more. The knock-on effects were felt far beyond Alexandria. Greek-speaking settlers – whether mercenaries, military veterans or simple economic migrants – actively sought out and engaged with the literary and scientific works in their own language as a way of maintaining and asserting their cultural identity.

An example is the collection of papers amassed by Ptolemaios son of Glaukias, the recluse in the Sarapieion during the reign of Ptolemy VI. Alongside recollections of his disturbed dreams and copies of his petitions to the government, he also treasured papyrus copies of plays by Menander and Euripides, and a treatise on the nature of the universe called the *Art of Eudoxos*. This last work, dated to the beginning of the second century, is the earliest illustrated scientific text to have survived from antiquity. Its blend of astronomy and astrology includes lunar and solar calendars, the rising and setting of important constellations, and the observation that the moon reflects the light of the sun. The coloured illustrations scattered throughout the text include diagrams of the sun and moon, and the signs of the zodiac. Ptolemaios made his own notes in the margin, showing an active engagement with the ideas contained in the work. That a relatively humble soldier living in provincial Egypt not only had access to, but read and enjoyed, a pioneering study by one of the greatest scientific thinkers of the day reveals a deep intellectualism in Ptolemaic Egypt.

The fact that poems, plays and treatises by the greatest Greek writers remained popular until the very end of Ptolemaic rule (and beyond), by which time Greek-speaking families had been established in the Egyptian countryside for centuries, emphasises the central place of literacy and literary culture in Hellenistic identity. But 'Greeks born in Egypt' did not have to restrict themselves to a single literary tradition. They also had access to, and embraced, Egyptian writings – albeit in translation. Even the *Art of Eudoxos*, a work steeped in Hellenistic learning, included illustrations of Egyptian deities: a mummified ibis, a baboon and a scarab beetle inside a circle. Ptolemaios also had in his possession a Greek edition of an Egyptian tale, *The Dream of*

Nectanebo, and instructional texts that sought to teach their readers how to get on in life.

These so-called 'teachings' were one of the most venerable genres of Egyptian literature, their origins stretching back to the Pyramid Age. The earliest examples stressed correct behaviour, reflecting the rigid hierarchies of pharaonic society. Later examples, from the second millennium, betrayed a more 'middle-class' mindset, with practical advice on how to raise a family, flatter one's boss and turn a profit. Later still, the work known as the *Teaching of Ankhsheshonqy* was probably composed in the late Ptolemaic period and gives a strong sense of the Egyptian worldview around the time of Ptolemy XII. The very setting of the work is redolent of the political vicissitudes that had characterised the reigns of the later Ptolemies: in the introduction, the narrator, Ankhsheshonqy, learns of a plan to assassinate the king, but says nothing. When the conspiracy comes to light, Ankhsheshonqy is imprisoned for his silence. It is the prospect of spending years behind bars that prompts him to ask permission to pen a series of helpful instructions to his son.

The maxims run to many hundreds, making the work one of the most extensive examples of its kind. The hints and tips are repetitious, sometimes contradictory, and lacking in any sense of structure, but are wonderfully revealing of the native Egyptian mindset in the first century. The work eschews the poetic verse structure of earlier teachings and is written in practical prose; the tone is cynical but humorous, seeing the inherent comedy in daily life, despite its trials and tribulations. Individual pieces of advice are pragmatic, down to earth and full of self-interest, with no attempt at high-minded moralising. For example, 'The wealth of a town is not taking sides', echoes the fence-sitting of Egyptian priests when faced with opposing royal factions. 'Do not scorn Pharaoh's business' and 'Do not speak of Pharaoh's business when drinking beer', would have been good advice at any period of Egyptian history, but 'Learn how to report to the palace of Pharaoh' surely reflects the popularity in Ptolemaic Egypt of petitioning the king directly. The lawlessness of the Egyptian countryside prompted the advice, 'Do not walk the road without a stick in your hand', while the parlous state of the rural economy under Ptolemy XII provoked the wonderful aphorism, 'A crocodile does not die of worry, it dies of hunger'. All things considered, it was perhaps wisest to, 'Put your affairs in the hands of god'.[4]

Hence, while Ptolemaic Egypt's Greek-speaking population enjoyed pondering the scientific marvels of the universe, for the native inhabitants of the Nile Valley quotidian concerns remained uppermost in the mind. The vast majority of advice in the *Teaching of Ankhsheshonqy*, written by and largely for an Egyptian readership, relates to family life in a rural village: the environment most familiar to most people. There are practical reminders – 'Spend according to your means' and 'He who does not gather wood in summer will not be warm in winter' – as well as business tips – 'Borrow money at interest and put it in farmland'. The advice has a lot to say about family relationships: 'Do not prefer one of your children to another; you do not know which one of them will be kind to you'; 'Do not open your heart to your wife or your servant; open it to your mother – she is a woman of discretion'; 'Do not let your son marry a woman from another town, lest he be taken from you'; and 'Do not violate a married woman'. And just knowing one's place was a good recipe for a quiet life: 'You may trip over your feet in a great man's house; do not trip over your tongue'.[5] The surviving examples of literature must represent a mere fraction of the original corpus, but the Ptolemaic period none the less emerges as an era of remarkable literary creativity, in both Greek and Egyptian.

Works composed in demotic sometimes permeated the Greek-speaking population, but the reverse was rarely if ever the case. Roman visitors to the Nile Valley seem to have been even more closed-minded, disdaining the local customs as primitive and laughable. Their haughtiness did little to endear them to the native population. When the Greek historian Diodorus visited Egypt in the reign of Ptolemy XII, around 60, he reported seeing a Roman being torn apart by an angry mob for inadvertently killing a cat. The unlucky tourist would have done well to read Ankhsheshonqy's advice, 'Do not laugh at a cat',[6] or even to have heeded the words of Herodotus, writing some 400 years earlier, who noted that when a fire broke out, the Egyptians were more concerned about saving any trapped cats than putting out the flames. But to the Romans, the Egyptians' obsession with worshipping animals was downright bizarre, atavistic and ridiculous. Where the Ptolemies had taken great pains to understand and respect pharaonic traditions, there would be no such accommodation with the Romans. Egypt's increasingly desperate attempts to preserve its political autonomy began to seem like a struggle for cultural survival, too.

In the late summer of 58, within months of the humiliating loss of Cyprus, Ptolemy XII's courtiers forced him to abdicate in favour of his eldest daughter, Berenike IV. The king's overthrow was backed by the Alexandrian mob, well accustomed to flexing its political muscles, and seems to have been inspired by a growing anti-Roman sentiment – only exacerbated by incidents such as the killing of the cat two years earlier. But if the Egyptians thought that removing Ptolemy XII would counter Roman influence, they were sorely mistaken. Not only did the move push Ptolemy even further into the arms of Rome, his daughter also found herself an unwilling pawn in Roman power politics.

The fundamental, inescapable problem was the weakness of the Ptolemaic dynasty compared to the might of Rome. As a contemporary Egyptian saying put it, 'The hissing of the snake is more effective than the braying of the donkey'.[7] At first, Berenike IV's fragile reign was bolstered by the presence of her mother, Cleopatra Tryphaina, as co-regent, but she herself disappeared from view before the end of 57, either through retirement or death. Strenuous efforts were then made to find a suitable consort to rule alongside her. There being no plausible candidate within the Ptolemaic royal family, courtiers turned their eyes abroad, prepared to consider all serious possibilities. Eventually, three princes of the defunct Seleukid royal house were identified. However, one died while negotiations were taking place, and the second was prevented from travelling to Egypt by Asia's new Roman governor, Aulus Gabinius. The third prince, bearing the archetypal dynastic name Seleukos, did manage to reach Alexandria, but Berenike took such an instant dislike to him that she promptly had him strangled.

Rome, of course, took a keen interest in the matter of the Egyptian succession. Preventing a Ptolemaic–Seleukid alliance was essential, but the bigger prize was a Roman puppet on the throne of Egypt. Rome's chosen candidate, and the eventual winner of Berenike's hand, was a young man of impeccable royal lineage who had the added advantage of being well known, both to Gabinius and to his mentor, Pompey.

The prince was Archelaos, a son of Mithridates VI whom Pompey had defeated a decade earlier. Archelaos arrived in Alexandria in the spring of 56 and wed his bride; but he never seems to have gained acceptance in the country at large, and his name is studiously omitted from contemporary papyri.

Ptolemy XII, meanwhile, had no intention of simply resigning his throne. Believing himself the best – the only – hope of securing Egypt's independence, he resolved to use all his connections to regain power. On leaving Egypt, accompanied by his second daughter, his first stop was Rhodes, a long-standing Ptolemaic ally. The island had the added attraction of a notable temporary resident: the influential Roman senator, Cato the Younger, who had recently overseen the annexation of Cyprus. Cato offered the deposed monarch advice on how best to plead his case with Roman politicians – advice, but no tangible support. Ptolemy journeyed on to Rome itself, arriving during the course of 57.

There, he was welcomed by none other than Pompey the Great, and stayed as a guest at his villa in the Alban Hills. The general argued the king's case in the senate, but met with significant opposition. Not only were many senators still wary of direct involvement in Egypt's internal affairs, they were also conscious of the opposing factions within Egypt itself. This was brought home when Berenike IV's government dispatched to Rome a delegation of 100 men, led by Dion of Alexandria, to argue *against* Ptolemy XII. The king, however, still had his network of friends and informers, and before the envoys could reach Rome, Dion and most of his followers were killed, poisoned by Ptolemy's agents. A shocked senate promised an investigation, but it never took place and the incident was hushed up, for other voices, other interests had entered the debate. Ptolemy's many Roman creditors realised that the king's restoration represented their only chance of recouping their considerable investment. Money triumphed over politics. Ptolemy, now confident of Roman backing, left the city at the end of 57 and took up residence in the temple of Diana at Ephesos, a more convenient location from which to plan an invasion of Egypt.

Over the next twelve months, the exiled king obtained formal offers of support from Pompey, Gabinius and the moneylender Rabirius – who had been promised payment of 10,000 talents if the mission were successful, making his entire fortune dependent on

Ptolemy's restoration. Also throwing his weight behind the plan was a twenty-seven-year-old Roman cavalry officer by the name of Marcus Antonius (Mark Antony). The senate refused to give its formal blessing to any military intervention, citing a supposed declaration of the Sibylline Oracle as an excuse for inaction; but with the support of his three powerful backers, the wind was in Ptolemy's sails.

In the autumn of 56, a force led by Gabinius entered Egypt from Syria, attacking the border post at Pelousion. In the ensuing battle, Archelaos, leading the defence, was killed, allegedly by Gabinius himself – the very man who had placed him at Berenike's side in the first place. Friendship counted for little in Roman politics. (Later, when forced to defend his actions, Gabinius claimed that Archelaos had been encouraging piracy in the eastern Mediterranean, threatening Rome's economic interests. But of course, by then, the accused was not around to defend himself.) Archelaos duly received a soldier's burial from another erstwhile friend, Mark Antony, and the invasion force moved on. The army marched through the Nile Delta, stopping at Memphis before heading north-westwards towards Alexandria. By mid-April 55, the city's defenders had surrendered and Ptolemy XII was restored to his throne. But, for the first time in history, it was a Roman army that had conquered Egypt.

The king's retribution was swift and decisive. He had his daughter Berenike IV and her leading supporters executed. His own regime was maintained at the point of a spear, thanks to a force of 2,000 – Roman soldiers and mercenaries from Germany and Gaul – who remained in Egypt under Gabinius' command. The Gabiniani, as they were known, soon went thoroughly native, settling and marrying local Egyptian women. But they continued to take their allegiance to the Ptolemaic dynasty seriously, not least as it was paying their wages. (In due course, the Gabiniani would support the Egyptian monarchy *against* Rome.)

Financing a mercenary bodyguard was not the king's only financial concern. No sooner had he been restored than his Roman creditors demanded repayment of their loans. However, the royal treasury had insufficient funds, even after sequestering the assets of those wealthy businessmen who had backed Berenike. The cost of funding an army of reconquest had depleted government reserves, and the prospect of imposing further, unpopular taxes was deeply unappealing to a king who had only just regained his throne. Ptolemy's solution was both ingenious and Machiavellian. He appointed his main creditor, Rabirius, as finance minister, thus giving a Roman banker full control over Egypt's state income. Rabirius acted exactly as Ptolemy had predicted, plundering the treasury, debasing the coinage, cutting government expenditure and raising taxes – all to protect his personal financial position. The ruling class was scathing, accusing Rabirius of having 'replaced the people who had usually been appointed and had traditionally succeeded their fathers and grandfathers in this office. Instead, he appointed unsuitable and boorish men after he had sold everything that was saved over the years.'[8] The reaction of the Egyptian populace was even more negative. Rabirius had to be placed in protective custody to save him from the retribution of the Alexandrian mob, whence Ptolemy graciously allowed him to escape into exile. With his tail between his legs, Rabirius returned home to Rome, only to face criminal charges of embezzlement. He was acquitted on a technicality following a famous defence by Cicero, but his finances and reputation lay in tatters. Ptolemy had let him carry the can to preserve the monarchy's reputation.

Nor did Gabinius escape unscathed from his intervention in Ptolemaic politics. Politician, general, provincial governor: not even his illustrious career could protect him from charges of treason, which were brought against him for having left his province and invaded Egypt without the senate's consent. When the trial came to the senate, Pompey persuaded Gabinius' opponents, including Cicero, to hold their tongues (money may have changed hands). Gabinius was acquitted of treason but found guilty on the lesser charge of extortion, because of the 10,000 talents he had accepted from Ptolemy XII. The flautist had finally learned how to play his adversaries.

To secure his legacy, Ptolemy now took steps to ensure a smooth succession after his death. On 31 May 52, he made his second daughter, Cleopatra, co-regent, and drew up a will stipulating that she and the elder of her two brothers (both of whom were named Ptolemy) should rule together when the time came. In a nice twist, he made the people of Rome the executors of his will.

As his long and tumultuous reign drew to a close, Ptolemy XII may have reflected on the balance of his achievements. On the negative side, he had bankrupted his country and handed the keys of the treasury to Rome, waved goodbye to the overseas possessions of Kyrenaika and Cyprus, and made himself dependent upon a mercenary force to stay in power. On the positive side, he had done just that: stayed in power. Against all the odds, where the Macedonian and Seleukid kingdoms had wavered and failed, Egypt was still an independent country, ruled by a Hellenistic dynasty. Autonomy had been bought at a terrible price, but it was still no mean achievement.

Preoccupied with appeasing Rome – 'A snake that is eating has no venom'[9] – Ptolemy XII might have been forgiven for neglecting his traditional duties as pharaoh. But with Egypt facing an existential threat throughout his reign, the help of the old gods could not be taken for granted, nor could the promise of their protection be ignored. Consequently, royal patronage of the native cults and their priesthoods became a central plank of government policy. Ptolemy XII's largesse benefited every part of the country, from the Sinai in the extreme north-east to Philae at the First Cataract.

The first beneficiary of this renewed interest in pharaonic religion was the priesthood of Ptah at Memphis. Earlier generations of high priests had carefully cultivated a close relationship with the ruling dynasty, but under Ptolemy XII the bonds grew even stronger. When the old high priest, Padibastet IV, died, the monarch, then just four years into his reign, took the highly unusual step of travelling to Memphis in person to appoint the next incumbent. The man receiving the royal seal of approval was Padibastet's son, Pasherenptah III. 'The youngling of Ptah' certainly lived up to his name: he was just fourteen years old. By appointing him head of the cult of Ptah and primate of Egypt, Ptolemy was accomplishing two objectives at once: respecting the age-old Egyptian tradition of a son succeeding his father, and ensuring that the king could effectively direct the actions of the clergy through a puppet high priest. Indeed, Pasherenptah was granted the titles 'the eyes of the king of Upper Egypt, the ears of the king of Lower Egypt' and 'prince upon the throne of Geb [Egypt]'. Basking in his unprecedented authority, the young high priest was certainly happy to do his monarch's bidding; no sooner had he been confirmed in office than he performed the coronation ceremony for Ptolemy XII according to the ancient rites: 'It was I who placed the collar and the uraeus on the king's head on the day of Unifying-the-Two-Lands and who performed for him all the rites in the jubilee temples.'[10]

To mark the occasion, Ptolemy took the additional cult title Neos Dionysos ('the new Dionysos'). Given the association between Dionysos and Osiris, this gesture is likely to have been well received by the native clergy. The new epithet would also have resonated with Egypt's Greek-speaking population who, by the first century, were pinning their hopes for salvation, not on their latest hapless monarch, but on the second coming of a 'new Dionysos on earth'. All across the Hellenistic world, from Pontos to Syria, struggling rulers of failing dynasties had tapped into this religious sentiment, presenting themselves as incarnations of the new Dionysos.

In reciprocal gratitude for Ptolemy's personal visit to Memphis, Pasherenptah subsequently travelled to Alexandria. The head of the Egyptian clergy paying homage to a Macedonian ruler in his palace by the 'Sea of the Greeks' was a powerful statement of indigenous approval. The visit evidently made a big impression on the high priest, too; as one of the pivotal events of his life, he would later recount it in detail on his funerary stela:

> I travelled to the residence of the kings of the Ionians which is on the shore of the Sea of the Greeks, to the west of the 'building site' [Alexandria]. The king of Upper and Lower Egypt, Lord of the Two Lands, the father-loving and sister-loving god, the new Osiris [Philopator Philadelphos Neos Dionysos] solemnly came out of his royal palace, and he proceeded to the temple of Isis ... He made many rich sacrifices to her. Then, riding forth in his chariot from the temple of Isis, the king ordered his chariot to stop ... I was named [royal] priest and he sent out a royal decree saying: 'I have appointed the High Priest of Memphis Pasherenptah to be my priest.' And I was given an annual stipend from the temples of Upper and Lower Egypt.[11]

As priest of the pharaoh, Pasherenptah now had the additional responsibility of ensuring the maintenance of the royal cult within the sacred precinct of Memphis. So close was the bond between king and priest that Ptolemy XII became a frequent visitor to Egypt's traditional capital; at least in Memphis he could be assured of a warm reception. On one occasion, he inspected the city by boat, travelling up and down the canal on the royal barge, before visiting the necropolis with a large entourage that included his family and baggage train. The royal party stayed in a lodge adjacent to the Sarapieion, with a direct view of the group of Dionysiac statues and the semicircle of Greek worthies. Here was the New Dionysos, the young Osiris, cementing his divine credentials in the eyes of all his subjects.

Other priesthoods, too, benefited from royal attention. A priest of Tanis, Panemerit, glorified in the titles 'first confidant of the king of Upper and Lower Egypt, venerable and august among the courtiers' in addition to his sacred office. He was not only a priest but also the governor of his province, with responsibility for supervising taxes and customs dues. His name suggests that, under Ptolemy XII, members of the native elite were once again welcomed into the inner circles of government, where they helped to forge the bonds between monarchy and people. It had taken two and a half centuries, but, finally, the Ptolemaic dynasty and its Egyptian subjects seem to have found a mutually acceptable modus vivendi.

A concrete expression of this rapprochement was an upsurge in temple construction and decoration. Despite the pressures on the public finances, Ptolemy XII prioritised the beautification of existing temples and the construction of new ones. Evidence of his programme of work has been found from Lower Nubia to the Fayum. At Dabod, within the old Dodekaschoinos, he commissioned a new granite sanctuary for the temple of Amun, while at Philae he decorated the outer face of the first pylon with scenes showing him in traditional poses, offering to deities and smiting the enemies of Egypt. The accompanying list of foes, written in hieroglyphics, included the Greeks – a fact that must have drawn a wry smile from the few native priests who could read the sacred writings. Also within the First Cataract region, work was undertaken at the temple of Osiris on the holy island of Biga – a fitting project for the 'new Osiris'.

In the heartland of Upper Egypt, the great edifices of Ombos and Apollonopolis continued to be the recipients of royal largesse. At the temple of Horus, a new court and massive entrance pylon, the latter adorned with images of Ptolemy XII smiting his enemies, were inaugurated in February 70. The flagpoles set against the gateway were so massive, at 130 feet high, they had to be fashioned from several logs of imported cedar, spliced together. Later in Ptolemy XII's reign, the great temple doors, also of Lebanese cedar, sheathed with copper, were installed. Each measured over thirty feet high, six feet wide and a foot thick.

Ptolemy also took pains to honour the temples of the Thebaid with their powerful priesthoods. He dedicated a new portico within the Karnak complex, and commissioned three new shrines nearby, as well as a birth house at Athribis.

Even in the Arsinoite nome, the most Greek-speaking of all Egyptian provinces, Ptolemy took pains to ensure the proper maintenance of pharaonic religion. A Greek inscription records a contract between the crown and temple officials. It guaranteed the clergy its privileges as long as the priests promised to restore the statues of earlier kings and dedicate new, pharaonic statues of Ptolemy XII and his family in the temple sanctuary.

Each of these projects was important to its local priesthood and community; each demonstrated that the king, despite his preoccupation with external affairs, was not neglecting the primary duty expected of an Egyptian pharaoh. Every commission strengthened Ptolemy's reputation among his native subjects and bought their continued loyalty. He could easily have stopped there, but he did not. Following his restoration in 55, he embarked on one of the most ambitious temple construction projects ever witnessed in the Nile Valley. The audacious plan was to build a vast new temple at Tentyris; theologically and architecturally, it would serve as the northern counterpart to Apollonopolis, which had been completed a few years earlier. The main workshop was moved from Apollonopolis to the new site, and work duly began on 16 July 54.

The choice of site was no accident: there had been a shrine of sorts at Tentyris for most of pharaonic history. The most recent structure still standing was a birth house of Nakhtnebef; Ptolemy had it carefully restored to provide a link with the last dynasty of native kings. As for the main construction site, the builders had to clear away the scattered remains of earlier epochs before they could start work on a grand new temple. Blocks bearing the royal cartouches of kings from the Old, Middle and New Kingdoms were carefully salvaged to be reused in the new construction and lend it an immediate air of antiquity and sanctity.[12]

According to texts inscribed on the walls of the crypt – the first part of Ptolemy's *grand projet* to be built – the original temple of

Tentyris had been founded earlier than the first dynasty, even before the unification of Egypt. The foundation charter was said to have been rediscovered, centuries later, in the reign of Khufu (builder of the Great Pyramid of Giza), in a chest in the royal palace of Memphis. The temple had subsequently been restored by the sixth-dynasty king, Pepi I, and renovated by the warrior pharaoh of the eighteenth dynasty, Thutmose III. While this account may have been fanciful, intended to link Ptolemy XII with the greatest pharaohs of history, it was true in spirit (and the involvement of Pepi I and Thutmose III has since been proven on the ground). What it demonstrates, above all, is the extraordinary historical sensitivity of the native clergy, their awareness of traditions stretching back 3,000 years, and their determination to carry those traditions forward into the future – whatever the uncertainties.

The crypts at Tentyris, which extend over three levels, were the most innovative aspect of the temple. The rest of the building's layout was modelled closely on that of Apollonopolis. While the latter was dedicated to Horus, falcon god of the sun and kingship, Tentyris honoured his mother, the cow deity Hathor, goddess of solar and royal power. These theological links were also expressed in practical terms: each year, in a festival that could trace its roots back fifteen centuries, the cult statue of Hathor travelled in her barque-shrine, by land and river, from Tentyris to Apollonopolis. On arrival, she joined with Horus, and the couple visited the necropolis of the divine ancestors. The accompanying festivities, which lasted some two weeks, were an occasion for great popular celebration throughout the local area.

For a king and a dynasty struggling to maintain their independence, the significance of the two deities, Hathor and Horus, was clear and compelling: divine mother and son, each embodying the ideas of cosmic authority and royal power, whose worship in the Nile Valley stretched back to a time before recorded history. By completing Apollonopolis and inaugurating Tentyris, Ptolemy XII fervently hoped to tap into this ancient, powerful magic. Moreover, the birth house at Tentyris celebrated the fruit of Horus and Hathor's 'sacred marriage': a new generation, embodied in the person of the king, that guaranteed the continuation of creation and monarchy alike. Ptolemy could only hope that reality would follow theology.

13

Dangerous Liaisons

The ancient Egyptians were accustomed to watching the heavens for signs and portents. New Year's Day, the start of the civil calendar, was marked by the appearance of the Dog Star, Sirius, above the horizon just before dawn. The high priest of Ra, the ancient sun god of Heliopolis, bore the venerable title 'Greatest of Seers', reflecting his office's time-honoured role in celestial observation. And the goddess of Tentyris, Hathor, to whom Ptolemy XII had dedicated his greatest building project, could trace her origins back to a predynastic mother deity, depicted as a cow with stars for ears and a star between her horns – the Milky Way in bovine form. The astrologers and astronomers who studied in the Library and Mouseion of Alexandria under the Ptolemies were thus only the latest in a long line of stargazers. In a country where the skies were generally cloudless, the close scrutiny of celestial bodies was part and parcel of daily life, and informed the Egyptians' understanding of their universe.

So it must have been with a sense of foreboding that the people of the Nile Valley witnessed a partial solar eclipse in the spring of 51. The blotting out of the sun – the creator of life – could only presage some profound change of cosmic significance. The death of Ptolemy XII that same month must have confirmed people's worst fears.[1] To be sure, the royal line was strong – the king had left two daughters and two sons – and he had taken steps to ensure a smooth succession by appointing his eldest surviving child, Cleopatra, as his formal co-regent; she was named as such in the sacred inscriptions inside the crypt at Tentyris. But, as Ptolemaic tradition dictated that no woman should rule alone, the late king's will had nominated the elder of Cleopatra's two brothers to reign alongside her. He was a boy of just ten. The people of Egypt knew only too well that a minor on the throne was a recipe for court intrigue and civil unrest.

Cleopatra, too, knew the dangers. Though just eighteen, she had seen a lot and learned a lot at her father's side. She had accompanied him to Rome during his period of exile in 58, witnessed at first hand his restoration, and observed the diplomatic balancing act of his final years on the throne. Intelligent and quick-witted, she was well aware of the history of her dynasty, its highs and lows, and of the delicate geopolitics of the time. She knew enough to realise that her father had bequeathed her a poisoned chalice. Keeping her fractious courtiers on side and appeasing the Alexandrian citizenry, while securing the continued loyalty of her Egyptian subjects and staying Rome's hand, would require superhuman powers of diplomacy, strategy and resilience. But as the heir of a proud Hellenistic dynasty that had retained its crown longer than any other, Cleopatra – the seventh ruling member of her family to bear that auspicious name – was up for the fight.

The first test, and the first opportunity to demonstrate her credentials as a legitimate pharaoh, came just days after her accession. As so often at key moments of Ptolemaic history, the occasion concerned a sacred bull. Memphis was not the only Egyptian city where a great bovid was worshipped as a god. Heliopolis had the Mnevis bull, regarded as an avatar of the sun god Ra. Koptos, north of Thebes, had its own version of the Apis, though sacred to the local god Min. And Hermonthis had the Buchis (Eg. Ba-akh, 'effective soul'), a manifestation of the local war god Montu. As befitted its martial associations, the Buchis took part in fights with other bulls in a special arena.

The latest Buchis had died around the same time as Ptolemy XII; Cleopatra VII, as the new sovereign, travelled all the way upriver to Hermonthis to preside at its burial (in a special catacomb called the Bucheion) and the coronation of its successor. According to a later inscription found at the site, the ceremonies on 22 March 51 were attended by both co-rulers, 'the king himself [Ptolemy XIII]' and 'the queen, Lady of the Two Lands [Cleopatra VII]'. The ten-year-old Ptolemy placed the crown on the head of the new Buchis, which had been brought from Thebes, while Cleopatra led the beast onto a great ship for a river-borne procession. The festivities were an occasion for popular rejoicing, but the inhabitants of the Thebaid had not come just to see a sacred bull: they were also drawn by the chance to see Egypt's new monarch. Cleopatra made sure they were not disappointed: 'As for the queen, everyone was able to see her.'[2]

Having performed the duties expected of her and observed the niceties of her father's will, Cleopatra seems to have moved swiftly to take sole charge. She sidelined her brother and effectively ruled alone for the next eighteen months, while she consolidated her grip on power. Documents from the first half of 51 were dated to Year 30 of Ptolemy XII and Year 1 of Cleopatra, to emphasise dynastic continuity and her own legitimacy as her father's heir. To reinforce the point, she adopted the dynastic cult title of Thea Philopator ('father-loving goddess'). By July of that year, she was being depicted on monuments as sole ruler. A stela set up in the Fayum showed Cleopatra, attired like a traditional pharaoh in kilt and double crown, with a bare (male) torso, offering to Isis.

The bond between the queen and the goddess Isis, forged in the earliest days of Cleopatra's regime, would become a defining feature of her reign. Other native cults likewise benefited from her patronage. At Ombos, she commissioned new relief decoration in the outer hypostyle hall, showing her performing cultic duties for the gods of the temple. She also continued work on her father's magnum opus, the temple of Hathor at Tentyris. While the main part of the building had been completed, the roof chapels – where the statues stored in the crypt were taken before sunrise every New Year's Day, to be revivified by the first rays of the sun – remained unfinished. This was such a crucial part of the whole sacred complex that Cleopatra made its completion one of the first priorities of her reign. The decoration of the roof chapels was begun in 50, and took three years. One of the most important elements was a circular zodiac set into the ceiling. It symbolised the great rhythm of the universe, which the New Year's festival was designed to perpetuate. Cleopatra commissioned the zodiac in August 50, the configuration of the constellations reflecting the night sky at that very moment. Three years later, the queen would be present in person to witness the inauguration of the roof chapels. The date chosen for the ceremony, 28 December 47, was a uniquely auspicious day when the full moon appeared at its zenith, a conjunction that occurred only once every 1,480 years. Astrological phenomena seemed to accompany Cleopatra wherever she went, as if her fate were written in the heavens.

Notwithstanding an early focus on the traditions of pharaonic Egypt, Cleopatra's Macedonian heritage could not be ignored, and Hellenistic custom meant that she could not hope to have things her own way for ever. By the autumn of 50, soon after the commissioning of the zodiac, fate conspired to place her brother on the throne by her side once again. In one document, dated to 27 October that year, Ptolemy XIII was even recognised as the senior ruler. The trigger for this abrupt change may have been a drastically poor harvest, exacerbated by the *anachoresis* that had plagued previous generations. Hunger riots swept Alexandria, and drastic action was needed to avoid a full-scale revolution. Ptolemy XIII seems to have taken advantage of the crisis to re-emerge from the shadows. His ordinance of October 50 (which named him first, Cleopatra second) ordered all the sellers of grain and beans in Middle Egypt to transport their entire harvests to Alexandria on pain of death. It was worth risking a rural uprising to prevent insurrection in the capital, for Ptolemies only reigned with the support of Alexandria's citizens. The following year, official documents introduced a dual dating system – 'Year 1 [of Ptolemy XIII] which is also Year 3 [of Cleopatra VII]' – while continuing to assert the brother's primacy.

Given that the king was still only twelve years old, the hand of his puppet master can surely be detected in these developments. Even before Ptolemy XII's death, the boy had been assigned official guardians, an army general (Achillas) and a rhetorician (Theodotos of Chios): any self-respecting Ptolemy had to be both a capable war leader and an educated scholar. But it was a third man who really pulled the strings. As an underage sovereign, Ptolemy had, from the moment of his accession, been assigned an official regent to act on his behalf. This shadowy figure, very much in the mould of Ptolemy V's regents 150 years earlier, was a eunuch by the name of Potheinos. By promoting his ward he boosted his own authority; within eighteen months of Ptolemy XIII's restoration, Potheinos had been appointed finance minister. The riches of Egypt, as well as the direction of government policy, were now in his hands.

Neither Potheinos, nor his protégé Ptolemy, nor indeed their rival Cleopatra, would remain in charge of Egypt's destiny for very long.

On the night of 10–11 January 49, in far-off Europe, the veteran Roman politician Julius Caesar crossed the River Rubicon at the head of his troops, challenging Roman authority and plunging the Republic into civil war. The Ptolemies' fateful entanglement with the rising power of the Mediterranean would now prove a death grip. Egypt's fate no longer depended on its own actions, but on the outcome of the wars of others.

It was not long before the fight for supremacy between Caesar and Pompey reached Egypt's shores. In the late spring of 49, by which time Caesar had seized most of the Italian peninsula and his rival had fled eastwards, Pompey's eldest son travelled to Alexandria to request military support for his father's cause. Given the close bonds that Ptolemy XII had established with the elder Pompey, Cleopatra VII felt bound to respond positively to this latest appeal. She duly made available fifty warships and 500 Gallic and Germanic cavalry drawn from the Gabiniani. Sending members of an occupying force to fight in Rome's own civil war must have felt like poetic justice.

If the gesture was appreciated by Pompey, it was far less popular among members of Cleopatra's own government. The Ptolemaic navy could ill afford to relinquish so many fighting vessels, and the Gabiniani had proven remarkably loyal to their new paymasters. It seemed to some at court that Cleopatra had fatally weakened Egypt's sea and land defences for no better reason than a naive sense of loyalty to an old ally of her father's. It was just the excuse that Ptolemy XIII's backers had been waiting for. By the end of the summer, they had ousted Cleopatra and declared their charge sole ruler of Egypt. Cleopatra left Alexandria and retreated to Thebes – how ironic for a Ptolemaic ruler to seek refuge in the heartland of Egyptian nationalism! But Cleopatra was more popular with her native subjects than most of her predecessors, for her early actions had not gone unnoticed.

If the queen thought that a grateful Pompey might cast her a lifeline, she would be bitterly disappointed. In the autumn of 49, when the Roman counter-senate met to confirm Pompey as its supreme commander, it also recognised Ptolemy XIII as monarch of Egypt, ignoring the provisions of Ptolemy XII's will. Some gratitude. Cleopatra's abandonment by Pompey should have served as a painful but important lesson: intervening in Roman politics was a fool's errand.

Recognising that her position in Egypt was no longer tenable, Cleopatra fled to Phoenicia, a region with longstanding links to the Ptolemaic dynasty. Some of the local inhabitants certainly seem to have rallied to her cause, the city of Askalon minting coins bearing her portrait. While she set about trying to raise an army to win back her throne, events continued to move fast in Rome's civil war. In early August 48, the opposing sides met at Pharsalos in Thessaly, central Greece. Caesar inflicted a serious defeat on Pompey, who fled the field and hastened to his only remaining ally, Egypt.

News of Caesar's victory and of Pompey's imminent arrival (with Caesar in hot pursuit) must have provoked consternation in Alexandria. Ptolemy XIII's advisers had allied the king with the losing side. Recognising the way the wind was blowing, they now planned a spectacular volte-face. On 28 September, Pompey's flagship moored off Pelousion and the general embarked on a smaller tender to take him ashore. There to receive him and watching from the beach was the teenaged Egyptian king, dressed in full royal regalia. But before the boat even reached the shore, Pompey was stabbed to death by a former colleague, the officer Lucius Septimius, now serving in the Egyptian army. The general's body was swiftly cremated, but the head, unceremoniously hacked off, was kept as gruesome evidence of the great Pompey's ignominious fate. Ptolemy and his coterie must have gleefully anticipated Caesar's gratitude for eliminating his rival.

Rarely in history can a political calculation have backfired quite so spectacularly. Pompey was Caesar's rival, to be sure, but he was also his son-in-law. And there was also the matter of Roman pride: it might have been acceptable for one Roman general to kill another on the battlefield, but for a respected leader to be knifed in the back on a foreign shore was an affront to Roman values. When Caesar sailed into the harbour at Alexandria on 2 October, to be presented with Pompey's severed head, he was outraged. With a force of 4,000 battle-hardened men, he marched straight to the royal palace and set up residence. In his own mind, he was now ruler in Egypt. Following Ptolemaic royal custom, he carried out highly symbolic acts, visiting the tomb of Alexander the Great and taking part in philosophical discussions with the city's leading scholars. Then he announced that it was his duty to settle, once and for all, the dispute between Ptolemy XIII and Cleopatra VII. He promptly ordered the warring siblings to stand down their armies, make haste to Alexandria and attend on him.

Ptolemy, with a sizeable military force at his command, including the remaining Gabiniani, and the backing of the Alexandrian citizenry, had no intention of being dictated to by a Roman. Entering the city at the head of his army, he made his way to the palace to confront Caesar. For Cleopatra, by contrast, getting to Alexandria was not so easy. But somehow, slipping past her brother's forces, she made it into the city and into the royal compound. That she was hidden in a bed-linen sack, as a later author claimed, seems somewhat improbable, but then Ptolemaic behaviour was strange at the best of times. Whatever means she used to gain entry, her arrival changed the course of history. On that autumn day in 48, the twenty-one-year-old queen came face to face with the fifty-two-year-old Roman general. The chemistry, or the politics, clearly worked. By the next morning, Caesar had decided to back her.

As rumours started to spread across the city that the ousted queen had done a deal with a presumptuous Roman conqueror, the incensed populace threatened to storm the palace. Caesar now displayed all his political acumen – and a good deal of sang-froid – by calmly appearing before the mob and reading aloud the will of Ptolemy XII, reminding the crowd that the late king had made Rome the guarantor of his wishes. The document confirmed brother and sister, Ptolemy XIII and Cleopatra, as joint rulers of Egypt, and that was that. To placate public sentiment, Caesar returned Cyprus to the Ptolemaic realm in a gesture of magnanimity. Ptolemy and Cleopatra's two younger siblings, the younger Ptolemy and Arsinoe, were declared joint rulers of the island. In the course of an eventful twenty-four hours, calm had been restored in Alexandria, the dynasty's internecine rivalry ended and Ptolemaic prestige restored.

The outcome benefited Cleopatra, now restored to her throne, and Caesar, the power behind it. But Ptolemy XIII and his backers were far from pleased. For the king's part, he was now forced to share power once again with his sister, and the two were not exactly enamoured of each other. For his supporters, the outcome was a disaster: with Caesar's backing, Cleopatra would rule the roost, and she was hardly likely to allow her brother's faction to retain influence at court. With such opposing interests at play, the peace could not hold.

Potheinos, who had the most to lose, took matters into his own hands. He ordered Ptolemy XIII's army of 20,000 men to march into Alexandria and occupy the city. Arsinoe was proclaimed co-ruler of Egypt in place of Cleopatra, and the army set about forming the citizens of Alexandria into militias, rallying them with anti-Roman rhetoric. Against these massed forces, Caesar and Cleopatra had only the 4,000 troops he had brought with him, so there was no question of a full-scale confrontation. But Caesar had been in trickier situations, and he knew how to stall for time while reinforcements were summoned.

His first move was to take Ptolemy XIII hostage; the king would prove a useful bargaining chip. Next, Caesar sought to protect his back. With the army at the gates of the palace quarter, he could ill afford the risk of a naval attack from the sea. He knew his geography, and any warship seeking to enter the harbour of Alexandria would have to pass by the island of Pharos, beneath the shadow of the great lighthouse. So, in his own matter-of-fact account, Caesar 'landed his soldiers, seized the Pharos, and placed a garrison on it'.[3] That dealt with the threat of a naval blockade, but there were already ships at anchor in the harbour that might be requisitioned by the enemy at any time. Caesar simply set fire to them. Unfortunately, the northerly Etesian wind was blowing onshore at the time. The flames from the burning ships quickly spread to the warehouses on the quayside, and then to the Great Library (or its off-site storage facilities – the sources are not clear). Perhaps as many as 400,000 papyrus scrolls went up in smoke. Alexandria would never recover its importance as a centre of learning.

With Caesar and Cleopatra trapped in the palace quarter, Ptolemy XIII might have moved to strengthen his position in the country at large. But, as so often in Ptolemaic history, disputes within the king's inner circle led instead to chaos and confusion. Buoyed by the mob's support, Arsinoe overreached herself and promoted her tutor, a eunuch named Ganymedes, to commander-in-chief of the nationalist forces. His first instinct was to play dirty, killing his predecessor Achillas, then deliberately contaminating the canals that supplied fresh water to the royal palace in Alexandria. Caesar responded by digging new wells and sending ships along the coast to search for springs. Discontent with Ganymedes' leadership gathered pace, and his officers mutinied, negotiating with Caesar to exchange the hapless Arsinoe for the imprisoned Ptolemy XIII. Once the king was released from captivity, he took up the war with renewed energy. Only the arrival of Caesar's reinforcements from Anatolia, bolstered by recruits from Petra and Judaea, turned the tide decisively against Ptolemy. He tried to flee by river, but so great was the crowd of his followers seeking to escape with him that the ship sank. Thus did the Nile claim the life of the thirteenth Ptolemy, while Caesar entered Alexandria as victor.

For a second time, he invoked the will of Ptolemy XII to confirm the royal succession, this time proclaiming Cleopatra co-ruler alongside her *younger* brother, the twelve-year-old Ptolemy XIV. To mark his triumph, Caesar sailed up the Nile with Cleopatra, accompanied by 400 ships full of Roman soldiers. It was a deliberate show of force and it sent a blunt message to the Egyptian population: Rome was now in charge, and while Cleopatra and Ptolemy XIV reigned, they did so at Caesar's pleasure. The point was driven home when he departed Egypt the following spring: he left behind three of his four legions. Caesar disingenuously tried to suggest that this occupying force was a generous gesture, designed 'to support the authority of the king and queen, neither of whom stood well in the affections of their subjects on account of their loyalty to Caesar, nor could be supposed to have given any firm foundation to their power in a government of only a few days' duration'. But the true purpose was never in any doubt: 'Caesar thought it beneficial to the smooth running and renown of our [Roman] empire that the king and queen should be protected by our troops, as long as they remained faithful to us, but if they were ungrateful they could be brought back into line by those same troops.'[4]

An army of occupation was not Caesar's only parting gift to Egypt. Nine months after he and Cleopatra had been holed up together in the palace of Alexandria, the queen celebrated the birth of a baby boy, 'Ptolemy called Caesar'. Egyptian monuments publicly announced that this child was the son of Julius Caesar and Cleopatra – the heir of both the Ptolemaic dynasty and Egypt's new conqueror. The boy's birth was a cause for celebration in the Ptolemaic lands. Cyprus, newly returned to the fold, minted coins showing Cleopatra holding her infant in her arms. The native Egyptians proclaimed Ptolemy Caesar (or Caesarion, 'Little Caesar', as he was affectionately known) as a young pharaoh. But in Rome his birth was regarded as scandalous, especially as Caesar was still married to his Roman wife (Calpurnia) and already had an adopted son, Gaius Octavius (known after his adoption as Octavianus). The conqueror of Egypt, however, was in no mood to let public opinion rain on his parade. When he returned to Rome in 46, having finished campaigning in the east, he invited Cleopatra and her brother to visit him as honoured guests. He even put them up in his estate. There, seemingly oblivious to Roman republican sentiment, Cleopatra held court as if she were back in Alexandria. Cicero, a lifelong anti-monarchist, fumed, 'I hate the queen ... Her arrogance, when she was living across the Tiber ... I cannot recall without profound bitterness'.[5] Meanwhile, back in Egypt, a low Nile flood led to a poor harvest and famine. The Egyptians starved while their king and queen lived it up in a foreign capital.

As for Caesar, he regarded his victorious homecoming from Egypt as the pinnacle of his career. To celebrate his legendary conquest – of the Egyptian queen as well as her kingdom – he staged a lavish military triumph through the streets of Rome with a distinctly Ptolemaic flavour: a public banquet for 22,000 guests, a parade of exotic animals, including giraffes and elephants carrying torches, and Dionysiac rituals. If it called to mind accounts of Ptolemy III's great procession, that was surely the point. There was one novelty, though: Arsinoe, the Egyptian royal couple's own sister, was paraded as captured booty.

In a further display of his unrivalled authority, Caesar introduced to Rome a brand-new calendar. It was based on the calculations of the Alexandrian astronomer Sosigenes, and it brought the civil and astronomical calendars into line by introducing a leap day every four years – an idea first suggested in Ptolemy III's Kanopos Decree of 238. Under Cleopatra's influence, Caesar began to promote other ideas of the Hellenistic east, including its customs and religion. Some Romans, no doubt, were fascinated, but others were appalled. Like a latter-day Alexander, Caesar seemed to have had his head turned by oriental fantasies. A bigamous relationship with an Egyptian queen and delusions of monarchical grandeur: where would it all end?

Cleopatra's special allure was the subject of endless fascination, even during her own lifetime. Of course, as monarch of Egypt, she had fabulous wealth, and unmarried queens of prosperous kingdoms rarely failed to attract ambitious suitors. The bounty of the Nile Valley was fabled, its fields supplying much of the Hellenistic world's grain and its mines copious quantities of gold. Rulers across the Mediterranean world were rapacious, and none more so than the strongmen of the later Roman Republic. Cleopatra's riches alone made her attractive to a succession of ambitious Roman politicians.

By comparison, her physical appearance was of little interest to her contemporaries. In the ancient world, especially among the ruling classes, marriages were contracted for financial or political gain, rarely if ever for love. Despite the assertion of the seventeenth-century French philosopher, Blaise Pascal, that 'If Cleopatra's nose had been shorter, the entire face of the world would have been different,'[6] facial features played little role in the public perception of a Hellenistic ruler. The coin portraits of the Ptolemies suggest a dynasty singularly lacking in Alexander the Great's matinee-idol looks. Ptolemy V and VI were mere infants when they came to the throne, their coins portraying them as callow youths. Ptolemy VIII does not seem to have resented his nickname Physkon ('fatty'), for corpulence betokened wealth and luxury. Cleopatra's own coins showed her with a large, hooked nose and jutting chin: hardly the modern ideal of feminine beauty.

Not that she was uninterested in cultivating her public image. Ptolemaic sovereigns had to appeal to their Greek-speaking and Egyptian subjects, and official portraiture reflected the different traditions and expectations of these two distinct constituencies. Royal statues made for display in Greek temples and public spaces, especially in Alexandria, were generally fashioned from either marble or bronze. They showed the monarch with the beneficent, slightly rapturous gaze associated with Alexander, and all the accoutrements expected of a Hellenistic ruler. Queens like Cleopatra were customarily shown wearing a long, close-fitting dress with shoulder straps, a crinkly undergarment (Gr. *chiton*) and a large overmantle (Gr. *himation*). By contrast, statues made for Egyptian contexts – temples to the native gods – followed pharaonic traditions of representation. The favoured materials were hard stones such as basalt and granite, for the purpose of a pharaonic statue was to celebrate the ruler for all eternity. There was little or no attempt at lifelike portraiture; rather, the attributes of kingship – crowns or headdresses, robes and insignia – were what mattered to distinguish a pharaoh from an ordinary mortal.

Though steeped in centuries of tradition, Egyptian iconography proved remarkably adaptable to changing political circumstances. A royal crown fitted a woman's head just as well as a man's. Greek cult names like 'the father-loving goddess' were easily translated into Egyptian, and fitted into a pattern of royal epithets that was as old as pharaonic culture itself. Since the foundation of the Egyptian state, monarchs had identified themselves as gods incarnate, so the Hellenistic dynastic cult was easily accommodated. There had even been occasional female pharaohs in the past, so Cleopatra VII was able to tap into pre-existing strands of royal ideology and representation to cultivate her image among her native subjects.

Yet the very fact of her gender was one of the reasons for her fame – or notoriety – among contemporary Greek and Roman commentators. One of the distinctive features of Ptolemaic Egypt was the status of women; their rights and freedoms were unknown elsewhere in the Hellenistic world. Queens regnant were even more unusual, until the Ptolemies arrived on the scene. In the early second century, Cleopatra I was the first female member of the dynasty to act as official regent. Her descendants, Cleopatra II and III, were equal participants in a dual or triple monarchy. On occasion, they were presented as the dominant partners, outranking their male co-rulers. Cleopatra VII took full advantage of these precedents to assert her own sovereignty. But a woman on the throne still struck many outside Egypt, especially in Rome, as aberrant – not to say abhorrent. The accusations laid at Cleopatra's feet by commentators – regal haughtiness, a love of luxury, a voracious sexual appetite – would never have been levelled against a male ruler. They would have been considered strengths.

Fabulous wealth, a carefully curated image and the novelty of femininity: any of these might have been enough to attract a suitor. But Cleopatra had other, personal qualities, that served her well in her role as queen and that others found compelling. Her ability to navigate the shifting geopolitics of her age, maintain her own freedom to manoeuvre and her kingdom's independence, speak of a shrewd, intelligent and strategic mind. The relative ease with which she communicated to different audiences – Egyptian, Greek and Roman – suggests a high degree of cultural awareness and abundant charisma. Add to these her undoubted skill at negotiating and influencing, and the reasons for Cleopatra's allure come into sharper focus. Even some Roman commentators felt moved to dispense with the lazy stereotype of the oriental siren and acknowledge her true attributes:

> For her beauty, as we are told, was in itself not altogether incomparable, nor such as to strike those who saw her; but conversation with her had an irresistible charm, and her presence, combined with the persuasiveness of her discourse and the character which was somehow diffused about her behaviour towards others, had something stimulating about it.[7]

Caesar certainly fell under her spell. But, as history had shown many times before, spells could be broken.

The assassination of Caesar by Brutus and Cassius on the Ides of March 44 sent shockwaves across the ancient world. The bloody deed plunged Rome into civil war and left Cleopatra dangerously exposed. With Caesar's killers on the loose, and with many in the eternal city sharing Cicero's low opinion of the Egyptian queen, Cleopatra knew she was no longer welcome or safe. Within a month, she and Ptolemy XIV left Rome and returned to Egypt. A few months later, Ptolemy was murdered in suspicious circumstances, leaving the way clear for Cleopatra to rule alone – or, rather, with her three-year-old son (now proclaimed pharaoh Ptolemy XV) at her side. The baby was given the cult title Theos Philopator kai Philometor ('the father-loving and mother-loving god') to emphasise his lineage as the son of Caesar and Cleopatra.

The public recognition of her heir – the future inheritor not only of the Ptolemaic kingdom but also, perhaps, of the nascent Roman empire – provided Cleopatra with the opportunity to reset her reign. Ever conscious of the influence of the native clergy, she followed the example of her father, Ptolemy XII, by reinforcing the pre-eminence of the priesthood of Ptah. She did this in her own unique way, by promoting the female members of the god's cult. For centuries, one of the most influential members of the Karnak priesthood, in Upper Egypt, had been the 'god's wife of Amun', an office second only to the high priest himself. To signify the special status of the Memphite clergy,

Cleopatra now created the role of 'wife of Ptah', granting it to the sister-in-law of the current high priest, Pasherenptah III.

But Cleopatra did not neglect the other cults of Egypt. The Thebaid remained the centre of native religious consciousness, so it was necessary to honour and placate its priesthoods, too. Hence, at Koptos, she dedicated a new chapel to the local fertility god, Min, with reliefs and inscriptions celebrating herself and her son. At Hermonthis, where Cleopatra had carried out her very first religious engagement as pharaoh, she commissioned a birth house. Such buildings had become a popular feature of Ptolemaic temples, emphasising the divinity of the ruling monarch and the unbroken line of succession stretching back to the time of the gods. In Cleopatra's time, underscoring these characteristics of sovereignty had never been more important. For while her legitimacy as the daughter of Ptolemy XII was not in question, her right to rule alone – in defiance of his will and contrary to longstanding Ptolemaic custom – most certainly was. At Hermonthis, she could both celebrate the birth of Ptolemy Caesar and cast herself in the role of divine mother. This resonated with the age-old Egyptian myth of the goddess Isis and her son Horus.

If Ptolemy Caesar was the incarnation of Horus, and Cleopatra the embodiment of Isis, then the murdered Julius Caesar could be equated with Osiris, king of the dead and lord of the underworld. As such, he deserved a magnificent monument where his memory might be celebrated for all eternity. Cleopatra ordered the construction of a vast edifice on the eastern shoreline of Alexandria, overlooking the port. The Caesareion, as it was called, was intentionally designed to outshine even the city's temple of Sarapis. It was as if Caesar, deified after death, had become the new patron god of the Ptolemaic dynasty and their capital city.

Promoting the cults of Caesar and his son might have helped buy the loyalty of the late commander's legions, still stationed in Egypt; however, navigating the political fallout from Caesar's murder was not so easy. With no legitimate son of his own under Roman law, his adopted son Octavianus (better known as Octavian) became his heir. In November 43, the senate granted Octavian, together with Mark Antony and Lepidus, wide-ranging powers to hunt down Caesar's killers and bring them to justice. But Roman politics were complex and febrile, as earlier Ptolemies had discovered to their cost, and

Cleopatra could ill afford to back the wrong side. She felt honour bound to support the triumvirate against Caesar's assassins, Brutus and Cassius, but it was not a certain bet. To complicate matters further, her disgraced and treacherous sister Arsinoe had been freed after Caesar's triumphal procession and was now living in Ephesos where she had become a rallying point for Cleopatra's domestic enemies. The governor of Cyprus, for example, defected early on to Cassius' camp, probably hoping that the defeat of the triumvirate would facilitate the overthrow of Cleopatra in favour of Arsinoe. Faced with such threats to her own throne, Cleopatra responded by building a fleet to assist Octavian and Antony; but shortly after setting sail, the ships were wrecked in a storm off the coast of north Africa, and work had to begin all over again.

There were also pressing domestic concerns that demanded her attention. In early 43, a massive volcanic eruption in far-off Alaska led to climatic disruption across the Mediterranean. The two years following the cataclysm were among the coldest in the northern hemisphere in recorded history. The unusually chilly and wet conditions resulted in crop failure, famine and widespread unrest. In northern Italy in April 43, Antony's troops faced starvation. The following year, Rome itself was 'wasted by famine'[8] and appealed to Egypt for supplies of grain; but Cleopatra had to refuse, citing her own country's food and health emergency. In 43 and again in 42, the Nile ran so low – according to the Roman philosopher Seneca, it failed to flood at all – that harvests were pitiful. Famine and disease stalked the land. Deploying the government's buffer stocks of grain and distributing food rations became Cleopatra's overriding concern. But such life-and-death decisions were hugely contentious: the citizens of Alexandria, with their political influence, had to be prioritised, even if that meant that others had to be left to fend for themselves. The historian Josephus excoriated Cleopatra for refusing 'to distribute the necessary grain to the Jews'.[9] In Thebes, by contrast, the regional governor Kallimachos was celebrated as 'saviour of the city' when he managed to feed the people and 'took religious care of all that appertained to the worship of the gods, as his grandfather had done'.[10]

Egypt's ability to stave off the worst effects of famine did not go unnoticed in Rome. The Nile Valley, already famed as the breadbasket of the Mediterranean world, looked like the best answer to Rome's concern for long-term food security. For Egypt's part, famine was alleviated, but at a huge cost to the Treasury, and the after-effect of climatic perturbations and disease was a significant decline in state revenue. An ever more rapacious Rome coincided with an increasingly weakened Egypt.

Faced with calamities at home and uncertainties abroad, the native Egyptians did what they had always done, and put their faith in the old gods. One of the most extraordinary personal testaments from this time was set down in February 42 to commemorate the exceptional life and untimely death of a woman from Memphis. The funerary stela of Taimhotep is a masterpiece of carving, its detailed scenes and finely executed hieroglyphs representing the very best traditions of pharaonic workmanship. Indeed, Taimhotep was the wife of the most important and influential Egyptian of the time, the high priest of Ptah, Pasherenptah. Even more striking than the quality of the stela, however, is its inscription. The text starts with prayers to the most important pharaonic deities of Ptolemaic Egypt: Sokar-Osiris, Memphite god of the underworld; Apis-Osiris (Sarapis), hailed as 'opener of the ways [to the underworld], king of the gods, lord of eternity and ruler of everlastingness'; the great Isis, 'mother of god, the eye of Ra, lady of heaven and mistress of all the stars'; Nephthys, Horus, Anubis and 'all the gods of the Memphite necropolis'. It is an appeal to the traditional deities who had guarded Egypt, and offered the promise of a glorious afterlife to its people.

What follows is an intimate account of Taimhotep's life, and a remarkable speech from beyond the grave to her husband. As the stela explains, Taimhotep was born on 17 November 73, in the ninth year of the reign of Ptolemy XII. She married Pasherenptah in 58, when she was not quite fifteen, and the young couple set about starting a family. But it did not go according to plan: 'I was pregnant by him three times but did not bear a male child, only three daughters.' Egyptian custom demanded a male heir, even more so when the future of an ancient and hereditary office like the high priesthood of Ptah was at stake. So Taimhotep turned to the god after whom she had been named: the deified sage and healer, Imhotep, whose greatest masterpiece, the Step Pyramid, still dominated the skyline of the Memphite necropolis twenty-six centuries after it was built. Up on the plateau, Imhotep was worshipped in his own sacred enclosure, the Asklepieion, while down below in the city of Memphis, he was regarded as the son of Ptah. Either way, people from the surrounding region in need of healing or a medical miracle turned to him to answer their prayers. Accordingly, Taimhotep 'prayed together with the high priest to the majesty of the god great in wonders, effective in deeds, who gives a son to him who has none: Imhotep son of Ptah. He heard our pleas … he made me conceive a male child.'[11] The longed-for son was born on the very feast day of Imhotep, 13 July 46. To honour the circumstances of his conception, 'He was given the name Imhotep and was also called Padibastet. Everyone rejoiced over him.'[12]

But the family's joy was to be short-lived. Less than four years later, on 15 January 42, Taimhotep died, aged thirty. In her final words to Pasherenptah, carved on her funerary stela, she urged her husband to eat, drink and be merry in the face of death:

> Oh my brother, my husband, friend and High Priest! Do not weary of drinking, eating, getting drunk and making love! Make merry! Follow your heart day and night! Do not let care enter your heart otherwise what use are your years upon earth? As for the west [the necropolis], it is a land of sleep: darkness weighs on that place where the dead dwell.[13]

Such sentiments had a long history in the Nile Valley: despite the Egyptians' apparent preoccupation with death, they had no wish to hasten its inevitability; even if they believed that a good death would be followed by the promise of rebirth, earthly life was still precious.

14

Serpent of Old Nile

Like all her Ptolemaic forebears, Cleopatra VII had to steer a delicate course. At one and the same time, she had to reassure her Egyptian subjects (for fear of native insurrection) while placating her Greek-speaking ones (for fear of the Alexandrian mob). Like her father, she also had to take heed of a third constituency that posed an existential threat to her kingdom and needed to be managed accordingly: Rome. A final challenge, unique to Cleopatra, was the need to justify her position as a queen regnant. The final years of her reign, from the death of her lover Julius Caesar to her own tragic demise, saw the queen consciously adopt different strategies, different identities, in an increasingly desperate attempt to keep the whole ship of state afloat.

Rome's civil war, which dragged on for two and a half years after Caesar's assassination, was brought to an end in the autumn of 42. The decisive battle was fought on the plains to the west of Philippi, the Macedonian city refounded by Alexander the Great's father, and involved huge opposing armies, numbering some 200,000 men in total. Octavian led a force against Brutus, while Antony commanded another division to engage Cassius. The third member of the triumvirate, Lepidus, stayed behind in Rome to attend to the business of government. As the battle unfolded, Brutus made early gains, pushing Octavian's forces back and even penetrating his camp. But, in another part of the plain, Antony defeated Cassius, who promptly took his own life. Brutus rallied the remaining troops and both sides retired to camp to lick their wounds. A second clash ended in Brutus' defeat and suicide. The triumvirate emerged victorious, with Antony as the hero of the hour.

His reward was to be given responsibility for organising Rome's eastern provinces, the very lands that had comprised Alexander's empire. Antony's victory at Philippi gave him immediate and unquestioned legitimacy: his territories were spear-won, and he was a military ruler in a familiar mould. Antony's prize included the erstwhile kingdom of Macedon, the lands of the defunct Seleukid empire and a collection of outlying provinces (such as Pontos and Lykia) that had fallen under Roman control. But the Hellenistic world was nothing without its third major component, the Ptolemaic realm. If Antony were to be lord of the east, an accommodation with Egypt was essential. A year after Philippi, Antony was at Tarsos, a port city situated at the mouth of the River Kydnos. From there, he sent a messenger to Alexandria, summoning Cleopatra to attend upon him.

For the queen, the calculation must have been simple: having lost one Roman protector in Caesar, this was her chance to gain another. Among all the major players in Roman politics, the victor of Philippi was a rising star and looked the best bet. Moreover, he had played an important role in the restoration of her father to the throne in 55, and she may well have met him at this crucial turning point in her life. Accepting Antony's invitation, she set out for Tarsos. Her arrival by boat, sailing up the Kydnos, was carefully calculated and brilliantly stage-managed. It created such an impression that writers down the centuries felt drawn to conjure it. Antony's biographer was one, painting the colourful spectacle in rapturous language:

> a barge with gilded poop, its sails spread purple, its rowers urging it on with silver oars to the sound of the flute blended with pipes and lutes. She herself reclined beneath a canopy spangled with gold, adorned like Aphrodite in a painting, while boys, like Cupids in paintings, stood on either side and fanned her. Likewise also the fairest of her serving-maidens, attired like Nereids and Graces, were stationed, some at the rudder-sweeps, and others at the reefing-ropes. Wondrous odours from countless incense-offerings diffused themselves along the river-banks.[1]

Cleopatra's royal barge had been transformed for the occasion into a tabernacle: here was Aphrodite coming to meet Dionysos. The oarsmen rowed to the sound of flutes – Ptolemy XII's favourite instrument and an important element in Dionysiac rituals. The queen's attendants were accoutred, not as mere royal servants but as figures from Greek legend – sea-nymphs and incarnations of beauty. The burning of holy incense reinforced the message that here was a goddess arriving to meet her consort.

The theatre certainly worked as far as the onlookers were concerned: 'a rumour spread on every hand that Aphrodite was come to revel with Dionysos for the good of Asia'.[2] Antony, too, seems to have fallen for the bait. (The fact that he was forty-two, Cleopatra twenty-eight, may have helped.) Instead of treating Cleopatra like a client monarch, he found himself doing her bidding. Within weeks, Arsinoe was murdered on Antony's orders, removing the last serious rival to the Ptolemaic throne. Antony also gave Kilikia, the province in which Tarsos was situated, to Cleopatra, to add to her Cypriot territories. Little by little, first with Caesar and then with Antony, Cleopatra was achieving her ambition of restoring the Ptolemaic realm to its former glory. Hers may not have been spear-won territory, but the return of Cyprus and part of Anatolia was a triumph, nonetheless. And none of her Greek subjects could ignore the *tryphé* of her arrival in Tarsos.

To seal his entente with Egypt, Antony visited Alexandria in the winter of 41/40, staying in the same palace quarters where Caesar had lodged seven years earlier. So much had changed in the intervening period – and so little. Cleopatra's first liaison with a Roman commander had resulted in the birth of Caesarion, Little Caesar. Nine months after Antony's sojourn, in the autumn of 40, she bore twins, a brother and sister. The boy was named Alexander, after the great Macedonian conqueror who continued to inspire would-be emperors like Antony. The girl was named Cleopatra, after her mother. In addition to their birth names, the babies were also given epithets to evoke the cosmic destiny of the Egyptian kingdom and its ruling dynasty. Alexander was Helios, the sun; his sister Selene, the moon: celestial twins to crown a match made in heaven.

A matter of weeks after the babies' birth, Rome's triumvirate officially agreed their respective areas of authority in a treaty signed at Brundisium (present-day Brindisi). Lepidus received the north African coast, including Carthage; Octavian the Iberian peninsula, Gaul and northern Italy; Antony was confirmed as master of the eastern territories, from Greece to the Euphrates, including the old Ptolemaic lands of Koile-Syria and Kyrenaika. The Italian peninsula was meant to be shared between the three men, but Octavian's interests ensured him virtual hegemony. In dividing the empire between them, they were, consciously or not, setting the battle lines for future conflict. The senate insisted on certain measures to try to prevent, or at least stall, another civil war. In October 40, it decreed that Antony should wed Octavian's sister, Octavia – her second marriage, his fourth. The fact that Octavia was pregnant with her first husband's child while Antony had just fathered two children with his unmarried lover, Cleopatra, mattered less than the underlying politics; the two great rivals, Antony and Octavian, were now brothers-in-law, bound to each other by family ties. Octavia loyally followed her new husband from province to province over the next four years, raising a large family of biological and adopted children.

A further requirement of the treaty of Brundisium was that Antony should launch a campaign against the Parthian empire, as retribution for the military defeat it had inflicted on Rome some thirteen years earlier. This was by no means a straightforward mission. Time and again, the Parthians had shown themselves capable of outwitting major armies. Beginning in the middle of the third century, they had overthrown Seleukid power in north-eastern Iran, before expanding their writ to include all of Mesopotamia and eastern Anatolia. Now, in a deliberate provocation to the Romans, the Parthians seized the whole of the Levantine coast except the port city of Tyre. Bringing them to heel would soak up all of Antony's energies (and fortune) for years to come. Perhaps that was Octavian's plan.

Antony's confirmation as overlord of Rome's eastern provinces, coming so soon after the birth of his twins, fundamentally altered his attitude towards Cleopatra. He now regarded her as his consort and equal. The erstwhile Macedonian and Seleukid kingdoms were his, the still extant Ptolemaic kingdom hers. Together, their domains encompassed virtually the entire Hellenistic world; and with the conquest of Parthia, he would be able to bequeath to his children the whole of Alexander the Great's empire, newly restored. To this end, he began to reorganise the eastern provinces – largely by gifting vast swathes to Cleopatra. She received Koile-Syria with its great timber stands of the Lebanon, the prized balsam and date groves in Judaea, the wealthy client kingdom of Nabataea, a number of estates on Crete and the city of Kyrene. The last must have been a particularly welcome gift: the earliest of the Ptolemaic colonies had returned to the fold.

Cleopatra's gamble seemed to have worked: a decade earlier, her liaison with Caesar had brought her Cyprus; now, her partnership with Antony had delivered most of the rest of her forefathers' hard-won empire. Egypt's economic fortunes had been turned around with the addition of new lands rich in natural resources and well situated for trade. Far from being down and out, under Cleopatra the Ptolemaic dynasty seemed to be on the way up again. To celebrate her astonishing diplomatic triumph, she had new coins minted in her Levantine territories; those issued by the city of Antiokheia bore Cleopatra's face on one side, Antony's on the other. And it was to Antiokheia that Antony sailed, towards the end of 37, to spend the winter with Cleopatra while he completed his reorganisation of the east.

For her part, she announced the renaissance in her dynasty's fortunes by adopting a new dating system. The year 37/36, the sixteenth of her reign, was renamed 'Year 16 which is also Year 1'. Only once before in the long history of pharaonic Egypt had a monarch taken such a step, and that was over a thousand years earlier. Cleopatra had restored Ptolemaic pride, both territorially and economically. The royal line looked secure, and the country was at peace. Her Greek-speaking subjects could not have asked for more. Aphrodite had indeed come among them.

Beyond the bustling streets of Alexandria, out in the Egyptian countryside, the indigenous inhabitants of the Nile Valley certainly appreciated stability and prosperity, but notions of imperial grandeur counted for less than respecting the age-old contract between the human and divine realms. A pharaoh's first and foremost duty was to honour the gods by beautifying and enlarging their temples, observing their festivals and daily rites, and thereby encouraging them to safeguard Egypt and its people. The poor Nile floods and disastrous harvests of 43 and 42 must have rocked native confidence in Cleopatra VII's reign. The gods were clearly punishing Egypt and had to be appeased if better times were to return. Cleopatra was astute enough to respond accordingly.

From the very beginning of her reign, she seems to have had more sympathy for, and interest in, her Egyptian subjects than any of her predecessors. According to Antony's biographer (who was no particular fan of the queen), she was the first of her dynasty to learn to speak Egyptian: a far cry from Ptolemy IV addressing his Egyptian troops in Greek on the eve of the Battle of Raphia. The close connections between the royal family and the high priests of Ptah, fostered by Cleopatra's father, were maintained and strengthened in her own reign. Both parties recognised the value of the relationship for their own survival.

But Cleopatra's links with the indigenous aristocracy went far deeper than ceremonial interactions with the Memphite clergy. According to another Roman writer, she numbered a native priest among her private counsellors, while several high-ranking Egyptian officials are known from her reign, who were immortalised in fine stone statues that must have been produced in the royal workshops. One such was the governor of Tentyris, Pakhom. Like the panjandrums of the pharaonic past, he gloried in a host of titles: 'prince and member of the elite, royal brother, general-in-chief, priest of the statues of pharaoh, guardian of the treasure of Horus of Apollonopolis … and of Hathor, Lady of Tentyris, priest of Isis who resides at Tentyris, priest of Isis, Lady of Philae … priest of Hathor … priest of Horus of Apollonopolis'.

As governor of Tentyris, Pakhom would have presided over the ongoing work of construction and decoration carried out in the local temple in Cleopatra's name. On the rear wall, huge reliefs were cut showing the queen and her son (named, properly, as 'Ptolemy Caesar') offering to the gods of the temple and performing cult ceremonies – scenes practically unchanged in their basic format for more than 2,000 years. The message of continuity, of timeless pharaonic tradition, was loud and clear. The resident priesthood would have appreciated this royal patronage: it not only made their temple one of the most stunning in the land, but by attracting pilgrims from far and wide it also swelled their coffers.

The decoration at Tentyris was lavish and exuberant, as if the artists and craftsmen were revelling in being able to express their native traditions. In one striking example, a series of reliefs on the outer wall of the temple depicted elements from the coronation ceremony.

For perhaps the first time in ancient Egyptian history, the full range of crowns worn by a monarch was depicted, arranged in neat rows as if laid out on the shelves of a royal wardrobe. Cleopatra VII and Ptolemy XV, though descended from generations of Greek-speaking foreigners, were asserting their right to bear all the traditional regalia of Egyptian kingship.

The renaissance of indigenous religion was mirrored at sites throughout Egypt in the later decades of Cleopatra's reign. At Apollonopolis, two giant stone falcons (representing the god Horus) were erected at the entrance to the temple. Each protected a smaller figure of a prince, nestling against the bird's breast. The weathering of centuries has destroyed the princes' faces, but they surely depict Caesarion between the ages of eight and eleven, and can therefore be dated to the beginning of Cleopatra's renaissance. At Karnak, the priests of Amun-Ra were happy to install a black basalt statue of Caesarion, depicted in pharaonic style, albeit with a few curly Greek locks peeping out from under the traditional headcloth. Elsewhere, there were men such as Hor son of Hor, who took great pride not only in worshipping the old gods (in Hor's case, the ibis-headed Thoth, god of writing and wisdom, and Amun-Ra, lord of Karnak and king of the gods) but also in ensuring that the shrines of old were properly maintained. In his autobiographical inscription, carved in neat hieroglyphs on the back pillar of a portrait statue, Hor boasted how he renewed the sacred precinct of Osiris near his home city, which had fallen into ruin ever since its mudbrick foundations had been undermined by the cutting of a new irrigation canal. Throughout Ptolemaic history, there must have been frequent examples of the state's economic priorities riding roughshod over local religious sensibilities; but under Cleopatra VII, some of these wrongs were righted – and with government support.

Little surprise, then, that when the high priest of Ptah, Pasherenptah III, died in office on 14 July 41, his lavish funeral was a model of tradition. Furthermore, the authorities saw to it that he was succeeded immediately by his brother-in-law Pasherenamun I, keeping this most important religious office in the family that had monopolised it for generations. Barely two years later, Pasherenptah's cherished son and heir, Imhotep (Padibastet V), was in turn named high priest by Cleopatra, even though he was just seven years and ten days old. Respecting the hereditary principle counted for more than the experience or abilities of the new incumbent – and that was the pharaonic way.

Cleopatra positioned herself not merely as the defender of pharaonic religion, but as an integral part of its dense fabric of belief. For a woman fulfilling the role of pharaoh there was one divine precedent in particular. The cult of Isis was one of the most ancient and venerable in the Nile Valley, a focus of native worship for 2,500 years; the fact that it had become popular with the country's Greek-speaking inhabitants in more recent times was an added bonus. When Greek merchants had first settled in the Nile Delta, the state had begun actively promoting the cult of Isis, perhaps conscious of its easy assimilation into other religious traditions. With each successive dynasty, it became more closely linked with the royal family, and Isis gradually subsumed the powers and attributes of other goddesses. In the thirtieth dynasty, and continuing under the Ptolemies, the temple of Isis on the island of Philae became one of the most important shrines in Egypt. The goddess's cult also spread around the Mediterranean, taken from port to port by Ptolemaic sailors and traders. Part of the reason for Isis' popularity was her multiple personae. She was the protector of Egyptians far from home, the avenging eye of the sun god and the divine mother. Something, in other words, for everyone.

The maternal aspect of Isis held particular resonance for Cleopatra following the birth of Caesarion. Coins issued at this time showed Cleopatra with the epithets and headdress of Isis. When she visited Rome as Caesar's guest in 46, he erected a gold statue of her next to the cult statue of Venus (whom the Romans equated with Isis) in the temple at the centre of the Forum Iulium. This gesture publicly acknowledged Cleopatra's divinity as the incarnation of Isis, and associated her with the goddess (Venus) from whom Caesar claimed descent. Though doubtless appreciated by Cleopatra, the move was highly provocative to many Romans, for the city authorities had traditionally taken a dim view of the Isis cult, regarding it as foreign and dangerous. Back in 58, the Senate had ordered the destruction of all statues and altars to Isis on the Capitoline Hill. So quickly were they rebuilt by her devotees that a similar order had to be issued just five years later, and again in 50 and 48. Four times the authorities mandated the erasure of the Isis cult from the capital; four times, her worshippers refused to be silenced.

While Cleopatra was being feted as the living Isis in Rome, her supporters were busy promoting her cult throughout her realms. The governor Kallimachos commissioned a new sanctuary of Isis in the Thebaid, to add to the Iseion established in nearby Ptolemais under Cleopatra's grandfather, Ptolemy IX. After Cleopatra's meeting with Antony in Tarsos, her association with Aphrodite and her Egyptian counterpart, Isis, was promulgated with renewed intensity. A statue of the Egyptian goddess was even set up on the Acropolis of Athens in the summer of 42 – an extraordinarily brazen gesture in one of Greek religion's most revered locations.

The reliefs on the rear wall of the temple of Tentyris represented the culmination of Cleopatra's indigenous religious strategy. Although the temple was officially dedicated to Hathor, the connections between this goddess and Isis were so close and so ancient that Cleopatra was able to portray herself as Isis – and Caesarion as Horus – without any offence to the resident deity or the temple clergy.

The queen's unique bond with her Egyptian subjects – quite unlike anything seen under her Ptolemaic predecessors – was the focus of particular celebration at the start of her renaissance. At the same time as changing the dating formula, Cleopatra also changed her title in the dynastic cult. In a highly significant move, she added the epithet Philopator ('father-loving') to that of Philopatris ('fatherland-loving'). It was a small but crucial signal. Here was a Ptolemy publicly allying herself with Egypt. The Nile Valley was her fatherland, too, and she was its patriotic monarch. Her message to the Egyptians: I am one of you, and I am with you.

Cleopatra's overtures to her Egyptian subjects were of scant interest to Rome. But Antony's gifting of Roman territories to a foreign ruler was quite another matter. No matter that the Treaty of Brundisium had allocated him oversight of the eastern provinces: they were not his personal property to be given away to whomsoever he pleased. The fact that he had made a present of them to his Egyptian paramour, while he was still married to Octavia, raised serious concerns about his longer-term intentions. For Cleopatra's enemies in Rome, her track record was all too clear: she had ensnared one great Roman general, and now she was doing the same again. Antony would need to be watched; Cleopatra brought to heel.

In the early months of 36, as winter turned to spring, Cleopatra left Antiokheia and returned to Alexandria, while Antony set off on his Parthian campaign. It was a total disaster. In keeping with the campaign's chaotic prosecution, the sources are confused about exactly what happened. Antony, with sixteen legions under his direct command, seems to have allied himself with the client kingdoms of eastern and central Anatolia (Galatia, Kappadokia, Pontos and Armenia) which together supplied thousands more infantry and heavy cavalry. In total, Antony must have had something like 100,000 troops at his disposal, together with siege engines and an eighty-foot-long battering-ram. The army's baggage train, loaded onto 300 wagons, was said to have stretched for five miles. The Parthian forces were concentrated along the Euphrates, so Antony decided to attack from the north-east, via Armenia and the neighbouring state of Atropatene, situated on the southern shore of the Caspian Sea. His army followed a well-trodden caravan route, but by the time it reached the agreed rendezvous, the baggage train, which had taken a different path, had been attacked and destroyed by the Parthian cavalry. Antony's army suddenly found itself deep in hostile territory with no supplies. His Armenian allies promptly deserted, and Antony was forced into an ignominious retreat, suffering yet more casualties in the process. By the time his army limped back into camp in Syria, it had lost some 20,000 infantry and 5,000 cavalry – perhaps two-fifths of the total force.

Humiliated on the battlefield, his troops in rags, Antony had only one recourse. He sent for Cleopatra. She had just given birth to their third child, named Ptolemy Philadelphos in emulation of his great ancestor, Ptolemy II. But it was neither grain nor gold that Antony needed; his requests were altogether more basic, and Cleopatra arrived in January 35 with fresh clothes for his soldiers. The ever-faithful Octavia had also taken it upon herself to bring fresh troops, provisions and money. She got as far as Athens, where she was met by a message from Antony instructing her to proceed no further. It was a declaration that their marriage had come to an end. Antony had made his choice; Octavia returned to Rome.

Despite his total failure to defeat the Parthians, Antony knew that his future reputation and authority depended upon the ultimate success of his assigned mission. He was determined to try again, once he had been refinanced and resupplied by the Ptolemaic treasury. First, however, there were matters back home to deal with. Lepidus had tried and failed to take over Sicily, and was forced to resign by Octavian. The triumvirate came to an abrupt end, and Octavian set about positioning himself as sole ruler. Antony was now his main opponent, and the easiest way to undermine Antony was to draw attention to his recent behaviour. How could a man who had abandoned his high-born Roman wife to consort – and father yet more bastards – with a foreign queen, hold any sort of position of power in the Republic? Antony was summoned to Rome, but chose to stay in his eastern stronghold. Twelve months of political infighting followed, but Antony remained resolute.

By 34 he was ready to resume his Parthian campaign. This time, Cleopatra accompanied him as far as the Euphrates. As Antony marched off to war, she spent the summer on a royal progress through her newly acquired territories. It was the first time in more than a century that a Ptolemy had journeyed through Koile-Syria as sovereign monarch. Cleopatra evidently relished the experience, even visiting one of her rivals, Herod of Judaea, and staying at his palace in Jerusalem. By the autumn, she had returned to Alexandria, and Antony had achieved a notable – if limited – victory against the perfidious Armenia. With its king in chains, Antony made haste to the Egyptian capital, in triumphant mood.

What followed was one of the most extraordinary sights the citizens of Alexandria had ever witnessed, even in a city used to spectacles. In a carefully stage-managed event that consciously harked back to the glorious reign of Ptolemy II, Antony celebrated his victory with a magnificent pageant through the streets. Just like the Grand Procession of two centuries earlier, it was replete with Dionysiac imagery. Antony himself appeared in the guise of the god, wearing a gold-embroidered gown with buskins on his feet and holding Dionysos' distinctive staff topped with a pine cone. According to a contemporary account, he 'drove into the city upon a chariot and he not only presented to Cleopatra all the other spoils but brought her the Armenian and his family in gold bonds'.[3] The captured king of Armenia was the least of the gifts that Antony gave out that day. In a lavish ceremony in the gymnasium, he donated swathes of his eastern territories to Cleopatra and their three children. To Alexander Helios he gave Armenia and Media, as well as Parthia beyond the Euphrates, anticipating its eventual defeat and annexation. Cleopatra Selene received Kyrenaika; Ptolemy Philadelphos, Koile-Syria and Kilikia. Cleopatra VII was confirmed as ruler of Egypt and Cyprus and proclaimed 'Queen of Kings and Queen of Egypt', while Ptolemy XV Caesar, now aged thirteen, was declared 'King of Kings and King of Egypt' and the legitimate heir of Julius Caesar. In Antony's eyes, all the recipients were accepting his role as suzerain, while they were merely client rulers. Cleopatra, no doubt, saw things rather differently: the 'Donations of Alexandria' acknowledged her and her children as heirs to the Ptolemaic empire, and restored that empire to its former glory. Another of Antony's gifts was said to have been the contents of the Pergamon library, a noted rival to the Great Library of Alexandria. Pergamon's 200,000 parchment rolls went some way to restoring the papyrus scrolls that Caesar had unwittingly sent up in smoke fourteen years earlier.

In the city, the people celebrated with gusto and souvenirs were produced as a permanent reminder of the day. A bronze statuette of the six-year-old Alexander Helios, sporting the distinctive pyramidal crown of Armenia, recalled the moment when Antony presented his children to the crowd, including Alexander Helios 'arrayed in Median garb, which included a tiara and upright *kidaris* [the tiered crown of the Persian kings]'.[4]

The Romans were aghast at Antony's behaviour. Triumphal processions in Rome itself were an acceptable tradition, but to hold one overseas, and to give away Roman possessions, crossed too many lines. Public opinion, stoked by Octavian, felt that Antony 'had bestowed the honourable and solemn rites of his native country upon the Egyptians for Cleopatra's sake'.[5] By his actions, Antony seemed to be signalling that he was abandoning Rome in favour of Alexandria, and that he intended to rule alongside Cleopatra as joint sovereigns of a new eastern empire.

Cleopatra shrugged off any such criticism. Capitalising on the success of the Donations, during which she had appeared dressed as Isis, she took the title 'the new Isis', proclaiming her role as the divine counterpart of Antony's Dionysos/Osiris. She also ordered the construction of a vast Greek temple to Antony, situated in a prime location overlooking the main harbour of Alexandria. Behind the temple stood a huge plaza, graced at its centre by a towering obelisk.⁶ She was consciously marrying Hellenistic and Egyptian traditions in honour of her new Roman spouse. Elsewhere in the city, she erected a colossal pair-statue of Antony and herself, in the guises of Osiris and Isis. The people of Alexandria responded in kind. A basalt pedestal, erected on 28 December 34, is all that remains of a large statue of Antony, presumably cast in bronze in Greek style. The inscription on the base runs, 'Antony the Great, lover without peer: Parasitos [set this up] to his own god and benefactor'.⁷

The reference to 'lover without peer' or 'inimitable lover' may have been a typically Alexandrian in-joke. For Antony and Cleopatra had recently established a secret society called 'The Inimitable Livers', a curious name for an equally curious group of people who prided themselves on their singular lifestyle. The society was dedicated to the cult of Dionysos, and its ceremonies featured much eating and drinking and general licence (to the long-term detriment, one imagines, of the Livers and their livers). According to one account, 'every day they feasted one another, making their expenditures of incredible profusion'.⁸ The Romans took this as yet another sign of the debauchery into which Antony had fallen, under Cleopatra's malign influence.

By the start of 33, the rosy glow of the Donations was beginning to fade. Antony still had unfinished business with the Parthian empire, and he returned to campaigning. But any plans for a major new advance into Parthian territory were scuppered when he received an ultimatum from Octavian to partition and share Armenia. If a new client state were to be added to Roman territory, Octavian wanted a piece of it. Relinquishing any hopes of ever conquering Parthia, Antony travelled at once to Ephesos and summoned Cleopatra to meet him there.

The queen now had to make one of the most important, fateful decisions of her reign. All her adult life, she had manoeuvred to keep the different factions happy: playing the Hellenistic monarch with new territorial acquisitions and conspicuous displays of *tryphé*; being a good pharaoh by honouring Egypt's traditional deities, building temples and speaking the native language; keeping Rome onside by offering support, first to Caesar, then to Caesar's friends. Now she had to choose between two strongmen vying for supremacy. Octavian was Caesar's legitimate heir and had the backing of the Roman people. Antony was her lover, and wildly popular with the citizens of Alexandria. The Mediterranean world was a big place, but not big enough for both men.

In the weeks before she departed for Ephesos, Cleopatra issued a royal ordinance. Such was the everyday stuff of government, but this particular document illustrated the corner into which Egypt's monarch had painted herself. Dated 23 February 33, the papyrus was addressed to a high-ranking official in Alexandria, asking him to notify other bureaucrats. The measures contained in the ordinance granted an extraordinary range of tax privileges to Antony's right-hand man, the Roman general Publius Canidius. Under pressure from Antony, Cleopatra was giving Canidius permission to export 10,000 sacks of wheat from Egypt and import 5,000 amphorae of wine from Kos, duty free. He was also being granted exemption – in perpetuity – from all taxes on his landholdings in Egypt. His tenants, his livestock and his grain-ships would also enjoy freedom from all taxes and liabilities. Customs dues and taxes were the lifeblood of the Egyptian economy. Now a monarch was giving away these revenues – for herself and her successors – to curry favour with her husband's supporters. Alongside the detailed clauses, carefully written by a government scribe, the papyrus bears a single word in a different hand: *ginesthoi* ('make it happen'). It is possibly Cleopatra's own writing, the only example to have survived. She was, in effect, signing her kingdom's death warrant.

And so Cleopatra set sail for Ephesos, casting her lot with Antony and burning her bridges with Octavian once and for all.

Later that year, Antony divorced Octavia. To rub salt into the wound, he sent men to Rome to eject his former wife from the marital home. Relations between Antony and his erstwhile brother-in-law sank to an all-time low. Octavian publicly attacked Antony – using his rival's liaison with the Egyptian queen to whip up anti-foreign sentiment – in the senate and among the people. Cleopatra was branded a danger to Rome and the world, while Antony was deprived of his consulship and military command. He was no longer a general or a statesman, but a renegade, a traitor, and Cleopatra was his co-conspirator. A final showdown was coming, and both sides made preparations for war.

Antony gathered his forces in Anatolia, bolstered by the 200 ships and 20,000 talents that Cleopatra had provided. She was gambling her nation's economic fortunes on a successful outcome. From Ephesos, the couple moved their campaign headquarters, first to the island of Samos, where they staged an elaborate dramatic festival in honour of Dionysos, then to Athens. They knew that Octavian's attack, when it came, would come from the west. Seeking divine assistance for the impending confrontation, they had statues of themselves – Antony as Dionysos, Cleopatra as Selene – set up on the Acropolis. But the Greek gods were not listening.

In the autumn of 32, Antony and Cleopatra moved their base for a third time, setting up their winter quarters at Patras in the north-west Peloponnese. A few months later, as soon as the snows had melted on the mountaintops and the cross-country routes reopened, hostilities commenced. To begin with, the much-anticipated clash was something of an anticlimax. Only a handful of minor skirmishes took place, along the west coast of Greece, and as spring turned to summer it seemed as if Octavian might have taken fright. There was even talk of a peace conference. But in fact, the small-scale coastal landings by Octavian's forces had been designed to divert Antony's attention. Octavian's field commander, Marcus Agrippa, was a brilliant strategist, and he successfully landed troops from Italy, cutting Antony's lines of communication with Egypt, while ships blockaded the coast. Antony and Cleopatra, hemmed in by land and sea, made their last stand at Aktion (Actium), situated on a promontory overlooking a large gulf on the west coast of Greece. In the face of a determined, well-organised enemy, sections of Antony's army deserted. On 2 September 31, in a desperate attempt to break out, his fleet sailed through the Bay of Actium, only to come under attack by a larger force, under Agrippa's command. Cleopatra's ships, waiting nearby, prevented the total annihilation of Antony's navy; but only 60 of their 230 ships escaped, with Octavian in hot pursuit.

Knowing that an attack on Alexandria would surely follow, Antony sailed for Kyrenaika, to reinforce the region's defences and prevent an assault on Egypt from the west. Cleopatra headed home. Fearful of the people's reaction to such a humiliating military defeat, the queen is said to have 'crowned her prows with garlands as if she had actually won a victory, and had songs of triumph chanted to the accompaniment of flute-players'.[9] Having made it safely into the royal palace, she took steps to refill her depleted coffers – her detractors later accused her of rapacious taxation and confiscations – while pretending that everything was fine. To strengthen her position, especially with her Greek-speaking subjects, she declared that Caesarion had come of age, and would now reign alongside her as equal co-ruler. This signalled a return to the norm of Ptolemaic rule and asserted confidence in the future succession. To mark the occasion, Cleopatra, now joined by Antony, staged a huge festival in Alexandria – keep calm and carry on.

A further striking example of this approach is found on an inscription from Upper Egypt. The upper part of a stela from Koptos is decorated in traditional pharaonic style, with a scene of Ptolemy XV making offerings to local and national deities. The cartouches are left empty, a telltale indicator of political uncertainty, but the accompanying text, written in the vernacular demotic script, lauds Cleopatra as 'the female pharaoh, the bodily daughter of kings who were on their part kings born of kings' and Caesarion as 'pharaoh Ptolemy, called Caesar, the father- and mother-loving god'. The bulk of the text is quintessentially Egyptian, combining bureaucratic legal contracts and provisions for the worship of sacred animals. One contract, between the priests of Koptos and a local guild of linen manufacturers, ensured financial support for the cult of a sacred bull. A second contract was signed with a guild of embalmers, ensuring payments and services for the mummification of the said bull and other sacred animals. Both documents were written exactly as they would have been on papyrus, but were carved in stone to stand for all time. They are dated to 21 September 31, less than three weeks after the Battle of Actium. It was a vote of confidence in continuity. But the confidence was misplaced.

In spring of the following year, Octavian launched his long-awaited attack on Egypt. In a classic pincer movement, he rode at the head of an army coming from Syria, while his lieutenant, Cornelius Gallus, moved in from Kyrenaika; Antony's attempts to secure Egypt's western approaches had been a failure. Desperate for reinforcements, Cleopatra even considered an anti-Roman alliance with the fiercely independent kingdom of Media, but she had no means of sending a mission to Asia: Antony's forces in Syria had defected to Octavian's side. With few options left to her, Cleopatra sent repeated embassies to Octavian, offering to abdicate in favour of her children. She received no reply.

In one final, frantic bid to save her dynasty, Cleopatra tried to send Caesarion to safety in India, with the intention of following him. She even had part of her fleet hauled overland to the Red Sea. But the perfidious Nabataeans, who had previously supported her, deserted her cause and burned her boats – literally and metaphorically. Trapped in Alexandria with Antony at her side, all she could do was wait for the inevitable. According to a later account she enlisted both Caesarion and Antony's eldest son, Antyllus, who was the same age, in her army, 'to arouse the enthusiasm of the Egyptians, who would feel that they had at last a man for their king, and to cause the rest to continue the struggle with these boys as their leaders, in case anything untoward should happen to the parents'.[10] If so, the decision sealed the lads' fate.

The border city of Pelousion fell quickly. Within a few days, a forced march through the Nile Delta brought Octavian's army to the outskirts of Alexandria, to be joined there by Gallus' troops coming from Kyrenaika. Antony bravely led his remaining troops out of the city to engage the enemy; but, outnumbered two to one, the result was a foregone conclusion. He escaped while the last of his infantry, cavalry and naval forces surrendered without a fight. On 1 August 30, Octavian entered Alexandria as conqueror of Egypt, terminating nearly three centuries of Ptolemaic rule.

Three deaths that day signalled the end of an era. Caesarion, the fifteenth Ptolemy to bear that noble dynastic name, was hunted down as he tried to flee southwards towards Nubia. Antyllus, Antony's son and heir, was likewise butchered without mercy, even though he had taken refuge in his father's temple. Octavian 'spared neither of them, claiming that they were men and were clothed with a sort of leadership'.[11] And Imhotep-Padibastet V, the ninth generation of his family to hold the office of high priest of Ptah, died aged just sixteen, almost certainly murdered on Octavian's orders. Three dynasties, all snuffed out in a matter of hours.

What happened next has passed into legend. Cleopatra sought refuge in the royal mausoleum, perhaps still hoping to negotiate with Octavian. Antony, however, realised the game was up and fell on his sword. Dying, he was hauled up into Cleopatra's apartment and expired in her arms. As for the queen, she initially refused to leave her sanctuary, but was eventually tricked into doing so; she was taken to the palace and placed under house arrest. Within a week, she had persuaded her guards of her willingness to succumb to Octavian's terms, namely her transport to Rome to be paraded in his triumphal procession. When the guards' backs were turned, she seized her chance. In the words of a Roman chronicler, 'thoroughly mindful was she even then, in the midst of her dire misfortune, of her royal rank, and chose rather to die with the name and dignity of a sovereign than to live in a private station'.[12] By the time the guards returned, the deed was done.

As Antony's own biographer was forced to admit, 'the truth of the matter no one knows'.[13] But the legend that quickly gained popularity – that Cleopatra had died by a snakebite – certainly made sense to her Egyptian subjects. For not only was the cobra an ancient symbol of royal power, worn on the brows of kings since the dawn of history, it had also, latterly, become closely associated with 'Isis, great of magic', a form of the goddess associated with miracles. As the living Isis, Cleopatra had been the goddess's earthly incarnation. Now, through the manner of her death, she had returned to join the pantheon.

The respect in which Cleopatra was held by her native subjects is illustrated by a small but telling incident that happened in the immediate aftermath of her demise. While Octavian ordered the immediate destruction of Antony's statues, 'those of Cleopatra remained standing'. A man named Archibios, described only as 'a friend of the queen', apparently offered the Roman conqueror 2,000 talents to spare her monuments.[14] Such a sum was enough to support Octavian's army for an entire year. The only way in which a bribe of this scale could have been gathered together in such a short time was by means of an appeal to the temple treasuries throughout the Nile Valley. That they responded to the call says a great deal about the indigenous support for Egypt's last Macedonian Greek ruler.

Later generations, too, continued to honour Cleopatra's name. In AD 373, an Egyptian temple scribe in the temple of Isis at Philae honoured his goddess by gilding a wooden statue of the queen – 400 years after her death. In Egyptian religious tradition, a statue was not a mere representation, but a living, breathing embodiment of its subject.

And the Egyptians fervently believed that true pharaohs never died. They passed through death to eternal life.

Epilogue: To the Victor the Spoils

In the autumn, the season of new growth, as green shoots began to appear in the well-watered fields along the banks of the Nile, a foreign ruler from across the sea made his way to Egypt's ancient capital. He did not come alone, but was accompanied by a sizeable detachment of his own soldiers; for this warrior had just conquered Egypt by force of arms, and was heading to Memphis to claim his prize and receive the homage of his new subjects.

In the city's main temple, dedicated to the local creator god Ptah, there was a special area set aside for his living embodiment, a sacred bull. The beast had its own stall, its own priests and lived a life of pampered bovine luxury. It was revered not just as Ptah's avatar but also as the guarantor of royal authority and national prosperity. Its cult stretched back to the dawn of history, an unbroken thread that had endured – through war and famine, invasion and turmoil – unchanged and unchanging. The sacred bull asserted by its very presence in the heart of Memphis that the Egypt of the pharaohs lived on.

As the animal paced back and forth in its stall, the attendant priests must have felt a degree of apprehension. Would their country's new ruler respect age-old tradition by venerating the bull in their care? As the sound of horses' hooves and marching men came into earshot, the moment of truth had arrived.

Octavian may have won control over all the old Hellenistic lands, but he was no latter-day Alexander. Whereas the ruler of Macedon had shown an openness, indeed a receptiveness, to exotic customs and ideologies, Octavian was a Roman through and through. His instinctive disdain for foreign ways bordered on xenophobia. In the days following his capture of Alexandria, he had been shown the sarcophagus of Alexander, paying it due respect 'by placing upon it a golden crown and strewing it with flowers'.[1] But, touching the body, Octavian had broken a piece off the nose. It was not a good omen. He had then been asked if he wished to see the mausoleum of the Ptolemies. He is said to have replied, 'My wish was to see a king, not corpses.'[2]

The priests of Memphis should have taken note. On arriving in Egypt's old capital, Octavian refused even to enter the Apis' sacred enclosure, declaring 'that he was accustomed to worship gods, not cattle'.[3]

Alexander's conquest of Egypt in 332 and the foundation of the Ptolemaic dynasty in 305 had each represented a new beginning for pharaonic civilisation. Octavian's conquest of 30 sounded its death knell. Under Roman rule, the Nile Valley became the dictator's personal fiefdom, a territory to be exploited and plundered at will – for Rome's sole benefit. Economic considerations had, of course, motivated many of the Ptolemies' policies towards Egypt; but they had been resident monarchs, their own fortunes inextricably bound up with the prosperity of the country at large. Octavian and his successors, by contrast, were absentee landlords. Their only interest was the revenue they could extract from their new asset. This explains Octavian's initial leniency towards the people of Egypt, even those who had opposed him: 'The truth was that he did not see fit to inflict any irreparable injury upon a people so numerous, who might prove very useful to the Romans in many ways.'[4] The same consideration also motivated his programme of public works: 'He reduced Egypt to the form of a province, and then to make it more fruitful and better adapted to supply the city with grain, he set his soldiers at work cleaning out all the canals into which the Nile overflows, which in the course of many years had become choked with mud.'[5]

Yet, despite this renewed focus on Egypt's agricultural economy – the basis of the country's prosperity since time immemorial – Roman rule represented a profound break with the past. Institutions were reorganised, the system of government replaced, local autonomy abolished in favour of central control, and prime agricultural land given away to relatives and favourites of the ruler. Many rural villages entered a swift decline and were ultimately abandoned, their residents forced by excessive taxation to seek their fortunes elsewhere. In Memphis, the quarters named after the city's different ethnic communities were redesignated by numbered arrondissements: no-nonsense efficiency in place of cherished identity. Emigration from the city soared, as many saw the opportunities available elsewhere in the Roman world as preferable to remaining serfs in their own land.

Religious life, too, felt the change. In Alexandria, the plaza behind the temple to Antony was completed but renamed the Forum Iulium, while the temple itself was finished as the Caesareum. Both thus became symbols of Roman sovereignty over Egypt. The Ptolemaic dynastic cult was abolished, to be replaced – soon afterwards – by the Roman imperial cult. In the country at large, Octavian and his successors went through the motions of maintaining the old cults (temple services at Tentyris formally began in February 29), but it was a veneer. Without a resident pharaoh to fulfil the age-old contract with the gods, traditional beliefs started to wither. Imhotep-Padibastet V's first cousin was declared the new high priest of Ptah – a stop-gap appointment to fill a void and ensure the immediate loyalty of the native clergy; but when he died a few years later, his office died with him, shorn of royal support. The appointment of a High Priest of Alexandria and All Egypt, held by a Roman commander, brought all the priesthoods under secular control; synods were discontinued; and temple lands were confiscated by the state. Even personal names referencing Egyptian gods started to fall out of fashion. What was the point in honouring deities who were no longer listening? The coins minted by Octavian from 28 onwards said it all: on the obverse, they bore the conqueror's head in profile; on the reverse, a crocodile (the quintessential emblem of Egypt) and the legend AEGYPTO CAPTA, 'Upon the conquest of Egypt'.[6]

Perhaps the most poignant and colourful description of Egypt's fall was penned, ironically, by a Roman author. Though proud of his countrymen's achievements, he was not insensible to the impact on the people and customs of the Nile Valley:

> Thus was Egypt enslaved. All the inhabitants who resisted for a time were finally subdued, as, indeed, Heaven very clearly indicated to them beforehand. For it rained not only water where no drop had ever fallen previously, but also blood; and there were flashes

of armour from the clouds as this bloody rain fell from them ... Elsewhere there was the clashing of drums and cymbals and the notes of flutes and trumpets, and a serpent of huge size suddenly appeared to them and uttered an incredibly loud hiss. Meanwhile comets were seen and dead men's ghosts appeared, the statues frowned, and Apis bellowed a note of lamentation and burst into tears.[7]

The sacred bull of Memphis thus became a metaphor, not for Egypt's sovereignty but for her subjugation.

Following the death of Antony and Cleopatra in August 30, their three children – Alexander Helios, Cleopatra Selene and Ptolemy Philadelphos – were taken prisoner and sent to Rome. The following year, they had to witness – nay, participate in – Octavian's victory procession through the city streets. In fact, Rome's new dictator staged not one but three triumphs, over three consecutive days. The first celebrated his subjugation of the Dalmatian tribes, the second his victory at Actium and the third his conquest of Egypt. As the children followed the soldiers and carts groaning with booty along the Via Sacra, they experienced for themselves what the unfortunate king of Armenia and his family had suffered just five years earlier.

Thereafter, the three siblings were taken in and raised by Antony's former wife, Octavia. The two boys promptly disappeared from history. But Cleopatra Selene, the daughter of Egypt's last independent sovereign, was too big a prize to be allowed to pass into obscurity. She could continue to serve Rome's interests by securing the loyalty of a client king. And so, around the year 20, she was married off to Juba II, king of Mauretania (present-day coastal Algeria and northern Morocco). Under her influence, her husband transformed his capital city – despite its loyal name of Caesarea – into a Little Alexandria. In time, it came to boast a noted library, a temple to the ancestors (adorned with portrait busts of Ptolemaic kings) and even imported Egyptian statuary: memories of a beloved homeland painstakingly recreated in exile.

It was in Caesarea, some years later, that Cleopatra Selene gave birth to a son. The boy's father was a Roman client king, while his grandfather had been a Roman general and statesman; but through his mother and grandmother, the baby had the blood of a great Hellenistic dynasty flowing in his veins. A dynasty that could trace its origins back to the conquests of Alexander the Great. A dynasty that had established the first of the successor kingdoms, and maintained its independence longer than any other.

Though born in a far-off land under Roman yoke, the newborn baby was heir to a royal line that had ruled over the ancient world's most prosperous realm for nearly three centuries; established and nurtured the greatest centre of science and scholarship in history; built astonishing temples in a land famed for its religious architecture; and presided over a melting pot of cultures – a crucible of innovation and creativity. With such an inheritance, there was never any doubt in Cleopatra Selene's mind as to what she would name her son.

Ptolemy.

Notes

INTRODUCTION: QUESTIONS OF IDENTITY

1. Dio Cassius 51.13.
2. Plutarch, *Life of Antony*: 85.
3. Dio Cassius 51.14.
4. Dio Cassius 51.15.
5. Pollard and Reid (2007): xiv.
6. McKechnie (2018): 1.

PROLOGUE: HAIL THE CONQUERING HERO

1. Arrian 3.1.
2. Arrian 3.1.
3. Diodorus Siculus 17.49.
4. Translated in Bosch-Puche (2014): 63.
5. Arrian 3.1.
6. Arrian 3.3.
7. Arrian 3.3.
8. Arrian 3.4.
9. Diodorus Siculus 17.51.
10. Arrian 3.1.
11. Arrian 3.2, quoting Aristander the Telmissian.
12. Diodorus Siculus 17.52.
13. Arrian 3.5.

1: RISE OF A DYNASTY

1. Translation after Ockinga (2018) and Ritner (2003).
2. Diodorus Siculus quoted in Lloyd (2002): 121.
3. Tomb inscription of Padiusir, translated in Wilkinson (2010): 465.
4. Manetho's magnum opus is usually dated to the reign of Ptolemy I, but may have been commissioned by Ptolemy II (Hölbl (2001): 27). A papyrus from el-Hibeh, dated to 241/40, which mentions a high-ranking official named Manetho, may indicate that he was still active at court, albeit very elderly, early in the reign of Ptolemy III (see Moyer (2011): 86).
5. The people of Rhodes melted down the bronze weapons abandoned by Demetrios' troops and used the metal to cast the famous Colossus of Rhodes, later acclaimed as one of the Wonders of the World.
6. The whole complex was razed to the ground in AD 391.

2: BRAVE NEW WORLD

1. Seleukos I's epithet was Nikator, 'bringer of victory'.
2. Dedicated to Seleukos I's son Antiochos I, the *Babyloniaka* was the Mesopotamian counterpart to Manetho's *Aigyptiaka*.
3. It is tempting to draw a parallel with a much later colonial possession, the Belgian Congo.
4. All quotes refering to the geography of Alexandria are from Strabo 17.1 (17.1.6; 17.1.6; 17.1.9; 17.1.1; 17.1.10; 17.1.8; 17.1.10; 17.1.8).
5. Diodorus Siculus 17.52, quoted in Pollard and Reid (2007): 29.
6. Theokritos, quoted in Grant (1982): 39.
7. Strabo 17.1.8.
8. The lighthouse was still working 900 years after it was built, when the Arabs conquered Alexandria in AD 642; it was still standing in AD 1165 (cf. Pollard and Reid (2007): 90–2).

3: GRAIN, GOLD AND GLORY

1. Letter to Kleon, translation after Lewis (1986): 44.
2. Letter from Tushratta of Mittani to Amenhotep III (EA17), translated in Moran (1992): 44.

3 After being mentioned by Pliny the Elder in Book VI of his *Natural History*, Berenike Panchrysos was abandoned and forgotten, and its very existence passed into myth. It was rediscovered at the modern site of Daraheib, just south of the modern border between Egypt and Sudan.
4 Strabo 16.4.7.
5 Burstein (2008): 146.
6 Revenue Laws of Ptolemy II, translation after Austin (2006): 519.
7 Decree of the League of Islanders on the acceptance of the *Ptolemaieia*, translated in Austin (2006): 451.
8 Both quotes from Rice (1983): 13, quoting Athenaeus of Naukratis, *The Learned Banqueters*, Book 5, itself quoting Kallixeinos of Rhodes, *On Alexandria*.

4: THE LIFE OF THE MIND

1 Archimedes, *The Sand Reckoner*, chapter 1, quoted in Pollard and Reid (2007): 104.
2 Also known as Lycophron the Obscure, because of his habit of using obscure or even made-up words, perhaps to obscure his true meaning; the results of his study of comedic texts was a tract, now lost, called *On Comedy*.
3 Canopus Decree.
4 Canopus Decree.
5 Canopus Decree.
6 Strabo 1.1.20.
7 Epitaph of Eratosthenes, quoted in Pollard and Reid (2007): 120.
8 Pappus of Alexandria, *Synagogue* ('Collection'), book 8, quoted in Pollard and Reid (2007): XX.
9 Athenaeus 1.22D, quoting Timon of Phlius.

5: FRAGILE STATE

1 Polybius 5.63.
2 Lewis (1986): 23, quoting P.Ent.11, dated to 242 BC.
3 Polybius 5.85.
4 Raphia Decree, translated in Austin (2006): 482–4.
5 Ptolemy II increased the number of nomes from 36 to 39.
6 Memorandum to an *oikonomos*, translated in Austin (2006): 561.

7 Memorandum to an *oikonomos*, translated in Austin (2006): 559.
8 All three quotes from Lewis (1986): 59.
9 Lewis (1986): 60, quoting P.Ent.11.
10 Polybius 14.12.
11 Polybius 5.34.
12 Polybius 5.34.

6: REBELLION AND RETRENCHMENT

1 Polybius 15.25.
2 Polybius 15.25.
3 Polybius 15.25.
4 A recently discovered inscription from Karia strengthens the evidence for an understanding between Philip V and Antiochos III.
5 Quoted in Hölbl (2001): 154.
6 Second Philae Decree.
7 Second Philae Decree.
8 Compare the legendary Saxon resistance leader, Hereward the Wake, who is said to have held out against Norman forces for years in the fens of East Anglia – a not dissimilar environment to the Nile Delta.
9 Decree of Memphis, translated in Austin (2006): 493.
10 Both quotes from the First Philae Decree.

7: THE HINGE OF FATE

1 Polybius 27.13.
2 Respectively Meretneith, regent for her son Den in the middle of the first dynasty, and Sobekneferu, last ruler of the twelfth dynasty (the existence of a ruling queen Nitiqret, at the end of the sixth dynasty, is disputed).
3 *The Teaching of Ani*, fiftieth maxim, translated in Wilkinson (2016): 310.
4 The document is, incidentally, the earliest dated Greek papyrus from Egypt.
5 Quoted in Hölbl (2001): 169.
6 Livy 45.12.
7 UPZ 59.13–16, quoted in Thompson (2012): 128.
8 Hölbl (2001): 91.

9 Polybius 31.10.
10 Polybius 31.10.

8: ONE COUNTRY, TWO CULTURES

1 Lewis (1986): 4.
2 Herondas, *Mimes*, quoted in Lewis (1986): 10.
3 Theokritos, quoted in Lewis (1986): 11.
4 The phrase, often encountered in demotic texts, is *Wynn ms n Kmy* (Goudriaan (1988): 117).
5 Grant (1982): 46, quoting one of the Zenon Papyri.
6 Rowlandson (1998): 172, quoting P.Ent.82.
7 Lewis (1986): 61, quoting P.Ent.79.
8 But see Bagnall (1988): 25 for the example of an Upper Egyptian family in the late second century; its members held public (military) office under their Greek names, but in private used Egyptian names, held Egyptian priesthoods and commissioned Egyptian tombstones.
9 Will of Dryton, translation after Lewis (1986): 99.
10 At the time of Napoleon's invasion of Egypt in AD 1798, customs tolls constituted 16.7 per cent of Egypt's national income, a picture that is unlikely to have changed much since the Ptolemaic period.
11 Grant (1982): 41, quoting P.Tebt.703.230.
12 Thompson (2012): 47.
13 Quoted in Grant (1982): 47.

9: OUT OF JOINT

1 Justinus 38.8.
2 *Oracle of the Potter*, translated in Austin (2006): 569–70.
3 Quoted in Ray (2001): 136.
4 Lewis (1986): 98, quoting W.Chr.10.
5 Amnesty decree of Ptolemy VIII, Cleopatra II and Cleopatra III, translated in Austin (2006): 502–6.
6 Apollonopolis (Edfu) building inscription, quoted in Hölbl (2001): 265.
7 Sadly, Ptolemy VIII's memoirs (*Hypomnemata*) survive only in quotations in Athenaeus (see Thompson (2009)).
8 Will of Ptolemy VIII, translated in Austin (2006): 501.

10: MOTHER'S RUIN

1. Justinus 39.3.1.
2. The full name was 'holy of birth with the living Apis, divine of creation, twin in [his] birthplace with the son of Isis' (*djeser-mesut hena Hep ankh, netjery-kheperu, sensen-meskhen[et] net sa-Iset*).
3. The Ptolemies divided the Arsinoite nome into three divisions, Themistos (W), Heracleida (N), Polemon (S), perhaps named after the original Macedonian governors; Kerkeosiris was located in the Polemon division.
4. Crawford (1971): 25, quoting P.Tebt. 703.57–60.
5. Ritner (n.d.), quoting P.London 465.
6. Ritner (n.d.), quoting P.Bouriant 10.
7. Ritner (n.d.), quoting P.Bad. II 16, date uncertain.
8. Ritner (n.d.), quoting P.Bouriant 12.
9. Pausanias 1.9.3.
10. The fourth name is unclear.
11. Polybius 9.11a.
12. Livy 31.2.3–4, quoted in Neatby (1950): 94–5.
13. Livy 31.2.3–4, quoted in Neatby (1950): 94–95.

11: KEEPING THE FAITH

1. Herodotus 3.28.
2. Of these eleven Apis burials, eight are attested in documents: in 281 (Year 5 of Ptolemy II), 187 (Year 19 of Ptolemy V), 164 (Year 6 of Ptolemy VI), 143 (Year 27 of Ptolemy VIII), 119 (Year 51 of Ptolemy VIII), 96 (Year 18 of Ptolemy X), 75 (Year 7 of Ptolemy XII) and 50/49 (Year 3 of Cleopatra VII) (see Thompson (2012): 107).
3. Names incorporating Ptah were taken by Ptolemies III, IV, V, VI, X and XIII.
4. Inscription of Djedhor, translation after Gorre (2009): 307.
5. Vienna Stela 82, translation after Gorre (2009): 322.
6. Herodotus mentioned a temple of Herakles in the region, suggesting that the sacred traditions of Thonis may have significantly predated the arrival of the Macedonians.
7. The precise ingredients were 'moulded and sieved bitumen, fir-tree resin, lotus essence, frankincense, oil, wax, fresh and dried turpentine resin, carob bean extract, herbs and spices diluted in wine, crushed precious

metals and minerals, honey and more frankincense' (Goddio and Masson-Berghoff (2016): 174).

12: FIGHT FOR SURVIVAL

1 Whether Tryphaina was the daughter of Ptolemy IX or Ptolemy X remains unclear; she was thus either Ptolemy XII's sister or cousin. To add to the confusion, she is referred to by some authors as Cleopatra V, by others as Cleopatra VI (cf. Bennett (1997); Hölbl (2001): 222).
2 Cleopatra Tryphaina seems to have fallen from favour around 69, when her images on the pylon at Apollonopolis were covered over.
3 Cicero, *Letters to Atticus* 2.5.1, quoted in Siani-Davies (1997): 316.
4 *Teaching of Ankhsheshonqy*, maxims 9.3, 9.7, 16.16, 25.10, 17.14, 10.5 and 11.23, respectively, translated in Lichtheim (1980): 159–84.
5 *Teaching of Ankhsheshonqy*, maxims 9.25, 9.17, 16.9, 13.11, 13.17–18, 15.15, 21.18 and 10.7, respectively, translated in Lichtheim (1980): 159–84.
6 *Teaching of Ankhsheshonqy*, maxim 16.15, translated in Lichtheim (1980): 159–84.
7 *Teaching of Ankhsheshonqy*, maxim 20.9, translated in Lichtheim (1980): 159–84.
8 Siani-Davies (1997): 338, quoting P.Med.Inv.68.53.
9 *Teaching of Ankhsheshonqy*, maxim 20.13, translated in Lichtheim (1980): 159–84.
10 Stela British Museum 866, translated in Gorre (2009): 330.
11 Stela British Museum 866, after the translation in Thompson (2012): 129.
12 Earlier royal builders attested at Tentyris include Pepi I (sixth dynasty), Mentuhotep II (eleventh dynasty), Amenemhat I and Senusret I (twelfth dynasty), most of the kings of the eighteenth dynasty and Ramesses II (nineteenth dynasty), spanning the twenty-second to the thirteenth centuries.

13: DANGEROUS LIAISONS

1 The precise date of Ptolemy XII's death is not known, but it must have occurred before 22 March 51; 7 March has been suggested as a plausible date (see Weill Goudchaux (2001): 133).
2 Weill Goudchaux (2001): 133, quoting a stela commissioned for the death of the Buchis in 29, within a year of Cleopatra VII's own death.

3 Caesar, *Civil War* 3.112, quoted in Pollard and Reid (2006): 164.
4 Both from Caesar, *Alexandrian War* 33, quoted in Meadows (2001): 25.
5 Cicero, *Letters to Atticus* 15.15.2, quoted in Williams (2001): 192.
6 'Le nez de Cléopatre: s'il eût été plus court, toute la face de la terre aurait changé', quoted in Quaegebeur (1988): 43.
7 Plutarch, *Life of Antony* 27.
8 Appian, *The Civil Wars* 5.25.
9 Josephus, *Against Apion* 2.5.60.
10 Ritner (n.d.) and Weill Goudchaux (2001): 137, citing Bernand (1992): no. 46.
11 Stela of Taimhotep, translated in Lichtheim (1980): 62.
12 Stela of Taimhotep, translated in Lichtheim (1980): 62.
13 Stela of Taimhotep, translation after Walker and Higgs (2001): 186.

14: SERPENT OF OLD NILE

1 Plutarch, *Life of Antony* 26; for an even more famous account of the same event, see Shakespeare, *Antony & Cleopatra*, Act 2, scene 2, lines 223–37.
2 Plutarch, *Life of Antony* 26.
3 Dio Cassius 49.40.3.
4 Plutarch, *Life of Antony* 54.
5 Plutarch, *Life of Antony* 50.
6 The obelisk is now in St Peter's Square, Rome.
7 Walker and Higgs (2001): 232, cat. 213.
8 Plutarch, *Life of Antony* 28.
9 Dio Cassius 51.3–5.
10 Dio Cassius 51.6.
11 Dio Cassius 51.6.
12 Dio Cassius 51.11.
13 Plutarch, *Life of Antony* 86.
14 Plutarch, *Life of Antony* 86.

EPILOGUE: TO THE VICTOR THE SPOILS

1 Suetonius, *Life of Augustus* 18.
2 Dio Cassius 51.16.

3 Dio Cassius 51.16.
4 Dio Cassius 51.16.
5 Suetonius, *Life of Augustus* 18.
6 The Roman city of Nemausus (present-day Nîmes) went a stage further, issuing coins bearing the image of a crocodile (symbolising Egypt, or even Cleopatra herself) chained to a palm branch with the ties of a laurel wreath fluttering above (symbols of Roman victory): see Walker and Higgs (2001): 260, cats 305–6.
7 Dio Cassius 51.17.

Sources

GENERAL

The most accessible general history of the Ptolemaic period is Hölbl (2001). This is usefully supplemented by Manning (2010), while Austin (2006) provides an anthology of key texts in translation.

INTRODUCTION: QUESTIONS OF IDENTITY

For papyri as a source of Ptolemaic history and the likely quantity of the material used in a single day by a typical government office, see Lewis (1986): 51. For the Zenon archive, see Rostovtzeff (1922), Lewis (1986): 7 and Buraselis et al. (eds) (2013): 43. For the Tebtunis papyri, see Crawford (1971). The art of Ptolemaic Egypt is contextualised in Bianchi (1988b).

PROLOGUE: HAIL THE CONQUERING HERO

The literature on Alexander the Great is voluminous; Cartledge (2004) is one of the more thoughtful contributions, while Grieb et al. (eds) (2014) offers a range of studies on aspects of the king's life and reign. For the siege and capture of Gaza by Alexander, ancient sources include Diodorus Siculus 17.8 and Arrian 2.27. The anecdote that Alexander carried a copy of the *Iliad* with him at all times is from Plutarch. Quintus Curtius 4.7.29 gives the figure of 800 talents handed over to Alexander by the Persian governor of Egypt; see also Cartledge (2004): xii. The papyrus notice pinned up by Alexander's general at the Memphite necropolis is published by Turner (1974). For Alexander's Egyptian titulary, see Hölbl (2001): 77–81; for his patronage of Egypt's temples, Abd el-Raziq (1984), Arnold (1999) and Ladynin (2014). Arrian 3.3 provides a full account of Alexander's visit to the Siwa oracle, an early reference to which is included in Pindar, *Pythian Odes* 4. The two fantastical accounts, involving serpents and ravens, were penned by Ptolemy son of Lagus (i.e. Ptolemy I) and Aristobulus, respectively, and are quoted in Arrian 3.3. The confirmation of Alexander's divinity by oracles of Apollo and Athena is from Strabo 17.1.43, quoting Callisthenes. The possibility of Alexander having been crowned as pharaoh at Memphis is discussed by Sekunda (2014), but for a different view see Winter (2005); Wojciechowska and Nawotka (2014) review the evidence for the likely date of this ceremony (14 March 331). For the foundation and construction of Alexandria, see Pollard and Reid (2007). The precise timing of the city's foundation in relation to Alexander's visit to Siwa and his second visit to Memphis remains uncertain: see Thompson (2022). That Alexander originally planned to found his new city on the island of Pharos is asserted by Quintus Curtius 4.8. For Lake Mareotis and the geographical setting of Alexandria, see Arrian 3.1, Grant (1982): 37 and Khalil (2008). The city's early temples are discussed by Arnold (1999): 138. Alexander's departure from Egypt is recounted by Arrian 3.6.

CHAPTER 1: RISE OF A DYNASTY

McKechnie and Cromwell (eds) (2018) provides a good series of studies on the reign of Ptolemy I. Adams (1997) offers an accessible summary of the events following Alexander's death, including the Wars of the Successors. For the sacking of Kleomenes, see Bingen (2007): 23. Moyer (2011): 277 has described the Ptolemaic monarchy as 'Janus-headed'. For a reliable study of the Satrap Stela, see Ockinga (2018). The official Egyptian name for Alexandria is discussed by Ritner in

Simpson (ed.) (2003): 393–7; and the much shorter, pejorative nickname by Quaegebeur (1988): 42, Chauveau (1999) and Depauw (2000). For Ptolemy I's temple building, as satrap and king, see Minas-Nerpel (2018); and, for his actions to legitimise himself in both Egyptian and Macedonian eyes, Moyer (2011): 88. The evidence for high-ranking Egyptians in government under the early Ptolemies is discussed by Bianchi (1988a): 13, Legras (2002), Lloyd (2002) and Verhoeven (2005). For the career of Somtutefnakht, see Hölbl (2001): 27. For the tomb chapels at Tuna el-Gebel (some of which were built in Egyptian style, others in Greek style), see Arnold (1999): 156–7. Redford (1986) discusses the etymology of Manetho's name, and Moyer (2011): 277 his writing of a history of Egypt. For the cult of Apis, see Thompson (2012): 107 and Thompson (2018): 18. The cult of Sarapis and the Sarapieion at Alexandria are discussed by Grant (1982): 230, Schmidt (2005), Masson-Berghoff and Goddio (2016).

CHAPTER 2: BRAVE NEW WORLD

Grant (1982) provides an accessible introduction to the wider Hellenistic world. For the Kingdom of Macedon, see Borza (1990) and Heskel (1997); for Rhodes, Buraselis et al. (eds) (2013), especially Gabrielsen (2013); and for the Seleukid empire, Strootman (2021). Ptolemaic relations with the Kingdom of Kush are discussed by Burstein (2021), while Kushite culture is analysed by Taylor (1991). Bagnall (1976) is the definitive study of the administration of Ptolemaic possessions outside Egypt. For Kyrenaika, see Marquaille (2003), and for the new constitution imposed on Kyrene by Ptolemy I, Austin (2006): 69–71. The new settlements founded throughout the Ptolemaic realms are examined by Mueller (2006). Ptolemaic Cyprus is discussed by Michaelides and Papantoniou (2018). Strabo 17.1.6–10 gives the most detailed first-hand account of ancient Alexandria; the geographer visited the city in the 20s BC, not long after the death of the last Ptolemaic ruler. Pollard and Reid (2007): 24–9 provides a comprehensive analysis of Strabo's description. Ptolemy's history of Alexander is discussed briefly by Hölbl (2001): 15 and Thompson (2018): 15.

CHAPTER 3: GRAIN, GOLD AND GLORY

McKechnie and Guillaume (eds) (2018) provides a useful series of essays on aspects of Ptolemy II's reign. For the career of Kleon, see Lewis (1986): 37–45. Thompson (2018) discusses the Macedonian expertise in land reclamation; and Hölbl (2001): 62–3, Ptolemy II's drainage works in the Fayum, including the thirty to forty new settlements founded in previously uninhabitable areas. For a useful summary, see also Römer (2019). For Apollonios' estate in the Fayum and the career of Zenon, see Rowlandson (1998): 7–8 and 95–6; Bowman (1986): 57; Hölbl (2001): 63; Lewis (1986): 165 n. 7; Buraselis et al. (eds) (2013): 42; and Rostovtzeff (1922). For Zenon's epigrams in memory of his favourite dog, and his largely male-dominated milieu, see Rowlandson (1998): 96.

Much has been written recently about the Ptolemaic gold mines in the eastern desert of Egypt; for the latest archaeological evidence, see Redon and Faucher (2015, 2016); Castiglioni and Castiglioni (1994, 1999, 2004); Castiglioni, Castiglioni and Vercoutter (1998). Diodorus Siculus 3.12.1–3 mentions the brutal conditions endured by the miners. For the Red Sea ports, see Meredith (1953) and Meredith (1957); Sidebotham and Wendrich (1996); Sidebotham (1999); Seeger and Sidebotham (2005). Burstein (2008) discusses Ptolemy II's overarching policy towards Nubia, with an emphasis on elephant hunting. For Ptolemy II's annexation of the Dodekaschoinos and subsequent Ptolemaic policy towards the region, see Török (1980).

The king's dominance of the League of Islanders, and the implications for Mediterranean trade, are examined by Buraselis et al. (eds) (2013), especially Buraselis (2013), Criscuolo (2013) and Gabrielsen (2013). For Ptolemy II's military activities, see Erskine (2013); for his foreign policy, Marquaille (2008); and for his economic policies, Thompson (1997) and Thompson (2008). A contemporary document describing the royal oil monopoly is translated in Austin (2006): 524–31. For the commodities exported from Alexandria, see Pollard and Reid (2007): 79. The posthumous deification of Arsinoe II and the foundations established in her honour are discussed by Rowlandson (1998): 7; Buraselis et al. (eds) (2013): 9; and Hölbl (2001): 101–3 (quoting Pliny the Elder's *Natural History*). The most detailed study of Ptolemy II's Grand Procession is Rice (1983), with further references in Buraselis et al. (eds) (2013): 8, 11. The date of the festival is uncertain: Thompson (1997): 242 suggests 279/8 BC, Hölbl (2001): 55, the winter of 275/4 BC. The story of the ageing Ptolemy II looking out from his palace window is mentioned by Thompson (2008): 27, quoting Athenaeus of Naukratis, *The Learned Banqueters*, itself quoting an earlier author, Phylarchos.

CHAPTER 4: THE LIFE OF THE MIND

The intellectual achievements of ancient Alexandria are discussed extensively in Grant (1982) and Pollard and Reid (2007). For the possibility that Ptolemy II commissioned the first Greek translation of the Torah, see Guillaume (2008). The Egyptian revolt of the 240s and subsequent native insurrections against Ptolemaic rule are analysed by Veïsse (2004). The Decree of Canopus is translated in Austin (2006): 470–5, and discussed by Hölbl (2001): 108–9. For the background to the decree and evidence of an earlier synod, see El-Masry et al. (2012). Hölbl (2001): 122–6 discusses the deification of Princess Berenike. The story about Ptolemy III writing a letter 'To All the World's Sovereigns' is from the works of Galen, quoted by Pollard and Reid (2007): 127. For the writing of the name of Syene/Aswan with the hieroglyphic signs of a protractor and plumb line, see Hölbl (2001): 65. For the career of Djedhor, see Lloyd (2002): 129.

CHAPTER 5: FRAGILE STATE

Masson-Berghoff and Goddio (2016): 129 discuss the shrine of Ptolemy IV within the Sarapieion at Alexandria, and Lewis (1986): 14 the need for an exit permit to leave Egypt. For the allotment of land to military settlers, see Lewis (1986) *passim*, and Stefanou (2013). The papyrus from the reign of Ptolemy II instructing a district official to take back the landholdings of recently deceased cavalrymen is translated by Austin (2006): 553–4. For the size of the army under Ptolemy IV, see Fischer-Bovet (2014): 80. The build-up to the Battle of Raphia is covered extensively by Polybius 5.63–65, and its prosecution by Polybius 5.83–85. The decree issued by Ptolemy IV after the battle is translated by Austin (2006): 482–4. For aspects of Ptolemaic local government, see Chauveau (2000): 73 and Hölbl (2001): 59. The memorandum to an *oikonomos* (P.Tebt.703) is translated by Austin (2006): 558–62, while Bagnall (1976): 3–10 provides a useful commentary. Lewis (1986): 58–67 discusses the correspondence of Diophanes. For Ptolemy IV's artistic accomplishments, see Grant (1982): 259 and Hölbl (2001): 133; for his royal yacht, see Thompson (2013).

CHAPTER 6: REBELLION AND RETRENCHMENT

Events at the beginning of Ptolemy V's reign are covered by Polybius 15.25.3–18. For the plot by Philip V and Antiochos III to divide the Ptolemaic realm between them, see Polybius 15.20, and for the Battle of Paneion, Polybius 16.18–19. The economic travails caused by the devaluation of bronze coinage are discussed by Chauveau (2000): 84–6. For Horwennefer's rebellion, see Clarysse (1978), Pestman (1995) and Veïsse (2022); Redon (2018): 19 notes the abandonment of the eastern desert fortress guarding the gold mines. For the Philae Decrees, see Recklinghausen (2018). The treatment of the Delta rebels – recalling Alexander's vengeance on the defeated governor of Gaza – is recounted (in lurid detail) by Polybius 22.17, and the final battles, waged in the central and north-eastern Delta, analysed by Nespoulous-Phalippou (2015). For the Decree of Memphis (the Rosetta Stone), see Ray (2007). Thompson (2012) is the unparalleled modern study of Ptolemaic Memphis; the most detailed account of Memphis to have survived from the ancient world is by Strabo 17.1.31–32. The proclamation to celebrate the enthronement of a new Apis bull in the latter part of Ptolemy V's reign is known as the First Philae Decree, studied by Recklinghausen (2018).

CHAPTER 7: THE HINGE OF FATE

Events at the beginning of Ptolemy VI's reign are covered by Polybius 22.3. For the status of women in the Ptolemaic dynasty, see Rowlandson (1998) and Minas-Nerpel (2022); Klotz (2013) offers a perspective from the Seleukid empire. The complaint of an Egyptian widow, dated July 256 (P.Mich.1.29), is discussed by Rowlandson (1998): 221, and the petition by the priests of Isis, dated 17 September 170, by Hölbl (2001): 169. Polybius 28.12.8 recounts the celebrations held to mark Ptolemy VI's coming of age. For the ambiguity surrounding the king's status during Antiochos IV's invasion, see Skeat (1961). Egypt's ham-fisted attempts to defend itself against a second invasion are in Polybius 29.23.4, and the dramatic events of the Day of Eleusis by a number of ancient authors, including Livy 45.12, Polybius 29.27 and Diodorus Siculus 31.2. The letter of 29 August 168 referring to 'times like these' (UPZ 59.13–16) is quoted in Hölbl (2001): 128. For Numenios' report of his trip to Rome, see Ray (1976): 20–9 and 128. Hölbl (2001): 160–73 and 257–93 discusses the Ptolemaic ruler cult. For the revolt led by Dionysios Petosarapis, see Diodorus Siculus 31.15a, and for the attempts to shore up native support, Lanciers (1987). Lewis (1986): 36 and Hölbl (2001): 182 mention the formation of the 'Special Account', while the resulting native rebellion is recounted in Diodorus Siculus 31.17b and analysed by Ray (1976): 1–6. Kruse (2013) discusses Nile patrols and river security. Tensions surrounding the royal visit to Memphis in 163 are mentioned by Thompson (2012): 201, and the unsuccessful plot by the governor of Cyprus by Polybius 33.5. The terms of Ptolemy VIII's surrender are given by Polybius 39.7 and Diodorus Siculus 31.33.

CHAPTER 8: ONE COUNTRY, TWO CULTURES

Bagnall (1988) provides a good introduction to the cultural divide in Ptolemaic Egypt, and the topic is discussed at length in Goudriaan (1988) and Lewis (1986). See also Clarysse (1995) for Greeks at Thebes. For the two different types of legal system, see Bagnall (1976): 7, Grant (1982): 46 and Yiftach (2015). Dhennin (2018) presents the results of recent excavations at Taposiris Magna. For the title 'king's cousin', see Lewis (1986): 29 and 57, and, for the career of Dryton, Lewis (1986): 88–103 and Vandorpe (2002). Discussions of the royal foundation of Ptolemais in Upper Egypt include Strabo 17.1.42, Grant (1982): 39, Thompson (2018): 12 and Madkour (2018). Banking in Ptolemaic Egypt, including the career of Nikanor, is analysed by Lewis (1986): 46–55. For aspects of the Ptolemaic economic system, see Bagnall (1976), Grant (1982), Lewis (1986) and Thompson (2012), *passim*, and for tax-farmers and tax-collectors, Clarysse and Thompson (2006): 74–5. The letter of complaint from a ship owner to the finance minister, dated December 258, is discussed in Thompson (2012): 58. The excavations at Plinthine are presented by Redon (2019). For agriculture and industry in Ptolemaic Memphis, see Thompson (2012). The death of a labourer in a vat of castor oil (UPZ 120.5–8) is cited in Thompson (2012): 11. Rostovtzeff (1922): 53 notes the presence of a large woollen factory in the city, established in the reign of Ptolemy II.

CHAPTER 9: OUT OF JOINT

The life and (troubled) times of Ptolemaios the recluse are discussed by Lewis (1986): 69–87, Ray (2001): 130–52 and Thompson (2012): 198–245. The bureaucratic journey of Ptolemaios' petition (UPZ 14) is quoted in Lewis (1986): 78–9; as John Ray (Ray (2001): 138) has remarked, 'Anyone who wonders why the Hellenistic monarchies folded up at the arrival of the Roman army may like to read UPZ 14.' For the posthumous deification of the murdered Ptolemy Memphites, see Chauveau (1991). Austin (2006): 502–6 translates the amnesty decree of 17 April 118 BC. For Ptolemy VIII's work at Berenike on the Red Sea coast, see Meredith (1957); and for his literary output, Hölbl (2001): 203 and Thompson (2009). For the voyage to India, captained by Eudoxos of Kyzikos, which took place around 117, see Hölbl (2001): 204 and Habicht (2013).

CHAPTER 10: MOTHER'S RUIN

Pausanias 1.9.1 covers Cleopatra III's scheming to secure the throne for her younger son. For Ptolemy IX's pharaonic titles, see Ritner (n.d.), and for his visit to Elephantine, de Meulenaere (1961); the inscription commemorating the visit (British Museum EA1020) is translated and analysed by Piejko (1992). Arnold (1999): 207–9 summarises Ptolemy IX's temple projects. The appointment of a priest of Sarapis to officiate in the dynastic cult is mentioned by Thompson (2012): 114–15.

Crawford (1971) remains the standard work on Menkhes the village scribe and life in Ptolemaic Kerkeosiris; see also Lewis (1986): 104–23. Diodorus Siculus 1.21.7 states that up to a third of the land was controlled by the temples; see also Crawford (1971): 93. A useful review of land ownership and management is Christensen et al. (2017). Bianchi (1988a): 18 cites the dearth of coins from Ptolemy IX's reign as a possible indication of a partial return to a barter economy. For the conflict between Ptolemy IX and Cleopatra III, and the sequence of letters written by Platon to Nakhthor, see Ritner (n.d.). The rumours about the reasons for Ptolemy X's downfall were reported by Porphyry and Strabo. The dedication of a temple of Isis at Ptolemais is mentioned by Hölbl (2001): 278, and the replacement of Pathyris by Hermonthis as the provincial capital by Vandorpe (1995). For Ptolemy IX's work at Medinet Habu, see Ritner (n.d.); for his jubilee, Thompson (2012): 116 and 143. Hölbl (2001): 213 cites the document reporting depopulation in the Herakleopolite province. For the Latin graffiti at Philae, see Devijver (1985) and Beness and Hillard (2003) plus references. The Egyptian delegation to Rome and the reciprocal embassy to Alexandria are recorded by the ancient authors Eutropius and Valerius Maximus, respectively, while Livy states that a formal diplomatic alliance was concluded at this time; see also Dio Cassius 10. For the similarities between Roman and Ptolemaic silver coinage, see Neatby (1950): 93, and for early Romans in Egypt, Crawford (1971): 136 n. 3 and Neatby (1950): 97. Meadows (2001) and Bianchi (1988a) provide further background on Egypt's relations with Rome. For Memmius' visit to the Fayum, see Hölbl (2001): 207.

CHAPTER 11: KEEPING THE FAITH

Thompson (2012) (esp. 180–7) provides a detailed overview of the cult of Apis at Memphis. For the relationship between the Ptolemaic royal family and the dynasty of high priests of Ptah, see Thompson (2012) and Gorre (2009). Wilkinson (2023) provides a useful overview of the reign of Ramesses II, and his own attempts to assert his legitimacy; for Ptolemaic awareness of Ramesside monuments and traditions, see Bianchi (1991). The papyrus describing the burial of an Apis bull is discussed in Thompson (2012): 185–7. Thompson (2012) is also the best source for the Memphite necropolis in the Ptolemaic period. For the interpretation of dreams, see Ray (2001): 140–1, and for the archive of Hor, Ray (1976). The remarkable site of Thonis-Herakleion is published in full by Goddio and Masson-Berghoff (eds) (2016). For individual aspects of the city and its festivals, see Masson-Berghoff and Goddio (2016) and Goddio and Masson-Berghoff (2016). Myśliewicz (1996) discusses the production of Dionysiac votive offerings (at Athribis in the Nile Delta). The identification of Osiris with Dionysos is from Herodotus 2.144. For aspects of traditional religion during the Ptolemaic period, see Goyon (1988) and Strudwick and Strudwick (1999): 198–203; and for Ptolemaic 'temple grammar' and the decoration of the temple of Horus at Apollonopolis, Wilson (1997) and Kurth (1998). Among the best discussions of Ptolemaic art are to be found in Smith (1981), Bianchi et al. (1988), Bianchi (1988b), Vassilika (1995) and Stanwick (2005).

CHAPTER 12: FIGHT FOR SURVIVAL

Egypt's entanglement with Rome in the aftermath of Ptolemy IX's death is referenced by a number of ancient authors, including Appian 1.102. For Ptolemy XII's nickname, see Strabo 17.1.11, and for his relations with Rome, Siani-Davies (1997). Crassus' advocacy for the annexation of Egypt is reported by Plutarch, *Crassus*, 13.2, and the civil disturbances in Egypt in the aftermath of the Third Mithridatic War by Appian 2.12.114 and Josephus, *Jewish Antiquities* 14.35. The new law relating to those who died intestate is referenced by Parsons (2009): 29, and the strike by farmers in the Herakleopolite nome by Hölbl (2001): 225. For the legal contracts from Oxyrhynchos, see Bulow-Jacobsen and Whitehorne (1982), Rea (1988) and Schubert (2019). For the *Art of Eudoxos* and other works amassed by Ptolemaios son of Glaukias, see Thompson (2012): 234–6. The *Teaching of Ankhsheshonqy* is translated by Lichtheim (1980): 159–84, and discussed by Smith (2001) and Tait (2001). The report of a Roman being torn apart by an angry mob for killing a cat is in Diodorus Siculus 1.83.1–9, and Herodotus' related observation, 400 years earlier, in Herodotus 2.66. The rise and (rapid) fall of Archelaos, husband of Berenike IV, is discussed by Siani-Davies (1997): 324–6; see also Strabo 12.3.34–35. Cicero's defence of Rabirius is documented in Cicero, *Pro Rabirio Postumo*. For the semicircle of Greek worthies at the Memphite Sarapieion, see Hölbl (2001): 283–4, and Thompson (2012): 17 and 129. The careers of Pasherenptah and Panemerit are analysed in Gorre 2009; Pasherenptah's funerary stela (BM866) is published in Walker and Higgs (2001): 184–5, cat. 192. For Ptolemy XII's temple projects, see Hussein (2016) and Arnold (1999); the Greek inscription from the Arsinoite nome guaranteeing the clergy its accustomed privileges is discussed by Bianchi (1988b): 73. For the temple of Tentyris, see Cauville (1999).

CHAPTER 13: DANGEROUS LIAISONS

The background to Cleopatra's reign is conveniently analysed by Weill Gouchaux (2001) and Meadows (2001). For the cult of Buchis, see Wilkinson (2003): 172–3. The stela commemorating the death of the Buchis in 29 BC is illustrated in Bianchi (1988b): 214, cat. 107; and the stela set up in the Fayum, showing Cleopatra as a male ruler, is Louvre E.27113, illustrated in Bianchi (1988b): 188, cat. 78. For the Tentyris zodiac and roof chapels, see Cauville (1999). Ptolemy XIII's ordinance of October 50 is referenced in Hölbl (2001): 231. The story that Cleopatra was smuggled into Caesar's presence in a bed-linen sack is from Plutarch, *Life of Caesar* 49; the same chapter also recounts the destruction of the Great Library of Alexandria by fire. For these events, see also Pollard and Reid (2006): 163–5. Caesar's despatch of coastal reconnaissance missions to search for freshwater springs is from his *Alexandrian War* 8, and the drowning of Ptolemy XIII from *Alexandrian War* 31. The famine in Egypt in 46 BC is mentioned in Crawford (1971): 106. For the status of Ptolemaic royal women, see Vassilika (1995): 120, and for the cult title of Ptolemy XV, Thompson (2012): 133. The Alaskan volcanic eruption of 43 BC and its climatic effects are discussed by McConnell et al. (2020) and Manning et al. (2017); the account of the Nile failing to flood for two years in succession is in Seneca the Younger IVA.2.16. For the stela of Taimhotep, see Bianchi (1988b): 230; Walker and Higgs (2001): 186–7, cat. 193; and Thompson (2012): 130.

CHAPTER 14: SERPENT OF OLD NILE

For the introduction of a double-dating system in Cleopatra VII's Year 16, see Bingen (2007): 57 and Walker and Higgs (2001): 175. The queen's linguistic abilities are referenced by Plutarch, *Life of Antony* 27, and her native Egyptian counsellors by Lucan 8.475–477. The statue of Pakhom, governor of Tentyris, is published in Walker and Higgs (2001): 180–2, cat. 189. Weill Goudchaux (2001): 139 identifies the weathered statues from the temple of Apollonopolis as images of Caesarion. For the black basalt statue of the same ruler, see Walker and Higgs (2001): cat. 171; for the statue of Hor son of Hor, Walker and Higgs (2001): 182–3, cat. 190; and for the funeral of Pasherenptah III, Walker and Higgs (2001): 186. Bianchi (1988b): 206 charts the fortunes of the cult of Isis, and Weill Gouchaux (2001): 132 and 134 its proscription by the Roman authorities. See also Weill Gouchaux (2001) for the erection of a statue of Isis on the acropolis of Athens. For the change of Cleopatra's dynastic cult title see Bingen (2007): 58 and 59; Gorre (2009): 620 n. 48; and for the only known instance of the new epithet, see Brashear (1980): no. 2376.

Antony's losses in the ill-fated Parthian campaign are recounted by Dio Cassius 49.27–33, and Plutarch, *Life of Antony* 50. His public renunciation of Octavia is from Plutarch, *Life of Antony* 53. For the Donations of Alexandria, see Hölbl (2001): 243–4, Weill Goudchaux (2001): 139, Meadows (2001): 28 and Williams (2001): 195. The bronze statuette of Alexander Helios as king of Armenia is illustrated and discussed in Walker and Higgs (2001): 250–1, cat. 270. For the colossal pair-statue of Cleopatra and Antony set up in Alexandria, see Ashton (2005). The royal ordinance bearing what has been claimed as Cleopatra's own handwriting is published in Walker and Higgs (2001): 180, cat. 188. Antony's ejection of Octavia from the marital home is from Plutarch, *Life of Antony* 57. For Antony and Cleopatra setting up statues of themselves on the acropolis, see Dio Cassius 50.15. The Battle of Actium and its aftermath are discussed by many authors, ancient and modern; for a convenient summary see Meadows (2001): 29–30. The stela from Koptos, dated less than three weeks after Actium, is illustrated and discussed in Walker and Higgs (2001): 174–5, cat. 173. For the death of Imhotep-Padibastet V, see Thompson (2012): 143 (his body would lie in a storeroom, unburied, for the next seven years). Ancient accounts of Cleopatra's death include Dio Cassius 51.10–11 and Plutarch, *Life of Antony* 85–6; for modern interpretations, see Weill Goudchaux (2001). For the rescue of Cleopatra's statues in the immediate aftermath of her demise, see Weill Goudchaux (1992); and for the dedication of a new statue 400 years after her death, Griffith (1937), Quaegebeur (1988): 41, and Weill Goudchaux (2001): 141.

EPILOGUE: TO THE VICTOR THE SPOILS

For Roman rule in Egypt, see Bowman (1986), Bagnall (2021) and Manning (2003): 241. The depopulation of rural villages is mentioned by Rostovtzeff (1922): 12–13, and the fate of Memphis by Thompson (2012): 247–57. Religious changes, including the abolition of the high priesthood of Memphis, are covered by Gorre (2009). The coins of Octavian bearing the legend AEGYPTO CAPTA are illustrated in Walker and Higgs (2001): 259, cats 295–6. Draycott (2022) provides a full biographical study of Cleopatra Selene.

Bibliography

ANCIENT WORKS

Appian, *Roman History*
  Volume III: *The Civil Wars, Books 1–3.26*. Trans. Horace White. Loeb Classical Library 4. Cambridge, MA: Harvard University Press, 1913
  Volume VI: *The Civil Wars, Book 5. Fragments*. Trans. and ed. Brian McGing. Loeb Classical Library 544. Cambridge, MA: Harvard University Press, 2020
Arrian, *The Anabasis of Alexander; or, The history of the wars and conquests of Alexander the Great*. Trans. E. J. Chinnock. London: Hodder and Stoughton, 1884
Athenaeus, *The Learned Banqueters. Volume I: Books 1–3.106e*. Trans. and ed. S. Douglas Olson. Loeb Classical Library 204. Cambridge, MA: Harvard University Press, 2007
Caesar, *Alexandrian War. African War. Spanish War*. Trans. A. G. Way. Loeb Classical Library 402. Cambridge, MA: Harvard University Press, 1955
Canopus Decree: E. A. W. Budge, *The Decree of Canopus*. Oxford: Oxford University Press, 1904
Cicero, *Pro Milone. In Pisonem. Pro Scauro. Pro Fonteio. Pro Rabirio Postumo. Pro Marcello. Pro Ligario. Pro Rege Deiotaro*. Trans. N. H. Watts. Loeb Classical Library 252. Cambridge, MA: Harvard University Press, 1931
Dio Cassius, *Roman History*
  Volume I: *Books 1–11*. Trans. Earnest Cary and Herbert B. Foster. Loeb Classical Library 32. Cambridge, MA: Harvard University Press, 1914

Volume V: Books 46–50. Trans. Earnest Cary and Herbert B. Foster. Loeb Classical Library 82. Cambridge, MA: Harvard University Press, 1917

Volume VI: Books 51–55. Trans. Earnest Cary and Herbert B. Foster. Loeb Classical Library 83. Cambridge, MA: Harvard University Press, 1917

Diodorus Siculus, *Library of History*

Volume I: Books 1–2.34. Trans. C. H. Oldfather. Loeb Classical Library 279. Cambridge, MA: Harvard University Press, 1933

Volume II: Books 2.35–4.58. Trans. C. H. Oldfather. Loeb Classical Library 303. Cambridge, MA: Harvard University Press, 1935

Volume VIII: Books 16.66–17. Trans. C. Bradford Welles. Loeb Classical Library 422. Cambridge, MA: Harvard University Press, 1963

Volume XI: Fragments of Books 21–32. Trans. Francis R. Walton. Loeb Classical Library 409. Cambridge, MA: Harvard University Press, 1957

First Philae Decree: www.attalus.org/docs/other/inscr_261.html, accessed 31 December 2023

Herodotus, *The Persian Wars*

Volume I: Books 1–2. Trans. A. D. Godley. Loeb Classical Library 117. Cambridge, MA: Harvard University Press, 1920

Volume II: Books 3–4. Trans. A. D. Godley. Loeb Classical Library 118. Cambridge, MA: Harvard University Press, 1921

Josephus, *Jewish Antiquities. Volume VI: Books 14–15*. Trans. Ralph Marcus and Allen Wikgren. Loeb Classical Library 489. Cambridge, MA: Harvard University Press, 1943

—— *The Life. Against Apion*. Trans. H. St J. Thackeray. Loeb Classical Library 186. Cambridge, MA: Harvard University Press, 1926

Justinus, *Epitome of Pompeius Trogus' Philippic Histories*. Trans. Revd. J. S. Watson. https://www.attalus.org/translate/justin6.html, accessed 23 December 2023

Livy, *History of Rome. Volume XIII: Books 43–45*. Trans. Alfred Schlesinger. Loeb Classical Library 396. Cambridge, MA: Harvard University Press, 1951

Lucan, *The Civil War (Pharsalia)*. Trans. J. D. Duff. Loeb Classical Library 220. Cambridge, MA: Harvard University Press, 1928

Pausanias, *Description of Greece. Volume I: Books 1–2 (Attica and Corinth)*. Trans. W. H. S. Jones. Loeb Classical Library 93. Cambridge, MA: Harvard University Press, 1918

Pindar, *Olympian Odes, Pythian Odes*. Trans. and ed. William H. Race. Loeb Classical Library 56. Cambridge, MA: Harvard University Press, 1997

Plutarch, *Lives*

 Volume III: Pericles and Fabius Maximus. Nicias and Crassus. Trans. Bernadotte Perrin. Loeb Classical Library 65. Cambridge, MA: Harvard University Press, 1916

 Volume VII: Demosthenes and Cicero. Alexander and Caesar. Trans. Bernadotte Perrin. Loeb Classical Library 99. Cambridge, MA: Harvard University Press, 1919

 Volume IX: Demetrius and Antony, Pyrrhus and Gaius Marius. Trans. Bernadotte Perrin. Loeb Classical Library 101. Cambridge, MA: Harvard University Press, 1920

Polybius, *The Histories*

 Volume III: Books 5–8. Trans. W. R. Paton. Loeb Classical Library 138. Cambridge, MA: Harvard University Press, 1923

 Volume IV: Books 9–15. Trans. W. R. Paton. Loeb Classical Library 159. Cambridge, MA: Harvard University Press, 1925

 Volume V: Books 16–27. Trans. W. R. Paton. Loeb Classical Library 160. Cambridge, MA: Harvard University Press, 1926

 Volume VI: Books 28–39, Fragments. Trans. W. R. Paton. Loeb Classical Library 161. Cambridge, MA: Harvard University Press, 1927

Quintus Curtius, *History of Alexander. Volume I: Books 1–5*. Trans. J. C. Rolfe. Loeb Classical Library 368. Cambridge, MA: Harvard University Press, 1946

Second Philae Decree: www.attalus.org/docs/other/inscr_260.html, accessed 31 December 2023

Seneca the Younger, *Natural Questions, Volume II: Books 4–7*. Trans. Thomas H. Corcoran. Loeb Classical Library 457. Cambridge, MA: Harvard University Press, 1972

Strabo, *Geography*

 Volume I: Books 1–2. Trans. Horace Leonard Jones. Loeb Classical Library 49. Cambridge, MA: Harvard University Press, 1917

 Volume V: Books 10–12. Trans. Horace Leonard Jones. Loeb Classical Library 211. Cambridge, MA: Harvard University Press, 1928

 Volume VII: Books 15–16. Trans. Horace Leonard Jones. Loeb Classical Library 241. Cambridge, MA: Harvard University Press, 1930

 Volume VIII: Book 17. General Index. Trans. Horace Leonard Jones. Loeb Classical Library 267. Cambridge, MA: Harvard University Press, 1932

Suetonius, *Lives of the Caesars. Volume I: Julius, Augustus, Tiberius, Gaius, Caligula*. Trans. J. C. Rolfe. Introduction by K. R. Bradley. Loeb Classical Library 31. Cambridge, MA: Harvard University Press, 1914

MODERN WORKS

Abd el-Raziq, Mahmud (1984), *Die Darstellungen und Texte des Sanktuars Alexanders des Großen im Tempel von Luxor*. Mainz: von Zabern

Adams, W. Lindsay (1997), 'The successors of Alexander', in Lawrence A. Tritle (ed.), *The Greek World in the Fourth Century: From the Fall of the Athenian Empire to the Successors of Alexander* (London and New York: Routledge), 228–48

Arnold, Dieter (1999), *Temples of the Last Pharaohs*. New York and Oxford: Oxford University Press

Ashton, Sally-Ann (2005), 'In search of Cleopatra's temple', *Egyptian Archaeology* 27, 30–2

Austin, Michel (2006), *The Hellenistic World from Alexander to the Roman Conquest: A Selection of Ancient Sources in Translation*, 2nd edn. Cambridge: Cambridge University Press

Bagnall, Roger S. (1976), *The Administration of the Ptolemaic Possessions Outside Egypt*. Leiden: Brill

—— (1988), 'Greeks and Egyptians: Ethnicity, Status, and Culture', in Robert S. Bianchi et al., *Cleopatra's Egypt: Age of the Ptolemies*. New York: The Brooklyn Museum, 21–5

—— (2021), *Roman Egypt: A History*. Cambridge: Cambridge University Press

Beness, J. Lea and Tom Hillard (2003), 'The First Romans at Philae (*CIL* 1^2.2.2937a)', *Zeitschrift für Papyrologie und Epigraphik* 144, 203–7

Bennett, Christopher J. (1997), 'Cleopatra V Tryphaena and the Genealogy of the Later Ptolemies', *Ancient Society* 28, 39–66

Bernand, A. (1992), *La prose sur pierre dans l'Egypte hellénistique et romaine*, 2 vols. Paris: Editions du Centre National de la Recherche Scientifique

Bianchi, Robert S. (1988a), 'Ptolemaic Egypt and Rome: An Overview', in Robert S. Bianchi et al., *Cleopatra's Egypt: Age of the Ptolemies*. New York: The Brooklyn Museum, 13–20

—— (1988b), 'The Pharaonic Art of Ptolemaic Egypt', in Robert S. Bianchi et al., *Cleopatra's Egypt: Age of the Ptolemies*. New York: The Brooklyn Museum, 55–80

—— (1991), 'Graeco-Roman uses and abuses of Ramesside traditions', in Edward Bleiberg and Rita Freed (eds), *Fragments of a Shattered Visage: The Proceedings of the International Symposium on Ramesses the Great*. Memphis, TN: Memphis State University, 1–8

Bianchi, Robert S. et al. (1988), *Cleopatra's Egypt: Age of the Ptolemies*. New York: The Brooklyn Museum

Bingen, Jean (2007), *Hellenistic Egypt: Monarchy, Society, Economy, Culture*. Edinburgh: Edinburgh University Press

Borza, Eugene N. (1990), *In the Shadow of Olympus: The Emergence of Macedon*. Princeton, NJ: Princeton University Press

Bosch-Puche, Francisco (2014), 'Alexander the Great's Egyptian Names in the Barque Shrine at Luxor Temple', in Volker Grieb, Krzysztof Nawotka and Agnieszka Wojciechowska (eds), *Alexander the Great and Egypt: History, Art, Tradition: Wrocław/Breslau 18./19. Nov. 2011*. Wiesbaden: Harrassowitz, 55–87

Bowman, Alan K. (1986), *Egypt After the Pharaohs: 332 BC–AD 642: From Alexander to the Arab Conquest*. Berkeley and Los Angeles: University of California Press

Brashear, William M. (1980), *Ptolemaïsche Urkunden aus Mumienkartonnage: Ägyptische Urkunden aus den Staatlichen Museen Berlin*. Berlin: Staatliche Museen Preussischer Kulturbesitz

Bulow-Jacobsen, A. and John Whitehorne (eds) (1982), *The Oxyrhynchus Papyri*, vol. XLIX. London: Egypt Exploration Society

Buraselis, Kostas (2013), 'Ptolemaic grain, seaways and power', in Kostas Buraselis, Mary Stefanou and Dorothy J. Thompson (eds), *The Ptolemies, the Sea and the Nile: Studies in Waterborne Power*. Cambridge: Cambridge University Press, 97–107

Buraselis, Kostas, Mary Stefanou and Dorothy J. Thompson (eds) (2013), *The Ptolemies, the Sea and the Nile: Studies in Waterborne Power*. Cambridge: Cambridge University Press

Burstein, Stanley M. (2008), 'Elephants for Ptolemy II: Ptolemaic policy in Nubia in the third century BC', in Paul McKechnie and Philippe Guillaume (eds), *Ptolemy II Philadelphus and his World*. Leiden and Boston: Brill, 135–47

—— (2021), 'The African encounter with Greece: the case of Kush', *Acta Classica* 64, 48–71

Cartledge, Paul (2004), *Alexander the Great: The Hunt for a New Past*. London: Macmillan

Castiglioni, Alfredo and Angelo (1999), 'Berenike Panchrysos', in Kathryn A. Bard (ed.), *Encyclopedia of the Archaeology of Ancient Egypt*. London and New York: Routledge, 172–5

Castiglioni, Alfredo and Angelo, and Jean Vercoutter (1998), *L'Eldorado dei Faraoni: alla scoperta di Berenice Pancrisia*. Novara: Istituto Geografico De Agostini

Castiglioni, Angelo and Alfredo (1994), 'Discovering Berenice Panchrysos', *Egyptian Archaeology* 4, 19–22

—— (2004), 'Gold in the Eastern Desert', in Derek A. Welsby and Julie R. Anderson (eds), *Sudan: Ancient Treasures*. London: British Museum Press, 122–6

Cauville, Sylvie (1999), 'Dendera', in Kathryn A. Bard (ed.), *Encyclopedia of the Archaeology of Ancient Egypt*. London: Routledge, 252–4

Chauveau, Michel (1991), 'Un été 145', *Bulletin de l'Institut Français d'Archéologie Orientale* 90, 135–68

—— (1999), 'Alexandrie et Rhakôtis: le point de vue des Égyptiens', in *Alexandrie: une mégapole cosmopolite: Actes du 9ème colloque de la Villa Kérylos à Beaulieu-sur-Mer les 2 & 3 octobre 1998*. Paris: Académie des Inscriptions et Belles Lettres, 1–10

Chauveau, Michel, trans. David Lorton (2000) *Egypt in the Age of Cleopatra*. Ithaca NY and London: Cornell University Press

Christensen, Thorolf, Dorothy J. Thompson and Katelijn Vandorpe (2017), *Land and Taxes in Ptolemaic Egypt*. Cambridge: Cambridge University Press

Clarysse, Willy (1978), 'Notes de prosopographie thébaine, 7. Hurgonaphor et Chaonnophris, les derniers pharaons indigènes', *Chronique d'Égypte* 53, 243–53

—— (1995), 'Greeks in Ptolemaic Thebes', in S. P. Vleeming (ed.), *Hundred-gated Thebes*. Leiden, New York and Köln: Brill, 1–19

Clarysse, Willy and Dorothy J. Thompson (2006), *Counting the People in Hellenistic Egypt*. Vol. 2: *Historical Studies*. Cambridge: Cambridge University Press

Crawford, Dorothy J. (1971), *Kerkeosiris: An Egyptian Village in the Ptolemaic Period*. Cambridge: Cambridge University Press

Criscuolo, Lucia (2013), 'Ptolemies and piracy', in Kostas Buraselis, Mary Stefanou and Dorothy J. Thompson (eds), *The Ptolemies, the Sea and the Nile: Studies in Waterborne Power*. Cambridge: Cambridge University Press, 160–71

De Meulenaere, H. (1961), 'Ptolémée IX Sôter II à Kalabcha', *Chronique d'Égypte* 36, 98–105

Depauw, Mark (2000), 'Alexandria, the Building Yard', *Chronique d'Égypte* 75, 64–5

Devijver, Hubert (1985), 'La plus ancienne mention d'une tribu romaine en Egypte', *Chronique d'Égypte* 60, 96–101

Dhennin, Sylvain (2008), 'An Egyptian animal necropolis in a Greek town', *Egyptian Archaeology* 33, 12–14

Draycott, Jane (2022), *Cleopatra's Daughter: Egyptian Princess, Roman Prisoner, African Queen*. London: Apollo

El-Masry, Yahia, Hartwig Altenmüller and Heinz-Josef Thissen (2012), *Das Synodaldekret von Alexandria aus dem Jahre 243 v. Chr.* Hamburg: Helmut Buske Verlag. Studien zur Altägyptischen Kultur Beihefte, Band 11

Erskine, Andrew (2013), 'Polybius and Ptolemaic sea power', in Kostas Buraselis, Mary Stefanou and Dorothy J. Thompson (eds), *The Ptolemies, the Sea and the Nile: Studies in Waterborne Power*. Cambridge: Cambridge University Press, 82–96

Fischer-Bovet, Christelle (2014), *Army and Society in Ptolemaic Egypt*. Cambridge: Cambridge University Press

Gabrielsen, Vincent (2013), 'Rhodes and the Ptolemaic kingdom: the commercial infrastructure', in Kostas Buraselis, Mary Stefanou and Dorothy J. Thompson (eds), *The Ptolemies, the Sea and the Nile: Studies in Waterborne Power*. Cambridge: Cambridge University Press, 66–81

Goddio, Franck and Aurélia Masson-Berghoff (eds) (2016), *Sunken Cities: Egypt's Lost Worlds*. London: Thames and Hudson/The British Museum

—— (2016), 'From myth to festivals', in Franck Goddio and Aurélia Masson-Berghoff (eds), *Sunken Cities: Egypt's Lost Worlds*. London: Thames and Hudson/The British Museum, 139–219

Gorre, Gilles (2009), *Les relations du clergé égyptien et des Lagides d'après les sources privées*. Studia Hellenistica 45. Leuven: Peeters

Goudriaan, Koen (1988), *Ethnicity in Ptolemaic Egypt*. Amsterdam: Gieben

Goyon, Jean-Claude (1988), 'Ptolemaic Egypt: Priests and the Traditional Religion', in Robert S. Bianchi et al., *Cleopatra's Egypt: Age of the Ptolemies*. New York: The Brooklyn Museum, 29–39

Grant, Michael (1982), *From Alexander to Cleopatra: The Hellenistic World*. London: Weidenfeld & Nicolson

Grieb, Volker, Krzysztof Nawotka and Agnieszka Wojciechowska (eds) (2014), *Alexander the Great and Egypt: History, Art, Tradition: Wrocław/Breslau 18./19. Nov. 2011*. Wiesbaden: Harrassowitz

Griffith, Francis Llewellyn (1937), *Catalogue of the Demotic Graffiti of the Dodecaschoenus*, vol. II. Oxford: Oxford University Press

Guillaume, Philippe (2008), ''Philadelphus' Alexandria as cradle of biblical historiography', in Paul McKechnie and Philippe Guillaume (eds), *Ptolemy II Philadelphus and his World*. Leiden and Boston: Brill, 247–55

Habicht, Christian (2013), 'Eudoxus of Cyzicus and Ptolemaic exploration of the sea route to India', in Kostas Buraselis, Mary Stefanou and Dorothy J. Thompson (eds), *The Ptolemies, the Sea and the Nile: Studies in Waterborne Power*. Cambridge: Cambridge University Press, 197–206

Heskel, Julia (1997), 'Macedonia and the North, 400–336', in Lawrence A. Tritle (ed.), *The Greek World in the Fourth Century: From the Fall of the Athenian Empire to the Successors of Alexander*. London and New York: Routledge, 167–88

Hölbl, Günther, trans. Tina Saavedra (2001), *A History of the Ptolemaic Empire*. London and New York: Routledge

Huß, W. (1991), 'Die in ptolemaiischer Zeit verfaßten Synodal-Dekrete der ägyptischen Priester', *Zeitschrift für Papyrologie und Epigraphik* 88, 189–208

Hussein, Hesham (2016), 'Searching for Ptolemy XII: inscriptions from Sinai', *Egyptian Archaeology* 48, 28–9

Khalil, Emad (2008), 'The Lake Mareotis Research Project', *Egyptian Archaeology* 33, 9–11

Klotz, David (2013), 'Who was with Antiochus III at Raphia? Revisiting the hieroglyphic versions of the Raphia decree (CG 31008 and 50048)', *Chronique d'Egypte* 88, 45–59

Kruse, Thomas (2013), 'The Nile police in the Ptolemaic period', in Kostas Buraselis, Mary Stefanou and Dorothy J. Thompson (eds), *The Ptolemies, the Sea and the Nile: Studies in Waterborne Power*. Cambridge: Cambridge University Press, 172–84

Kurth, Dietrich (1998), 'A World Order in Stone – The Late Temples', in Regine Schulz and Matthias Seidel (eds), *Egypt: The World of the Pharaohs*. Köln: Könemann, 296–311

Ladynin, Ivan A. (2014), 'The Argeadai Building Program in Egypt in the Framework of Dynasties' XXIX–XXX Temple Building', in Volker Grieb, Krzysztof Nawotka and Agnieszka Wojciechowska (eds) (2014), *Alexander the Great and Egypt: History, Art, Tradition: Wrocław/Breslau 18./19. Nov. 2011*. Wiesbaden: Harrassowitz, 221–40

Lanciers, C. (1987), 'Die Stele CG 22184: Ein Priesterdekret aus der Regierungszeit des Ptolemaios VI. Philometor', *Gottinger Miszellen* 95, 53–61

Legras, Bernard (2002), 'Les experts égyptiens à la cour des Ptolémées', *Revue historique* 624, 963–91

Lewis, Naphtali (1986), *Greeks in Ptolemaic Egypt: Case Studies in the Social History of the Hellenistic World*. Oxford: Oxford University Press

Lichtheim, Miriam (1980), *Ancient Egyptian Literature*, vol. III: *The Late Period*. Berkeley, Los Angeles and London: University of California Press

Lloyd, Alan B. (2002), 'The Egyptian elite in the early Ptolemaic period. Some hieroglyphic evidence', in Daniel Ogden (ed.), *The Hellenistic World: New Perspectives*. London: Duckworth/The Classical Press of Wales, 117–36

Madkour, Haitham (2018), 'New light on the chronology of Ptolemais Hermiou through Hellenistic stamped amphora handles', *Zeitschrift für Papyrologie und Epigraphik* 207, 73–88

Manning, J. G. (2003), *Land and Power in Ptolemaic Egypt. The Structure of Land Tenure*. Cambridge: Cambridge University Press

—— (2010), *The Last Pharaohs: Egypt Under the Ptolemies 305–30 BC*. Princeton and Oxford: Princeton University Press

Manning, Joseph G., Francis Ludlow, Alexander R. Stine, William R. Boos, Michael Sigl and Jennifer R. Marlon (2017), 'Volcanic suppression of Nile summer flooding triggers revolt and constrains interstate conflict in ancient Egypt', *Nature Communications* 8, article number 900

Marquaille, Céline (2003), 'The Ptolemaic ruler as a religious figure in Cyrenaica', *Libyan Studies* 34, 25–42

—— (2008), 'The foreign policy of Ptolemy II', in Paul McKechnie and Philippe Guillaume (eds), *Ptolemy II Philadelphus and his World*. Leiden and Boston: Brill, 39–64

Masson-Berghoff, Aurélia and Franck Goddio (2016), 'Greek kings and Egyptian gods', in Franck Goddio and Aurélia Masson-Berghoff (eds), *Sunken Cities: Egypt's Lost Worlds*. London: Thames and Hudson/The British Museum, 73–137

McConnell, Joseph R., Michael Sigl, Gill Plunkett et al. (2020), 'Extreme climate after massive eruption of Alaska's Okmok volcano in 43 BCE and effects on the late Roman Republic and Ptolemaic Kingdom', *Proceedings of the National Academy of Science* 117 (27) (June 22, 2020), 15,443–9

McKechnie, Paul and Jennifer A. Cromwell (eds) (2018), *Ptolemy I and the Transformation of Egypt, 404–282 BCE*. Leiden and Boston: Brill

McKechnie, Paul and Philippe Guillaume (eds) (2008), *Ptolemy II Philadelphus and his World*. Leiden and Boston: Brill

Meadows, Andrew (2001), 'Sins of the fathers: the inheritance of Cleopatra, last queen of Egypt', in Susan Walker and Peter Higgs (eds), *Cleopatra of Egypt: From History to Myth*. London: British Museum Press, 14–31

Meredith, David (1953), 'The Roman remains in the Eastern Desert of Egypt', *Journal of Egyptian Archaeology* 39, 95–106

—— (1957), 'Berenice Troglodytica', *Journal of Egyptian Archaeology* 43, 56–70

Michaelides, Demetrios and Giorgios Papantoniou (2018), 'The advent of Hellenistic Cyprus', in Anna Cannavó and Ludovic Thély (eds), *Les royaumes de Chypre à l'épreuve de l'histoire*. Athens: École Française d'Athènes, 267–90

Minas-Nerpel, Martina (2018), 'Pharaoh and Temple Building in the Fourth Century BCE', in Paul McKechnie and Jennifer A. Cromwell (eds), *Ptolemy I and the Transformation of Egypt, 404–282 BCE*. Leiden and Boston: Brill, 120–65

—— (2022), 'The Creation of New "Cultural Codes": The Ptolemaic Queens and Their Syncretic Processes with Isis, Hathor, and Aphrodite', in Jeffrey Spier and Sara E. Cole (eds), *Egypt and the Classical World: Cross-Cultural Encounters in Antiquity*. Los Angeles: J. Paul Getty Museum, chapter 4. https://www.getty.edu/publications/egypt-classical-world/04 Accessed 31 December 2023

Moran, William L. (1992), *The Amarna Letters*. Baltimore, MD: The Johns Hopkins University Press

Moyer, Ian S. (2011), *Egypt and the Limits of Hellenism*. Cambridge: Cambridge University Press

Mueller, Katja (2006), *Settlements of the Ptolemies: City Foundations and New Settlement in the Hellenistic World*. Leuven: Peeters

Myśliwiec, Karol (1996), 'In the Ptolemaic workshops of Athribis', *Egyptian Archaeology* 9, 34–6

Neatby, Leslie H. (1950), 'Romano-Egyptian Relations During the Third Century B.C.', *Transactions and Proceedings of the American Philological Association* 81, 89–98

Nespoulous-Phalippou, Alexandra (ed.) (2015), *Ptolémée Épiphane, Aristonikos et les prêtres d'Égypte: Le Décret de Memphis (182 a.C.): Édition commentée des stèles Caire RT 2/3/25/7 et JE 44901*. Montpellier: Université Paul Valéry

Ockinga, Boyo G. (2018), 'The Satrap Stele of Ptolemy: A Reassessment', in Paul McKechnie and Jennifer A. Cromwell (eds), *Ptolemy I and the Transformation of Egypt, 404–282 BCE*. Leiden and Boston: Brill, 166–98

Parsons, Peter (2009), 'New Greek Texts from Oxyrhynchus', *British Academy Review* 14, 28–31

Pestman, P. W. (1995), 'Haronnophris and Chaonnophris: Two Indigenous Pharaohs in Ptolemaic Egypt (205–186 BC)', in S. P. Vleeming (ed.), *Hundred-gated Thebes*. Leiden, New York and Köln: Brill, 101–37

Piejko, Francis (1992), 'The Relations of Ptolemies VIII and IX with the Temple of Chnum at Elephantine', *The Bulletin of the American Society of Papyrologists* 29.1/2, 5–24

Pollard, Justin and Howard Reid (2007), *The Rise and Fall of Alexandria, Birthplace of the Modern World*. London: Penguin

Quaegebeur, Jan (1988), 'Cleopatra VII and the Cults of the Ptolemaic Queens', in Robert S. Bianchi et al., *Cleopatra's Egypt: Age of the Ptolemies*. New York: The Brooklyn Museum, 41–53

Ray, John (1976), *The Archive of Hor*. London: Egypt Exploration Society
—— (2001), *Reflections of Osiris: Lives from Ancient Egypt*. London: Profile Books
—— (2007), *The Rosetta Stone and the rebirth of Ancient Egypt*. London: Profile Books
Rea, J. R. (1988), *The Oxyrhynchus Papyri*, vol. LV. London: Egypt Exploration Society
Recklinghausen, Daniel von (2018), *Die Philensis-Dekrete: Untersuchungen über zwei Synodaldekrete aus der Zeit Ptolemaios' V. und ihre geschichtliche und religiöse Bedeutung*. Wiesbaden: Harrassowitz
Redford, Donald B. (1986), 'The Name Manetho', in Leonard H. Lesko (ed.), *Egyptological Studies in Honor of Richard A. Parker*. Hanover, NH: University Press of New England, 118–21
Redon, Bérangère (2018), 'La prise en main du desert Oriental par les Lagides: nouvelles données archéologiques', in Jean-Pierre Brun, Thomas Faucher, Bérangère Redon and Steven Sidebotham (eds), *Le désert oriental d'Égypte durant la période gréco-romaine: bilans archéologiques*. Paris: Collège de France
—— (2019), 'An Egyptian grand cru: wine production at Plinthine', *Egyptian Archaeology* 55, 28–33
Redon, Bérangère and Thomas Faucher (2015), 'Gold mining in Early Ptolemaic Egypt', *Egyptian Archaeology* 46, 17–19
—— (2016), 'Samut North: "heavy mineral processing plants" are mills', *Egyptian Archaeology* 48, 20–2
Reymond, E. A. E. (1981), *From the Records of a Priestly Family from Memphis*. Wiesbaden: Harrassowitz
Rice, Ellen E. (1983), *The Grand Procession of Ptolemy Philadelphus*. Oxford: Oxford University Press
Ritner, Robert K. (n.d.), *Ptolemy IX (Soter II) at Thebes*. Chicago: Oriental Institute. https://isac.uchicago.edu/sites/default/files/uploads/shared/docs/ptolemy_soter_II_at_thebes.pdf, accessed 1 August 2023
Römer, Cornelia E. (2019), *The Fayoum Survey Project: The Themistou Meris*. Vol. A: *The Archaeological and Papyrological Survey*. Leuven, Paris and Bristol, CT: Peeters
Rostovtzeff, Michael (1922), *A Large Estate in Egypt in the Third Century B.C.: A Study in Economic History*. Madison, WI: University of Wisconsin
Rowlandson, Jane (ed.) (1998), *Women and Society in Greek and Roman Egypt*. Cambridge: Cambridge University Press
Schmidt, Stefan (2005), 'Serapis – ein neuer Gott für die Griechen in Ägypten', in Herbert Beck, Peter C. Bol and Maraike Bückling (eds),

Ägypten Griechenland Rom: Abwehr und Berührung: Tübingen: Ernst Wasmuth, 291–304

Schubert, Paul (2019), 'Transmission of Cleruchic Land: A Model to Describe the Procedure', *Archiv für Papyrusforschung und Verwandte Gebiete* 65, 280–316

Seeger, John and Steven Sidebotham (2005), 'Marsa Nakari: an ancient port on the Red Sea', *Egyptian Archaeology* 26, 18–20

Sekunda, Nicholas (2014), 'The Importance of the Oracle of Didya, Memphis 331 BC', in Volker Grieb, Krzysztof Nawotka and Agnieszka Wojciechowska (eds), *Alexander the Great and Egypt: History, Art, Tradition: Wrocław/Breslau 18./19. Nov. 2011*. Wiesbaden: Harrassowitz, 107–17

Siani-Davies, Mary (1997), 'Ptolemy XII Auletes and the Romans', *Historia* 46.3, 306–40

Sidebotham, Steven (1999), 'Berenike', in Kathryn A. Bard (ed.), *Encyclopedia of the Archaeology of Ancient Egypt*. London and New York: Routledge, 170–2

Sidebotham, Steven and Willemina Wendrich (1996) 'Berenike: Roman Egypt's maritime gateway to Arabia and India', *Egyptian Archaeology* 8, 15–18

Simpson, William Kelly (ed.) (2003), *The Literature of Ancient Egypt*. New Haven: Yale University Press

Skeat, T. C. (1961), 'Notes on Ptolemaic chronology, II. "The twelfth year which is also the first": the invasion of Egypt by Antiochus Epiphanes', *Journal of Egyptian Archaeology* 47, 107–12

Smith, Mark (2001), 'Ankhsheshonqy', in Donald B. Redford (ed.), *The Oxford Encyclopedia of Ancient Egypt*, vol. 1 (New York: Oxford University Press), 94

Smith, W. Stevenson, rev. William Kelly Simpson (1981), *The Art and Architecture of Ancient Egypt*. New Haven, CT: Yale University Press

Stanwick, Paul E. (2005), 'Ägyptische Statuen der Ptolemaër', in Herbert Beck, Peter C. Bol and Maraike Bückling (eds), *Ägypten Griechenland Rom: Abwehr und Berührung*. Tübingen: Ernst Wasmuth, 244–51

Stefanou, Mary (2013), 'Waterborne recruits: the military settlers of Ptolemaic Egypt', in Kostas Buraselis, Mary Stefanou and Dorothy J. Thompson (eds), *The Ptolemies, the Sea and the Nile: Studies in Waterborne Power*. Cambridge: Cambridge University Press, 108–31

Strootman, Rolf (2021), 'The Seleukid Empire', in Rachel Mairs (ed.), *The Graeco-Bactrian and Indo-Greek World*. London and New York: Routledge. DOI: 10.4324/9781315108513-3

Strudwick, Nigel and Helen (1999), *Thebes in Egypt: A Guide to the Tombs and Temples of Ancient Luxor*. Ithaca, NY: Cornell University Press

Tait, John (2001), 'Demotic literature', in Donald B. Redford (ed.), *The Oxford Encyclopedia of Ancient Egypt*, vol. 1. New York: Oxford University Press, 378–81

Taylor, John H. (1991), *Egypt and Nubia*. London: British Museum Press

Thompson, Dorothy J. (1997), 'The infrastructure of splendour: census and taxes in Ptolemaic Egypt', in Paul Cartledge, Peter Garnsey and Erich Gruen (eds), *Hellenistic Constructs: Essays in Culture, History, and Historiography*. Berkeley, Los Angeles and London: University of California Press, 242–58

——— (2008), 'Economic reforms in the mid-reign of Ptolemy Philadelphus', in Paul McKechnie and Philippe Guillaume (eds), *Ptolemy II Philadelphus and his World*. Leiden and Boston: Brill, 27–38

——— (2009), 'Review of P. Nadig, "Zwischen König und Karikatur. Das Bild Ptolemaios' VIII. im Spannungsfeld der Überlieferung"', *The Classical Review*, 59.1, 203–5

——— (2012), *Memphis Under the Ptolemies*, 2nd edn. Princeton, NJ: Princeton University Press

——— (2013), 'Hellenistic royal barges', in Kostas Buraselis, Mary Stefanou and Dorothy J. Thompson (eds), *The Ptolemies, the Sea and the Nile: Studies in Waterborne Power*. Cambridge: Cambridge University Press, 185–96

——— (2018), 'Ptolemy I in Egypt: Continuity and Change', in Paul McKechnie and Jennifer A. Cromwell (eds), *Ptolemy I and the Transformation of Egypt, 404–282 BCE*. Leiden and Boston: Brill, 6–26

——— (2022), 'Alexander and Alexandria in Life and Legend', in Richard Stoneman (ed.), *A History of Alexander the Great in World Culture*. Cambridge: Cambridge University Press, 14–41

Török, László (1980), 'To the History of the Dodekaschoenos', *Zeitschrift für Ägyptische Sprache und Altertumskunde* 107, 76–86

Turner, E. G. (1974), 'A Commander-in-Chief's Order from Saqqâra', *Journal of Egyptian Archaeology* 60, 239–42

Vandorpe, Katelijn (1995), 'City of Many a Gate, Harbour for Many a Rebel. Historical and Topographical Outline of Greco-Roman Thebes', in S. P. Vleeming (ed.), *Hundred-gated Thebes*. Leiden, New York and Köln: Brill, 203–39

——— (2002), *The Bilingual Family Archive of Dryton, His Wife Apollonia and Their Daughter Senmouthis*. Brussels: Comité Klassieke Studies, Subcomité Hellenisme, Koninklijke Vlaamse Academie van België voor Wetenschappen en Kunsten

Vassilika, Eleni (1995), *Egyptian Art*. Cambridge: Cambridge University Press

Veïsse, Anne-Emmanuelle (2004), *Les révoltes égyptiennes: recherches sur les troubles intérieurs en Egypte du règne de Ptolémée III à la conquête romaine*. Leuven: Peeters

——(2022), 'The 'Great Theban Revolt', 206–186 BCE', in Paul J. Kosmin and Ian S. Moyer (eds), *Cultures of Resistance in the Hellenistic East*. Oxford: Oxford University Press, 57–73

Verhoeven, Ursula (2005), 'Die interkulturelle Rolle von Priestern im ptolemaïschen Ägypten', in Herbert Beck, Peter C. Bol and Maraike Bückling (eds), *Ägypten Griechenland Rom: Abwehr und Berührung*. Tübingen: Ernst Wasmuth, 279–84

Walker, Susan and Peter Higgs (eds) (2001), *Cleopatra of Egypt: From History to Myth*. London: British Museum Press

Weill Goudchaux, Guy (1992), 'Archibios. Sauveur des «éffigies» de Kléopâtre VII', in *Sesto Congresso Internazionale di Egittologia: Atti*, vol. I. Turin: International Association of Egyptologists, 651–6

——(2001), 'Cleopatra's subtle religious strategy', in Susan Walker and Peter Higgs (eds), *Cleopatra of Egypt: From History to Myth*. London: British Museum Press, 128–41

Wilkinson, Richard H. (2003), *The Complete Gods and Goddesses of Ancient Egypt*. London: Thames and Hudson

Wilkinson, Toby (2010), *The Rise and Fall of Ancient Egypt*. London: Bloomsbury

——(2023), *Ramesses the Great: Egypt's King of Kings*. London and New Haven: Yale University Press

Williams, J. H. C. (2001), '"Spoiling the Egyptians": Octavian and Cleopatra', in Susan Walker and Peter Higgs (eds), *Cleopatra of Egypt: From History to Myth*. London: British Museum Press, 190–9

Wilson, Penelope (1997), *A Ptolemaic Lexikon: A Lexicographical Study of the Texts in the Temple of Edfu*. Leuven: Peeters

Winter, Erich (2005), 'Alexander der Große als Pharao in ägyptischen Tempeln', in Herbert Beck, Peter C. Bol and Maraike Bückling (eds), *Ägypten Griechenland Rom: Abwehr und Berührung*. Tübingen: Ernst Wasmuth, 204–15

Wojciechowska, Agnieszka and Krzysztof Nawotka (2014), 'Alexander in Egypt: Chronology', in Volker Grieb, Krzysztof Nawotka and Agnieszka Wojciechowska (eds) (2014), *Alexander the Great and Egypt: History, Art, Tradition: Wrocław/Breslau 18./19. Nov. 2011*. Wiesbaden: Harrassowitz, 49–54

Yiftach, Uri (2015), 'Law in Ptolemaic and Roman Egypt', in Edward M. Harris and Mirko Canevaro (eds), *The Oxford Handbook of Ancient Greek Law* (online edn, Oxford Academic, 6 August 2015), https://doi.org/10.1093/oxfordhb/9780199599257.013.11, accessed 3 August 2023

Acknowledgements

The completion of this book provides an appropriate, if long overdue, opportunity to thank the two people who got me started as an author of authoritative yet accessible ancient history: my friend and colleague Dr John Guy, for that crucial first conversation and introduction, and many subsequent, inspirational discussions about history and history-writing; and my former agent, Peter Robinson, whose suggestion it was that I might at some point write a history of the Ptolemies. I thank him for planting the seed – even if it has taken many years to germinate and flower! I am also very grateful to my agents for this book, Georgina Capel and Veronica Goldstein, and my editors, Ian Marshall and Juliet Brooke at Bloomsbury and Matt Weiland at W. W. Norton, and all their colleagues, for their enthusiasm and support for this project.

My deepest gratitude goes to my colleague Dr Dorothy Thompson, perhaps our greatest authority on Ptolemaic Egypt, who took the time and trouble to read and comment on an earlier draft of this book. Her detailed feedback saved me from a number of errors of fact or interpretation, and provided valuable new references and insights. I am humbled to have been the beneficiary of her lifetime of scholarship. I would also like to thank Dr Sarah Cullis for an invaluable reference.

I could not have carried out the research for this book without the extraordinary resource, right on my doorstep, of the Cambridge University Library; as always, I am grateful to the library staff for their unfailing help. I also benefited, as the accompanying expert on a Nile cruise in the spring of 2023, from the opportunity to revisit a host of Ptolemaic sites, and reacquaint myself with the extraordinary – and often overlooked – artistic and architectural accomplishments of the period. I would like to thank all my fellow travellers on that memorable trip.

Last but not least, my thanks are due to Michael Bailey for his unstinting love and support: they mean everything.

Index

Abu Sha'ar: harbour 70
Abukir Bay 218
Abydos 127, 128
Achillas (general) 252, 256
Actium, Battle of (31) 281, 282, 288
Acutius, C. 204, 205
Adikhalamani 186
Adulis, island of Massawa (Eritrea) 89
Aegean, the 22, 41–2, 44, 72, 123, 124, 135, 157, 175, 188, 223
Aeschylus 94
Aetolian League 41, 119
Agathoklea 121, 122, 123
Agathokles 105, 121, 122–3
agriculture: in Egypt 13, 61–2, 63–7, 88, 91, 97, 106, 111–12, 125, 132, 146, 151–2, 166, 168, 170, 184–5, 193, 195–7, 198, 204, 234, 235, 286–7; Macedonian 40; Mesopotamian 45
Agrippa, Marcus 281
Ahmose II 42
Aigai (Vergina) 25
Alexander the Great (Alexander III of Macedon) 4, 5, 25, 39, 41, 147; education 8, 21; influenced by Homer 8–9; and Ptolemy I 3, 18, 21–2, 29, 37, 59, 85; conquers Rhodes 42; captures Gaza 8, 9; conquers Egypt 9–10, 24, 29, 35, 157, 286; honours Egyptian cults 10, 11, 32, 37, 149, 209; crowned at Memphis 7, 10–11, 12–13, 15, 216; as ruler of Egypt 11–13; and Zeus-Ammon 13, 14–15; travels to Siwa 13–14; issues coins 15; founds Alexandria 1, 15–17, 51, 158; reorganises Egypt's administration 17; resumes campaigning 17–18; and Nubian elephants 70; death 18, 22, 31, 39; burial of his body at Memphis 25–6, 215; reburial in Alexandria by Ptolemy 29, 34, 37, 55, 147; visited by Octavian 286; as cult figure 75, 78, 121, 147–8, 200; golden statue 79; third reburial 148
Alexander IV 23, 24, 27, 28, 29, 30
Alexander Balas 154, 155
Alexander Helios 269, 277–8, 288; statue 278
Alexander of Aetolia 86
Alexandria 1–2, 3, 15–18, 29, 54, 51–5, 57, 104, 105, 106, 120, 122–3, 128–9, 144–5, 149, 151, 152, 157, 170, 173, 174, 176, 177, 182, 190, 193, 199, 200, 202, 205, 206, 207, 232, 233, 235–6, 239, 241, 244, 255, 256, 277, 278–80, 282–4; agora 53; Berenikeion 138; Brucheion 54; burial of Alexander 29, 34, 37, 55, 147; burial of Nakhthorheb 34; canals 16, 51, 53, 54, 55, 256; Canopic Gate 55; Canopic Way 55; as centre of learning 55–6, 87, 95, 96–7; coinage 61;

Eunostos 53; founded by Alexander 15–18, 23, 31, 51, 52, 147, 158; Gate of the Moon 55; Gate of the Sun 55; Great Harbour 52, 53, 57; Great Library 6, 85, 86, 87, 92–3, 94, 98–9, 116, 174, 249, 256; Greek-speakers 54, 56, 158, 267; gymnasium 53–4; Heptastadion 52; hippodrome 54; hunger riots 252; Jews 49, 54, 151; Kibotos 53; Mouseion 56, 61, 81–2, 83, 85, 86, 87, 95, 98–9, 116, 249; necropolis 53, 55; Paneion 54; Ptolemaieia festivals 76–7; Rhakotis (district) 31, 53; royal palace 1, 176, 199; stadium 53; Sarapieion 38, 53, 104; Soma (Mausoleum) 148; statues of Ptolemy II's mistresses 138; Street of the Soma 55; temple to Mark Antony 287; temple of Poseidon 54; theatre 53; and trade 42, 48, 51, 55, 72, 74; Treasury 69, 138, 146, 154; university 99
Alexandria-in-Arakhosia (Kandahar) 44
Amenemhat III, pyramid temple of 207
Amenhotep (god) 186
Amenhotep III 12
Ammon *see* Amun; Zeus-Ammon
Ammon, Libya (god) 13
Amun (god) 11, 12, 13, 47, 149, 194, 216, 218; temples to 13, 46
Amun, Lord of Gereb (god) 219
Amun-Ra (god) 273
anachoresis (flight from the countryside) 151, 184, 204, 252
Anatolia 14, 27, 28, 44, 88, 103, 117, 135, 138, 140, 157, 202, 233, 257, 269, 280; central 23, 117, 276; coastal 38, 64, 71, 72, 80, 86, 89; eastern 270; southern 23, 17; western 57, 117, 133, 162
Anemhor 217
animals: sacred 3, 7, 90, 160, 178, 184, 185, 214, 238, 282; *see also* bulls, sacred
Ankhsheshonqy 237, 238
Ankhwennefer 127–8, 129
Antaeopolis 186

Antigonids 41
Antigonos I, the One-Eyed, of Macedonia 23, 26, 27, 28, 29, 34, 41, 48–9
Antigonos III, of Macedonia 103
Antioch 108
Antiochos 43
Antiochos I, of the Seleukids 71
Antiochos II, of the Seleukids 80, 88
Antiochos III, of the Seleukids 103, 104–5, 108, 109, 117–18, 123, 124, 125, 135, 138, 161
Antiochos IV, of the Seleukids 142, 143, 144–5, 150, 216; death 153
Antiochos V, of the Seleukids 153
Antiochos VIII, of the Seleukids 183, 199, 201, 231
Antiochos IX, of the Seleukids 199, 231
Antiochos X, of the Seleukids 231, 232, 233
Antiochos XIII, of the Seleukids 233
Antiokheia 43, 44, 233; coins 271; sanctuary 199
Antipatros ix–x, 23, 26, 27, 41, 59
Antirrhodos, islet of 42, 52
Antyllus 283
Anu (god) 45
Anubis (jackal god) 194, 213
Apameia 44
Apedemak (lion god) 47
Aphrodite (goddess) 138, 269, 275
Apis (sacred bull) 10, 18, 37, 90, 131, 133, 135, 149, 169, 185, 192, 210–11, 216; burials 211–13
Apollo (god) 194; oracle of (near Miletos) 14, 15
Apollodorus (a Greek) 115
Apollonia/Setenmontu 162–4, 165, 182
Apollonios, governor of Libya 17
Apollonios (Ptolemy II's finance minister) 63–5, 66–7, 167, 169
Apollonios (brother of Ptolemaios) 177, 179–80
Apollonios of Rhodes 93, 94; *Argonautica* 93
Apollonopolis (Edfu) 69, 70, 126, 185, 187–8, 222, 247; Mysteries of Osiris 219–20; priests 222, 223; temple of

INDEX

Horus 100, 185, 221–2, 224, 225, 245–6, 273; texts 222–3
Arabia 9, 45, 49, 55, 66, 70, 78, 118
Archelaos 239–40, 241
Archibios 284
Archimedes 97–8; *On Conoids and Spheroids* 98; *On the Sphere and Cylinder* 98; *Measurement of a Circle* 98; *On the Equilibrium of Planes* 98; *On Spirals* 97–8; *Quadrature of the Parabola* 98; *The Sand-Reckoner* 97
Arensnuphis (god) 187, 194
Argead dynasty 21, 23, 27, 49, 41
Aristarchos of Samos 86, 91, 99, 174
Aristoboulos 151
Aristotle 8, 21, 56, 81, 85; *The Constitution of the Athenians* 235
Armenia 276, 277, 278, 279; king 118, 288
Arqamani (Ergamenes), king of Nubia 71, 186
Arrhidaios *see* Philip III, of Macedon
Arsinoe (port) 89
Arsinoe (mother of Ptolemy I) 21
Arsinoe (I) 74–5
Arsinoe II 75–6, 108, 138, 148, 217
Arsinoe III 121, 122, 123, 137
Arsinoe (sister of Ptolemy XIII and Cleopatra) 255, 256–7, 258, 263, 269
Arsinoite nome *see* Fayum, the
Art of Eudoxos 236
Artakama 22, 59
Askalon: coins 254
Astarte (goddess) 133, 178, 179; temple 134
astrology/astronomy 45, 82, 86, 91, 94, 97, 99, 236, 249, 251–2
Atbara, River 46
Athena, oracle of (Ionia) 14
Athens 40, 41, 43, 56, 72, 73, 74, 81, 94, 103, 147, 149, 275, 276, 281; libraries 93
Athribis: temple to Repyt 192; birth house 246

Babylon 18, 22, 25, 26, 27, 28, 88; Settlement of (323) 23

Babylonia (Iraq) 43, 45
Bactria (Afghanistan) 44, 45, 71, 118
Bahariya Oasis: temple to Amun-Ra and Horus 12
Balakros (general) 17
banks and banking, Egyptian 45, 61, 126, 164–5, 242
Bastet (cat goddess) 139, 194, 213
Batis, governor of Gaza 9
Belistiche 138
Berenike (garrison town) 70
Berenike (port) 89, 186
Berenike I 59, 60, 138
Berenike II 89–91, 104, 138, 148
Berenike III 201, 230
Berenike IV 239, 240, 241
Berenike (daughter of Ptolemy II) 88
Berenike, Princess (daughter of Ptolemy III): cult and statues 90–91
Berenike Panchrysos (All-Gold Berenike), Nubia 68–9
Berenike Troglodytika (Berenike-of-the-Cave-Dwellers) 69–70, 71, 72
Berossus: *Babyloniaka* 45
Biga, island of: temple of Osiris 245
birth houses 33, 99, 187, 188, 246, 247, 262
Bithynia 44, 74
Book of the Dead 35
bronzes 47, 140, 169; coins 74, 125; gates 132; statues 149, 259, 278, 279
Brundisium (Brindisi), treaty of (40) 269, 270, 275
Brutus 261, 263, 267
Buchis (sacred bull) 210, 250
bulls, sacred 7, 10, 209; *see* Apis; Buchis; Mnevis
Buto, temples of 30, 31
Byzantion 105, 147

Caesar, Julius 4, 233, 234, 253, 254–61, 262, 274
Caesarion *see* Ptolemy XV Caesar(ion)
Calpurnia 258
Cambyses, of Persia 33
canals 16–17, 51, 53, 54, 55, 62, 70, 111, 112, 213, 219, 220, 244, 256, 273, 286
Canbidius, Publius 280

Cannae, battle of (216) 119
Carthage/Carthaginians 73, 118, 119, 153, 175, 205, 206, 269
Cassius 261, 267, 273
Cato the Younger 240
Celtic tribes 41
Chandragupta Maurya 43
Charmion 2
Chios, island of 74
Chremonidean War (267–261) 72–3
Chremonides (Athenian general) 73
Cicero 232, 233, 234, 242, 258
Cleopatra, Lower Nubia (military colony) 150
Cleopatra I 135, 136, 137–8, 140, 141, 142, 248, 260; death 141
Cleopatra II 149, 153, 174, 175–6, 181–2, 183, 184, 189–90, 217, 229, 260
Cleopatra III 173, 175–6, 182, 183, 189–90, 192, 199–200, 201, 229, 231, 260
Cleopatra IV 199
Cleopatra VII 1–4, 5; appearance 259; appointed co-regent 242, 249–50; presides over burial of Buchis 250–51; rules alone 251; and Isis 251; completes temple at Tentyris 251–2; supports Pompey in fight against Caesar 253; flees from Egypt 253–4; meets Caesar 255; is restored to the throne 255–7; has son by Caesar 257–8; as his guest in Rome 274; feted as the living Isis 274–5; her fame 258–61; her final years as queen 267; summoned to Tarsos by Mark Antony 268–9; their liaison and the birth of twins 269, 270–71, 275–80; and her subjects 271–2, 273; and Mark Antony's defeat by Octavian 281–3; death 2, 283–4, 288
Cleopatra (co-regent with Ptolemy VI) 141, 143
Cleopatra Selene 199, 200, 201, 231, 232, 233, 269, 278, 288–9
Cleopatra Thea 154, 183
Cleopatra Tryphaina 231–2, 239
clepsydra 96
cleruchs 106, 107, 110, 113, 152, 176, 184, 196, 197, 198, 235
coinage 15, 29, 45, 56, 61, 74, 125, 137, 141, 164, 170, 198, 200, 205, 223, 242, 254, 257, 259, 271, 274, 287
Contra-Latopolis: temple to Isis 192
Copernicus, Nicolaus 86
Corinth 79; Isthmus of 103
Crassus, Marcus Licinius 232, 234
Crete 175, 206, 271
customs/customs dues 73–4, 132, 167, 184, 245, 280
Cyclades, the 42, 72, 175
Cyprus: invaded by Ptolemy I 27, 37; falls to Demetrios 28, 37, 106; retaken by Ptolemy 50–51; and Macedonian–Seleukid plot 123; a new military governor appointed by Cleopatra I 138; captured by Seleukids 144; restored to Ptolemy VI by Rome 145, 152, 153, 154, 175; Ptolemy VIII and Cleopatra III in exile 176, 182; and Ptolemy IX 189, 190, 199–200, 201, 202, 231; and Ptolemy XII 234–5, 239, 242; returned to Cleopatra by Caesar 255, 257, 269, 271, 278

Dabod 186; temple of Amun 245
Dakka 186
Dalmatian tribes 288
Dardanelles 89
Darfur 46
Darius I, of Persia 99, 211
Darius III, of Persia 9, 15
Deinokrates of Rhodes 17
'Delian problem', the 94
Delos, island of 72, 76, 147, 168
Demeter (goddess) 138
Demetrios (son of Antigonos the One-Eyed) 28, 37, 41, 42, 106
Demetrios (son of Seleukos IV) 153, 154
Demetrios II 154, 155, 182–3
Demetrios of Phaleron 56, 60–61, 81, 82, 85
Dexiphanes the Knidian 57

Dinnos 205
Dinokrates of Rhodes 54–5
Diodorus Siculus 4, 238
Dion of Alexandria 240
Dionysios Petosarapis 151, 174
Dionysos (god) 38, 77, 117, 147, 268, 269, 277, 281; association with Osiris 187, 219, 220, 244, 245, 278; cult of 104, 215, 232, 279; festival and Grand Procession in Alexandria 77–9; temples to 162
Diophanes (military commander) 113–15
Dioskouroi (gods) 194
Diospolis Parva: garrison 162
Djed-djehuty-iufankh, the Elder 35
Djed-djehuty-iufankh, the Younger 35
Djedhor 99
Dodekaschoinos, the 150, 186, 191, 245
Doloaspis, governor of Egypt 17
Dream of Nectanebo, The 236–7
Dryton 161–3, 182
'dynasties', Egyptian 36

Eastern Desert, Egypt 67
Ebers Papyrus 84
economy, Egyptian 50, 64, 106, 163–4, 165, 166–8, 169, 170, 185, 198, 201, 204, 224, 233, 237, 280; *see also* agriculture; banks and banking; customs; grain; oil
Elephantine, island of 32, 186, 190–91, 221
elephants 26, 43, 47, 70–72, 108, 109, 118, 124; divine 47
Eleusis 145, 151; Day of 145, 146, 150, 207, 216
Eleutheros, River 45, 49
emerald mines 70
Ephesos 80, 88–9, 135, 279, 280, 281
Erasistratos 84–5, 86, 99
Eratosthenes of Kyrene 94–6, 99; *Chronology* 94; *Geographika* 95; *On Ancient Comedy* 94
Esthladas 163, 164, 182
Euclid 82–3, 86, 97, 99; *Catoptrics* 82; *Conics* 83; *Data* 82; *Elements* 82, 235; *Fallacies* 83; *On Divisions* 82; *Optics* 82; *Phenomena* 82

Eulaios 141, 142, 143
Eumenes of Kardia 23, 27, 28
eunuchs 9, 141, 152, 252, 256
Euripides 94, 235, 236
Eurydike 59

Fabius, C. 205
faience industry 169
famine 7, 88, 128, 165, 258, 263–4, 285
farmers *see* agriculture
Fayum, the (Arsinoite nome) 16, 32, 61–3, 64, 65, 76, 107, 113, 115, 139, 143, 144, 147, 158, 168, 170, 193–4, 196, 205, 207, 246; 'Great Lake' 61–2; stela 251
Fertile Crescent 45

Gabiniani, the 241, 253, 255
Gabinius, Aulus 239, 240, 241, 242
Gallus, Cornelius 282, 283
Ganymedes (eunuch) 256
Gaza, Palestine 8–9, 34, 108, 123, 201
Geb (god) 187
Gebel Barkal (mountain) 46
geographers 4, 52, 94–5, 99
geometry 82, 83, 95, 97, 98, 99
Glaukias 177–8, 179, 236
gold mining/gold smelting 40, 67–9, 70, 86, 126, 259
grain 27, 41, 43, 47, 49, 55, 62, 67, 70, 74, 86, 88, 90, 111, 119, 120, 154, 166, 167–8, 170, 195, 205, 206, 232, 252, 259
Great Southern Rebellion (205–186) 129
Greek settlers/speakers 5–6, 16, 33, 37, 38, 45, 48, 54, 61, 63, 65–6, 75, 107, 110, 113, 115, 120, 125, 126, 132, 133, 141, 144, 146–9, 152, 157–63, 167, 168, 169, 175, 188, 194, 198, 214, 220–21, 224, 236, 244
gymnasia 44, 53, 65, 132, 158

Hades (god) 38
Halikarnassos: garrison 72
Hannibal 118, 119, 206
Hapy (god) 219
Harsiyotef, ruler of Kush 68

Hathor (goddess) 247, 249, 272; temple to 251, 275
Heliopolis 10; Mnevis bull 210, 250; temple of Ra 36, 76
Hellenomemphites 133
Henen-nesut (Herakleopolis) 34
Hera (goddess) 138
Herakleides 159–60
Herakleopolitan province 234
Herakles (god) 133, 219
Hermonthis 176, 186, 203; Buchis 210, 250–51
Hermopolis 34, 111; temple of Thoth 32
Hermpolite nome 111
Herod of Judaea 277
Herodotus 210–11
Herondas 157
Herophilos of Khalkedon 83, 84, 86
Hesiod 86; statue 215
Hierax (general) 203
Hindu Kush 17, 22, 39
Hippodamos of Miletos 54
Hippokrates 83, 84
Homer 86–7, 116; *Iliad* 8–9, 235; *Odyssey* 15, 52; statue 215
Hor 214, 273
Horus (god) 12, 99, 100, 109, 141–2, 187, 194, 216, 224, 247, 262, 264, 275; temples and shrines to 100, 104, 185, 187, 194, 221–2, 245–6, 247, 272, 273
Horwennefer ('pharaoh') 126–7, 128, 177
Horwerra (god) 187
houses 158, 194–5, 213; see also birth houses
Hydaspes, Battle of the (326) 70
hydrostatics 98

ibis 160, 169, 214, 236; see also Thoth
Illyria 119
Imhotep (Asklepios) (god) 186, 213, 264–5
Imhotep-Padibastet V 273–4, 283
immigrants 36, 59, 106, 133–4, 194; see also Greek settlers/speakers
imports 53, 54, 70, 71, 74, 88, 90, 162, 166, 184, 245, 280, 288
incense trade 55, 70, 77
India 18, 39, 45, 78, 118, 147, 188, 283; elephants 26, 44, 70, 71, 108, 118; spices 55, 70, 79
Ionia/Ionians 14, 89, 132, 133, 164, 168, 244
Iras 2
irrigation systems 5, 46, 62–3, 97, 111, 115, 130, 166, 194, 198, 273
Isis (goddess) 38, 75, 138, 141–2, 148, 178, 186, 194, 251, 262, 278; cult of 188, 274, 275; temples to 16, 48, 68, 99, 185, 192, 203, 284
Issos, Battle of (333) 9, 34
Itanos, Crete 175, 206

Jerusalem 125, 277; Maccabean revolt (167–160) 150
Jews 49, 134, 194, 202, 263; and Maccabean Revolt 150
Josephus 263
Juba II, of Mauretania 288
Judaea/Judaeans 49, 125, 200–1, 233, 270

Kalabsha 186
Kallimachos, governor of the Thebaid 263, 275
Kallimachos of Kyrene 93–4, 263, 275; *Causes (Origins)* 93–4; *List of Those who Distinguished Themselves in All Branches of Learning…* 93
Kanopos 15, 55, 149, 218, 219; Decree (238) 100, 258; foundation of (238;) 149
  temple of Osiris 99
Kappadokia 23, 26, 28, 44
Karia/Karians 64, 71, 74, 133, 135
Karnak 11, 12; statue of Caesarion 273; temples 99, 186, 192, 203, 246
Karomemphites 133
Kassandros of Macedon 27, 28, 29, 41
Kaunos 64
Kerkeosiris 193, 194–9
Kerma 46
Khababash 31–2

Kharga Oasis: temple 99
Khnum (god), priesthood and temple of 191–2, 221
Khoiak ceremonies 219–20
Khonsu (god) 11, 219; temples to 11, 99, 186, 192, 218–19
Kilikia 231, 269, 278
Kineas 143–4
Kleanthes of Assos: *Against Aristarchos* 86
Kleomenes III, of Sparta 103, 104
Kleomenes, governor of Sinai 17, 23–4
Kleon (engineer) 61, 62–4
Knidos, Anatolia 162
Koile-Syria 49, 50, 105, 108, 117, 123, 125, 135, 137, 142, 143, 144, 154, 175, 206, 270, 277, 278; immigrants from 133–4; natural resources 49, 88, 117, 270
Komanos 143–4
Konon of Samos 97
Kopais, Lake, Boeotia 62
Koptos 250; stela 282
Kordofan 46
Kos, island of 140, 208, 231
Krateros 23, 26
Krokodilopolis 61, 62, 140, 193
Ktesibios 96, 97; clepsydra 96; *On Pneumatics* 96; water organ 96
Kush/Kushites 46–7, 68, 127, 129, 186, 191
Kyrenaika, Libya 24; under Ptolemy I 26, 27, 48, 49, 50, Ptolemy III 89, 206, Ptolemy IV 107, Philip V 123, Ptolemy VI 152–3, Ptolemy VIII 154, 173, 175, and Ptolemy IX 190; and Rome 200, 232, 270, 281, 282; and Ptolemy XII 235, 242; under Cleopatra Selene 278
Kyrene, Libya 24, 37, 48, 89, 94, 173, 174, 271; temples 48, 188

Lagos 21
'Lake of Pharaoh' 169, 212
land ownership 111, 196–7, 235
Laodike 88, 138
Laodikeia 44

Latopolis 202
League of Islanders 41–2, 72
Lebanon 48, 49, 55, 270
legal affairs 114, 115, 127, 128, 139, 140, 143, 160–61, 162, 163, 164, 184, 214, 235, 282
Lenaios 141, 142, 143
Lentulus, Lucius Cornelius 135
Leontopolis (Tell el-Yahudiya) 151
Lepidus, Marcus 207, 262, 267, 269, 270, 277
Letopolis 216
Levantine, the 48–9, 179, 270, 271
Libya/Libyans 13, 17, 24, 28, 39, 40, 48, 107, 188; see also Kyrenaika; Kyrene
Lochias promontory 52, 57
Lucius Septimius 254
Lucullus 207, 208
Luxor 12, 72, 149
Lycophron of Khalkis 86
Lykia 23, 28, 135, 268
Lykopolis, northern (Segin al-Kom) 126, 130, 131; southern (Asyut) 128
Lysander (general) 13
Lysimachos (Ptolemy IV's uncle) 104
Lysimachos of Thrace 23, 27, 28, 29, 60, 74

Maccabean Revolt (167–160) 150
Macedon/Macedonia/Macedonians 21, 23, 31, 34, 35, 39, 40–42, 45, 59, 61, 62, 118, 146, 149, 209, 216; town planning 69; and Ptolemy II 72–3, 80; and Ptolemy III 103–4; soldiers 105, 106, 107, 124, 177, 179, 180; women 139, 140; monarchs and priests 209, 216, 217, 218, 244; and Rome 206, 233, 267–8, 270, 284, 285; and Cleopatra 252, 284; *see also* Alexander the Great; Antigonos I; Philip II; Philip V; Ptolemy I; Ptolemy VIII *and below*
Macedonian Companions 17, 22, 33
Macedonian Wars: First (214–205) 119–20; Second (200–197) 124, 135; Third (171–168) 142, 144, 145
Magas 28, 104
Malichos 114–15

Manetho of Sebennytos 36, 38, 209; *Aigyptiaka* 36
Marduk (god) 45
Mareotis, Lake 15, 16–17, 53, 55
Mark Antony (Marcus Antonius): and invasion of Egypt 241; in the hunt for Caesar's killers 262; supported by Cleopatra 262–3; his troops face starvation 263; defeats Cassius at Philippi 267–8; and Cleopatra 268–9, 270, 271, 275–6, 279, 280; fathers her children 269, 270, 276; confirmed as master of the eastern territories 269–70; marries Octavia 270, 276; his Parthian campaign 270, 276–7, 279; opposed by Octavian 277, 279–80; celebrates victory in Alexandria 277–8; summons Cleopatra to Ephesos 279, 280; divorces Octavia 280; defeated by Octavian 280–83; death 283; statues destroyed 279, 281, 284
marriage 139, 140, 162–3, 175–6, 259; sibling 75, 141
mathematicians 45, 82–3, 86, 94, 95, 97–8, 99
Mazaces, governor of Persia 9
Medes 108
Media (Iran) 105, 108, 278, 282
medicine and anatomy 83–5, 99, 213, 224, 264–5
Medinet Habu 203–4
Megakles 17
Memmius, Lucius 27
Memphis 53, 105, 109, 130, 132–3, 144, 147, 149, 153, 167, 168–70, 175, 179, 182, 193, 203, 204, 210, 216–17, 243–5, 287; accession of Alexander the Great 7, 10–11, 12–13, 15, 216; accession of Ptolemy I 31, 37; accession of Ptolemy V 131–2, 134; Anoubieion 186, 213, 214, 216; Apis sacred bulls/Temple 7, 10, 37, 131, 135, 149, 169, 181, 185–6, 209, 210, 211–13, 215, 285, 288; Arsinoeion 75–6; Asklepieion 213, 214, 264–5; Boubastieion 213; Decree (Rosetta Stone) 131–2, 149; ethnic groups 133–4; Jews 134; necropolis 178, 209, 212, 213–14, 215–16, 244–5, 264; Nilometer 132; priesthood/temple of Ptah 10, 131, 138, 139, 170, 210, 212, 213, 216, 217–18, 243, 285, 286; Sarapieion 178, 181, 212–13, 214–15
Menander 235, 236
Mendes, temple at: stela 75
Menelaos 27, 28, 147
Menes 229
Menkhes/Asklepiades 160–61, 193, 194, 195, 196, 197–9
mercenaries 8, 24, 49, 66, 103, 105, 107, 124, 176, 197, 202, 205, 236, 242; Gabiniani 241, 253, 255
Meroë 46–7
Mesopotamia 44, 45, 88, 270
Methana 175
Miletos 14, 15, 54, 80
Min (god) 250
Mithridates VI, of Pontos 207, 208, 231, 240
Mithridatic Wars: First 207–8, 231; Third 233
Mnevis sacred bulls 90, 185, 210, 250
Montu (god) 99, 186, 250
Mount Kasion, Battle of (170) 143
mummification 53, 83, 139, 178, 194, 215, 220; of animals and birds 5, 160, 194, 213, 214, 236; of sacred bulls 37, 211–12, 282
Mut (goddess) 218, 219
Myos Hormos (Quseir) 70

Nabataea/Nabataeans 271, 283
Nabu (god) 45
Nakhthor 202
Nakhthorheb (pharaoh) 11, 34, 129, 217
Nakhtnebef, King 100; birth house of 246
Napata, Kingdom of Kush 46
Napoleon Bonaparte 132
Nastasen, ruler of Kush 68
Naukratis 48, 126, 133, 144, 157; temple 32
Naxos, island of 72

Nechesia: harbour 70
Nero, Emperor 232
Nesisty Padibastet (high priest) 217
Nes-Shu 35
Nesyt 162
New Paphos, Cyprus 51
New Year/New Year's Day, Egyptian 91–2
Nikanor (banker) 165
Nile, River 7, 26, 62, 88, 98, 152, 167, 190, 271; Cataracts 46, 68, 69, 71, 95, 150, 186, 191, 204–5, 209, 219, 245; inundation 91, 92, 190–91, 204–5, 219; *see also below*
Nile Delta 15, 17, 29, 32, 110–11, 130–31, 143, 167
Nile Valley 3, 5, 18, 23, 29, 36, 40, 62, 64, 70, 127, 128, 133, 176, 193, 249, 259, 271; cult of Isis 274; faience industry 169; Greek settlers 157, 158; Nubian *see* Dodekaschoinos; provincial governors 17, 110–11, 223; and Romans 232–3, 238, 263–4; temples 6, 32, 75, 149, 158, 186, 192, 246, 247, 284
Nilopolis (Delas) 211
nomarchs (provincial governor) 17, 99, 111, 113
Nubia 30, 46, 47, 55, 69, 71; cults/gods 47, 187; elephants 70, 71–2; gold mines 68–9; Lower Nubia 68, 150, 185, 186, 187, 191, 203; Nile Valley 46, 150; Upper Nubia 68
Numenios 145

Octavian (Gaius Octavius) 258, 262, 263, 267, 269, 270, 277, 278, 279, 281, 282–7, 288; coins 287
Ogulnius, Q. 205
oikonomos ('household manager') 111–12
oil imports and production 49, 65, 73, 74, 112, 166, 168, 169, 178
Olympias 27
Olympic Games 12

Ombos (Kom Ombo) 187, 245, 251; temple sanatorium 224
Onias IV 150–51
Ophellas (general) 24, 28
Oracle of the Potter 177
Orontes, River 43
Osiris (god) 37, 38, 75, 127, 178, 186, 187, 188, 194, 219, 262, 279; and Dionysos 244, 245, 278; Mysteries of 188, 219–21; temples to 99, 127, 245, 273; *see also* Kerkeosiris
Osorapis (god) 37–8; *see also* Sarapis
Oxus River 44
Oxyrhynchos (Bahnasa) 32, 211; documents found on rubbish dumps 235

Paabeithis: temple 32
Padibastet IV (high priest) 217–18, 243
Padibastet V *see* Imhotep-Padibastet V
Padiusir of Hermopolis 34, 35, 36, 209
Pakhom, governor of Tentyris 272
Palestine 27; *see also* Gaza
Pamphylia 23
Pan (god) 124
Paneion, Battle of (202) 124–5, 135
Panemerit 245
Panopolis 152
Pantaleon 17
Paos 176, 182
Paphlagonia 23
papyri: Egyptian 4–5, 10, 61, 66, 73, 74, 87, 106, 110, 139–40, 144, 159, 164, 170, 212, 215, 235, 236, 256, 278, 280, 282; funerary 216; Greek 4; Edwin Smith Surgical 83–4; temple 222
Parates (barber) 114
Parthia/Parthians 118, 270, 276–7, 278, 279
Pascal, Blaise 259
Pasetenbast (Psenobastis) 159
Pasherenamun I 273
Pasherenptah III 243, 244, 264, 265, 272, 273
Pathyris (Gebelein) 127, 162, 163, 165, 202, 203
Patras 281

Pelousion 9, 10, 17, 26, 74, 108, 143, 182, 199, 241, 254, 283
Pepi I 247
Perdikkas (general) 22, 23, 25–6
Pergamon 44, 119; Library 278
Peripatetic school 56
Perseus, ruler of Macedon 142, 145
Persia/Persians 7, 8, 9, 10, 11, 15, 25, 31–5, 41, 43, 45, 59, 68, 90, 105, 108, 109, 209, 211
Petisis 17
Peukestas (general) 10, 17, 209
Pharos, island of 15, 16, 52, 53; lighthouse 1, 57, 95, 256
Pharsalos, Battle of (48) 254
Philadelpheia 65, 143, 158
Philae, island of 186–7, 188, 204–5; temple of Isis 68, 99, 129–30, 150, 185, 224, 245, 274, 284
Philip II, of Macedon 21, 23, 40–41, 62
Philip III (Arrhidaios), of Macedon 23, 24, 27, 29, 32
Philip V, of Macedon 119, 122, 123, 124, 206
Philippi 62; Battle of (42) 267, 268
Philometris, Lower Nubia (military colony) 150
Philotera 70, 71
Phoenicia 27, 45, 48, 49, 50, 105, 123, 133, 254
Phoenike (Finiq), Treaty of (205) 120
Phoenico-Egyptians 133–4
Phrygia 23, 28
pigeon lofts 195
Pindar 13, 86, 235; statue 215
Piraeus, Athens 16
Plato 81; statue 215
Platon 202–3
Plinthine 167
Polemon 17
Polybius 4
Polyperchon 27
Pompey the Great (Gnaius Pompeius Magnus) 233, 234, 239, 240–41, 253, 254
Pontos 44, 74, 207, 233, 244, 268, 376
Popilius Laenas, Caius 145
Potheinos 252, 256

Praxagoras of Kos 83, 86
Ptah (god) 7, 130, 136, 216, 217, 265, 285; priesthood of 10, 131, 138, 139, 210, 216, 217, 218, 224, 243, 261–2, 264, 272, 273, 283, 286, 287; temple at Karnak 203; temple at Memphis 133, 170, 203, 211, 212, 213, 217, 285
Ptolemaic decree (238) 89–91
Ptolemaios (general) 124
Ptolemaios (recluse) 177, 178–9, 181, 214, 236–7
Ptolemais, Egypt 48, 127, 129, 147, 157, 162
Ptolemais, Libya 89
Ptolemais Ake, Phoenicia (Acre) 200–1
Ptolemais-of-the-Arabs 114
Ptolemais-of-the-Hunts, Nubia 71
Ptolemy I Soter x, 3, 5; birth 21; personality 22, 60; education 81; and Alexander the Great 18, 21–2; as satrap of Egypt 23–5, 26, 29–30, 110–11, 209–10; gains Kyrenaika 24, 48; presides over Alexander's burial and reburial 25–6, 29, 34, 37, 55, 147, 215; and Wars of the Successors 26–7, 37, 70; crowned in Memphis 31, 37, 216; invasdes Cyprus 27, 28, 37, 50–51; extends his control 28; seizes the Levantine littoral 48–9; adopts royal titles 28–32, 146; relocates capital to Alexandria 29, 51, 210; his throne 79; develops Egyptian sacred architecture 32–3, 185, 194; wins over native elite 33–4, 35, 36–7; provides for burial of Apis bull 37, 211; invents a new god 37–8, 76; foreign policy 40, 41–2, 43, 45–6, 47–9, 59, 76, 147; army 105–6; restarts goldmining 67; annexes Sidon 50; makes Alexandria great centre of learning 55–7, 81, 85, 94, 99; writes biography of Alexander 59, 85; marriages 59; names son as co-ruler 60, 229; death 60; statue 79; his cult 138, 147, 162
Ptolemy II Philadelphos: personality 60, 80; appointed co-ruler 60, 229; secures throne 60–61; and Aristarchos

85–6, 87; and Zenodotos 87; his plans for transforming Egypt 61–4, 66, 157; and sacred buildings 214, 221; and banking 164, 165; his need for gold 67–9, and elephants 70–72; consolidates power 72, 73, 185; his court poet 158; foreign policy 72–4, 205, 206; self-promotion 72, 74; marriages and mistresses 74–6, 138, 141; establishes Ptolemaieia festival 76–9; and war with Seleukids 80; cult 147, 148; death 87

Ptolemy III Euergetes 87, 147; triumphs in Third Syrian War 88; domestic troubles 88; signs peace treaty with Seleukids 88–9; and the priests 217, 218; lauded in synod's 238; decree 89–91; fails to reform Egyptian calendar 91–2, 258; and expansion of Alexandrian Library 92–3, 94; and Archimedes 97; founds temple at Apollonopolis 99–100, 185, 187, 221; builds at Karnak 192; and ruler cult 100, 147, 148, 149; foreign policies 103–4, 206; death 103

Ptolemy IV Philopator 104, 127; and Sosibios 104, 105, 121; his favourite mistress 121; appoints new military commanders 113; army 107–8; and Battle of Raphia 108–9, 136, 216, 272; signs treaty with Seleukids 109; orders search for stolen statues 109, 149; on victory tour of Egypt 110; intellectual pursuits and decadence 116–17; and foreign conflicts 117–18, 119, 120, 206; and ruler cult 148, 185; death 120, 121, 122, 125

Ptolemy V Epiphanes 137; proclaimed co-regent 121, 122, 123, 124, 134, 206–7; coinage 259; under Rome's protection 207; signs peace treaty with Seleukids 125, 161; marriage 135–6, 141; gains Ptolemais 127, loses Thebes 128; and end of Fifth Syrian War 128, 131; crowned in Memphis 131, 216; and Decree of Memphis 131–2, 149; sponsors decoration and construction in Memphis 185–6; chooses Memphis as setting for synod 218; and civil war 128–9, 130–31; and ruler cult 148; death 137

Ptolemy VI Philometor: accession 137; and Cleopatra I 137–8, 140, 141; rules jointly with siblings 143; comes of age 143; marriage to Cleopatra II 141, 174; settlement with Antiochos IV 144–5; and the 'Day of Eleusis' 145–6, 149, 150; appearance 149–50, 259; grants Jews of Alexandria self-governance 151; conflict with Ptolemy VIII 144, 145, 151, 152–3, 154, 229; and Seleukid dynastic crisis 153–4; takes back Koile-Syria 154; crowned king of Asia 154; founds temple in Ombos 187; orders documents to be labelled in Greek 215–16; in Memphis 217; death 155, 173, 175

Ptolemy VII Neos Philopator x

Ptolemy VIII Euergetes II: conflict with Ptolemy VI 144, 145, 151, 152–3, 154, 229; exiled 152; recalled and acclaimed as ruler 173; purges enemies 174; marries Cleopatra II 174; welcomes Roman embassy 175; his various vices 175; nickname 174, 259; marries Cleopatra III 175–6; and civil war 176, 177, 181, 182, 197, 198; murders his son, Ptolemy Memphites 181–2; in triple monarchy 183; issues royal decree (118) 183–5; and temple construction 186–8, 189, 221, 224; in Memphis 217; and crown officials 221; a controversial monarch 188; his will 188, 200; death 188, 189

Ptolemy IX Soter II: accession 189–90; visits Elephantine 190–92, 221; honours local deities 192; and temple construction and decoration 192, 203–4, 221, 222, 225, 275; promotes cult of Apis 192; and civil unrest 198; divorces Cleopatra IV 199; flees to Cyprus 199, 231; issues

coins 200; bequeaths his kingdom to Rome 200; at war with Cleopatra III and Ptolemy X 200–1, 230; re-enters Egypt 202, 203; stages second coronation in Memphis 204; and Rome 207–8, 232–3; death 230
Ptolemy X Alexander 199–200, 201, 202, 207, 222, 230, 231
Ptolemy XI Alexander II 230
Ptolemy XII Neos Dionysos; becomes co-regent with Tryphaina (Cleopatra) 231–2; a flautist 232, 268–9; and Rome 232–5, 239; presides over Alexandria as centre of learning 236, 237; forced to abdicate 239; supported by Pompey, Gabinius and Mark Antony 240–41; restored to his throne 241; appoints Rabirius as finance minister 241–2; makes his daughter co-regent 242; his achievements 242–3; and the priesthood 243–5, 261; his coronation 243; and temple construction 245–7, 249; his will 251, 253, 255, 257; death 249
Ptolemy XIII 250, 252, 253, 254, 255, 256–7
Ptolemy XIV 257, 261
Ptolemy XV Caesar(ion) 257–8, 261, 262, 269, 273, 274, 275, 278, 282, 283
Ptolemy Apion 189, 200, 232
Ptolemy Eupator 173
Ptolemy Keraunos 59–61
Ptolemy Memphites 175, 181–2, 183
Ptolemy Philadelphos 276, 278, 288
pumps, water 97
Punic Wars: First (264–241) 73, 118, 206; Second (218–201) 118, 206; Third (149–146) 175
Pydna, Battle of (168) 145
Pyramid Texts 35
Pyrrhus, king of Epirus 205
Pythagoras 86

Ra (sun god) 10, 11, 216, 250; high priest of 249; temple of 37
Rabirius Postumus, Caius 234, 240, 242
Ramesses II 11, 210

Raphia (Rafah) 135–6; Battle of (217) 108, 109, 110, 116, 117, 120, 124, 125, 138, 197, 272
Repyt (goddess) 192
Rhodes 37, 42–3, 55, 74, 105, 119, 147, 162, 168, 240
Roman Republic 73, 119–20, 124, 134, 135, 140, 142, 144, 145, 146, 153, 154, 155, 175, 182, 200, 204–8, 230, 231, 232–5, 238, 263–4, 286–8; *see also* Caesar, Julius; Mark Antony; Octavian; Pompey the Great; Punic Wars; Rabirius Postumus
Roxane 18, 23, 28

Saguntum 118
Sais 33, 130
Salamis, Cyprus 28, 51
Samaria 125
Samos, island of 72, 86, 281
Samothrace, island of 143
Samut, Egypt 67; gold mines 126
Sappho 235
Sarapis (god) 38, 48, 51, 56, 76, 148, 178, 192, 194; cult 38, 148–9; temple to 69–70
Sardinia 119
Sardis 117
Satrap Stela, the 29–30, 31
Sceptics, the 94
Scipio Aemilianus (general) 175
Scopas (general) 124
sculpture 5, 47, 74, 215
'Sea of the Greeks' (Mediterranean) 15, 31, 51, 158, 218, 244
Sebennytos 34, 36
Sebiumeker (creation god) 47
Sekhmet (goddess) 178
Seleukeia 43, 44
Seleukeia-in-Pieria 199
Seleukeia-on-the-Tigris 45
Seleukid kingdom/empire 43–5, 49, 70, 80, 88, 89, 104–5, 108–9, 117, 118, 120, 123–5, 135, 136, 137, 142, 144–6, 150, 153–5, 175, 182–3, 199, 200–1, 206, 231, 233, 239, 270; *see also* Antiochos I–XIII; Syrian Wars *and below*

Seleukos I 26, 27, 28, 29, 43, 44, 45, 49, 60, 71
Seleukos II 88
Seleukos IV 137, 142, 153
Seleukos, Prince 239
Sellasia, Battle of (222) 103
Seneca 263
Seth (god) 109, 222
Shedyt, the Fayum 61; shrine to Sobek 61
shipbuilding/ships 49, 66, 152, 170, 250, 256, 257; grain-ships 280; warships 253, 254, 256, 257, 263, 280, 281
Shu (god) 187
Sicily 73, 119
Sidon 49, 50, 123, 124
Sile 34
Siwa, oasis of 13, 14; oracle 14; temple of Zeus-Ammon 18, 25
slaves 9, 47, 49–50, 63, 119, 128, 141, 152, 169
Smith (Edwin) Surgical Papyrus 83–4
Sobek (crocodile god) 187, 194
Soloi, Cyprus 51
Somtutefnakht 34
Sophilos: mosaic floor 72
Sophocles 94, 235
Sosibios of Alexandria 104, 105, 108, 121, 122
Sosigenes 258
Sostratos: Pharos lighthouse 57
Sotades (poet) 75
Sparta/Spartans 13, 24, 40, 72, 73, 103, 104
spice trade 47, 49, 79, 167
Stoics, the 44, 86
Strabo 4, 52, 53, 56, 95
Stratonikeia 44
Sulla (general) 207, 208, 230
Susa: mass wedding 59
Syene (Aswan) 95, 129; temple of Isis 99
Syracuse 98, 118, 119, 158
Syria 27, 28, 30, 43, 44, 49–50, 71, 72, 89, 104, 135, 142, 143; see also Koile-Syria; Syrian Wars
Syrian Wars 45; First (274–271) 71, 72; Second (260–253) 80, 88; Third (246–241) 88; Fourth (219–217) 105, 169; Fifth (202–195) 123–4, 125, 128, 131, 135; Sixth (170–168) 146, 175

Taimhotep 264, 265
Tanis 32, 186, 245
Taous and Tawê 181
Taposiris Magna 167
Tarsos 268, 269
taxation/taxes 49–50, 70, 73, 76, 88, 120, 126, 127, 151, 157, 165–7, 170, 184, 193, 197, 234, 280
Teaching of Ankhsheshonqy 237–8
Tebtunis 194; temple 32
Temnos, Anatolia 140
temple building 11–12, 16, 32–3, 38, 75–6, 99–100, 116, 126, 169–70, 185, 186–7, 218–19, 221–2, 224, 245–6
Tentyris (Dendera) 201, 219, 249; birth house of Nakhtnebef 246; Mysteries of Osiris 219–20; temples 201, 224, 246–7, 251, 272–3, 275, 287
Terenuthis: temple 32
Tetosiris 115
textile industry 168–9
Thasos, island of 74
Thebaid, the 126, 128–9, 152, 161, 176, 186, 202, 203, 211, 246, 251, 262, 275
Thebes, Boetia 56
Thebes (Luxor) 147, 162; Horwennefer's rebellion 126–9; a nuptial contract from 140; a second rebellion 152; Paos as commander 176; remains rebellious 186, 202, 203, 210; temples 192, 201, 203; as religious capital 210; and Cleopatra 250, 253; see also Thebaid, the
Theodotus of Chios 252
Theokritos (court poet) 75, 158
Thera, island of 175
Thmuis: mosaic floor 72
Thonis-Herakleion 218, 219; Mysteries of Osiris 219, 220; temples 218–19
Thoth (god) 32, 35, 194, 273
Thrace 23, 27, 29, 60, 62, 74, 88, 89, 138, 194
Thutmose III 8, 11, 247

Tigris, River 43
Timotheos of Athens 38
town planning 54–5, 69, 158
trade 5, 15, 28, 40, 42–3, 44, 45, 46, 47, 48, 49, 53, 54, 56, 57, 61, 66–7, 70, 72, 74, 120, 213, 215, 271, 274; slaves 49–50; spices 167; textiles 169; *see also* grain; oil
Tryphaina 183, 199, 231–2
Tuna el-Gebel: Padiusir's tomb chapel 35
Tyre 49, 105, 270

Udjahorresnet 33
Usir-Hep (Osiris-Apis; Osorapis) 37–8

vineyards 64, 65, 76, 133, 168, 170, 184

Wadi Allaqi 69, 70
Wadi Hammamat 70
Wars of the Successors 27, 37, 39, 41, 70
water, devices for raising 97, 98
water clocks 96
wine 49, 50, 55, 65, 70, 74, 77–8, 147, 157, 167, 168, 280; *see also* vineyards
women: Egyptian 139–41; Macedonian 139, 140

Xois 186

Zenodotus of Ephesos 85, 86–7, 93
Zenon 64–5, 66, 73–4, 107, 140, 165
Zeus (god) 13, 14, 38, 76, 133; statues 1, 57; temples to 162
Zeus-Ammon 13, 14, 18; temples to 13, 14, 18, 25

Image Credits

Alexander: Bridgeman Images; Pharos of Alexandria: The Print Collector/Alamy Stock Photo; Ptolemy I: CM Dixon/Print Collector/Getty Images; Ptolemy II: © Zev Radovan/Bridgeman Images; Eratosthenes: Ancient Art and Architecture/Alamy Stock Photo; Dendera crowns: Mike P Shepherd/Alamy Stock Photo; Harvest scene: DeAgostini/Getty Images; Rosetta Stone: © The Trustees of the British Museum; Gilded furniture decoration: © NPL – DeA Picture Library/Bridgeman Images; Terracotta water jar: © The Met, shared under a Creative Commons CC0 1.0 Universal licence; Terracotta mercenary: © The Trustees of the British Museum; Stele dedicated to the Bull Buchis: © Sandro Vannini / Bridgeman Images; Bust of Serapis: Lanmas / Alamy Stock Photo; Offering table: © The Trustees of the British Museum; The Nile mosaic of Palestrina: GRANGER – Historical Picture Archive/Alamy Stock Photo; Hypostle Hall: Nick Brundle Photography/Getty Images; Temple of Sobek relief: © NPL – DeA Picture Library/C. Sappa/Bridgeman Images; Back of gold-winged Ba amulet: Art Media/Print Collector/Getty Images; Underwater archaeology in Thonis-Herakleion: Christoph Gerigk © Franck Goddio/Hilti Foundation; Temple of Horus: Kitti Boonnitrod/Getty Images; Temple of Philae: Matt Champlin/Getty Images; Papyrus from the Book of the Dead: Luisa Ricciarini/Bridgeman Images; Wall relief of Cleopatra III, Cleopatra II and Ptolemy VIII in Kom Ombo: eFesenko/Alamy Stock Photo; Ptolemy V: Dirk Sonnenwald, licensed Public Domain Mark 1.0. Berlin, Münzkabinett der Staatlichen Museen, 18203067; Ptolemy VI Philometor: © Peter

Willi/Bridgeman Images; Ptolemy IX: © 2024 Museum of Fine Arts, Boston/Bridgeman Images. All rights reserved/Edwin L. Jack Fund/Bridgeman Images; Caesar Augustus: CPA Media Pte Ltd/Alamy Stock Photo; Mark Antony: Chronicle/Alamy Stock Photo; Marble head of Cleopatra VII: DEA/S. VANNINI/Getty Images; Aegupto Capta/Crocodile Roman coin: © The Trustees of the British Museum; Cleopatra VII coin: © The Trustees of the British Museum; Cleopatra VI and Caesarion wall relief in Dendera: robertharding/Alamy Stock Photo.

A Note on the Author

Toby Wilkinson is an Egyptologist and the prize-winning author of thirteen books on the history and culture of the Nile Valley, ancient and modern. Lauded by the *Daily Telegraph* as 'the foremost Egyptologist of his time', his works include *The Rise and Fall of Ancient Egypt*, which won the Hessell-Tiltman Prize. He studied Egyptology at the University of Cambridge and is currently a Fellow of Clare College, Cambridge, a Fellow of the Society of Antiquaries and a Fellow of the Royal Historical Society.

A Note on the Type

The text of this book is set in Linotype Stempel Garamond, a version of Garamond adapted and first used by the Stempel foundry in 1924. It is one of several versions of Garamond based on the designs of Claude Garamond. It is thought that Garamond based his font on Bembo, cut in 1495 by Francesco Griffo in collaboration with the Italian printer Aldus Manutius. Garamond types were first used in books printed in Paris around 1532. Many of the present-day versions of this type are based on the *Typi Academiae* of Jean Jannon cut in Sedan in 1615.

Claude Garamond was born in Paris in 1480. He learned how to cut type from his father and by the age of fifteen he was able to fashion steel punches the size of a pica with great precision. At the age of sixty he was commissioned by King Francis I to design a Greek alphabet, and for this he was given the honourable title of royal type founder. He died in 1561.